Culturally Sustaining Pedagogies:
Teaching and Learning for Justice in a Changing World
DJANGO PARIS & H. SAMY ALIM, EDS.

Choice and Agency in the Writing Workshop:
Developing Engaged Writers, Grades 4–6
FRED HAMEL

Assessing Writing, Teaching Writers: Putting the
Analytic Writing Continuum to Work in Your Classroom
MARY ANN SMITH & SHERRY SEALE SWAIN

The Teacher-Writer: Creating Writing Groups
for Personal and Professional Growth
CHRISTINE M. DAWSON

Every Young Child a Reader: Using Marie Clay's
Key Concepts for Classroom Instruction
SHARAN A. GIBSON & BARBARA MOSS

"You Gotta BE the Book": Teaching Engaged and
Reflective Reading with Adolescents, Third Edition
JEFFREY D. WILHELM

Personal Narrative, Revised:
Writing Love and Agency in the High School Classroom
BRONWYN CLARE LAMAY

Inclusive Literacy Teaching: Differentiating Approaches in
Multilingual Elementary Classrooms
LORI HELMAN, CARRIE ROGERS, AMY FREDERICK, & MAGGIE STRUCK

The Vocabulary Book:
Learning and Instruction, Second Edition
MICHAEL F. GRAVES

Reading, Writing, and Talk: Inclusive Teaching Strategies
for Diverse Learners, K–2
MARIANA SOUTO-MANNING & JESSICA MARTELL

Go Be a Writer!: Expanding the Curricular Boundaries of
Literacy Learning with Children
CANDACE R. KUBY & TARA GUTSHALL RUCKER

Partnering with Immigrant Communities:
Action Through Literacy
GERALD CAMPANO, MARÍA PAULA GHISO, & BETHANY J. WELCH

Teaching Outside the Box but Inside the Standards:
Making Room for Dialogue
BOB FECHO, MICHELLE FALTER, & XIAOLI HONG, EDS.

Literacy Leadership in Changing Schools:
10 Keys to Successful Professional Development
SHELLEY B. WEPNER, DIANE W. GÓMEZ, KATIE EGAN CUNNINGHAM,
KRISTIN N. RAINVILLE, & COURTNEY KELLY

Literacy Theory as Practice:
Connecting Theory and Instruction in K–12 Classrooms
LARA J. HANDSFIELD

Literacy and History in Action: Immersive Approaches to
Disciplinary Thinking, Grades 5–12
THOMAS M. MCCANN, REBECCA D'ANGELO, NANCY GALAS,
& MARY GRESKA

Pose, Wobble, Flow:
A Culturally Proactive Approach to Literacy Instruction
ANTERO GARCIA & CINDY O'DONNELL-ALLEN

Newsworthy—Cultivating Critical Thinkers, Readers, and
Writers in Language Arts Classrooms
ED MADISON

Engaging Writers with Multigenre Research Projects:
A Teacher's Guide
NANCY MACK

Teaching Transnational Youth—
Literacy and Education in a Changing World
ALLISON SKERRETT

Uncommonly Good Ideas—
Teaching Writing in the Common Core Era
SANDRA MURPHY & MARY ANN SMITH

The One-on-One Reading and Writing Conference:
Working with Students on Complex Texts
JENNIFER BERNE & SOPHIE C. DEGENER

Critical Encounters in Secondary English:
Teaching Literary Theory to Adolescents, Third Edition
DEBORAH APPLEMAN

Transforming Talk into Text—Argument Writing, Inquiry,
and Discussion, Grades 6–12
THOMAS M. MCCANN

Reading and Representing Across the Content Areas:
A Classroom Guide
AMY ALEXANDRA WILSON & KATHRYN J. CHAVEZ

Writing and Teaching to Change the World:
Connecting with Our Most Vulnerable Students
STEPHANIE JONES, ED.

Educating Literacy Teachers Online:
Tools, Techniques, and Transformations
LANE W. CLARKE & SUSAN WATTS-TAFFEE

Other People's English: Code-Meshing,
Code-Switching, and African American Literacy
VERSHAWN ASHANTI YOUNG, RUSTY BARRETT,
Y'SHANDA YOUNG-RIVERA, & KIM BRIAN LOVEJOY

WHAM! Teaching with Graphic Novels Across
the Curriculum
WILLIAM G. BROZO, GARY MOORMAN, & CARLA K. MEYER

The Administration and Supervision of Reading Programs,
5th Edition
SHELLEY B. WEPNER, DOROTHY S. STRICKLAND,
& DIANA J. QUATROCHE, EDS.

Critical Literacy in the Early Childhood Classroom:
Unpacking Histories, Unlearning Privilege
CANDACE R. KUBY

Inspiring Dialogue:
Talking to Learn in the English Classroom
MARY M. JUZWIK, CARLIN BORSHEIM-BLACK,
SAMANTHA CAUGHLAN, & ANNE HEINTZ

Reading the Visual:
An Introduction to Teaching Multimodal Literacy
FRANK SERAFINI

Race, Community, and Urban Schools:
Partnering with African American Families
STUART GREENE

continued

For volumes in the NCRLL Collection (edited by JoBeth Allen and Donna E. Alvermann) and the Practitioners Bookshelf Series
(edited by Celia Genishi and Donna E. Alvermann), as well as other titles in this series, please visit www.tcpress.com.

CULTURALLY SUSTAINING PEDAGOGIES

Teaching and Learning for Justice in a Changing World

EDITED BY

Django Paris ● **H. Samy Alim**

TEACHERS COLLEGE PRESS

TEACHERS COLLEGE | COLUMBIA UNIVERSITY

NEW YORK AND LONDON

Published by Teachers College Press, 1234 Amsterdam Avenue, New York, NY 10027

The book cover art—"We're Building the World We Need"—was designed by Favianna Rodriguez, an Afro-Peruvian, transnational, interdisciplinary artist and cultural organizer based in Oakland, CA (www.favianna.com). The piece represents a society in which children, adults, and elders are empowered and engaged in decision-making about their education, communities, and lives.

For reprint permission and other subsidiary rights requests, please contact Teachers College Press, Rights Dept.: tcpressrights@tc.columbia.edu

Chapter 4 is adapted with permission from Teresa L. McCarty and Tiffany S. Lee (2014), "Critical Culturally Sustaining/Revitalizing Pedagogy and Indigenous Education Sovereignty," *Harvard Educational Review*, 84(1, Spring), 101–124. Copyright © 2014 by President and Fellows of Harvard College. All rights reserved. For more information, please visit http://hepg.org/her-home/issues/harvard-educational-review-volume-84-number-1/herarticle/critical-culturallysustaining-revitalizing-pedago

Chapter 10 is adapted with permission from Jonathan Rosa and Nelson Flores, (2015), "Undoing Appropriateness: Raciolinguistic Ideologies and Language Diversity in Education," *Harvard Educational Review*, 85(2, Summer), 149–171. All rights reserved. For more information, please visit http://hepg.org/her-home/issues/summer-2015/herarticle/undoingappropriateness

Library of Congress Cataloging-in-Publication Data is available at loc.gov

ISBN 978-0-8077-5833-5 (paper)
ISBN 978-0-8077-5834-2 (hardcover)
ISBN 978-0-8077-7570-7 (ebook)

Printed on acid-free paper
Manufactured in the United States of America

24 23 22 21 20 19 18 17   8 7 6 5 4 3 2 1

We teach what we value.
—*Gloria Ladson-Billings*

Contents

PART II: ENVISIONING CSP FORWARD
THROUGH THEORIES OF PRACTICE

Shout Outs

Photograph by Jennifer A. Martin

The Culturally Sustaining Pedagogies Retreat in Half Moon Bay, California, May 3–4, 2015, together known as The Half Moon Bay Crew (HMBC). (From left to right: Timothy San Pedro, Jason Irizarry, Carol Lee, Kris Gutiérrez, Gloria Ladson-Billings, Django Paris, Valerie Kinloch, Mary Bucholtz, Courtney Peña, Norma González, Teresa McCarty, Stacey Lee, Casey Wong, Adam Haupt, H. Samy Alim. Not pictured: Dolores Inés Casillas, Michael Domínguez, Nelson Flores, Amanda Holmes, Patrick Johnson, Tiffany Lee, Jin Sook Lee, Jonathan Rosa, Daniel Walsh.)

This photo captures the warmth, the love, the strong sense of intellectual community, the positive vibes and spirits that carried us through that entire weekend. This retreat and our subsequent gathering at AERA in Washington, D.C., on April 12, 2016, carried us through the work of writing and revising these past few years. Much *much* love for all of the intellectual exchange, the lively debates, the loving critiques, the sense of mission, the intergenerational building, and the edifying and soul-reviving (soul-sustaining) feeling that comes from being part of a collective working toward social and educational justice. We cannot thank you all enough! Looking forward to our many collaborations and future work together as a collective!

Django sends love and thanks to Rae Paris for continuing to show us what it means to write, teach, and live to sustain our communities. Huge gratitude to our editor, Emily Spangler, for her deep commitment to getting this project into the hands and hearts of educators. Ups as well to Donielle Prince at the Center for Race, Ethnicity, and Language (CREAL) for her crucial help in compiling, editing, and formatting the manuscript.

Finally, big love and respect to our families, near and far, and to the youth, educators, and communities whose culturally sustaining teaching and learning are the heart of this work, forward.

—Django and Alim

CHAPTER 1

What Is Culturally Sustaining Pedagogy and Why Does It Matter?

H. Samy Alim
University of California, Los Angeles

Django Paris
Michigan State University

Across the centuries, countless philosophers and teachers—and legions of students—have asked that age-old educational question: What is the purpose of schooling? In the context of the United States and other nation-states living out the legacies of genocide, land theft, enslavement, and various forms of colonialism, the answer to this question for communities of color has been rather clear: The purpose of state-sanctioned schooling has been to forward the largely assimilationist and often violent White imperial project, with students and families being asked to lose or deny their languages, literacies, cultures, and histories in order to achieve in schools. In the United States and beyond, this saga of cultural and linguistic assault has had and continues to have devastating effects on the access, achievement, and well-being of students of color in public schools.

Continued social and educational inequality coupled with the massive demographic changes sweeping the United States and Europe, among other regions, have brought to the fore an urgent, more pressing iteration of this age-old question: What is the purpose of schooling *in pluralistic societies*? This has been the most important question for us over the past several years as we have worked to offer a needed change in stance and terminology in pedagogical theory and practice—*culturally sustaining pedagogy* (CSP; Alim & Paris, 2015; Paris, 2012; Paris & Alim, 2014). CSP seeks to perpetuate and foster—to sustain—linguistic, literate, and cultural pluralism as part of schooling for positive social transformation. CSP positions dynamic cultural dexterity as a necessary good, and sees the outcome of learning as additive rather than subtractive, as remaining whole rather than framed as broken, as critically enriching strengths rather than replacing deficits. Culturally sustaining pedagogy exists wherever education sustains the lifeways of communities who have been and continue to be damaged and erased through schooling.

The more we write and think about CSP, the more we are convinced that we are dealing with fundamental questions about teaching and learning. At the same time, our theorizing has taken us far beyond the traditional kinds of questions that are commonly asked in much of education research, questions that too often obscure, confound, or remain silent on issues of systemic racial and intersectional inequalities that continue to be part of the fabric of schooling. In essence, by proposing schooling as a site for sustaining the cultural ways of being of communities of color rather than eradicating them, CSP is responding to the many ways that schools continue to function as part of the colonial project. We seek to disrupt the pervasive anti-Indigeneity, anti-Blackness, and related anti-Brownness (from anti-*Latinidad* to Islamophobia) and model minority myths so foundational to schooling in the United States and many other colonial nation-states (Alexander, 2007; Dumas, 2014; Dumas & ross, 2016; S. Lee, 2005; Lomawaima & McCarty, 2006; Woodson, 2000).

In our work with CSP we begin matter-of-factly with the knowledge that our languages, literacies, histories, and cultural ways of being as people and communities of color are not pathological. Beginning with this understanding—an understanding fought for across the centuries (Kendi, 2016)—allows us to see the fallacy of measuring ourselves and the young people in our communities solely against White middle-class norms[1] of knowing and being that continue to dominate notions of educational achievement. Du Bois (1965), of course, theorized this well over a century ago with his conceptualization of *double consciousness*, "This sense of always looking at one's self through the eyes of others, of measuring one's soul by the tape of a world that looks on in amused contempt and pity" (p. 45). In this work we are committed to envisioning and enacting pedagogies that are not filtered through the glass of amused contempt and pity (e.g., the "achievement gap"), but rather are centered on contending in complex ways with the rich and innovative linguistic, literate, and cultural practices of Indigenous, Black, Latinx, Asian, Pacific Islander, and other youth and communities of color.

In our conceptualization of CSP, we have moved away from (sometimes even progressive) pedagogies that are too closely aligned with linguistic, literate, and cultural hegemony. Instead, we have worked with others to develop a pedagogical agenda that does not concern itself with the seemingly panoptic *White gaze* (Morrison, 1998) that permeates educational research and practice with and for students of color, their teachers, and their schools.[2] In a 1998 interview, Nobel laureate Toni Morrison responded to misguided critiques of her books with the rebuttal, "As though our lives have no meaning and no depth without the White gaze. And I have spent my entire writing life trying to make sure that the White gaze was not the dominant one in any of my books."

As we think about teaching and teachers, we ask: What would our pedagogies look like if this gaze (and the kindred patriarchal, cisheteronormative, English-monolingual, ableist, classist, xenophobic, Judeo-Christian gazes)[3] weren't the dominant one? What would liberating ourselves from this gaze and the educational expectations it forwards mean for our abilities to envision new and recover community-rooted forms of teaching and learning? What if the goal of teaching and learning with youth of color was not ultimately to see how closely students could perform White middle-class norms, but rather was to explore, honor, extend, and, at times, problematize their cultural practices and investments?

We ask this question knowing that so-called educational "integration" has always framed success in terms of a unidirectional assimilation into whiteness (for example, as a result of *Brown v. Board of Education*, they weren't busing White students into Black neighborhoods and firing White teachers—see Walker, 2013). For Morrison, as soon as she jettisoned this White gaze, she found herself in a new territory that allowed for boundless creativity, a world of imagination and possibility. "This was brand-new space," she said, "and once I got there, it was like the whole world opened up, and I was never going to give that up." What kinds of transformative experiences can we offer our students, such that a "whole world" of learning opens up for them, one that, like Morrison, they would never want to give up (versus one that continually gives up on them)? What can educators of color and other educators in solidarity with us learn from Morrison's courage and conviction to de-center whiteness, to envision a world where we owed no explanations to White people about the value of our children's culture, language, and learning potential?[4]

It is important to note that in de-centering whiteness, we are not putting aside issues of (so-called) access and equity; we are reframing them. For too long, scholarship on "access" and "equity" has centered implicitly or explicitly around the White-gaze-centered question: How can "we" get "these" working-class kids of color to speak/write/be more like middle-class White ones (rather than critiquing the White gaze itself that sees, hears, and frames students of color in everywhichway as marginal and deficient)? For equally long, as Fairclough (1992) and Rosa and Flores (Chapter 10, this volume) have pointed out, much of additive scholarship has focused on the cultural and linguistic practices of our students, rather than the listening and framing practices of "Whitestream institutions" (Urrieta, 2010). We believe that equity and access can best be achieved by centering the dynamic practices and selves of students and communities of color in a critical, additive, and expansive vision of schooling. Instead of being oppressive, homogenizing forces, CSP asks us to reimagine schools as sites where diverse, heterogeneous practices are not only valued but *sustained*. In fundamentally reimagining the purpose of education, CSP demands a critical, emancipatory vision of schooling that reframes the object of critique from our children to oppressive systems.

These are not just theoretical questions for us; our experiences as teachers of color deeply inform our work on CSP. We have been confronted with the racially discriminatory context of U.S. education our entire lives—first as students and then as teachers. Between the two of us, we have participated in the complex and imperfect work of sustaining our students and communities through education for nearly forty years as elementary, middle school, high school, and now university educators. These experiences anchor our theorizing and our practice of culturally sustaining pedagogies.

LOVING CRITIQUES OF ASSET PEDAGOGIES AND NEW DIRECTIONS

As we continued to build from our own experiences as teachers and students, we came together to further conceptualize CSP in 2014 through a series of respectful and generative loving critiques of previous asset pedagogies, as we sought to problematize and extend three areas of scholarship and practice: (a) previous conceptualizations and enactments of asset pedagogies, (b) asset pedagogies that consider the longstanding practices of communities of color without taking into account contemporary enactments of communities, and (c) asset pedagogies that do not critically contend with problematic elements expressed in some youth (and adult) cultural practices. Below we trace and extend these loving critiques as we build toward the future of CSP.

Our first engagement is with previous conceptualizations and enactments of asset pedagogies, which begins with an understanding of the emergence of these necessary approaches to teaching and learning. Building on the court rulings of the 1960s and 1970s and the subsequent policies that required schools to attend to the languages (e.g., African American Language, Chinese, Navajo, Spanish) and (less so) cultures of communities of color (e.g., *Lau v. Nichols, Martin Luther King, Jr. Elementary School Children v. Ann Arbor School District*)[5], collaborations between researchers and teachers proved that the deficit approaches to teaching and learning that had echoed across the decades (centuries, really) were untenable and unjust (Cazden & Leggett, 1976; Heath, 1983; Labov, 1972; Moll, 1992; Smitherman, 1977). These deficit approaches viewed the languages, literacies, and cultural ways of being of many students and communities of color as deficiencies to be overcome in learning the demanded and legitimized dominant language, literacy, and cultural ways of schooling.

With this research as a foundation, asset pedagogies were enacted and understood in ever more complex ways by teachers and researchers throughout the 1990s and into the 2000s (Garcia, 1993; Ladson-Billings, 1994; C. D. Lee, 1995; McCarty & Zepeda, 1995; Moll & Gonzalez, 1994; Nieto, 1992; Valdés, 1996). These revolutionary pedagogies repositioned the linguistic, literate, and cultural practices of working-class communities—specifically poor communities of color—as resources and assets to honor, explore, and extend in accessing White middle-class dominant cultural norms of acting and being that are demanded in schools.

One of the most important pedagogical statements of this asset pedagogies movement was Ladson-Billings's (1995) landmark article *Toward a Theory of Culturally Relevant Pedagogy*. Indeed, the term *culturally relevant pedagogy* (CRP) has become ubiquitous in educational research circles and in teacher education programs.[6] This speaks to the lasting conceptual value of the term and, more importantly, Ladson-Billings's illumination of the concept through her work with successful teachers of African American students. We, like countless teachers and university-based researchers, continue to be inspired by what it means to make teaching and learning relevant to the languages, literacies, and cultural practices of students in our communities. And we understand our work with CSP as founded upon the original formulation of CRP. Indeed, as Ladson-Billings (2014) recently wrote, "culturally sustaining pedagogy uses culturally relevant pedagogy as the place where the beat drops" (p. 76).

Ladson-Billings's (1995) original formulation of CRP, where the "beat drops" for us, laid the groundwork for pedagogies that maintain the long-standing cultural practices of communities of color while students also learn to critique dominant power structures. And yet we believe that much of the work being done under the umbrella of CRP comes up far short of these goals. It is also true that the term "relevant" does not do enough to explicitly support the goals of maintenance and social critique. It is quite possible to be relevant to something without ensuring its continuing and critical presence in students' repertoires of practice (Gutiérrez & Rogoff, 2003), and its presence in our classrooms and communities. We believe that the term CRP and, just as important, the way it has been taken up in teacher education and practice needs to be revised forward from the crucial work it has done over the past two decades. We make this call with deep respect for the work we have cited to this point, for it has allowed us all to move beyond rationalizing the need to include the linguistic, literate, and other cultural practices (e.g., Hip Hop) of our communities meaningfully as assets in educational spaces. Rather, we begin with this as a given and ask, *for what purposes and with what outcomes?*

As such, CSP explicitly calls for schooling to be a site for sustaining the cultural ways of being of communities of color. We believe that the term, stance, and practice of CSP are increasingly necessary in the context of the new students of color majority in U.S. public schools: 2014 was the first year students of color were the majority in U.S. public schools, whereas in 1970, 80% of students were White (Strauss, 2014).[7] Indeed, given these extraordinary demographic shifts in and far beyond schools (Taylor, 2014), promoting linguistic and cultural dexterity is no longer only about equally valuing all of our communities—it is also about the skills, knowledges, and ways of being needed for success in the present and future. As our society continues to shift, CSP must be part of a shifting *culture of power* (Delpit,

1988). We cannot continue to act as if the White middle-class linguistic, literate, and cultural skills and ways of being that were seen as the sole gatekeepers to the opportunity structure over a quarter-century ago have remained so or will remain so as our society changes. Simply put, the future is a multilingual and multiethnic one, regardless of attempts to suppress that reality. For too long we have taught our youth (and our teachers) that Dominant American English (DAE) and other White middle-class normed practices and ways of being alone are the key to power, while denying the languages and other cultural practices that students of color bring to the classroom. Ironically, this outdated philosophy will not grant our young people access to power; rather, it may increasingly deny them that access.

Yet, despite these contemporary shifts, a vocal number of researchers, whose work is deeply flawed theoretically and methodologically, continue to argue that youth of color suffer from "a language gap" (see Avineri & Johnson, 2015, for a resounding critique of this research). This research not only upholds what Alim (2004) and Alim and Smitherman (2012) have referred to as *linguistic supremacy*, but it is also sadly out of step with our new demographic reality. CSP, then, is necessary to honor, value, and center the rich and varied practices of communities of color, *and* is a necessary pedagogy for helping shape access to power in a changing nation.

As evidenced by the "language gap" research, the demographic and cultural changes sweeping the United States and other nations present an opportunity and an imperative, but they are no guarantee of educational and social equity in the short term. Indeed, many indices of equality are going in the opposite direction, as a backlash against the reality of our racially and culturally shifting future is in full effect. Evidence of this backlash includes explicit assimilationist monolingual/monocultural educational policies (for example, Arizona HB2281, ["standard"] English Only laws in several states, the prevalence of decontextualized, monolingual literacy programs for students of color, and wildly disproportional discipline, push-out (not "dropout"), and incarceration rates for students of color).[8] And these educational policies, of course, are embedded in the larger context of continued institutional and environmental racism, including police brutality and mass incarceration, unsafe water, and the disposability of Black, Brown, and Indigenous bodies and, more generally, the nation's poor (Hill, 2016).[9]

In this context, the goals of CSP are even more urgent, especially when coupled with the emergence of recent research from Arizona (Cabrera et al., 2014) and California (Dee & Penner, 2016) that shows that students of color have more success across subjects in school (even on dominant, narrow measures) when given the opportunity to enroll in ethnic studies courses that center their experiences. In Chapter 6 of this volume, Timothy San Pedro shares a powerful narrative of James, a Native student (Ute and Pima tribes) who recommitted to driving across the border between his reservation and the city to attend high school because he was motivated by a new class being offered on Native American literature, the first of its type at his school. After deciding to drop out of school, news of this class was, according to James, "the only reason" he came to school:

> just the fact that I'm Native. Just the fact that we're talking about things [in the Native American literature classroom] that I'm familiar with, ya know? Kinda like the ceremony and stuff. The different tribes and stuff and that's where I feel comfortable, you know? I think it's better that we learn about Native American stuff other than the stuff like in my history classes. Whatever they learn about: Columbus or whatever. That stuff don't interest me, ya know? This stuff—*this stuff*—interests me.

In this case, James's narrative, by decentering "Columbus or whatever" and centering Native cultures, practices, languages, literatures, and histories in a critical framework, speaks quite literally to CSP as an anti-settler-colonial, anti-imperial project. Given the results of the emerging research on the value of ethnic studies, and the myriad examples of educational narratives like James's, any future attempts to ban race and ethnic studies or to pass English-Only laws must be seen as part and parcel of the political project of whiteness—that is, as oppressive, restrictive policies that are passed with the express intent of limiting the progress of communities of color.[10]

SUSTAINING DYNAMIC COMMUNITY PRACTICES

Our second loving critique examines how contemporary research and practice too often draw over-deterministic links between languages, literacies, cultural practices, and race/ethnicity. As we seek to perpetuate and foster a pluralist present and future through our pedagogies, it is crucial that we understand that the ways in which young people are enacting race, ethnicity, language, literacy, and their engagement with culture is always shifting and dynamic. Indeed, the vast majority of asset-oriented research, and the pedagogies it documents or enacts, has been focused solely on abstract or fixed versions of the culturally situated practices of our communities.

Although these practices (e.g., Indigenous languages and cultural ways of knowing, African American language and cultural ways of knowing) have historically been and continue to be the target of deficit approaches, contemporary linguistic, pedagogical, and cultural research has pushed against the tendency of researchers and practitioners to assume static relationships between race, ethnicity, language, and cultural ways of being (Alim, Rickford, & Ball, 2016; Gutiérrez & Rogoff, 2003; Irizarry, 2007;

Paris, 2011; Wyman, McCarty, & Nicholas, 2014). Such assumptions have led to the unfortunate simplification of asset pedagogies as solely about considering longstanding practices while simultaneously ignoring the shifting and changing practices of students and their communities. The result has been the simplification of what teachers are seeking to sustain as only, for example, African American Language (AAL) among Black students or Spanish among Latinx students (a one-to-one mapping of race and language). And this goes, of course, beyond language, where communities of cultural practice, such as Hip Hop cultures, are assumed to be a cultural source for teaching with only Black or even with Black and Brown students.

To move us out of this overly deterministic rut while continuing (of course) to attend to sustaining the cultural practices that have sustained and strengthened us, CSP shifts toward contemporary understandings of culture as dynamic and fluid, while also allowing for the past and present to be seen as merging, a continuum, or distinct, depending on how young people and their communities live race/ethnicity, language, and culture. In Chapter 12 of this volume, for example, Holmes and Gonzalez argue for the need to focus on "elder epistemologies" and practices as they have sustained Indigenous communities for centuries. In fact, as Carol Lee (Chapter 15, this volume) argues, in the contexts of genocide, land theft, and slavery—the foundational, settler colonial experiences of Indigenous peoples and enslaved Africans—acts of historic and cultural resistance and *survivance* (Vizenor, 1994) allowed Indigenous and African-descended communities to sustain practices and belief systems (and their very lives) in the face of racialized White terror. As a collective, we argue that these cultural practices and ways of knowing should certainly be sustained, even as we make room for how youth of today are reworking this set of knowledges to meet their current cultural and political realities.

As examples of these cultural reworkings, we draw from our research (Alim, 2011; Paris, 2011) in local and international contexts. In this work, we examine how young people both rehearse longstanding versions of racial/ethnic and linguistic identities and, importantly, offer new ones (Alim & Reyes, 2011; Irizarry, 2007; Martinez, 2017; Paris, 2009, 2011). In his research, Django worked with youth in a California high school and community to explore the important ways Black students navigated identities through the longstanding practices of AAL and Hip Hop cultures. What he discovered was that in addition to Black youth, many Mexicana/o, Mexican American, and Pacific Islander youth (U.S.-born and born in Samoa, Fiji, and Tonga) also navigated identities through their participation in AAL and Hip Hop cultural practices. Moreover, they did so while simultaneously participating in their longstanding community practices of, for example, Spanishes or Samoan and other cultural practices (clothing, ways of believing) passed down from the elders in their ethnic communities.

In this way, much like the global youth practices documented in Alim's studies of global linguistic flows (2009) and global ill-literacies (2011), youth were fashioning new linguistically and culturally dexterous ways of being Latinx or Fijian that relied on longstanding cultural practices while they also relied on emerging ones. Therefore, our pedagogies must address the well-understood fact that what it means to be Black or Latinx or Pacific Islander (as examples) both remains rooted *and* continues to shift in the ways culture always has.

While conceptions of time, heritage, and the stakes for sustaining particular practices vary across contexts for communities (see Holmes and Gonzalez, Chapter 12 of this volume), these examples show that while it is crucial that we work to sustain Black, Latinx, Asian, Pacific Islander, and Indigenous languages and cultures in our pedagogies, we must be open to sustaining them in ways that attend to the emerging, intersectional, and dynamic ways in which they are lived and used by young people. Indeed, applications of the most lasting frameworks for asset pedagogies—the *funds of knowledge* (Moll & Gonzalez, 1994), the *third space* (Gutiérrez, 2008; Gutiérrez, Baquedando-Lopez, Alvarez, & Chiu 1999), and *culturally relevant pedagogy*—have too often been enacted by teachers and researchers in static ways that look only to the important ways that racial/ethnic difference was enacted by previous generations. As youth continue to develop new, complex, and intersecting forms of racial/ethnic identification in a world where cultural and linguistic recombinations flow with purpose, we need pedagogies that speak to our shifting cultural realities or, as Pennycook (2007) put it, pedagogies that "go with the flow."

A final caveat in our discussion of culture and pedagogy: Too often cultural practices, activities, and ways of being and doing are invoked in ways that obscure the racialized, gendered, classed, dis/abilitied, languaged (and so on) bodies of the people enacting them. In short, we cannot separate culture from the bodies enacting culture and the ways those bodies are subjected to systemic discrimination. CSP, then, is about sustaining cultures as connected to sustaining the bodies—the lives—of the people who cherish and practice them. Further, as argued by Waitoller and King Thorius (2016), focusing on the body allows us to view overlapping and intersecting oppressions as opportunities for those of us committed to CSP to form strategic alliances against exclusion.

FURTHER INWARD: CRITICAL REFLEXIVITY

In our final loving critique, we seek to move beyond critiquing the dominant pedagogies that perpetuate educational injustice, and turn our gaze inward on our own communities and cultural practices as people and scholars of color. Here, we are primarily interested in creating generative spaces for asset pedagogies to support the practices of youth and communities of color, while maintaining a critical lens vis-à-vis these practices. Providing the example of Hip Hop as a form of the cultural and community practice that pedagogies should sustain, we argue that rather than avoiding problematic practices or keeping them hidden beyond the White gaze, CSP must work with students to critique regressive practices (e.g., homophobia, misogyny) and raise critical consciousness. We as authors are implicated in this final critique, as we have been throughout this work; our own research on and practice of Hip Hop pedagogies have not always taken up these problematic elements in the direct ways that we forward here.

And so we migrate further inward, to what Alim has called "ill-literacies" (Alim, 2011)—counterhegemonic forms of youth literacies—and ask, "What happens when ill-literacies get *ill*?" In other words, what happens when rather than challenging hegemonic ideas and outcomes, the cultural practices of youth actually reproduce them, or even create new ones? Most of the research and practice under the asset pedagogies umbrella, including the frameworks of the *funds of knowledge,* the *third space,* and *culturally relevant pedagogy,* too often view youth cultures through a purely "positive" or "progressive" lens. This is true as well for the research and pedagogical traditions founded upon these frameworks, like the hugely influential Hip Hop pedagogies movement.

The vast majority of Hip Hop education research has focused pedagogies on the many progressive, justice-oriented aspects of Hip Hop. There are good reasons for this. For one, there is of course much in Hip Hop's past and present that is explicitly concerned with social justice. Also, most advocates of Hip Hop pedagogies are consciously engaging in a project that views deficit thinking as a product of White supremacy and the racism (and classism, cisheteronormativity, xenophobia, etc.) that it engenders. As we have stated, however, we build on this important work by engaging in reflexive analyses that are not bound by how educational systems that privilege White middle-class norms view the practices of communities of color.

In nearly all of the U.S.-based research on Hip Hop pedagogies, and all of the globally produced research in this area, youth's spoken, rhymed, and written texts are seen only as challenging prescriptive, restrictive, and anti-democratic notions of culture, citizenship, language, literacy, and education. With a few important exceptions (Hill, 2009; Low, 2011; Love, 2012; and some chapters in Petchauer & Hill, 2013), studies rarely look critically at the ways in which youth might reify existing hegemonic discourses about, as examples, gender, race, sexuality, and citizenship. In other words, Hip Hop pedagogies have tended to be largely celebratory and have ignored the contradictory forces found within all popular cultural forms (Giroux, 1996). However, the simultaneously progressive and oppressive currents in these innovative youth practices must be interrogated and critiqued, as has been done consistently for noneducation-based Hip Hop research, such as Rose (1994), Perry (2004), Neal (2006), Haupt (2008), Williams (2017) and Alim et al. (2010, 2011). Simply put, a reading of most of the asset-based pedagogies literature would make it appear that youth practices present us with no internal inconsistencies. Being participants and scholars of and with communities of color, we take it as a given that practices of youth of color often work explicitly toward social justice, but critically, we must pay attention to both the liberatory and nonliberatory currents within these practices.

Many Hip Hop pedagogies, from Alim's critical Hip Hop language pedagogies (2004) to Emdin's work on Hip Hop and science education (2010), for example, argue for the use of rap battles—improvised verbal duels—in classroom learning. Yet few take up the fact that the Hip Hop battle can sometimes be a masculinist space that excludes young women, queer youth, and young men of color who do not identify as Black (even as young women, queer youth, and youth who are not Black continue to "roc the mic"). CSP must contend with the possibility that Hip Hop pedagogies that utilize rap battles (as one among many examples of Hip Hop pedagogical practices) may seemingly serve the needs of many students of color, particularly young, able-bodied, cishetero men, but may unwittingly reproduce forms of exclusion in our classrooms and communities. (For example, the field rarely produces gendered analyses of classroom participation when using Hip Hop.)

The revoicing of ableist, racist, (trans)misogynistic, homophobic, patriarchal, and xenophobic discourses does occur in some forms of commercial rap (and in some rap produced by youth in our communities). We must work toward CSPs that sustain the many practices and knowledges of communities of color that forward equity (like much of Hip Hop does) and help youth, teachers, and researchers expose those practices that must be revised in the project of cultural justice. Our goal is to find ways to support and sustain what we know are remarkable ways with language, literacy, and cultural practice, while at the same time opening up spaces for students themselves to critique the ways that they might be—intentionally or not—reproducing discourses that marginalize members of our communities. As Low (2011) has argued, the very real and difficult tensions found within youth cultures are not reasons to inhibit their use in schools, but rather to demand their use in the development of more critical approaches.

Although we have used Hip Hop education here as an example, it is important to note again that these damaging discourses are present across *all* cultural communities and practices, including those within which we and our young people are socialized. As Tricia Rose recently argued in her June 2016 keynote address at Cambridge University's Hip Hop Studies Conference, in line with our notion of loving critique, "to love something is not to affirm it all the time; we need transformational love." Ultimately, sustaining those practices within our communities that promote equity across race, gender, sexuality, language, class, and ability and revising those that don't will help us thrive and, ultimately, will allow us to get free (Smith, 2016).

REFLECTING FORWARD:
WHERE WE ARE AND WHERE WE NEED TO GO

CSP must extend the previous visions of asset pedagogies by demanding explicitly pluralist outcomes that are not centered on White middle-class, monolingual/monocultural norms and notions of educational achievement—and that call out the imposition of these norms as harmful to and discriminatory against many of our communities. CSP must also resist static, unidirectional notions of culture and race that center only on longstanding cultural practices of communities without also attending to continual shifts and cultural reworkings. Finally, CSP must be willing to seriously contend with the sometimes problematic aspects of our communities, even as we celebrate our progressive, social justice-oriented movements and approaches.

We are in many ways at the asset-based, critical pedagogical edge. For us, as we hope is clear by now, we are not interested in offering pedagogical quick fixes or "best practices" that teachers can drop into the same old tired curriculum that deadens the souls of vast numbers of children of color in U.S. schools. Nor are we, as we wrote earlier in this chapter, interested in asking questions that fall neatly within the bounds of conventional educational research and practice.

As such, this volume is a product of a collective of researchers and teachers who share the explicit purpose of thinking through the implications of CSP, pushing its theoretical boundaries, growing its practice through case study and critique, and bringing theory and practice together to offer a way forward toward reaching our goal of developing a more pluralistic and just future. As part of this collective effort, we organized a retreat in Half Moon Bay, California, in order to flesh out and think through the challenges and potential of CSP in times of radically changing demographics, ongoing justice movements, and severe political and social backlash. Out of that retreat we took on the name "Half Moon Bay Crew," connoting the love and respect we developed prior to, during, and since our intensive retreat.

In reflecting forward on the present and future of CSP, we think it's necessary to once again ask the question: What are we seeking to sustain through CSP? The simple, perhaps taken-for-granted assumption behind the development of CSP is: We sustain what we love (to remix Ladson-Billings's oft-heard assertion, "we teach what we love"). CSP calls for sustaining and revitalizing that which has over the centuries sustained *us* (Chapters 3, 4, and 15, this volume) as communities of color struggling to "make it"—to resist, revitalize, and reimagine—under enduring colonial conditions that constantly work to diminish our intellectual capacities, cultures, languages, and, yes, our very lives. As we mention love and lives here, we hold up the work of Black queer and trans women and all who have forwarded #BlackLivesMatter (Garza, 2014). This movement for Black lives and distinct, coalitional, intersectional justice work in Native (most especially in this moment, the Indigenous sovereignty, land, and Water Protectors at Standing Rock[11]), Latinx, Asian and Pacific Islander, and LGBTQ communities, in many ways led by young people, is calling out systemic racism across institutions, including schools. And it has transformed our thinking about the need for CSP as being literally about sustaining our minds and bodies as communities of color within a schooling system that has often had the exact opposite goals.

At the end of the day, the term *culturally sustaining pedagogy* is only as important as the ideas behind it and the enactments it engenders. Our collective knows well that naming matters, that terms like *culturally relevant pedagogy, cultural modeling, third space*, and *funds of knowledge* remain lasting concepts (after all, folks in this volume coined these terms and concepts!). But as Kris Gutiérrez (Chapter 14, this volume) has said in our meetings, we also know that "bad things happen to good ideas." Yet it is the decades of educational justice work done through these terms, these concepts, that matters most. And we are hopeful that CSP can join in such justice work at a time when we must be ever more explicit about critiquing the oppressive systems that limit our life experiences and centering our cultural communities in teaching and learning.

We believe that a critical centering of the valued ways of youth and communities of color in education is a radical act, an act made possible by the work of many in our collective and across the centuries of struggle in our communities, an act that disrupts a schooling system centered on ideologies of White, middle-class, monolingual, cisheteropatriarchal, able-bodied superiority. In this book, we focus on and examine educational spaces that instead center cultural, linguistic, and literate pluralism as part of schooling for racial justice and positive social transformation. We believe that CSP, like all critical asset-based approaches, is at heart about survival—a survival we want to sustain through education—and about changing the conditions under which we live and work by opening up new and revitalizing community rooted ways of thinking about education beyond, as Morrison reminded us, "the White gaze." We want to create conditions where children of color can both survive and thrive. Toward this effort, we agree wholeheartedly with Carol Lee, who shares in her chapter in this volume:

[I]f particular cultural practices and belief systems allowed people of African descent in the U.S. and the diaspora to survive and thrive through enslavement and Jim Crow—America's two centuries of legal apartheid—then it seems reasonable that sustaining these practices and

strategic transformations in response to changing conditions is a worthwhile goal.

The gravity of this statement, and this work writ large, is laid to bear
starkly and beautifully by Lee, and provokes further critical questions:
Under the latest iterations of White Supremacist, capitalist, cisheteropatriarchal ideologies, systems, and practices, what knowledges must we sustain in order to overcome and survive when faced with a power that seeks
to sustain itself above and beyond—and sometimes shot through—our
bodies? CSP is indeed about providing our children with the opportunities
to survive and thrive, but it is also centrally about love, a love that can
help us see our young people as whole versus broken when they enter
schools, and a love that can work to keep them whole as they grow and
expand who they are and can be through education.

CSP: A CONCEPTUAL AND EMPIRICAL PROJECT

Like the asset pedagogies from which it builds, CSP is both a conceptual
and an empirical project. We seek to offer visions of teaching and learning and evidence of teaching and learning at once. Across the long-term,
community-engaged studies in this volume, community accountability
and local affordances and constraints mean that CSP takes on necessarily different forms across different contexts. Even within this necessary
and expected variation, key features across the chapters include a critical
centering on dynamic community languages, valued practices and knowledges, student and community agency and input, historicized content and
instruction, a capacity to contend with internalized oppressions, and an
ability to curricularize all of this in learning settings.

Some of the chapters in this volume, all anchored to long-term engagements with communities and learning settings, are empirical/conceptual
(practice leads theorizing), and others are conceptual/empirical (theorizing leads practice). This split is not dichotomous, as we understand forg-
ing practice and theory as concurrent, reciprocal, and iterative processes.
As such, we organize the volume into two sections that, together, map
out where we are and where we need to go in our collective work with
CSP. Part I, "Enacting Culturally Sustaining Pedagogies: Students, Teachers, and Schools," offers several theoretically driven empirical cases of
robust CSPs centered on critical engagements with languages, literacies,
literatures, performances, and knowledges in classrooms and schools. By
showing how CSP works across settings, these chapters extend the theory
through situated practice. In Part II, "Envisioning CSP Forward Through
Theories of Practice," we offer practice-anchored theoretical contributions that push on and strengthen current conceptions of CSP to chart our

present and future. Together, the two sections offer the dialogic interweaving of research, theory, and practice necessary to fully understand and move forward with CSP for educational and cultural justice with students and communities in a changing world.

As we continue to think through the promises and challenges of culturally sustaining pedagogy, we are hopeful that our work in this volume can join young people, educators, communities, and scholars in our collective struggle against an educational system that contains us and toward one that sustains us.

NOTES

1. White middle-class norms of language, literacy, and cultural ways of interacting demanded for access and achievement in school have been documented and contrasted with the norms of working-class communities of color (and, less so, working-class White communities) across four decades of scholarship. Regarding White norms of "standard" or Dominant American English language use, see, for example, Labov (1972), Smitherman (1977), Garcia (1993), and Alim (2004). Regarding White middle-class literacy norms, see, for example, Heath (1983) and Kirkland (2013). Regarding White-centered cultural norms of interacting (including language), see Valdés (1996), Romero (1994), Lee (2005), and Leonardo (2009).

2. Tuck & Yang (2014) refer to this as the *colonial settler gaze*, which includes attention to race and racism but also explicitly indexes land theft and genocide against Indigenous peoples as foundational U.S. nation-state projects.

3. While we largely focus our argument here and in this volume more generally on race and racism within a nation-state context founded on ideologies of White supremacy, we recognize intersecting forms of oppression and resistance, including gender, sexuality, dis/ability, spirituality, and class, among others. See Waitoller & King Thorius (2016) for a particularly cogent discussion of CSP at the intersection of race and dis/ability.

4. Though it is easy to single out "White people," as they more often occupy positions of power in the United States and beyond, what we mean here, really, is *anybody* who resinscribes White Supremacist ideologies. As Pulitzer Prize–winning author Junot Diaz noted in a 2012 address at Stanford University, "White people act like we need them for everything. The truth is: We don't even need you for the maintenance of White Supremacy!" In other words, he was less hopeful that White Supremacy would be dismantled by focusing on the efforts of White people alone (though surely much focus is needed there). Rather, he urged People of Color to look inward critically to discover powerful ways to disrupt oppressive systems, to liberate

ourselves from the panoptic White gaze. See *Junot Díaz and the Decolonial Imagination,* edited by Monica Hanna, Jennifer Harford Vargas, and José David Saldívar (Duke, 2016), for more on these ideas.

5. *Lau v. Nichols* was brought and won on behalf of Chinese-speaking Chinese American students in San Francisco who claimed a lack of equal educational opportunity based on language discrimination. The Supreme Court's 1974 decision for the plaintiffs relied on the 1964 Civil Rights Act, which explicitly banned educational discrimination based on race or national origin. *MLK Elementary School Children v. Ann Arbor School District,* more commonly known as the 1979 "Black English Case," was brought and won by families of 11 Black students in Ann Arbor, MI, who had been diagnosed as "linguistically handicapped" by the district's speech pathologist. The families contended that the children had been misdiagnosed and miseducated as a result of their strong use of AAL (see Smitherman, 1981).

6. Other important terms and formulations that have looked to forge asset pedagogies with students of color include, but are not limited to, *culturally responsive pedagogy* (Gay, 2000), *culturally congruent pedagogy* (Au & Kawakami, 1994), *culturally compatible pedagogy* (Jacob & Jordan, 1987), *engaged pedagogy* (hooks, 1994), and *critical care praxis* (Rolón-Dow, 2005). We focus on the term and formulation of *culturally relevant pedagogies* because it has become the most used shorthand term and concept in teacher education, teacher practice, and research on teaching and learning.

7. In citing this demographic shift, it is crucial, of course, to note that Indigenous communities have been living and learning, have been educating their children and young people for millennia on their lands, though U.S. public schooling for Native peoples has historically been one of the institutions responsible for the forced and violent loss of culture and land associated with the settler colonial nation-state (Lomawaima & McCarty, 2006; Tuck & Yang, 2014).

8. See the U.S. Department of Education Civil Rights Data for examples of this massive disproportionality.

9. Given the campaign and outcome of the 2016 U.S. presidential election, this backlash and context of continued racism will continue unabated, and by all indications will increase, though it is important to note that the larger context of settler colonialism and White supremacy supersedes electoral outcomes (as seen in the Black Lives Matter and Standing Rock movements beginning under Democratic leadership.)

10. At the time of writing, California had recently passed a state bill to develop a model ethnic studies curriculum for voluntary adoption by any public school, and several large urban districts, like San Francisco, Los Angeles, and San Diego, had recently implemented ethnic studies courses for

all secondary students. These developments are evidence of successes in a long and continuing struggle in research and practice to center students and communities of color meaningfully in school teaching and learning.

11. For more on the Standing Rock movement, including the role of schooling, see Hayes, 2016, and Schwartz & Prakash, 2016.

REFERENCES

Alexander, N. (2007). Mother-tongue education and the African renaissance, with special reference to South Africa. In H. S. Alim & J. Baugh (Eds.), *Talkin Black talk: Language, education, and social change* (pp. 142–152). New York, NY: Teachers College Press.

Alim, H. S. (2004). You know my steez: An ethnographic and sociolinguistic study of styleshifting in a Black American speech community. Durham, NC: Duke University Press.

Alim, H. S. (2009). Intro: Straight outta Compton, straight aus München: Global linguistic flows, identities, and the politics of language in a global Hip Hop nation. In H. S. Alim, A. Ibrahim, & A. Pennycook (Eds.), *Global linguistic flows: Hip Hop Cultures, youth identities, the politics of language* (pp. 1–24). New York, NY: Routledge.

Alim, H. S. (2011). Global ill-literacies: Hip Hop cultures, youth identities, and the politics of literacy. *Review of Research in Education, 35*(1), 120–146.

Alim, H. S., & D. Paris. (2015). Whose Language Gap? Critical and Culturally Sustaining Pedagogies as Necessary Challenges to Racializing Hegemony. *Journal of Linguistic Anthropology, 25*(1), 66–86.

Alim, H. S., Lee, J., & Carris, L. M. (2010). "Short fried-rice-eating Chinese MCs" and "good-hair-havin Uncle Tom niggas": Performing race and ethnicity in freestyle rap battles. *Journal of Linguistic Anthropology, 20*(1), 116–133.

Alim, H. S., Lee, J., Carris, L. M. (2011). Moving the crowd, "crowding" the emcee: The production of Black normativity in freestyle rap battles. *Discourse & Society, 22*(4), 422–440.

Alim, H. S., & Reyes, A. (2011). Complicating race: Articulating race across multiple social dimensions. *Discourse & Society, 22*(4), 379–384.

Alim, H. S., Rickford, J., & Ball, A. (Eds.). (2016). *Raciolinguistics: How language shapes our ideas of race.* New York, NY: Oxford University Press.

Alim, H. S., & Smitherman, G. (2012). *Articulate while Black: Barak Obama, language, and race in the U.S.* New York, NY: Oxford University Press.

Au, K., & Kawakami, A. (1994). Cultural congruence in instruction. In E. Hollins, J. King, & W. Hayman (Eds.), *Teaching diverse populations: Formulating knowledge base* (pp. 5–23). Albany, NY: SUNY Press.

Avineri, N., & Johnson, E. (2015). Invited forum: Bridging the "language gap." *Journal of Linguistic Anthropology, 25*(1), 66–86.

Cabrera, N. L., Milem, J. F., Jaquette, O., & Marx, R. W. (2014). Missing the (student achievement) forest for all the (political) trees: Empiricism and the Mexican American studies controversy in Tucson. *American Educational Research Journal, 51*(6), 1084–1118.

Cazden, C., & Leggett, E. (1976). *Culturally responsive education: A discussion of LAU remedies II.* Prepared for the U.S. Department of Health, Education, and Welfare. U.S. National Institute of Education, Washington, D.C.

Dee, T., & Penner, E. (2016). *The causal effects of cultural relevance: Evidence from an ethnic studies curriculum.* Working paper, The National Bureau of Economic Research, Cambridge, MA.

Delpit, L. (1988). The silenced dialogue: Power and pedagogy in educating other people's children. *Harvard Educational Review, 58*(3), 280–298.

Du Bois, W. E. B. (1965). *The souls of Black folk.* New York, NY: Avon Books. (Original work published 1903.)

Dumas, M. J. (2014). "Losing an arm": Schooling as a site of Black suffering. *Race and Ethnicity in Education, 17*(1), 1–30.

Dumas, M. J., & ross, k. m. (2016). "Be real Black for me": Imagining BlackCrit in education. *Urban Education, 51*(4), 415–442.

Emdin, C. (2010). *Urban science education for the hip hop generation.* New York, NY: Sense Publishers.

Fairclough, N. (1992). The appropriacy of appropriateness. In N. Fairclough (Ed.), *Critical discourse awareness* (pp. 233–252). London, UK: Longman.

Garcia, E. (1993). Language, culture, and education. *Review of Research in Education, 19*, 51–98.

Garza, A. (2014, October 7). A herstory of the #BlackLivesMatter movement. Retrieved from http://www.thefeministwire.com/2014/10/blacklivesmatter-2/

Gay, G. (2000). *Culturally responsive teaching: Theory, research, and practice.* New York, NY: Teachers College Press.

Giroux, H. (1996). *Fugitive cultures: Race, violence, and youth.* New York, NY: Routledge.

Gutiérrez, K. (2008). Developing a sociocritical literacy in the third space. *Reading Research Quarterly, 43*(2), 148–164.

Gutiérrez, K., Baquedano-Lopez, P., Alvarez, H., & Chiu, M. (1999). Building a culture of collaboration through hybrid language practices. *Theory into Practice, 38*, 87–93.

Gutiérrez, K., & Rogoff, B. (2003). Cultural ways of learning. *Educational Researcher, 35*(5), 19–25.

Hanna, M., Vargas, J. H., & Saldívar, J. D. (Eds.). (2016). *Junot Díaz and the decolonial imagination.* Durham, NC: Duke University Press.

Hayes, K. (2016). From #NoDAPL to #FreedomSquare: A tale of two occupations. Retrieved from http://www.truth-out.org/news/item/37378-from-nodapl-to-freedomsquare-a-tale-of-two-occupations

Heath, S. B. (1983). *Ways with words.* New York, NY: Cambridge University Press.

Hill, M. L. (2009). *Beats, rhymes and classroom life: Hip Hop pedagogy and the politics of identity.* New York, NY: Teachers College Press.

Hill, M. L. (2016). *Nobody: Casualties of America's war on the vulnerable, from Ferguson to Flint and beyond.* New York, NY: Atria Books.

hooks, b. (1994). *Teaching to transgress.* New York, NY: Routledge.

Irizarry, J. (2007). Ethnic and urban intersections in the classroom: Latino students, hybrid identities, and culturally responsive pedagogy. *Multicultural Perspectives, 9*(3), 21–28.

Jacob, E., & Jordan, C. (1987). Moving to dialogue. *Anthropology and Education Quarterly, 18*(1), 259–261.

Kendi, I. (2016). *Stamped from the beginning: The definitive history of racist ideas in America.* New York, NY: Nation Books.

Kirkland, D. E. (2013). *A search past silence: The literacy of young Black men.* New York, NY: Teachers College Press.

Labov, W. (1972). *Language in the inner city.* Philadelphia, PA: University of Pennsylvania Press.

Ladson-Billings, G. (1994). *The Dreamkeepers: Successful teachers of African American children.* San Francisco, CA: Jossey-Bass.

Ladson-Billings, G. (1995). Toward a theory of culturally relevant pedagogy. *American Educational Research Journal, 32*(3), 465–491.

Ladson-Billings, G. (2014). Culturally relevant pedagogy 2.0: The remix. *Harvard Educational Review, 84*(1), 74–84.

Lau v. Nichols, 93 S. Ct. 2786, 412 U.S. 938 (Supreme Court 1973).

Lee, C. D. (1995). A culturally based cognitive apprenticeship: Teaching African American high school students skills in literary interpretation. *Reading Research Quarterly, 30*(4), 608–630.

Lee, S. (2005). *Up against Whiteness: Race, school, and immigrant youth.* New York, NY: Teachers College Press.

Leonardo, Z. (2009). *Race frameworks: A multidimensional theory of racism and education.* New York, NY: Teachers College Press.

Lomawaima, K. T., & McCarty, T. L. (2006). *To remain an Indian: Lessons in democracy from a century of Native American education.* New York, NY: Teachers College Press.

Love, B. L. (2012). *Hip Hop's li'l sistas speak: Negotiating Hip Hop identities and politics in the new South.* New York, NY: Peter Lang.

Low, B. E. (2011). *Slam school: Learning through conflict in the Hip Hop and spoken word classroom.* Stanford, CA: Stanford University Press.

Martin Luther King Jr., etc. v. Ann Arbor Sch. Dist., 473 F. Supp. 1371 (E.D. Mich. 1979).

Martínez, D. C. (2017). Imagining language solidarity for Black and Latinx youth in English language arts classrooms. *English Education, 49*(2), 179–196.

McCarty, T. L., & Zepeda, O. (1995). Indigenous language education and literacy: Introduction to the theme issue. *The Bilingual Research Journal, 19*(1), 1–4.

Moll, L. (1992). Literacy research in community and classrooms: A sociocultural approach. In R. Beach, J. L., Green, M. L., Kamil, & T. Shanahan (Eds.), *Multidisciplinary perspectives in literacy research* (pp. 211–244). Urbana, IL: National Conference on Research in English and National Council of Teachers of English.

Moll, L., & Gonzalez, N. (1994). Lessons from research with language minority children. *Journal of Reading Behavior, 26*(4), 23–41.

Morrison, T. (1998, March). From an interview on *Charlie Rose*. Public Broadcasting Service. Retrieved from http://www.youtube.com/watch?v=F4vIGvKpT1c

Neal, M. A. (2006). *New Black man*. New York, NY: Routledge.

Nieto, S. (1992). *Affirming diversity: The sociopolitical context of multicultural education*. New York, NY: Longman.

Paris, D. (2011). *Language across difference: Ethnicity, communication, and youth identities in changing urban schools*. Cambridge, MA: Cambridge University Press.

Paris, D. (2012). Culturally sustaining pedagogy: A needed change in stance, terminology, and practice. *Educational Researcher, 41*(3), 93–97.

Paris, D., & Alim, H. S. (2014). What are we seeking to sustain through culturally sustaining pedagogy? A loving critique forward. *Harvard Educational Review, 84*(1), 85–100.

Pennycook, A. (2007). *Global Englishes and transcultural flows*. New York, NY: Routledge.

Perry, I. (2004). *Prophets of the hood: Politics and poetics in Hip Hop*. Durham, NC: Duke University Press.

Petchauer, E., & Hill, M. L. (Eds.). (2013). *Schooling hip-hop: Expanding hip-hop based education across the curriculum*. New York, NY: Teachers College Press.

Rolón-Dow, C. (2005). Critical care: A color(full) analysis of care narratives in the schooling experiences of Puerto Rican girls. *American Educational Research Journal, 42*(1), 77–111.

Romero, M. E. (1994). Identifying giftedness among Keresan Pueblo Indians: The Keres study. *Journal of American Indian Education, 34,* 1–16.

Rose, T. (1994). *Black noise: Rap music and Black culture in contemporary America*. Middletown, CT: Wesleyan University Press.

Schwartz, R., & Prakash, N. (2016). Meet the inspiring woman who's educating the children of the Standing Rock protesters. *Fusion*. Retrieved from http://fusion.net/story/373249/standing-rock-nodapl-protesters-defenders-water-school/?utm_source=facebook&utm_medium=social&utm_campaign=fusion

Smith, M. D. (2016). *Invisible man, got the whole world watching: A young black man's education*. New York, NY: Nation Books.

Smitherman, G. (1977). *Talkin and testifyin: The language of Black America*. Detroit, MI: Wayne State University Press.

Smitherman, G. (Ed). (1981). *Black English and the education of Black children and youth*. Detroit, MI: Wayne State University Press.

Strauss, V. (2014, August 21). For first time, minority students expected to be majority in U.S. public schools this fall. *The Washington Post*. Retrieved from http://www.washingtonpost.com/blogs/answer-sheet/wp/2014/08/21/for-first-time-minority-students-expected-to-be-majority-in-u-s-public-schools-this-fall/

Taylor, P. (2014). *The next America: Boomers, millennials, and the looming generational showdown*. New York, NY: Public Affairs/Perseus Book Group.

Tuck, E., & Yang, K. W. (2014). R-words: Refusing research. In D. Paris & M. T. Winn (Eds.), *Humanizing research: Decolonizing qualitative inquiry for youth and communities* (pp. 223–247). Thousand Oaks, CA: SAGE.

Urrieta, L. (2010). *Working from within: Chicana and Chicano activist educators in whitestream schools*. Tucson, AZ: University of Arizona Press.

Valdés, G. (1996). *Con respeto: Bridging the distances between culturally diverse families and schools*. New York, NY: Teachers College Press.

Vizenor, G. (1994). *Manifest manners: Postindian warriors of survivance*. Middletown, CT: Wesleyan University Press.

Waitoller, F. R., & King Thorius, K. A. (2016). Cross-pollinating culturally sustaining pedagogy and universal design for learning: Toward an inclusive pedagogy that accounts for dis/ability. *Harvard Educational Review*, 86(3), 366–389.

Walker, V. S. (2013). Ninth annual Brown lecture in education research. Black educators as educational advocates in the decades before Brown v. Board of Education. *Educational Researcher*, 42(4), 207–222.

Williams, Q. E. (2017). *Remix multilingualism: Hip hop, ethnography, and performing marginalized voices*. New York, NY: Bloomsbury.

Woodson, C. G. (2000). *The mis-education of the Negro*.: Trenton, NJ: Africa World Press. (Original work published 1933.)

Wyman, L., McCarty, T., & Nicholas, S. (Eds.). (2014). *Indigenous youth and multilingualism: Language identity, ideology, and practice in dynamic cultural worlds*. New York, NY: Routledge.

PART I

ENACTING CULTURALLY SUSTAINING PEDAGOGIES: STUDENTS, TEACHERS, AND SCHOOLS

CHAPTER 2

"You Ain't Making Me Write"
Culturally Sustaining Pedagogies and Black Youths' Performances of Resistance

Valerie Kinloch
University of Pittsburgh

CHRISTINA AND A WAY IN

Christina, an 18-year-old Afro-Jamaican female from Perennial High School in the U.S. Northeast, stood 4 feet 5 inches tall in midsize heels, and she offered a stare that could cut through steel. This girl was on fire: She had a tough exterior, a strong sense of self-confidence, and an intriguing disposition that reflected a combination of responsibility and concern on the one hand, and impracticality and disinvestment on the other hand. She walked as if to say, "I don't care who you are . . . I'm coming through." Christina came through, day after day, within an English classroom where I initially met her, and within the out-of-classroom spaces where I came to know her as more than a girl on fire. She was a girl whose fire represented ways of surviving in a world of peers and adults who often misunderstood, criticized, and/or dismissed her.

"You *taaaalllll*," were her first words to me. "You, like, so tall I can't even see your . . . I just can't see all of you." I interpreted her comment not just as a joke about height—granted, I am a Black woman who stands 6 feet tall—but also as a confession about Christina not being fully seen by people. When I laughed, she exclaimed, "You don't know me. I don't know you. If you want to keep it that way, fine. I'mah let you know straight up, this me. You don't have to want me here, but that's too bad." She did a sharp side turn, as if she were cutting corners in a Cadillac, or cutting me, for that matter. The smoke from her fire fully engulfed the classroom, and I had one of two choices to make: (a) remain silent and lose face as the English teacher in a class of 29 high school seniors staring at me, or (b) recognize that Christina was publicly performing a narrative of resistance to feelings of alienation and miscommunication that resulted from her daily interactions with teachers, administrators, and peers at the school.

I responded, "Nice to meet you. Guess we'll learn a lot about each other." She replied, "Yeah, right. Whatever, Mizz." Her "Mizz" was pronounced with a long, drawn-out, bee-buzzing-sounding "z." Without pause, she insisted, "By the way, Mizz, you teaching this class, you need to know upfront you ain't making me write. I don't write. We don't write in here." Christina walked away and class began, but not before I came to recognize her fire as fierceness and her refusal to name herself as a writer as her attempt to protect herself from my gaze.

DEREK ON WANTING SOMETHING

Derek, a 17-year-old Black male from Truth High School in the U.S. Midwest, was 5 feet 6 inches tall, head half-bowed and eyes dreaming of something that appeared very far away. He was neither passive nor quiet, but, as he explained, "always thinking about something better": a better school, better interactions with peers, better relationships with teachers and administrators, and better life opportunities. "Better" appeared in his facial reaction and in each word that came out of his mouth. Some of his peers and teachers at Truth High did not always understand his deep desire for better, as marked by those occasions when they would publicly refer to him as "different," "angry," "trouble," and/or "troubled."

We first met in the hallway leading to Ms. Washington's English classroom. I accidentally bumped into him, and he mean-mugged me. In other words, he threw me a hard, intense look complete with an exaggerated and aggressive facial expression as if to ask, "Why you looking at me? You don't want any of this." I said, "My bad." And he stared. I reached my hand toward his shoulder, and his mean-muggin' intensified. I knew the code implied in that gesture, so I let it go until I saw him walk into the same classroom I was going into. I asked who he was, and he questioned, "You talking to me?" Again, I let it go. Later, a student suggested I not bother Derek since "he don't wanna be here anywayz" (there was that same bee-buzzing-sounding "z" that Christina had given me years before). But my mind, heart, and soul knew I couldn't leave him be.

For days, I thought about his question, "You talking to me?" and how he asked it—as if he both dared and wanted me to answer it. The next time I ran into Derek was near the school's front office. Again he stared at me, and I said, "Hey Derek. How you doing?" The stare faded when he responded, "Good." But his reply turned distant: "Wait. How you know my name, son? You talking to me?" Then he said, "Why you here?" Instead of giving a long, drawn-out answer, I said, "To collaborate, to write, with students." Derek responded, "You trying to collaborate with me? That's why you said my name? You want something . . . I ain't into that writing." He walked away before I could answer.

INVITATIONS INTO LEARNING

My initial encounters with Christina and Derek provide more expansive ways for me to see, listen to, and work in collaboration with young people in urban schools. Christina's strategies of undermining me with language and Derek's accusations that I called him by name because I wanted something signify performances of resistance that often get misread in educational spaces as angry, hostile, and quasi-violent. I use the phrase *performances of resistance* to refer to a mode of communication or a particular, directed way of responding to the negative gaze, the degrading treatment, and the hurtful assumptions many youth of color receive from others, peers and adults alike. They engage in performances of resistance (e.g., eye-rolling, sharp verbal responses, silence, a seemingly disinterested disposition, absence, etc.) as a way to protect and safeguard themselves from the harmful, potentially painful, damaging forms of interaction they often encounter from others who might misread, misunderstand, ridicule, and denigrate them. Given that schools are primary sites of ideological struggle—for racial and linguistic equality, for educational equity, against the criminalization and disenfranchisement of students of color—young people's performances of resistance are not uncommon (see Penn, Kinloch, & Burkhard, 2016).

How educators read these performances, however, is crucial to the ways they come to know, hear, and see young people beyond assumed personas and stereotyped images, and in light of the complex ways young people get positioned within dominant discourses about failure and underachievement. For me, these performances are connected to the reality that Derek and Christina do not see themselves as writers inside school, and that school (e.g., the educational system, standardized curricula, the controlling White gaze) has contributed to creating and sustaining these resistances. As Christina shared, "You ain't making me write. I don't write," and as Derek assured me, "I ain't into that writing" because, as he later explained to me, "school ain't safe."

Derek and Christina are two of many youth of color with whom I have worked who have resisted identifying as writers in school. From Eva, Aureliano, Phillip, and Samantha to Damian, Karen, Rendell, and others, the declarations ring loud: "I don't write well like them" (Eva, 2011); "I'm not a writer, either. I don't do much on that front" (Aureliano, 2012); and "I used to like writing . . . but what I like to do doesn't happen in school as you see from this essay bleeding in bright red [from a teacher's written comments]" (Phillip, 2008). Connected to their refusal to identify as writers in school is an even larger concern: Many youth of color are intentionally placed under surveillance and are taught that survival, achievement, and success can happen only if they follow the rules, meet above and beyond the expectations, and perform in specific ways that, ultimately, *other* who they are (e.g., their familial, community, and racial identities, linguistic practices, and cultural and intellectual traditions). This othering, circulated through official school-sanctioned practices, expectations, and behaviors, is a dangerous form of mis-education (Coates, 2015; Hill, 1998; Woodson, 1933/1990) that does not recognize, care about, or seek to sustain the lives, cultures, histories, languages, and literacies of students of color.

In this chapter, I present qualitative data on the literacy engagements and classroom performances of Christina and Derek as I consider the deeper implications of their comments in relation to culturally sustaining pedagogy (CSP) and youth performances of resistance. My inquiry is guided by the question: What is the import of CSP on the literacy engagements of young people who resist being seen as writers inside school? Addressing this question through a CSP framing allows me to argue that Christina and Derek's resistances are directly connected to constraints imposed upon them by "a monocultural and monolingual society based on White, middle-class norms of language and cultural being" (Paris, 2012, p. 95). Given that such norms position some Black students as violent, delinquent, and academically inadequate, there is a strong need for sustaining pedagogies that argue against the ongoing pathologizing of Black lives, languages, and literacies. Such pedagogies must purposefully situate Blackness, Black cultural practices, and Black people within assets-based, rather than deficit-oriented, perspectives.

I wholeheartedly believe that Christina and Derek demonstrate agency and resolve despite (and/or because of) their performances of resistance. The examples I share in this chapter point to the significance of CSP in youth literacy lives in ways that reframe Christina and Derek's performances of resistance from hopeless to hopeful.

CULTURALLY SUSTAINING PEDAGOGIES (CSP)

To interrogate Derek and Christina's resistances to being seen as writers inside school, I turn to CSP. Conceptually, CSP recognizes the import of multiculturalism and multilingualism for students, teachers, and other agents of educational change. It also "seeks to perpetuate and foster—to sustain—linguistic, literate, and cultural pluralism as part of schooling for positive social transformation" (Alim & Paris, Chapter 1, this volume). CSP relies on Ladson-Billings's (1995) formulation of culturally relevant pedagogy (CRP) to deepen students' cultural competences and literacy practices from multiple sociocultural contexts. According to Ladson-Billings (1995, CRP) "empowers students intellectually, socially, emotionally, and politically by using cultural referents to impart knowledge, skills, and attitudes" (pp. 17–18). It also encourages teachers to have high expectations for students and to recognize the realities and causes of social inequities.

This understanding of CRP pushes me toward CSP because CSP disrupts dominant narratives that superficially affirm differences and diversities while maintaining the status quo. Maintenance of the status quo comes at the expense of the lives, literacies, and languages of Black students and other students of color, many of whom are regularly criminalized inside class-rooms and assaulted within their own communities. Teachers and research-ers have no choice but to delve deeply into (and expand on) meanings of cultural relevance and responsiveness if the languages and literacies of youth of color are to be sustained.

Additionally, for CSP to be effective, then collaborative, collective, crit-ical, and loving environments must be fostered that support young people's cultural identities, academic investments, and critiques of White middle-class values. Such environments must not only honor and examine youth heritage practices and community engagements, but also provide them with access to opportunity and power. To do this, we must work to combat and eradicate oppressive, racist educational policies that advantage monoculturalism, that debase the linguistic virtuosities of communities of color, and that recode terms such as *relevance* and *responsiveness* to mark tolerance over accep-tance, normalization over difference, demonization over humanization, and hate over love.

Thus, my utilization of CSP points to a necessary extension of CRP that seeks to sustain the literacy, heritage, and community practices of youth of color.[1] My concern is with understanding what CSP means for Black stu-dents generally, and for Derek and Christina specifically, who attend schools that have neither fully honored nor sustained their identities.[2] Do Christina and Derek fit into this conceptualization of CSP—a pedagogy that takes a critical stance to prepare students to confront the classist, racist, and sexist realities of succeeding in mainstream contexts? What is the import of CSP on their literacy engagements?

LEARNING TO "SEE ALL OF YOU"

To examine students' resistances to being seen as writers inside schools, I provide ethnographic data collected across two different contexts: from a senior-level English class at Perennial High School during the 2006–2007 academic year, and from a junior-level English class at Truth High School during the 2012–2013 academic year. Perennial High is a public school that employed 24 teachers and served 330 students across grades 9–12. At the time of this study, 29% of the students identified as Black, 69% as Hispan-ic, and 1% as Asian, identification markers used by district officials. The school, founded in the early 1990s by a university professor, is a Title I and an Empowerment School[3] with an interdisciplinary curriculum, an extended day program, and a multiyear arts and language requirement. It was within this context and in my role as a visiting English teacher that I worked with Christina and her peers.

Nearly 600 miles from Perennial is Truth High, a Title 1 urban public school that employed 47 certified teachers and served 800 students across grades 9–12. During my time at Truth, 81.5% of the students identified as Black, 11.5% as White, 5% as Hispanic, and 1% as Asian; and of the total percentage of enrolled students, 20% identified as physically disabled, identification descriptions used by district officials. Originally founded in the mid-1970s as a junior-senior school that enrolled nearly 1,200 students, Truth High is located in a longstanding White residential community. It was at Truth High that I collaborated with Derek and his peers by facilitating writing workshops alongside Ms. Tori Washington, an educator in the district with more than 17 years of teaching experience.[4]

From my time at Perennial and Truth high schools, I collected required and voluntary student writings, responses to questionnaires, and school statistics. I conducted conversational interviews with students and school personnel, and maintained observational fieldnotes. Also, I employed a qualitative research approach framed by critical literacy to categorize recurring themes related to youth resistances to being seen as writers. Doing so allowed me to think deeply about data across two phases: (1) an ethnographic phase, in which I coded observations from fieldnotes, transcripts from interviews, teaching materials, and archival data on the schools and local communities; and (2) a narrative analytic phase, in which I documented student writings and highlighted processes they used in the production of texts. Both phases revealed students' interests in completing nonrequired school activities (e.g., reading sci-fi and street lit, blogging, writing in personal journals, engaging in spoken word performances) and their resistances to school-sanctioned tasks (e.g., reading canonical texts, completing 5-paragraph essays, filling in worksheets, sitting in assigned desks). In what follows, I provide qualitative data and examples from Christina and Derek to show the *what, how,* and *why* of CSP.

CHRISTINA IS A GIRL ON FIRE

In the opening anecdote, I reference some of Christina's performances of resistance through verbal and nonverbal forms of communication and her attitude that "straight up, this me." In part, her resistances speak to how she thinks others feel about her ("You don't have to want me here") and how she views her writing identity ("I don't write"). Daily, Christina tried to convince me that she is an A student, as indicated by her comments: "Anywayzzz, here's my homework. . . . It's an A 'cause I worked hard on it, okay" and "Y'all say just do the work and that's what I do." Christina's belief that she is an A student does not mean she sees herself as a writer, which is evident in her confession, "I'mah A student, that don't mean I'm a writer. I ain't never said that!" For Christina, "How I write ain't from my soul. That don't factor into anything. How I write is by filling up the page so y'all be like, 'She write a lot. OK, she got an A.'"

Christina's resistances are also related to how she believes others see her—as uncaring, disruptive, and "dumb." Her assuredness that she is an A student is one way for her to protect herself from criticism, about which she confesses, "I always get that from y'all." Christina performs what others have come to expect from her, a performance that signifies compliance ("just do the work") and resistance ("I ain't never said that"). Her *performances of resistance* are attempts to protect herself from the unrelenting gaze of others who do not see her as capable enough or academically sophisticated. The many one-on-one conversations I had with Christina revealed a young woman who never felt valued in school and was positioned, to use her words, as a "dumb Black girl nobody taught to write." Her confessions were situated in the painful reality that her cultural and linguistic ways of being were not worth accepting, honoring, and affirming because she did not act, write, talk, or look like those who enjoyed the benefits of White privilege.

I observed how Christina measured her self-worth through what Du Bois (1965) refers to as "a peculiar sensation . . . this sense of always looking at one's self through the eyes of others, of measuring one's soul by the tape of a world that looks on in amused contempt and pity" (p. 45). Christina's comments—"accept me for what I show you" and "how I write ain't from my soul"—reflected her desire to decide for herself how she should be "measured." She did not write from her soul because schooling taught her to "give what they want . . . that's all I do." Thus, Christina's performances of resistance were also her attempts to reject embodied narratives—not intelligent, not good enough, too loud—that others had placed upon her.

The following snapshot of how Christina writes and believes others judge her derived from her response to a class-generated question, "How do you define community?":

> My neighborhood not so bad or to, to good. Its getting better than expected. Its just write. Know one gets hearts [hurt] they anymore. They talk . . . and don't fight. I think. They were good and bad things that was said and also happen in the neighborhood. But we have move on for the better and will do better. I wrote on neighborhood, maybe thats the same as community. Now you no my sites. . . . Y'all go 'head judge me. I say what true. . . . Y'all could laugh or roll eyes at me, so what.

A narrow, classist reading of Christina's response through the lens of Dominant Academic English (DAE)[5] would exclusively focus on issues with word choice, misspellings, and points of departure from the topic that could indicate a narrative of academic failure.[6] Additionally, reading her response through a *raciolinguistic ideology* would conflate, or flatten, her racialized identity "with linguistic deficiency unrelated to any objective linguistic practices" (Flores & Rosa, 2015, p. 150). According to Flores and Rosa (2015), such an ideology would "produce racialized speaking subjects who are constructed as linguistically deviant even when engaging in linguistic practices positioned as normative or innovative when produced by privileged white subjects" (p. 150). Hence, the need to critique and resist the White gaze in order to understand how Christina's response represents a narrative of possibility, as marked by her belief, for her community explicitly and herself, implicitly, that "we . . . will do better." This narrative of possibility allows me to reject deficit readings of Christina's academic ability in favor of a culturally sustaining perspective that both hears and seeks to sustain her voice and linguistic dexterity, while still supporting her in strengthening that dexterity. When I asked Christina to reflect on her writing, she shared: "It's not as lengthy as it could be, but you ain't askin' 'bout length." She continued, "Like my neighborhood could do better, I know I could be better, but y'all just gonna judge me anyways, so why try better?" Christina's writing is less about academic failure (as measured by DAE) and more about academic possibility—the opportunities afforded by African American Language (AAL) and CSP—which is evident in her wanting to "be better" and not wanting to be judged in light of enacted performances of resistance.

Additional narratives of possibility surfaced throughout the academic year. During a student-facilitated writing workshop, Christina asked if she could revisit the above writing sample with the entire class. When her peers agreed, she stated: "I could've learned if I was not so . . . bad. I'm not understood in this school and that, like, comes out in how I act and talk and even write. I'm working on it. It's hard when nobody listens to you or wants you around." She continued, "I shared my journal and it ain't that good, but I hope y'all connected to it." One of Christina's peers, Damya, quickly replied, "You act out because you think we don't like you? That impacts how you write and talk? That's powerful. You need to reject failure . . . be comfortable being you." Another student, Juan, asked Christina to consider "why you do what you do," while Carlos added, "Be you. Show that side more because we in this game together." He explained that "this game," or schooling, as he later named it, tries "to make you someone you don't recognize when looking in the mirror. It wants us sounding like somebody else when we open our mouth." Juan, Damya, and Carlos knew how to play the game (DAE, schooling) without relinquishing their identities to monolingual, monocultural norms based in White, middle-class standards. Christina was beginning to learn, and her involvement in a CSP classroom proved crucial.

As students listened to Christina read her revised journal, they realized she was not too different from them. They offered encouraging words that invited her to disrupt pervasive discourses of failure that contend that Black students are hostile and not intelligent. Christina became committed to interacting with peers, and she sought opportunities (e.g., volunteering to read in class) and spaces (e.g., English class, the school library) to display her learning, given that systemic inequalities hindered these opportunities from already being available. Carlos's comment, "we in this game together," helped her to question her actions (e.g., name-calling, hiding behind the length of her writings). Eventually Christina admitted: "I still ain't no writer yet. I used to not share 'cause you get tired of being laughed at. Maybe I [she paused]. We'll see, Mizz."

Just as much as Christina held firmly to her use of AAL to assert her identity, she also used it to sustain her self-worth in school as she acquired new and extended avenues of academic expression. In this way, her fire was being sustained rather than silenced or disciplined. Instead of allowing school to continue to transform her into a compliant student, or, as Carlos explained, "sounding like somebody else when we open our mouth," Christina maintained her cultural ways of being by refusing monolingualism. She contributed to creating a classroom environment and viewing herself in ways that rejected unidirectional and deficit readings of multiple racial, cultural, and linguistic identities.

"TRY BETTER": DEREK AND WRITING FOR CHANGE

In the second anecdote, I write about Derek's performances of self—his dead stare, his comment that I wanted something, and his hesitation to engage in a conversation. His resistances ("You talking to me?") masked who he was and what he regularly contemplated ("something better"). In Ms. Washington's class, Derek frequently sat quietly in a desk positioned in a corner near the front of the room. He sometimes slouched in his desk with one hand perched on his cheek. At other times, he sat up with a bold presence as if intently listening to directives from Ms. Washington. When I think about Derek, I am reminded of Christina. While their classroom behaviors differ—Christina appears aggressive, while Derek appears standoffish—the ways others judge them through a racialized lens as angry and troublemakers are all too similar and problematic.

During a co-teaching session with Ms. Washington, I asked students if they saw themselves as writers. Some said yes, some said maybe, and Derek said, "Nope." As Ms. Washington continued the discussion, I went to sit next to Derek, and when I asked him directly if he considered himself a writer, he stared at me before lowering his head and replying, "Nah." I retorted, "Do you like writing?" to which he said, "Nah." I asked, "If you could write on anything, what would it be?" He looked at me and said, "I don't know. I don't really write. I mean, I know how to . . . I'm not a writer." His head lowered slightly, and I sat there.

Derek was "not a writer," or at least that's what he tried to convince me. At the end of class, Ms. Washington and I talked about motivating students to see themselves as writers. According to Ms. Washington, "Our students are critical thinkers and writers. They have to see that." I replied: "They might not think so because we ask them to write in certain ways. Too many of us go from saying, 'Be yourself, just write,' to demanding, 'But don't write like that, don't talk like that.' Then students don't write and don't see themselves as writers." Reflecting on this conversation helps me to see that Ms. Washington and I wanted to "support young people in sustaining the cultural and linguistic competence of their communities while simultaneously offering access to dominant cultural competence" (Paris, 2012, p. 95).

The following week, as Ms. Washington and I facilitated a writing session, she said to students: "We want you to write an essay on, if you could change anything in the world, then what would it be, and why?" Derek stared at the floor after Ms. Washington wrote the prompt on the board. Over the next class sessions, he did not participate in peer-to-peer writing exchanges. However, near the end of one class session, he left the room only to return a few seconds later to ask Ms. Washington and me to read his essay. At that point, I noted that his disposition shifted, and when I asked Ms. Washington about it, she shared, "He's got a lot going on in his life, so I try to be present and patient. I care. I hope he sees that." In follow-up conversations with Derek, it became obvious to me that he did notice how Ms. Washington interacted with him—"I know she care, but I gotta care more." Throughout the year, Derek was learning to "care more," and his decision to voluntarily share his essay was indicative of this point. It was also indicative of someone who was working against his earlier claim that he was "not a writer."

His essay opened with, "If I could change anything I wanted to change, I would change my attitude and behavior toward my peers, the staff at my school, and most importantly, my family." He continued: "I do have some troubles following directions that are given to me by adults. I try my hardest to control that problem, but most of the time I be bored so I give adults a hard time for no reason at all. I would give almost anything in the world to just be normal and not be disrespectful or rude anymore." Derek was aware that his behavior—how he acts, how people perceive him at school, how he sees himself—is marked as "disrespectful." He has internalized White middle-class norms of behavior (respectful/disrespectful, normal/rude, in control/out of control) that have marginalized many young Black males and females and their ways of being in the world. Derek was also aware of a major factor in his behavior: "I think I disrespect adults a lot because I don't have my dad in my life."[7] His awareness led him to ask questions about why. Take the following excerpt from his essay as an example:

> I have not seen my dad in about a good year. My dad does not call on holidays or my birthday, he don't even try to put his self in my life. Why? I do not know, maybe its cause he has too many kids to keep

up with. I try not to let this bother me as much because I still have my mom, my grandma, my older brother, sister, and my uncle. I really don't need my dad at all. I just really want to graduate so I can tell him that I did it all without him, maybe that will encourage him to be in his younger kids' lives.

The story Derek has chosen to share in relation to the question, "If you could change anything in the world, then what would it be, and why?" invited him to write a narrative of (be)longing: He wants to belong in, and graduate from, school. Simultaneously, he longs to understand why his father is currently not in his life. Derek's narrative further develops when he admits that his attitude is hampering his success: "I'm a junior in high school and I'm acting like I'm in the 4th grade, and that's not good at all." He continues: "What if I do graduate and it's time to go out into the real world? I don't want to end up on the streets or even worse, in jail." Derek knows the options, however one-sided and racist, that school is laying out for him: assimilate to specific ways of doing school and being a student, or fail and, possibly, end up in jail. In contrast to these limited and unjust possibilities is Derek's desire to sustain his worth, value, and identity.

The story Derek shares, the moves he makes, and the stances he takes in his writing demonstrate a sophisticated communicative style. In fact, his narrative speaks to his storied ways of communicating, which are connected to his storied ways of being, knowing, performing, and working to/for change. This latter point surfaces near the conclusion of his essay when he writes:

> I'm done playing the blame game. It's all me and it's time I just accept the fact that I messed up and change. My man Gandhi once said, "Be the change you wish to see in the world." If I could live up to this quote, then I would, but I feel like something is holding me back. But we all know that's just an excuse, so I'm just going to try and live everyday in peace.

His way of seeing self cannot be divorced from the pervasive narratives of social inequalities and racialized expectations of behavior and language that are placed upon Black and Brown bodies. Derek unfairly takes the majority of the blame for his actions, probably because he is carrying the weight of the world on his shoulders or, as he says, "being grown too soon for everybody." Like many other youth of color, Derek turns to the myth of individual accountability, meritocracy, and respectability and assumes that changing his behavior would change the structural and ideological barriers that already exist and define him as less than, not good enough, and wrong. In seeking to sustain his identity—his current and future selves—Derek wants to gain access to opportunities that will not hold him back, and in order to do so, he must come to accept that he is not wrong or, according to poet June Jordan (2005), "*I am not wrong: Wrong is not my name* / My name is my own my own my own / and I can't tell you who the hell set things up like this" (p. 311; author's original emphasis).

Because many people do not see this reflexive side of Derek, he appears distant and uncaring. However, a close reading of his written text demonstrates that Derek is not only dealing with his father's absence, but also trying to figure out ways to not be overcome with this burden in his attempt to change and "live everyday in peace." An even closer reading reveals that Derek's resistances to being seen as a writer are unrelated to his ability to produce written texts. His resistances point to his fear of being a disappointment ("It breaks my mother's heart every time I do something wrong") and a success ("I want to go to college, too, but it don't look like that's going to happen"). To borrow a phrase from Christina, Derek's writing reveals a desire to "try better" within the context of a CSP classroom, which has implications for the sustainability of his identities in the larger world.

WRITING AS RESISTANCE

On the surface, Derek's writing addresses the assigned prompt with details, evidence, and emotions. Underneath the surface is a narrative that signifies his desire to belong and protect himself from others. In that regard, Derek's narrative is not too different from Christina's. They both feel as if they are not welcomed in their school community. As Derek indicated, "Most days, I wake up and think today is going to be a good non-disrespectful day, but like always, I find some way to mess it up,"[8] and "they're [colleges] not going to want someone like me." As Christina shared: "They gotta judge me. I don't like that. But I'mah try," and "you get tired being laughed at." Derek and Christina engage in performances of resistance that position them as active agents who struggle against being ostracized in school, be it through the norms of "proper" behavior or the requirements of DAE. The ways they are constructed as "bad" or "disrespectful" do not encapsulate the complexities of their identities and academic performances, but serve to name how others read them within racialized narratives that plague schools and their inability to serve Black students. Just as much as these constructions do not fully account for Christina and Derek's resistances to being seen as writers, they also do not account for the value of non-DAE cultural practices that already exist and operate in classrooms.

Christina's resistances have a lot to do with her belief that she is academically underprepared: "I ain't *really* good doing school. I know that, but they [her peers] be encouraging me now." Her resistances also have to do with her awareness that others will judge "my behavior and talk and how I be writing. You can't win." Christina's classroom performances are attempts to do schooling in ways that safeguard her from the negative gaze she receives from teachers and peers. Yet this safeguarding is disrupted when Christina's peers offer her support at a critical juncture in her life—just before she graduates high school and leaves behind the people and structures that have allowed her performances of resistance to go largely misinterpreted for years.

Derek's resistances have less to do with how he writes and more to do with his disengagement with school and school's disengagement with him. Similar to Christina, Derek feels as if he "can't win." His references to his father not being in his life and his desire for good days tell a story about resistances. Derek believes he is a disappointment to others. Yet his confession that he knows Ms. Washington cares provides an opening for Derek to call into question his resistances as he moves toward being seen as a writer—and more importantly, a human being—in school and in the world.

As much as their writing styles differ, Derek and Christina's writings exhibit power, passion, and presence. In her revised writing sample, Christina argues for community improvement, as evidenced by references to the community as "getting better because people are caring about other people there." She also mentions school as a community site where people can "actually like each other, work together, too." Although Christina still believes she is not "understood in school," she more fully embraces her ability to use "my language of comfort to be who I am." Her writings, stances, and desire to do well in school in light of how she performs narratives of resistance encourage me to reflect on how culturally sustaining pedagogy might transform public school classrooms.

Derek's writing also demonstrates passion. He not only confesses to giving "adults a hard time," but also to trying "my hardest to control that problem." Ms. Washington's writing assignment encouraged Derek to consider "what I'd like to change about me and what I want to keep as me." His thinking about self, to include a focus on his attitude and desire for change, are not simply Derek's concerns. They should be the concerns of teachers who want to create classrooms and implement practices that are culturally sustaining for Black students and other students of color who are "linguistically and culturally flexible across multiple language varieties and cultural ways of being" (Paris & Alim, 2014, p. 96; also see Chapter 1, this volume). Thus, I am left to think about how Derek's resistances to being seen as a writer speak to his fear of academic success and his reluctance to critique those structures (as well as people and narratives) that have painted him as "trouble."

It is important to note here that, understandably, Derek and Christina do not trust easily and are often not willing to express their own thoughts in class. They struggle to foster authentic interactions with their peers and teachers. Although they are moving to such a place and are beginning to recognize the support networks that are present, it is clear that their performances of resistance continue to influence their academic engagements. This is important to acknowledge, given the concrete challenges that both students face in terms of their academic trajectories, and given the larger lessons educators must learn about creating loving, critical, and welcoming schooling environments.

IS THIS CULTURALLY SUSTAINING?

CSP acknowledges the complexities of identities, lived conditions, and performances of resistance that are a part of the schooling experiences of many students of color. It facilitates and centers student learning, and it encourages teachers to have an unbreakable commitment to educational equity and cultural, racial, and social justice. Christina's resistances to being seen as a writer and having people "see all of you" represent how her literate identities have been devalued in schools. She performs schooling by drawing attention away from "what I can't do." Many of Derek's resistances result from his feelings of abandonment. He performs schooling in ways that disconnect and protect him from others. Their performances of resistance, however, must be viewed as invitations into learning and not as indications of deficiency or failure.

One way for teachers to view students' resistances as invitations into learning is by working with students to co-construct classroom spaces that support multiple literacy engagements and perspectives. Hence, the why of CSP: It is necessary because it not only validates who students are and their ways of knowing, it also locates students at the center of classrooms through assets-based, humanizing perspectives that lead to pluralism. This why has far-reaching implications for how students of color sustain their heritage and community practices, how they access power and opportunity in schools, and how they see themselves—racially, ethnically, linguistically, intellectually, socially, politically, and civically—in the world. In this way, students reject narratives of failure that demonize their intellectual acuity and cultural competences, and they accept narratives of belonging that locate them within the process and project of schooling.

This latter idea leads to the how of CSP. That is, we must do this work by rejecting racist, classist, deficit-oriented educational approaches that undermine the rich languages, literacies, and identities of racially and ethnically diverse students. And yet I realize that this is not an easy task, especially when rejections of such approaches often reinforce them, and when acts of disruption of the status quo unintentionally perpetuate the status quo. Indeed, racism and internalized oppression are real. The need for equitable educational opportunities and access to material resources is real. So, too, are the performances of resistance of countless students of color in public schools. The how of CSP leads me to argue that teachers need to be supported in placing more attention on deconstructing pervasive narratives of failure that prevent many students of color from extending their linguistic, literate, and cultural selves in ways that resist tendencies toward assimilation and individualism.

Theoretically, the what of CSP is that it is a pedagogy that does not tolerate differences as sidebars to dominant ways of schooling that have always relegated to the margins the languages, literacies, and cultural practices of students of color. CSP provides opportunities to interrogate Christina's assertion, "I don't write," just as much as it affords space for Derek to reflect on Gandhi's sentiments about being "the change you wish to see." Such interrogations can happen through student writings, because of student resistances, and in light of the sophisticated experiences students bring to schools. CSP encouraged Christina and Derek to work with others to reveal the complexities of their identities and to reject failure. This point is evident in Derek's confession, "Schools, the institution, don't care if I fail . . . I need to stop getting caught in the cycle." Derek is attempting to not get "caught" and Christina is "trying better." Their attempts must be supported by CSP educators who are committed to (a) placing multiculturalism, multilingualism, and racial, cultural, and social justice at the center of teaching and learning; (b) turning the gaze away from White middle-class expectations and onto the heritage and community practices of youth of color; and (c) facilitating young people's critiques of racist institutional barriers that have long hindered and that continue to hinder their academic success.

As teachers, I think it would behoove us to utilize CSP—in the construction of our classroom spaces, in the design of curricula, and in how we see, listen to, interact with, and respond to students—in humanizing and loving ways. Derek, like many youth of color, continues to feel alienated in school and gets caught in other people's positioning of him as angry and quasi-violent. Christina has a long way to go in nuancing her use of DAE and AAL, and in how she sees herself in the world. In part, sustaining their identities across their learning depends on their relationships with adults who understand the value of CSP when working with youth of color inside schools and communities.

NOTES

1. It is important to note that my utilization of CSP is highly informed by CRP as well as by cultural modeling and critically conscious research. Cultural modeling is a framework whose aim "is to facilitate students' learning generative concepts in academic subject matters by helping them to make connections between the target knowledge and forms of knowledge they have constructed from their home and community experiences" (Lee, Rosenfeld, Mendenhall, Rivers, & Tynes, 2004, p. 42). Critically conscious research is "a commitment to equity, social justice, and the valuing of multiple languages and literacies" (Willis et al., 2008, p. 130). It requires researchers to use transformative theoretical frameworks and analytical approaches.

2. I am not singularly attacking public schools for failing to honor and sustain the literacies, lives, and identities of Black students, but the

system of inequity and inequality that allows many of our public schools to underfunction because of a lack of necessary resources, infrastructures, and services (Kinloch, Burkhard, & Penn, in press).

3. Title I Schools receive extra federal funding "to ensure that all children have a fair, equal, and significant opportunity to obtain a high-quality education and reach, at a minimum, proficiency on challenging State academic achievement standards and state academic assessments" (see http://www2.ed.gov/policy/elsec/leg/esea02/pg1.html). Empowerment Schools are "schools at which principals have greater autonomy in exchange for agreeing to take on greater responsibility for producing results in terms of student academic achievement" (see http://schools.nycenet.edu/region6/midwood/empowerment.html).

4. In earlier publications, I used the pseudonym Janice Moore to write about the teacher in this study, whose real name is Tori Washington. She has given me permission to use her real name.

5. I use dominant academic English (DAE) to emphasize privilege, power, exclusion, and dominance in discussions of language, literacy, race, culture, schooling, and identity.

6. Christina employs AAL and grammar, as marked by the regularization of the verb form with tense (happen vs. happened), use of one verb form for plural and singular with number indicated by subject (things that was vs. things that were), and optional copular (neighborhood not so bad; what true).

7. While Derek admits that his "disrespect" has to do with his father not being present, I believe it also has to do with dominant norms and values that unfairly blame single-parent households for young people's alleged "acting-out" behaviors. We must seriously interrogate this blame game, and as we do, we must find ways to honor and understand the experiences young people such as Derek share with us. In this way, I am not supporting simple absent Black father narratives, but rather seeking to better understand Derek's lived experiences and performances of resistance.

8. Derek's sentiments here point to his internalization of individual accountability. While the ways he interacts with others and in particular spaces do matter, the how and why of his interactions get misread by racist, classist expectations of schooling that automatically view him (his actions, behaviors, performances, identities) as indicative of someone who is wrong and "disrespectful." These expectations point to larger issues related to respectability politics.

REFERENCES

Coates, T. (2015). *Between the world and me*. New York, NY: Spiegel & Grau.
Du Bois, W. E. B. (1965). *The souls of Black folk*. New York, NY: Avon Books. (Original work published 1903.)

Flores, N., & Rosa, J. (2015). Undoing appropriateness: Raciolinguistic ideologies and language diversity in education. *Harvard Educational Review, 85*(2), 149–171.

Hill, L. (1998). *The miseducation of Lauryn Hill* [CD]. Philadelphia, PA: Ruffhouse, Columbia.

Jordan, J. (2005). Poem about my rights. In J. Jordan (Ed.), *Directed by desire: The collected poems of June Jordan* (pp. 309–312). Port Townsend, WA: Copper Canyon Press.

Kinloch, V., Burkhard, T., & Penn, C. (in press). When school is not enough: Understanding the lives and literacies of Black youth. *Research in the Teaching of English.*

Ladson-Billings, G. (1994). *The dreamkeepers: Successful teachers of African American children.* San Francisco, CA: Jossey-Bass.

Ladson-Billings, G. (1995). Toward a theory of culturally relevant pedagogy. *American Educational Research Journal, 32,* 465–491.

Lee, C. D., Rosenfeld, E., Mendenhall, R., Rivers, A., & Tynes, B. (2004). Culturally modeling as a frame for narrative analysis. In C. Daiute & C. Lightfoot (Eds.), *Handbook of research on multicultural education* (pp. 39–62). Thousand Oaks, CA: Sage.

Paris, D. (2012). Culturally sustaining pedagogy: A needed change in stance, terminology, and practice. *Educational Researcher, 41*(3), 93–97.

Paris, D., & Alim, H. S. (2014). What are we seeking to sustain through culturally sustaining pedagogy? A loving critique forward. *Harvard Educational Review, 84*(1), 85–100.

Penn, C., Kinloch, V., & Burkhard, T. (2016). The languaging practices and counternarrative production of Black youth. In S. Nichols (Ed.), *Educational policies and youth in the 21st century: Problems, potential, and progress* (pp. 23–38). Charlotte, NC: Information Age Publishing.

Willis, A. I., Montavon, M., Hunter, C., Hall, H., Burkle, L., & Herrera, A. (2008). *On critically conscious research: Approaches to language and literacy research.* New York, NY: Teachers College Press.

Woodson, C. G. (1990). *The mis-education of the Negro.* Trenton, NJ: Africa World Press. (Original work published 1933.)

CHAPTER 3

Language and Culture as Sustenance

Mary Bucholtz, Dolores Inés Casillas, and Jin Sook Lee
University of California, Santa Barbara

Our multiliteracies operate in contentious spaces.

—Elisa, student researcher-activist

Spanglish is a skill, not a mistake.

—Isabel, student researcher-activist

For scholars, educators, and activists committed to culturally sustaining pedagogy, the U.S. public discourse on the education of low-income students of color ranges from disheartening to infuriating: The moralistic revival of so-called character education in schools for Black and Brown students, driven by a bizarrely influential study of preschoolers' willpower to withstand the siren song of marshmallows (Mischel, Shoda, & Rodriguez, 1999). The white elite's unflagging fascination with the thoroughly debunked notion of a "language gap" between poor children of color and their white middle-class counterparts (Hart & Risley, 1995). The establishment of militaristic, testing-obsessed, "no-excuses" charter academies for poor youth of color (Moskowitz & Lavinia, 2012), which so thoroughly terrorize students that they wet themselves rather than dare ask permission to use the restroom (Taylor, 2015). The racist and classist view of poverty as a moral failing, articulated by neoconservatives such as *New York Times* columnist David Brooks (2015), who, to take but one notorious example, gratuitously maligns Freddie Gray's character and educational attainment but neglects to mention this young Black man's horrific state-sponsored murder at the hands of Baltimore police officers.[1]

As scholarly critiques of these and similar pronouncements have shown (e.g., Avineri et al., 2015; Flores & Rosa, 2015; Giroux, 2015; Golann, 2015; Lack, 2009; Rose, 2014; Smitherman, 2000; Zentella, 2014), throughout this discourse runs the common theme of deficit: the notion that youth of color lack the language, the culture, the family support, the academic skills, even the moral character to succeed and excel. But the true deficiency lies with such commentators, who—despite draping themselves in the trappings of scholarship—rely on deeply problematic ideological assumptions rather than solid empirical evidence about the nature and experience of social inequality. As a result, advocates of the deficit viewpoint repeatedly fail to recognize not only the devastating effects of structural racism but also the considerable community-based resources available to young people to counter these processes in their own lives.

One of the most important yet most devalued resources available to youth of color is their language. Young people in general, and young people of color in particular, are frequently disparaged by adults for undermining their own "professional" self-presentation and even "destroying the language" by speaking in ways that are deemed "uneducated," "improper," "illogical," "sloppy," "lazy," "broken," and "ungrammatical." Abundant linguistic research has demonstrated, however, that youth, especially those from economically, racially, and/or linguistically marginalized communities, are in fact innovative, flexible, and sophisticated language users, and that language is central to young people's creation of their identities (e.g., Alim, 2004; Bucholtz, 2011; Mendoza-Denton, 2008; Paris, 2011; Reyes, 2007; Rosa, in press; Wyman, McCarty, & Nicholas, 2014). Recognizing the importance of language in the lives of youth of color, Django Paris and Samy Alim include the valorization of language as a central component of culturally sustaining pedagogy, or CSP (Paris, 2012; Paris & Alim, 2014a).

In this chapter, we expand on the importance of language in CSP by arguing that the linguistic repertoires of youth of color must be sustained in educational contexts because language is a crucial form of sustenance in its own right, providing the basis for young people's complex identities as well as their social agency. Our discussion is supported by examples taken from a social-justice-centered program informed by the CSP perspective. We focus on the experiences and insights of two Latina high school students within the program, who drew on their linguistic creativity and resourcefulness in ways that challenged widespread racialized ideologies of Spanish-English bilingual youth as linguistically deficient (see also García, 2009). As these students' stories indicate, a commitment to CSP enables educators to recognize and support the agency of young people of color by working with them to sustain and develop their identities as linguistic and cultural experts.

In the title of their 2014 essay, Paris and Alim ask, "What are we seeking to sustain through culturally sustaining pedagogy?" They offer the following answer to their question: "CSP seeks to perpetuate and foster—to sustain—linguistic, literate, and cultural pluralism as part of the democratic project of schooling and as a needed response to demographic and social change" (2014b, p. 88). Importantly, within CSP the concept of culture is not limited to longstanding traditional or heritage-based cultural practices that students participate in as members of their families and communities; it is these forms of culture that are the most visible to and valued by educators, leading in some cases to oversimplified or essentialist assumptions about how to bring students' cultures into classrooms. Rather, CSP also encompasses realms of cultural practice that tend not to be recognized as such and are instead often pathologized as evidence of cultural, intellectual, or moral deficiency: the newly emergent linguistic and cultural practices of families and communities undergoing often rapid change, as well as the innovative forms of language and culture that are created by young people themselves in peer interaction. In addition to sustaining family-, community-, and peer-based cultural practices, CSP strives to ensure that students gain full access to the practices associated with larger institutional and structural power as well as the tools to critique the processes of power.[2] In short, a pedagogy that truly sustains culture is one that sustains cultural practices too often excluded from classroom learning and leverages these as resources both for achieving institutional access and for challenging structural inequality. In this way, CSP fosters the full range of young people's expertise and thereby has the potential to transform schooling into a force for social justice.

The motivating premise of CSP, then, is that *culture is to be sustained.* This premise rests in turn on a second premise, which is immanent in but has not yet been fully discussed in the groundbreaking work on CSP: *Culture sustains.* That is, it is culture, produced primarily via language, that endows experience with meaning and provides a deeply held sense of identity and social belonging. It is precisely because of the central role of language and culture in sustaining selfhood that there is a vital need for pedagogical practices that sustain students' language and culture in classrooms and other learning contexts. For this reason, CSP is an especially necessary framework for educators who seek social justice for their students of color, whose sense of self is constantly under attack from schooling practices and policies that racialize and thereby devalue, distort, and erase their language, culture, and identity.

In the following pages, we discuss two examples of how, within a CSP approach, youth of color in a California classroom found new ways of understanding their language and culture as sustenance for their identities. Through this process, as we show, students not only engaged in transformative learning experiences but also undertook courageous and powerful agentive acts to advance sociolinguistic justice—that is, "self-determination for linguistically subordinated individuals and groups in sociopolitical struggles over language" (Bucholtz et al., 2014, p. 145)—in their school and community.

SCHOOL KIDS INVESTIGATING LANGUAGE IN LIFE AND SOCIETY (SKILLS)

The context of our discussion is a university–community partnership based at the University of California, Santa Barbara. Since 2010, faculty, graduate students, and undergraduates have been collaborating with educators and students in the Santa Barbara area within a social-justice-centered program combining research, academic preparation, and activism. This program, School Kids Investigating Language in Life and Society (SKILLS), closely aligns with the goals of CSP. Since its inception, SKILLS has involved over 800 public school students from six urban, rural, and suburban municipalities in two counties on California's Central Coast. SKILLS youth participants have ranged in age from 6 to 19, with most of high school age; nearly all students are of Latina/o background, come from working-class families, and are the first generation in their family to be college-bound. Although the program takes different forms at each partner site, depending on the interests and needs of the participants, the overall focus is the critical examination of language, culture, race, power, and identity in the United States, with a central goal of fostering sociolinguistic justice. The 5-month curriculum guides students to investigate a variety of topics through original research and activism. The results of their work are shared both on the SKILLS website (www.skills.ucsb.edu) and at the daylong SKILLS conference held annually at UC Santa Barbara.[3]

The SKILLS program strives to achieve the goals of CSP in three ways:

1. By supporting and developing the full repertoire of cultural and linguistic practices that young people engage in with their communities, families, and peer groups.
2. By facilitating students' access to the language and culture of institutional power.
3. By guiding students to critically scrutinize and directly challenge social inequality or exclusion, whether in the practices that perpetuate institutional power or in those that they themselves employ and encounter in their everyday lives (see also Paris & Alim, 2014b).

To accomplish these aims in the classroom, the SKILLS program is innovative both in how teaching takes place and in what is taught. The program seeks to go beyond the usual one-way transmission of knowledge in conventional classrooms. Instead, similar to other proponents of CSP and related perspectives (e.g., Alim, 2007; Cammarota, 2011; Irizarry, 2009), SKILLS takes a youth-centered approach that emphasizes the agency, expertise, and self-determination of young people as researcher-activists and positions scholars and educators as learners alongside their youth partners (Bucholtz, Casillas, & Lee, 2016; Lee & Bucholtz, 2015). The class has no tests, no exercise drills, and very little homework; learning takes place through discussion, activities, written reflections, and original research and community action projects conceptualized and implemented by teams and individual students.

SKILLS also differs sharply from traditional schooling in the content of its classes. With the guidance of the teaching team, student researcher-activists systematically explore a wide variety of issues regarding language, culture, race and racialization, power, and identity that are directly relevant to their lives. These issues may include slang and youth language; translanguaging and hybrid language practices; language brokering; individual, familial, and community language shift; peer policing of language and identity; and linguistic racism, among others. Such topics are central to students' everyday lived experience and sense of self, yet they are rarely if ever addressed in subject area classes at the high school level, which by policy privilege written language over spoken language, academic language over everyday language, and English over Spanish and other languages.[4] Thus the SKILLS curricula follow CSP principles in valorizing and sustaining students' own linguistic and cultural practices rather than only those prized by the educational system.

The two students who are the focus of our discussion participated in the SKILLS program at one of our four partner sites in Spring 2014. This site was Mission City High School's 12th-grade college preparation class for first-generation college-bound students. The 25 students, all of them Latina/o, received college credit at no cost for their participation in the SKILLS program through a partnership with a local community college. The class was led by two graduate student teaching fellows, Zuleyma Carruba-Rogel and Audrey Lopez, in collaboration with the partner teacher and a team of undergraduate mentors and research assistants. Each of the teaching fellows conducted original research within the classroom based on video recordings of program activities as well as ethnographic fieldnotes and other forms of data collected by the researchers and their undergraduate research assistants. The following discussion draws on chapters written by Audrey and Zuleyma for an edited volume about the SKILLS program (Carruba-Rogel, in press; Lopez, in press). Although our goals in this chapter are not precisely the same as those of the authors in their original work, we are deeply indebted to them for sharing their important research with us. Below, we consider the linguistic expertise and social agency of two bilingual students of Mexican American heritage, Isabel and Elisa, whose achievements within the SKILLS program were a focus of the graduate students' research.[5] These young women's experiences can help scholars and educators to better understand language and culture as sustenance within a CSP framework.

SUSTAINING PRACTICES, SUSTAINING IDENTITIES

The examples of Isabel and Elisa provide two different illustrations of how CSP can sustain the linguistic and cultural practices of young people of color, and how these practices in turn sustain youth identities. In both cases, through their work within the SKILLS program the students discovered new ways of conceptualizing culturally meaningful linguistic practices that were devalued by adults in their lives, and these new perspectives facilitated their use of language to publicly claim their identities as bilingual Latina youth. For Isabel, this involved the valorization of translanguaging practices and using these to sustain her identity in a community setting of mostly Spanish-dominant adults. For Elisa, learning that her linguistic practice of everyday interpreting between Spanish speakers and English speakers was an important topic of scholarly research provided sustenance for her identity in the face of English hegemony in the institutional context of her school.

Isabel's Spanglish Translanguaging

Our first example, focusing on Isabel, took place at a special Family Night event at Mission City High School. Because most of the parents of the SKILLS youth participants worked during the day and would be unable to attend the SKILLS Day conference at UCSB, Zuleyma, Audrey, and the SKILLS students decided to host an alternative event so that the student researcher-activists could share their ongoing work on a linguistic autobiography project with their parents and other family members. The student presenters were encouraged to use whatever linguistic practices they preferred in order to address their audience; most students presented in Spanish, and several presented in English, with simultaneous interpreting provided by bilingual UCSB undergraduates.

Isabel was the only student who chose to present her linguistic autobiography through what she termed Spanglish, the way of speaking that she most closely associated with her own identity. As a linguistic practice that creatively combines elements of Spanish and English, Spanglish is a form of translanguaging, which Ofelia García and her colleagues define as "the deployment of a speaker's full linguistic repertoire without regard for watchful adherence to the socially and politically defined boundaries of named (and usually national and state) languages" (Otheguy, García, & Reid, 2015, p. 283). Because Spanglish does not conform to monolingual ideologies of grammatical correctness, and because it is usually associated with racialized Latina/o bodies (Chapter 10, this volume), this practice is often stigmatized by Spanish-dominant and English-dominant speakers alike as an indication of linguistic deficit in both languages. Yet Isabel's oral presentation at Family Night was anything but deficient: She spoke fluidly and confidently, artfully weaving together Spanish and English as she wove together the threads of her life, from her religious faith to her passion for tattoos and cartoons, from her use of slang to a serious personal issue that she and her family were facing. The following is the beginning of Isabel's presentation; although by its very nature translanguaging practices like these cannot be "translated" straightforwardly into a single language, we have tried to give some sense of her meaning. (Portions of Isabel's speech that have been "translated" into English are marked with italics.)

Mi nombre es Isabel Sanchez, y- \<looking at microphone\> Wait, is this thing even on? Is it on? Okay. \<Zuleyma: Le tienes que, le tienes que gritar.\> Okay! I'm sorry! \<laughs; Zuleyma laughs\>	*My name is Isabel Sanchez, and- \<looking at microphone\> Wait, is this thing even on? Is it on? Okay. \<Zuleyma: You have to, you have to shout into it.\> Okay! I'm sorry! \<laughs; Zuleyma laughs\>*
Um, es mi vida de my autobiography de linguistics. Y lo hace en inglés y español. Spanglish! \<laughs\>	*Um, \<this\> is my life of my linguistic autobiography. And I'll do it in English and Spanish. Spanglish! \<laughs\>*
Yo me considero mexicana- Mexican American! \<laughs; audience laughs\>	*I consider myself Mexican-Mexican American! \<laughs; audience laughs\>*
So, eh, mi nombre que yo me considero es Isabel Carina Sanchez de la Vega Herrera.	*So, uh, my name that I consider myself is Isabel Carina Sanchez de la Vega Herrera.*
Porque es el nombre de mi mamá, y de mi abuela, que tanto quiero. Pero ya mi mamá me dijo que soy Isabel Carina Sanchez.	*Because that's my mom's name, and my grandma's, who I love so much. But then my mom told me that I'm Isabel Carina Sanchez.*
Y cumplí mis quince, cuando yo put up there. \<looks at Power-Point slide\>	*And I had my fifteenth birthday, when I put up there. \<looks at PowerPoint slide\>*
Yo me considero católica, que es San Juda Tadeo, y en esa parte, yo n- sé que necesito estar al respecto. No debo decir malas palabras, que eso es parte de una, parte que me ha considerado, (que me ha sido acerca con) el padre de mi iglesia. Ehm, Guadalup- Nues- Our Lady of- Nuestra- \<laughs\> Our Lady of Guadalupe! \<laughs\>	*I consider myself Catholic, which is Saint Jude Thaddeus, and in that area, I don't- I know that I need to be respectful. I shouldn't say bad words, that that's part of a, part that I've considered myself, (that I've been near with) the priest at my church. Um, Guadalup- Our- Our Lady of- Our- \<laughs\> Our Lady of Guadalupe! \<laughs\>*
Y me llaman Sissi. Porque mi prima Diane no sabía decir mi nombre Isabel cuando estaba chiquita. Y solo una persona afuera mi familia me llama eso. \<laughs\> . . .	*And they call me Sissi. Because my cousin Diane couldn't say my name Isabel when she was little. And only one person outside my family calls me that. \<laughs\> . . .*

Yo habla diferentes terms, como con mi familia yo digo, "Qué onda," "Chales," "Qué on-" \<laughs, points to mother in audience\> Yo puedo hablar igual a la mamá. \<laughs\> Aquí I'm like, "Battle!" "What's up then?" Yeah. \<laughs\>	*I speak different* terms, *like with my family I say,* "What's up?" "Hell, no!" "What's u-" \<laughs, points to mother in audience\> *I can talk like my mom.* \<laughs\> *Here* I'm like, "Battle!" "What's up then?" Yeah. \<laughs\>

Isabel's presentation involved translanguaging from the very outset, from her title PowerPoint slide ("My Life/Mi Vida") to her alternation between Spanish and English in order to manage the interactional demands of public speaking: Spanish for greeting her audience and introducing herself and English for off-record asides as she tested the microphone. But she put her commitment to Spanglish on record as well, quite literally, by announcing that she would be presenting her linguistic autobiography "en inglés y español—Spanglish!" This act of linguistic identity was matched by Isabel's acts of ethnoracial and national identity. Not only did she identify herself bilingually as both "mexicana" and "Mexican American," but she visually represented these affiliations on a PowerPoint slide that displayed two pieces of an American flag with a Mexican flag between them.

Isabel also showcased her linguistic dexterity in other ways. When she described the different slang that she uses at home and at school, she introduced this topic with the academic vocabulary item *terms*, which was part of the register of linguistics she had learned in the SKILLS class, rather than a more ordinary word like *words*. And she went on to offer a performance of her slang use that was rich both in Spanish and English youth language and in translanguaging practices.

Isabel spoke honestly, engagingly, and at times movingly; her utter fearlessness and her dazzling smile charmed the crowd, who applauded her enthusiastically. Yet in traditional schooling, in which whiteness and monolingualism are hegemonic, there is no place for this young woman's linguistic and cultural expertise. The rigid English-only policies of California's public schools, part of larger monolingual policies and practices in U.S. education (Fillmore, 2004), barred Isabel from using any Spanish in her conventional subject area classes to talk, write, or read, formally or informally, about her own bilingual life. Meanwhile, the only Spanish-medium classes available at her school, Spanish for heritage speakers, enforced a highly prescriptive variety of the language that was alien to most bilingual students and that negatively sanctioned bilingual youths' innovative practices of translanguaging.

Hence, Isabel's presentation was a small but significant political challenge to an educational system that rejected her linguistic knowledge, enabling her, for the first time, to publicly and proudly display her expertise as a bilingual youth to an adult audience. Her agentive choice to tell her linguistic life story in her own language—Spanglish—was supported by Zuleyma and Audrey's teaching within the SKILLS program, rooted in the CSP principle to sustain rather than disparage young people's linguistic practices. The class discussion of bilingualism in particular made a considerable impact on Isabel: The instructors challenged the widely held ideology that translanguaging is a sign of linguistic deficiency in both Spanish and English and showed students that it is instead an advanced bilingual ability. This is more than a mere linguistic fact; in its acknowledgment of speaker skill, it goes to the very heart of identity. Thus Isabel's experience in SKILLS sustained her rich repertoire of linguistic and cultural practices and hence her identity as both *mexicana* and Mexican American.[6]

However, even when educators work to sustain students' linguistic and cultural practices, these efforts may not be taken up by other adults in young people's lives. At the end of the student presentations at Family Night, Isabel's mother expressed great pride in her daughter but also remarked that Isabel's Spanish was *mocho,* 'choppy,' not recognizing that her daughter's linguistic practices were not a deficient form of Mexican Spanish but a highly skilled and innovative form of California Spanglish in which Spanish and English are seamlessly integrated into a single whole (Carruba-Rogel, in press). This devaluation of Spanglish is common among Spanish speakers in the United States, for a variety of complex reasons (Sánchez, 1983; Zentella, 2007).

But what might be perceived as "errors" in Isabel's presentation are in fact evidence of language contact and change, normal and natural linguistic processes in any living language. Therefore, her use of regularized verb forms such as *lo hace,* 'I'll do it,' and *yo habla,* 'I speak' (rather than the Spanish verb forms *lo hago* and *yo hablo*), or her movement between Spanish and English renderings of *Our Lady of Guadalupe/Nuestra Señora de Guadalupe* should be understood not as mistakes but as the innovative and hybrid resources available to advanced speakers of Spanglish.[7] Such resources provide a strong foundation for developing further skills in multiple varieties of both English and Spanish, alongside—not instead of—Spanglish. The CSP perspective taken within the SKILLS program acknowledges the significance of young people's cultural and linguistic practices for sustaining identity without denying or downplaying the complexities and contestations that such practices often generate, both within and beyond community boundaries (see also Carruba-Rogel, in press; Paris & Alim, 2014b).

Elisa's Bilingual Language Brokering

Our second example of how CSP sustains identity by sustaining the language and culture of youth of color is taken from Elisa's experiences. Where for Isabel the SKILLS program provided sustenance for her identity as a young Latina whose language differed from adult norms in her community, for Elisa, SKILLS offered sustenance for her identity as a Spanish speaker in the institutional setting of the school, where English was hegemonic. The two young women's situations differed in another important way as well: While neither the school nor the community recognized Isabel's Spanglish as a valid and valuable linguistic practice, Elisa's Spanish was acknowledged as a useful skill in both of these settings, since it provided a means of communication between Spanish-dominant adults in the Latina/o community and English-dominant adults in the educational system and other institutional domains (see also Valdés, 2015). Nevertheless, Spanish was not valued on an equal footing with English in the school context, as demonstrated by both policy and practice.

In the face of this institutional ambivalence toward Spanish, CSP sustained Elisa's bilingual identity by sustaining her practice as a language broker. As part of the SKILLS curriculum that Audrey and Zuleyma developed, they introduced the students to the concept of language brokering, or young bilinguals' everyday work of providing interpretation and translation services for family and community members (Orellana, 2009; Valdés, 2003). Because this was a practice that many students engaged in in their daily lives, it led to a lively discussion that extended over two class periods. During the second discussion, Audrey invited Elisa to comment on her experiences as a language broker. Elisa responded as follows:[8]

> Well, I feel really happy that I'm able to help, because I've experienced it in so many ways. I've done it with my family, in school, out of school. And the one that I really like the most—I'm not saying I don't like my family, but I feel really happy that I do it when I go and interpret for other schools. For like the Open House, and the parents come and visit the class, and hear the teacher speak: "Oh, this is what the course is gonna be about." And the last time I did it, it was a first-grade class. And then there's parents that don't speak English. And I'm able to translate and interpret whatever the teacher says. So that they can get the message and get more involved in their students' education. Because I feel like without me, that wouldn't be possible. So I'm really happy that I can help these kids out, because you don't know what their future's going to be like. So hopefully I'll help.

Elisa's response focused on her experiences of brokering outside the home as a member of Mission City High School's interpreters club, a program that built on the expertise of bilingual youth by training them to serve as interpreters in educational settings such as parent–teacher conferences. This opportunity not only enabled Elisa to take pride in her bilingual abilities, but also to use them to help advance social and educational justice. Describing her experiences interpreting for the parents of 1st-graders, she noted, "So I'm really happy that I can help these kids out, because you don't know what their future's going to be like. So hopefully I'll help." Elisa's characterization of her emotional experience inspired similarly emotional reactions from the instructors: Immediately following her comments, Zuleyma exclaimed, "You're making my heart sing! I'm so happy!" and Audrey added an emotional "Aw!"

In this situation, the instructors sustained Elisa's and her classmates' bilingual practices in a number of ways. They did so in the first instance simply by providing students with an academic term to name their experience and by recognizing the expertise required to perform the very demanding task of language brokering. But further, Audrey and Zuleyma also engaged in CSP by inviting discussion of students' experiences as language brokers and then emotionally validating such experience. This validation in turn sustained students' bilingual identities: Elisa's joy and pride in the work she did as a language broker—an emotion vicariously shared by her instructors—became tied to her identity as someone who could help others by virtue of her linguistic expertise.

If a CSP approach truly sustains the language and culture of youth of color, and these in turn sustain young people's identities, then the impact of CSP should be evident not only in specific vivid moments like those described above but also over longer periods of time. And indeed, the sustaining effects of Audrey's and Zuleyma's teaching were even clearer at the end of the program. For their final presentations for the SKILLS Day conference at UCSB, Isabel and Elisa formed a research team with two other students to carry out a project that they called "El Poder de Poder: Appreciating Our Linguistic Abilities" (the title translates as 'The Power of Power'). At SKILLS Day Isabel spoke of the importance of Spanglish for her cultural and linguistic identity, proudly stating, "Spanglish is a skill, not a mistake," and explaining that encountering this idea within the SKILLS program gave her a more positive perspective on her bilingual linguistic abilities. For her part, Elisa spoke with remarkable sophistication about her challenges to the school's hegemonic monolingualism, as she put it, which we discuss below, "Our multiliteracies operate in contentious spaces." The student researcher-activists' powerful presentations demonstrated to a large audience of adults—university faculty, graduate and undergraduate students, staff, and the general public—as well as to their peers within the SKILLS program that for these young people of color, language and culture provide essential sustenance for identity.

In fact, the effects of the SKILLS program's commitment to sustaining youth language and culture reached even further. Inspired by her experiences in Zuleyma and Audrey's class and with the support of her instructors, Elisa initiated a one-student political campaign to change the English-only policy of the school's commencement ceremony for graduating seniors. Elisa discovered this policy when she was selected as a commencement speaker. When she submitted the text of her speech in Spanish, school personnel told her that she would have to give the speech in English. Elisa argued that this requirement would prevent her family from understanding what she was saying at one of the proudest moments of her and their lives. Under the school's monolingual policy, and in the context of wider racialized ideologies of English hegemony in U.S. society, Spanish was framed as at best a way station to English and at worst an obstacle to communication, not as a resource to be sustained or as a source for sustaining students' identities. The idea that Spanish could take precedence over English contradicted the school's ideology that Spanish is only appropriate as a brokering tool, with the end goal being communication in English.

Yet in the end, Elisa's persuasive arguments convinced the administration to change the policy. She gave her speech in Spanish, and an English translation that she provided was printed in the commencement program. This was the first time in the school's history that a student had been permitted to give a commencement address in Spanish; thanks to Elisa's work, all student commencement speakers now have the option of giving their speeches in Spanish. Her activism, and the work of linguistic and cultural sustenance that helped inspire it, thus successfully challenged a monolingual policy at her own school and paved the way for other bilingual commencement speakers to use their home language to celebrate their academic accomplishments with their families.

The experiences and accomplishments of Isabel and Elisa as researcher-activists within the SKILLS program illustrate how practices of CSP sustain young people's linguistic and cultural practices, creating a space in which young people's abilities are recognized and prized, and hence sustain students' identities. More broadly, such practices help youth to connect their own experiences and actions to a larger history of working collectively toward social justice for communities of color. For Isabel, CSP provided sustenance for her identity within her community by valorizing her use of Spanglish despite its differences from adult ways of speaking. For Elisa, CSP sustained her identity within the institutional context of the school by supporting her work as a language broker as well as her efforts to undo a discriminatory language policy. And for both students, the SKILLS program's legitimation of linguistic practices associated with youth and Latina/o identities challenged the notion of school as an English-only white public space (Hill, 1999). Thus, in sustaining students' language and culture within the classroom, CSP also extends beyond the classroom to sustain lives that are too often devalued by hegemonic practices and policies.

CSP: TRANSFORMING LEARNING, TRANSFORMING SOCIETY

In this chapter we have argued that language and culture are not only resources to be sustained, but are themselves forms of sustenance that nurture the identities of young people of color. For this reason, CSP offers a necessary refinement of the earlier concepts of culturally relevant pedagogy (Ladson-Billings, 1995) and culturally responsive pedagogy (Gay, 2000). These frameworks, importantly, call for students' cultural practices to be central to the learning process. But where terms such as *relevant* and *responsive* position culture solely as the target of pedagogical practice, CSP connects culture directly to sustenance, as both its target and its source.

As deficit discourses continue to circulate and escalate, the dignity and humanity of youth of color are under constant assault in the U.S. public sphere (see also Paris & Winn, 2014). Young people from racialized groups have been framed—in both senses of the word—as lacking in the qualities and abilities needed to succeed in the educational system and beyond. Language has been a particular focus of such attacks, as young people engage in ways of speaking that do not conform to adult norms and so are dismissed as inappropriate, incorrect, and deficient. Educators are in a crucial position to challenge these pernicious misrepresentations by creating pedagogies that sustain students' linguistic and cultural practices. Such pedagogies are transformative not only of the learning process but also of the larger social sphere. When young people's language and culture are recognized as valid and valuable, and when young people themselves are respected as linguistic and cultural experts, then educators and students become partners in learning and in using their collective knowledge to bring about social change. Youth of color come to understand their language in a new light: as creative and innovative rather than "wrong," as a powerful symbol of family and community belonging rather than as a marginalized practice. Sustained by this knowledge, young people like those we discuss in this chapter may act to dismantle the artificial boundaries that exclude their language from public spaces, bringing "informal" language into formal settings and introducing bilingual practices into monolingual domains. These acts of sociolinguistic justice will of course often be met with resistance—and such opposition makes educators' sustenance of youth agency and identity all the more necessary.

Thus, CSP is an ethical imperative for educators and allies of young people of color. To sustain culture is to sustain the lives of those who enact it, and, conversely, to devalue culture is to devalue the lives of those who enact it. It is in this fundamental sense that language and culture are resources to be sustained as well as sources of sustenance for identity.

NOTES

Acknowledgments: We wish to express our deep appreciation for the important intellectual contributions and inspiration of the student researcher-activists in the 2014 School Kids Investigating Language in Life and Society (SKILLS) program at Mission City High School, especially Elisa and Isabel. Our sincere thanks also go to our administrator and teacher partners for welcoming SKILLS into their school. We are deeply grateful to the graduate student teaching fellows who taught the class, Zuleyma Carruba-Rogel and Audrey Lopez, for generously sharing their research, their insights, and their experiences with us for this chapter. Special thanks to Lizette Wences and Cheryl Lee for assistance with the transcription and editing of video clips. We gratefully acknowledge the many UCSB sponsors of the 2014 SKILLS program, especially the Center for California Languages and Cultures, the Crossroads Initiative, the Institute for Social, Behavioral, and Economic Research, and the Office of Education Partnerships. Finally, we thank the editors as well as the other participants in the Half Moon Bay Collective for their valuable feedback.

1. The U.S. Department of Justice, which investigated the Baltimore Police Department for a year after the murder of Freddie Gray, found that the police department "engages in unconstitutional practices that lead to disproportionate rates of stops, searches and arrests of African-Americans, and excessive use of force against juveniles and people with mental health disabilities," among other serious violations of the law (Grinberg, 2016).

2. As Paris (2012, p. 94) points out, these are also the goals of Gloria Ladson-Billings's (1995) culturally relevant pedagogy, which serves as a key inspiration and foundation for CSP.

3. The website also contains complete curricula from various implementations of the SKILLS program as well as team research on the program. Elsewhere we discuss the process of developing and implementing an education partnership between university members and local communities (Bucholtz, Casillas, & Lee, 2015).

4. By contrast, these topics are regularly covered in college-level curricula in sociolinguistics and linguistic anthropology, fields that students rarely encounter even in college; such courses serve as the general model for the content of SKILLS classes.

5. By school district policy, the names of all students and schools have been changed.

6. Another example of CSP in the SKILLS classroom was the instructors' validation of Isabel's preferred term for her translanguaging practice, *Spanglish*, a label that some linguists reject (Otheguy & Stern, 2011).

7. While in Spanish verb forms change depending on the subject, a common outcome of language contact and change is to maintain consistent verb forms regardless of the subject. Thus Isabel's consistent use of the most common verb form, the third person singular (*hace, habla*), should be understood not as disordered Spanish but as principled Spanglish. However, a fixation on grammatical form itself perpetuates racialized linguistic inequality: The dominance of the ideology of language-as-code over an alternative ideology of language-as-practice is one of the key reasons that normal processes of language variation, contact, and change are treated as deviant and deficient in educational settings (García & Wei, 2013).

8. We have edited and simplified the original transcript as presented in Lopez (in press).

REFERENCES

Alim, H. S. (2004). *You know my steez: An ethnographic and sociolinguistic study of styleshifting in a Black American speech community.* Durham, NC: Duke University Press.

Alim, H. S. (2007). Critical Hip Hop language pedagogies: Combat, consciousness, and the cultural politics of communication. *Journal of Language, Identity, and Education, 6*(2), 161–176.

Avineri, N., et al. (2015). Invited forum: Bridging the "language gap." *Journal of Linguistic Anthropology, 25*(1), 66–86.

Boler, M. (1999). *Feeling power: Emotions and education.* New York, NY: Routledge.

Brooks, D. (2015, May 1). The nature of poverty. *The New York Times,* p. A27.

Bucholtz, M. (2011). *White kids: Language, race, and styles of youth identity.* Cambridge, UK: Cambridge University Press.

Bucholtz, M., Casillas, D. I., & Lee, J. S. (2015). Team collaboration and educational partnership in sociocultural linguistics. *American Speech, 90*(2), 230–245.

Bucholtz, M., Casillas, D. I., & Lee, J. S. (2016). Beyond empowerment: Accompaniment and sociolinguistic justice in a youth research program. In R. Lawson & D. Sayers (Eds.), *Sociolinguistic research: Application and impact* (pp. 25–44). London, UK: Routledge.

Bucholtz, M., Lopez, A., Mojarro, A., Skapoulli, E., VanderStouwe, C., & Warner-Garcia, S. (2014). Sociolinguistic justice in the schools: Student researchers as linguistic experts. *Language and Linguistics Compass, 8*(4), 144–157.

Cammarota, J. (2011). A sociohistorical perspective for participatory action research and youth ethnography in social justice education. In B. A. U. Levinson & M. Pollock (Eds.), *A companion to the anthropology of education* (pp. 517–529). Malden, MA: Blackwell.

Carruba-Rogel, Z. N. (in press). The complexities in *seguir avanzando*: Incongruences between the linguistic ideologies of students and their *familias*. In M. Bucholtz, D. I. Casillas, & J. S. Lee (Eds.), *Feeling it: Language, race, and emotion in Latina/o youth learning.* New York, NY: Routledge.

Fillmore, L. W. (2004). Language in education. In E. Finegan & J. R. Rickford (Eds.), *Language in the USA: Themes for the twenty-first century* (pp. 339–360). Cambridge, UK: Cambridge University Press.

Flores, N., & Rosa, J. (2015). Undoing appropriateness: Raciolinguistic ideologies and language diversity in education. *Harvard Educational Review, 85*(2), 149–171.

García, O. (2009). Racializing the language practices of U.S. Latinos: Impact on their language. In J. A. Cobas, J. Duany, & J. R. Feagin (Eds.), *How the United States racializes Latinos: White hegemony and its consequences* (pp. 101–115). New York, NY: Routledge.

García, O., & Wei, L. (2013). *Translanguaging: Language, bilingualism and education.* Basingstoke, UK: Palgrave Macmillan.

Gay, G. (2000). *Culturally responsive teaching theory, research, and practice.* New York, NY: Teachers College Press.

Giroux, H. (2015, October 23). Culture of cruelty: The age of neoliberal authoritarianism. *Counterpunch.* Retrieved from http://www.counterpunch. org/2015/10/23/culture-of-cruelty-the-age-of-neoliberal-authoritarianism/

Golann, J. W. (2015). The paradox of success at a no-excuses school. *Sociology of Education, 88*(2), 103–119.

Grinberg, E. (2016, August 9). Baltimore police have racial bias, Justice Department reports. CNN. Retrieved from http://www.cnn.com/2016/08/09/us/baltimore-justice-department-report/

Hart, B., & Risley, T. (1995). *Meaningful differences in the everyday experience of young American children.* Baltimore, MD: Brookes.

Hill, J. H. (1999). Language, race, and white public space. *American Anthropologist, 100*(3), 680–689.

Irizarry, J. G. (2009). Reinvigorating multicultural education through youth participatory action research. *Multicultural Perspectives, 11*(4), 194–199.

Lack, B. (2009). No excuses: A critique of the Knowledge Is Power Program (KIPP) within charter schools in the USA. *Journal for Critical Education Policy Studies, 7*(2), 126–153.

Ladson-Billings, G. (1995). Toward a theory of culturally relevant pedagogy. *American Educational Research Journal, 32,* 465–491.

Lee, J. S., & Bucholtz, M. (2015). Language socialization across learning spaces. In N. Markee (Ed.), *Handbook of classroom discourse and interaction* (pp. 319–336). Malden, MA: Wiley-Blackwell.

Lopez, A. (in press). "Without me, that wouldn't be possible": Latina/o youth discussions of language brokering. In M. Bucholtz, D. I. Casillas, & J. S. Lee (Eds.), *Feeling it: Language, race, and emotion in Latina/o youth learning.* New York, NY: Routledge.

Mendoza-Denton, N. (2008). *Homegirls: Language and cultural practice among Latina youth gangs.* Malden, MA: Blackwell.

Mischel, W., Shoda, Y., & Rodriguez, M. L. (1999). Delay of gratification in children. *Science, 244*(4907), 933–938.

Moskowitz, E., & Lavinia, A. (2012). *Mission possible: How the secrets of the Success Academies can work in any school.* San Francisco, CA: Jossey-Bass.

Orellana, M. F. (2009). *Translating childhoods: Immigrant youth, language, and culture.* New Brunswick, NJ: Rutgers University Press.

Otheguy, R., García, O., & Reid, W. (2015). Clarifying translanguaging and deconstructing named languages: A perspective from linguistics. *Applied Linguistics Review, 6*(3), 281–307.

Otheguy, R., & Stern, N. (2011). On so-called Spanglish. *International Journal of Bilingualism, 15*(1), 85–100.

Paris, D. (2011). *Language across difference: Ethnicity, communication, and youth identities in changing urban schools.* New York, NY: Cambridge University Press.

Paris, D. (2012). Culturally sustaining pedagogy: A needed change in stance, terminology, and practice. *Educational Researcher, 41*(3), 93–97.

Paris, D., & Alim, H. S. (Eds.). (2014a). Symposium: Culturally sustaining pedagogy. *Harvard Educational Review, 84*(1).

Paris, D., & Alim, H. S. (2014b). What are we seeking to sustain through culturally sustaining pedagogy?: A loving critique forward. *Harvard Educational Review, 84*(1), 85–100.

Paris, D., & Winn, M. T. (Eds.). (2014). *Humanizing research: Decolonizing qualitative inquiry with youth and communities.* Los Angeles, CA: Sage.

Reyes, A. (2007). *Language, identity, and stereotype among Southeast Asian American youth: The other Asian.* Mahwah, NJ: Erlbaum.

Rosa, J. (in press). *Looking like a language, sounding like a race: Exclusion and ingenuity in the making of Latin@ identities.* New York, NY: Oxford University Press.

Rose, M. (2014, October 22). Character education: A cautionary note. Brookings Institution Center on Children and Families. Retrieved from http://www.brookings.edu/research/papers/2014/10/22-character-education-cautionary-note-rose

Sánchez, R. (1983). *Chicano discourse: Socio-historic perspectives.* Rowley, MA: Newbury House.

Smitherman, G. (2000). *Talkin that talk: Language, culture and education in African America.* New York, NY: Routledge.

Taylor, K. (2015, April 6). At Success Academy charter schools, high scores and polarizing tactics. *The New York Times.* Retrieved from http://www.nytimes.com/2015/04/07/nyregion/at-success-academy-charter-schools-polarizing-methods-and-superior-results.html

Valdés, G. (2003). *Expanding definitions of giftedness: The case of young interpreters from immigrant communities.* Mahwah, NJ: Erlbaum.

Valdés, G. (2015). Latin@s and the intergenerational continuity of Spanish: The challenges of curricularizing language. *International Multilingual Research Journal, 9*(4), 253–273.

Wyman, L., McCarty, T. L., & Nicholas, S. E. (Eds.). (2014). *Indigenous youth and bi/multilingualism: Language identity, ideology, and practice in dynamic cultural worlds.* New York, NY: Routledge.

Zentella, A. C. (2007). Dime con quién hablas y te diré quién eres: Linguistic (in)security and Latino unity. In J. Flores & R. Rosaldo (Eds.), *The Blackwell Companion to Latino Studies* (pp. 25–39). Malden, MA: Wiley-Blackwell.

Zentella, A. C. (2014). TWB (Talking while Bilingual): Linguistic profiling of Latina/os, and other linguistic *torquemadas. Latino Studies, 12*(4), 620–635.

CHAPTER 4

Upholding Indigenous Education Sovereignty Through Critical Culturally Sustaining/Revitalizing Pedagogy

Tiffany S. Lee
University of New Mexico

Teresa L. McCarty
University of California, Los Angeles

Education for Native American students is unique in that it implicates not only issues of language, "race"/ethnicity, social class, and other forms of social difference, but also tribal sovereignty: the right of a people to self-government, self-education, and self-determination, including the "right to linguistic and cultural expression according to local languages and norms" (Lomawaima & McCarty, 2006, p. 9). Tribal sovereignty is inherent, predating the U.S. Constitution, but is also recognized within the Constitution and in treaties and case law. The cornerstone is a legally and morally codified tribal–federal relationship of *trust responsibility* that entails the "federal responsibility to protect or enhance tribal assets . . . through policy decisions and management actions" (Wilkins & Lomawaima, 2001, p. 65). Although many education issues facing Native Americans are similar to those of other racialized communities, the experiences of Native Americans have been and are profoundly shaped by a unique relationship with the federal government and their status as originary peoples and sovereigns.

For education researchers working in Indigenous settings, culturally based and culturally responsive schooling have long been tied to tribal sovereignty (Beaulieu, 2006; Castagno & Brayboy, 2008; Demmert, McCardle, Mele-McCarthy, & Leos, 2006). This chapter builds on this work, arguing that tribal sovereignty must include education sovereignty. Regardless of whether schools operate on or off tribal lands, in the same way that schools are accountable to state and federal governments, so too are they accountable to the Native American nations whose children they serve.

With this as our anchoring premise, we take up Paris's (2012) and Paris and Alim's (2014) call for culturally sustaining pedagogy (CSP). Extending foundational work on culturally responsive education by Cazden and Leggett (1978) and Ladson-Billings (1995), Paris (2012) explains that CSP goes beyond being responsive to the cultural experiences of minoritized youth by seeking "to perpetuate and foster—to sustain—linguistic, literate, and cultural pluralism as part of the democratic project of schooling" (p. 95). Paris further explains that CSP democratizes schooling by "supporting both traditional and evolving ways of cultural connectedness for contemporary youth" (p. 95).

Here, we extend this conversation to new realms. Native communities are in a fight for cultural and linguistic survival in which Paris and Alim's (2014) question—"What are we seeking to sustain?"—takes on heightened meaning. As Brayboy (2005) notes, Indigenous peoples' desires for tribal sovereignty are interlaced with ongoing legacies of colonization, ethnicide, and linguicide. Colonial schooling has been the crucible in which these contested desires have been molded, impacting Native peoples in ways that have separated their identities from their languages, lands, and worldviews. Thus, we argue that in Native American contexts, CSP must also include *culturally revitalizing* pedagogy.

We propose critical culturally sustaining/revitalizing pedagogy (CSRP) as an approach to address the sociohistorical and contemporary contexts of Native American schooling. As Grande (2004) points out, education reforms that fail to critically examine the enduring forces of colonialism are "deeply insufficient," veiling "the incessant wounds of imperialism" (p. 19). We define CSRP as having three components. First, CSRP attends directly to asymmetrical power relations and the goal of transforming legacies of colonization. Second, CSRP recognizes the need to reclaim and revitalize what has been disrupted by colonization. For many Indigenous communities this centers on endangered languages, and thus, we focus on language education policy and practice. Finally, Indigenous CSRP recognizes the need for community-based accountability. Respect, reciprocity, responsibility, and caring relationships—what Brayboy, Gough, Leonard, Roehl, and Solyom (2012, p. 436) call "the four Rs"—are fundamental to community-based accountability. CSRP serves the needs of Indigenous communities as defined by those communities.

CSRP also necessitates engaging the complex emotions entangled with the legacy of colonization. Paris and Alim (2014) call this an *inward gaze*—a position of reflection and resistance to colonization as it has been internalized by youth and shapes their understandings of their lives and identities. We take this up later in the chapter.

Our lens into these processes is our ethnographic work with Indigenous-serving schools in the U.S. Southwest. We begin with background information on the social contexts that frame the work of these schools. Using two case examples, we explore the ways in which educators employ CSRP to destabilize dominant policy discourses, even as these educators operate, in their words, "under the radar screen" of dominant-policy surveillance. The cases illuminate the complexities and contradictions of practicing CSRP in schools that aim to exert educational control while confronting colonial influences embedded in curriculum, pedagogy, standards, policies, and Indigenous communities themselves. We conclude with a vision for a democratizing policy orientation that resists reductive pedagogies and engages the possibilities and tensions within CSRP.

SETTING THE EDUCATIONAL AND SOCIOLINGUISTIC SCENE

In 2012, 5.2 million people in the United States self-identified as American Indian or Alaska Native, and 1.2 million people self-identified as Native Hawaiians or "Other Pacific Islanders" (Hixson, Hepler, & Kim, 2012; Norris, Vines, & Hoeffel, 2012). These figures include 566 federally recognized tribes and 617 reservations and Alaska Native villages. The 2010 census also showed that 67–92% of American Indians and Alaska Natives reside outside of tribal lands (Norris et al., 2012), suggesting the increasing numbers of Native American children attending urban public schools.

More than 780,000 American Indian, Alaska Native, and Native Hawaiian school-age children are served by federal Bureau of Indian Education (BIE) schools; tribal or community-controlled schools operated by local Native school boards; state-supervised public schools, including charter schools; and private and parochial schools. Nearly 90% of Native American students attend public schools, and in more than half of these schools they constitute less than a quarter of school enrollments (Lomawaima, 2015). Off-reservation public schools are much less likely to have Native teachers or teachers with Indigenous cultural competency, which complicates but does not vitiate the possibilities for CSRP and Indigenous educational sovereignty.

Adding to the complexity of schooling for Native American learners is the diversity of the 170 Native American languages spoken and the threats to that diversity. Only one in ten Native children ages 5 to 17 reports speaking a Native American language (Siebens & Julian, 2011). The cause of language loss among younger generations is directly linked to federally attempted ethnicide and linguicide. Beginning in the 1800s and lasting well into the 20th century, such policies were carried out through punitive English-only instruction in distant boarding schools (Lomawaima & McCarty, 2006). These policies had multigenerational impacts, one of which, say Hermes, Bang, and Marin (2012), is that many Native children and their families "have no choice" but to use English in school, work, and "routine daily practices" (p. 398). This has made language revitalization a paramount educational goal.

Native American communities have taken a variety of approaches to language revitalization. Many revitalization programs operate in family homes and communal settings (Hinton, 2013). Many programs are situated within reservation settings, but some of the most successful Native American language and culture revitalization programs (e.g., Hawaiian) have operated for decades in large urban settings. Each revitalization effort must be understood according to locally defined needs, goals, and resources. What is shared among these projects is a strong belief that Indigenous languages reflect distinctive knowledges that children have a right to and need for full participation in their communities. To explore these issues in depth, we turn to our cases.

INTRODUCING THE CASES

The two case studies are based on our individual research at each site. Both cases should be understood in light of persistent disparities in educational opportunities and outcomes for Native American learners. National studies of American Indian and Alaska Native schooling continue to document ongoing disparities between the school performance of Native American and White mainstream students (Brayboy & Maaka, 2015). Similar disparities are found in graduation rates, postsecondary completion, and disproportionate representation in special education (Castagno & Brayboy, 2008). This national database also documents limited instruction in Native language and culture content. Further, although Native students increasingly enter school speaking English as a first language, they often speak varieties of English influenced by their Native languages and are subjected to school labeling practices that stigmatize them as "limited English proficient." "Schools are clearly not meeting the needs of Indigenous students," Castagno and Brayboy (2008) conclude, "and change is needed if we hope to see greater parity in these (and other) measures of academic achievement" (p. 942). The cases here represent schools and educators that have determinedly embarked on this path of needed change.

Since 2005, Tiffany Lee has been a researcher, coordinator, parent, and governing council member at the first case study site, the Native American Community Academy (NACA).[1] In this capacity she has observed and been involved in the successes and challenges of NACA to fulfill its mission while adhering to state mandates. Her research at NACA took place between 2008 and 2010 and involved in-depth interviews, focus groups, and recorded daily observations of language teaching. Lee undertook one component of this research, and she and her colleagues undertook another as part of a larger statewide study of American Indian education in New Mexico (Jojola et al., 2011).

Between 2009 and 2011, Teresa McCarty conducted research at the second case study site, Puente de Hózhǫ́ (Bridge of Beauty in Spanish and English; hereafter PdH). This research was part of a larger national study to evaluate promising practices for enhancing Native American students' academic achievement, including the role of Native languages and cultures in successful student outcomes (Brayboy, 2010). Data for the PdH study included ethnographic observations of classroom instruction and Native teachers' monthly curriculum meetings; individual and focus group interviews with key program personnel, parents, and youth; document analysis (e.g., school mission statements, teachers' lesson plans, and student writing samples); and photographs intended to capture how the local Native language and culture were represented in the school's visual environment.[2]

In both cases, our methodology was ethnographic and praxis-driven, with the intent of collaborating with local stakeholders in their efforts to effect positive change. As a guiding research ethic, we foregrounded community interests based on respect, relationships, reciprocity, and accountability to participants' communities (Brayboy et al., 2012). We regularly shared data and our interpretations with program participants. To supplement our qualitative data, we also collected state-required achievement data.

NACA: Sustaining "the Seeds"

> Someone planted the seed for me to start learning my language
> . . . and I'm excited to have the opportunity to try and do that for
> these students.
>
> —Mr. Yuonihan, NACA Lakota language teacher

The Native American Community Academy is a public charter school serving middle and high school students in Albuquerque, New Mexico, a city of 600,000 in a state that is home to 23 Native American nations. Charter schools have played a growing role in Native peoples' efforts to gain control over their children's education (Ewing & Ferrick, 2012). The school's founders proposed NACA as a charter school because charter status afforded greater autonomy, enabling the school to provide an academic focus tailored to community needs. Although NACA gained some degree of control, it must still adhere to state regulations, including state-determined English standardized tests—a challenge for charter schools whose missions are connected to community, culture, and wellness.

Approximately 5,500 Native American students are served by the Albuquerque public schools. These students represent Native nations within and outside New Mexico. Additionally, many students are of mixed heritage (e.g., Navajo/Cochiti Pueblo; Lakota/Anglo; Isleta Pueblo/Latino/a). NACA students reflect this diversity, and come from 60 different Native nations and 16 non-Native ethnic backgrounds. Ninety-five percent of the student body identifies as Native American. As more Native people move outside their Native nations' boundaries, this population of school-aged children continues to grow, making schools such as NACA particularly noteworthy as examples of CSRP and Indigenous educational sovereignty.

In fall 2006, NACA opened with approximately 60 students in 6th and 7th grades. Today it serves approximately 400 students in grades K, 1, and 6–12 (Figure 4.1). With the goal of serving local Native communities by offering a unique approach to Indigenous education, the school integrates an academic curriculum, a wellness philosophy, and Native culture and language. NACA's mission is to provide a well-rounded education focused on "strengthening communities by developing strong leaders who are academically prepared, secure in their identity and healthy" (NACA, 2012a) and aligns with Indigenous educational philosophies of holistic attention to students' intellectual, physical, emotional, and social development within a community and cultural context (Cajete, 2000).

Teachers and staff identified core values directly related to the school's mission—respect, responsibility, community/service, culture, perseverance, and reflection—and expressed an expectation that students and staff will display behavior and attitudes that represent each core value. NACA staff members have designed activities to integrate those values into their curriculum and teaching methods, and to instill a foundation for students' cultural identity as part of CSRP. As one example, a community member, Carrie, discussed a weekly morning ritual that draws on Native songs and communal gathering practices: "They gather in a circle on Monday mornings, and they begin with the drum. They actually sing together. . . And that's so important. . . . [It] makes it feel like it's a community and it's unified" (Figure 4.2).

The challenge in teaching NACA's core values has been to confront generalizations and stereotypes about those values. Native American people are often portrayed as one culture and one people, essentializing their diverse beliefs and traditions. Given NACA students' diverse backgrounds, teaching to each student's community values is unfeasible. Consequently, maintaining the integrity of new school-based rituals for exemplifying

Figure 4.1. 2015 NACA Community Feast Day photo of students and staff.

Photograph by Azella Humetewa

Figure 4.2. Eleventh- and 12th-grade students in their morning circle.

Photograph by Leroy Silva

school values becomes a constantly negotiated endeavor. In some cases, teachers, staff, and parents utilize specific traditions of particular communities. In other instances, school-based practices are jointly created by teachers, students, and staff, who are mindful to avoid essentializing Indigenous peoples. For example, the morning circle that Carrie described is adapted based on traditions of many Native communities. The head of the school discussed it this way: "The morning circle is an extension of traditional protocols for openings/closings where blessings, songs, and information dissemination happens in a circle" (Anpao Duta Flying Earth, personal communication, 2013).

Building community through NACA's core values occurs in the classroom as well. To create meaningful connections to the school's core values, some teachers use assessment practices that reflect a holistic view of student performance. Lakota language teacher Mr. Yuonihan describes assessing more than students' content knowledge. He also focuses on their development as caring and empathetic human beings and the quality of relationships they have with one another. He said, "Another way that I evaluate if they're receiving some of the things that I'm teaching them is how they treat each other out here when they're not in class." He looks for his students to demonstrate respect, compassion, and helpful behavior with others, as these are attributes associated with Native language practices and how Native people treat one another. Likewise, he strives to create a reciprocal and respectful relationship with his students. He described how he explains this to his students:

> The relationship that we're gonna have in this classroom—I'm gonna treat you like one of my nieces or nephews, so that it does not end once we are out of this class. It does not end once you've graduated from NACA.

Indigenous languages are inseparable from this educational approach. Language is vital to cultural continuity because it embodies both everyday and sacred knowledge and is essential to ceremonial practices. Language is also significant for sustaining Indigenous knowledge systems, communities, cultural identifications, and connections to land. Additionally, strong Native language and culture programs are highly associated with ameliorating persistent educational inequities by enhancing education relevancy, family and community involvement, and cultural identity (Arviso & Holm, 2001; Lee, 2014; McCarty, 2012).

Reflecting students' linguistic and cultural backgrounds, NACA offers five locally prevalent Native languages: Navajo, Lakota, Keres, Tiwa, and Zuni. While there are several more Native languages represented by students, NACA respects the sovereign authority of the local communities and takes seriously its commitment to community accountability. Hence, the school seeks permission from local communities to teach their languages. Keres, for example, has seven dialects representing seven Pueblo nations. Teaching Keres involves collaborating and gaining permission from each of those communities.

Teaching Native languages to students is a culturally sustaining and revitalizing practice. NACA language teachers make clear the importance of having autonomy and flexibility for teaching values that instill cultural identity through language-based methods. Teaching the language is also associated with creating a sense of belonging—a way to strengthen students' cultural pride and knowledge of the cultural protocols associated with their Native heritage. As Navajo mentor teacher Ms. Begay noted, through this pedagogy educators are able to teach students

> the etiquette of when someone comes to visit you, how you tell them come in, *wóshdéé'*, and they shake your hands, and you also address them by who they are to you. If it's an aunt, uncle, grandma, grandpa, then you always ask them to have a seat and offer them a drink and something to eat.

This aspect of teaching Native languages connects deeply to local cultural communities. The teachers engage in CSRP as they teach the protocols of using the language, rather than simply language mechanics, and emphasize the connections among language, culture, and identity. NACA teachers believe it is their responsibility to pass on the language. They share the view that schools must be able to accommodate and respect this high level of community-oriented education. Ms. Tsosie, for instance, discussed the value of using Native-language immersion as a community-oriented, natural process for learning Navajo: "When you say *immersion,* it ties back to your homeland, your environment. And it makes more sense when you do it in that type of a setting [or] environment, than, like, in a classroom."

Language and culture revitalization also requires adapting to nontraditional teaching practices. For example, the Navajo language teachers use teacher/mentor pairing where two teachers co-instruct. They also utilize Situational Navajo teaching methods, which involve teachers in creating everyday situations (i.e., cooking, cleaning) to foster conversations that require verb use and physical responses (Holm, Silentman, & Wallace, 2003). Teaching Native languages is particularly challenging in an environment where students may not have strong Native-language support at home; as a consequence, when students do not comprehend what the teacher is saying, it is difficult to "stay in" the Native language. NACA teachers have found the teacher/mentor pairing extremely helpful in surmounting this challenge. As Ms. Tsosie commented, "I think it's nice if you co-teach with another teacher; it's so much easier just to stay in the language. [Otherwise] sometimes I feel like I'm talking to myself." Similarly, Ms. Begay believes that collaborative language immersion teaching strengthens teachers' language abilities: " . . . if you co-teach with someone, I think it's a little easier. At least you can bounce ideas off of one another."

One of the prime tensions in implementing CSRP at NACA is the need to address monolingual, monocultural norms embedded in standardized testing while prioritizing community-based values. As is well documented, in the era of No Child Left Behind (NCLB) and its recent reauthorization, the Every Student Succeeds Act, scores on English standardized tests can have staggering consequences (Valenzuela, Prieto, & Hamilton, 2007). At NACA, students take the state-required courses in math, English reading and writing, science, and social studies. Teachers and administrators create a curriculum that integrates Native perspectives through these and other courses while attending to state standards. The Navajo Government course, for example, meets social studies requirements, and the Native Literature course enhances reading and writing skills while embedding Native perspectives.

School data indicate that NACA is making progress according to dominant-society standards: in 2011–2012, 8th-graders demonstrated a 21% increase in their math scores, a 20% increase in their reading scores, and a 9% increase in their writing scores from the previous year (NACA, 2012b). The student retention rate is above 95% (Kara Bobroff, NACA executive director, personal communication, 2012), and students in the first graduating class of 2012 were admitted into a multitude of universities (NACA, 2012c).

Measuring outcomes defined by NACA's mission and community interests is a challenge. Standardized tests do not assess students' levels of wellness, the strength of their cultural identity, and their commitment to their communities. Additionally, the NACA community recognizes that the state does not use the school's goals in their assessments of the school. The tension between community and dominant-policy goals is a source of continued discussion at NACA. When asked how NACA is doing at providing an Indigenous education as they define it, one staff member remarked,

> It's what we strive for, but . . . we aren't there yet; too hard to figure out how to do both an Indigenous education and a college prep education, especially when they [define] students by test scores and grades. (NACA, 2013, p. 11)

In light of persistent achievement disparities for Native Americans, who have experienced centuries of educational malpractice, Native-operated charter schools represent one option for reversing that history. Schools such as NACA can open new spaces for experiential and collaborative teaching and learning by integrating Native American languages and knowledges throughout the curriculum and by honoring community decisionmaking in the languages taught. This exemplifies community-based accountability. One crucial outcome at NACA has been teachers' assertion of their inherent power as Indigenous education practitioners, as they make a difference in revitalizing Native languages through culturally sustaining practices. The significant factor is that NACA honors teachers' ideas and supports strategies that often fall outside of mainstream schooling practices.

Puente de Hózhǫ́: "Fighting for Our Kids"

> We're fighting for our kids to have the right to learn their language and culture!
>
> —PdH teacher

Nestled at the base of mountains sacred to Native peoples, in Flagstaff, Arizona, Puente de Hózhǫ́—a trilingual Navajo-Spanish-English public magnet school—serves Native and non-Native students in grades K–5. Arizona is home to 22 Indigenous nations; it is also a state in which more than a quarter of the population is Latino/a, and where an English-only statute requires that English learners be instructed solely in English. PdH aims to provide a multilingual, multicultural alternative to this policy. The school's motto, "The Power of Two" (languages and cultural knowledge systems), reflects this goal (Figure 4.3).

The name Puente de Hózhǫ́ signals the school's vision to connect and valorize the three predominant ethnic and linguistic groups of the local community—Spanish and Mexican American traditions, Navajo (Diné) language and culture, and English and Anglo American traditions (Fillerup, 2011). As described by school founder Michael Fillerup (2005), in a district in which 26% of the students are American Indian and 21% are Latino/a, "local educators were searching for innovative ways to bridge the seemingly unbridgeable" equity gap experienced by poor children and children of color (p. 15).

Figure 4.3. Entrance sign at Puente de Hózhǫ́ Trilingual Magnet School, with the school motto in three languages.

Photograph by Teresa L. McCarty

Begun in 2001 as a kindergarten program, PdH has grown into a public elementary school serving approximately 450 students. As a magnet school, PdH enrolls students across many ethnic and social class backgrounds. Most of the school's approximately 120 Native American students, who comprise 27% of school enrollment, are Navajo, although, as with NACA, many come from racially and ethnically mixed families. As one bilingual teacher described this, "We are all intermixed . . . , and that is the way the real world is and that makes it beautiful."

Native students at PdH speak English as their primary language. While many come from Flagstaff and reservation border areas, Native teachers note that some come from the "heart of the [Navajo] reservation," seeking the "language-rich, Navajo-English instruction" that the school provides. As a graduate explained, "My parents really wanted me to learn Navajo so I can . . . talk to my grandmother and grandfather . . . and the elders."

PdH students enroll either in a Spanish-English dual-language program for native English- and native Spanish-speaking students, or a Navajo immersion program for Native students learning Navajo as a second language. In the Navajo-medium program, kindergartners receive 80% of their instruction in Navajo, with English instruction increased until a 50-50 balance is attained in grades 4 and 5.

This language programming reflects the expressed desires of Diné and Latino/a parents for a culturally sustaining and revitalizing educational alternative. As Fillerup (2011) explains, "Spanish-speaking parents wanted their children to not only learn English but to become literate in Spanish and continue to develop their Spanish language skills"; Diné parents "wanted their children to learn the Diné language" as a heritage language (p. 148). Following a series of community meetings, the district established an experimental program to respond to the aspirations of a multiethnic community. In practice, students in both programs interact regularly in art, physical education, music, and school activities designed to cultivate their multilingual, multicultural competence. As one PdH educator noted, "We merge multiple worlds. . . . they [students] are all being prepared for a further world, the global world."

Like other Native American language revitalization efforts, PdH grows out of a larger Indigenous self-determination movement. Its pedagogic approach has been influenced by Māori-medium schooling in Aotearoa/New Zealand and Hawaiian-medium schooling in Hawai'i (Hill & May, 2011; Wilson & Kamanā, 2011). The goal is an instructional program in which "each child's language and culture [are] regarded not as a problem to be solved but as an indispensable resource, the very heart and soul of the school itself" (Fillerup, 2008, para 3). In the Diné program, Navajo content and ways of knowing are integrated throughout the curriculum and school environment. This is signaled at the school entrance, where expansive student-created wall murals depict the Navajo girls' puberty ceremony (*Kinaaldá*) and the red-rock canyon lands of *Diné Bikeyah* (Navajoland) (Figure 4.4). Throughout the school the print environment displays vivid images of academic content in Navajo, Spanish, English, and other languages.

Navajo culture is integrated into the school curriculum in several ways. Four overarching themes organize curriculum content: earth and sky, health, living things, and family and community (Fillerup, 2011). A Navajo teacher described what the family and community theme looked like in her classroom:

> So our first month will be about . . . self-esteem, . . . your clanship, your kinship, who you are, where you come from [known in Navajo as *k'é*] . . . "You are of the Diné people, you should be proud of who you are and how you present yourself as a Navajo person." That's all intertwined with [cultural] stories as well.

During this research project, the song *Shí Naashá*—literally "I Walk About" but translated culturally by teachers as "I'm Alive"—was prominent in every Navajo-language classroom (Figure 4.5). The song commemorates

Figure 4.4. Student-created mural with Diné artist Shonto Begay, depicting the traditional practice of the morning run in the Navajo girls' puberty ceremony, *Kinaaldá*.

Photograph by Teresa L. McCarty

the Navajo people's survival and return to Diné Bikeyah from a federal concentration camp where thousands were incarcerated and perished between 1863 and 1868. Teachers incorporate the song into social studies and language arts lessons centered on Navajo history. Reflecting a critical pedagogical stance, one teacher remarked, "The song tells the story of how our people actually survived."

PdH educators thus understand their work as countering the repressive, compensatory focus of colonial language policies—a critical, decolonizing stance that characterizes CSRP. Teachers speak of reversing past pedagogic practices, including their own. For example, when asked if her children spoke Navajo, one Navajo teacher explained her choice to socialize them in English, her second language: "When I was a young parent, I really didn't know what it meant . . . to value the language that you were raised in . . . we were just barely getting over the shame . . . that we were minorities and we were not of value." PdH represents a redirection of this approach. One educator stated:

> This school is predicated on [the assumption] that learning more than one language is a *good* thing. . . . We know English is the dominant language, but . . . we believe that all three languages should be on equal terms. . . . This is what we strive for.

PdH teachers' experiences testify to the painful self-critique out of which culturally sustaining and revitalizing pedagogy is born. In their own

Figure 4.5. "Shí Naashá" ("I'm Alive") classroom poster commemorating the Navajo people's survival of federally attempted genocide and return from a concentration camp in Fort Sumner, New Mexico, in the late 19th century.

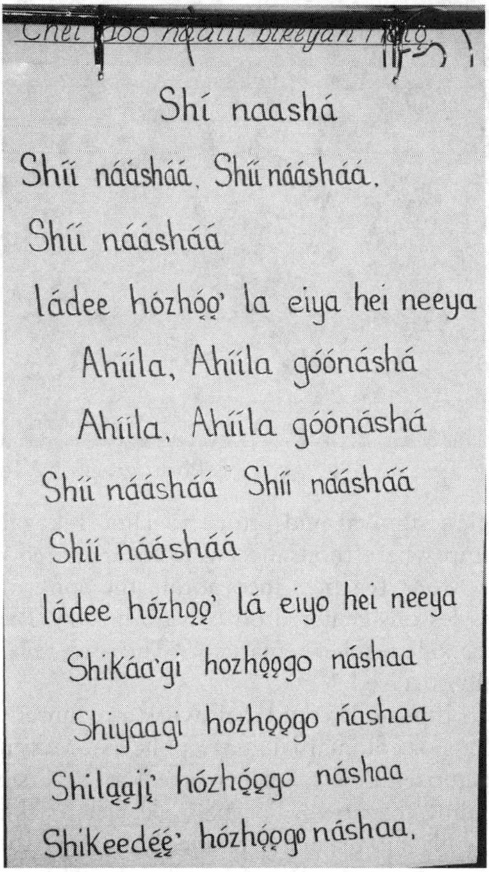

Photograph by Teresa L. McCarty

schooling, all five Diné teachers in the study had experienced the forced severing of their heritage language. "I was raised . . . when the Navajo language was suppressed," one teacher recalled. Another teacher remembered being mocked for using Navajo in school: "So from then on I was like, okay, I'm just going to stop . . . using [Navajo] . . . because it's not something that [White teachers] want to hear." Yet another teacher related that she studied Spanish and French in high school, even though her school offered a Navajo-language elective: "I didn't take Navajo because I didn't want people to know I could speak Navajo."

Like parents at NACA, PdH parents want their children to do well in school by dominant-language and -culture standards. This is also part of the school's efforts to be accountable to the community it serves. Keeping test scores "respectable," Fillerup (2005) observes, enables PdH educators to fulfill the school's mission (pp. 15, 16). In recent years PdH has ranked among the highest-performing schools in the district, surpassing schools serving more affluent, native English-speaking students (Dawn Trubakoff, principal, personal communication, 2015). Importantly, and reflective of international research on second-language acquisition, students with the strongest performance on English assessments began attending PdH in kindergarten and had the longest experience in the program.

The PdH community views the school's impacts as extending well beyond English-language test scores. As one teacher noted, "Hearing parents comment on how much their kids have learned or that their child may be the only one of all the cousins that [is] speaking to their grandparents [in Navajo]—this tells us that we are doing something [worthwhile]." "Most parents don't speak Navajo," another teacher explained, and "I may be *it*," the only source for learning the Navajo language. "Parents trust us to teach their children the language that is so valuable to them," yet another teacher reflected.

Like NACA, PdH illuminates both the promise and the tensions in implementing CSRP in an urban public school setting. By offering two distinct but organizationally integrated bilingual-bicultural education programs, PdH educators make themselves accountable to the linguistically and culturally diverse community they serve. At the same time, the school affirms the sovereignty of the Native American nation in which many of its students are enrolled. PdH does this through alternate institutional arrangements—it is a voluntary public magnet school—and by adhering to state requirements for teacher certification, curriculum, and testing. Like NACA, the PdH community has managed to negotiate systemic constraints by emphasizing high academic expectations, a content-rich curriculum, and children's heritage language and culture as essential resources for learning.

PROJECTING AN "INWARD GAZE" AND PROBLEMATIZING ESSENTIALISMS

We have examined two ethnographic cases in an effort to illuminate the complex contours of CSRP. We recognize that these are smaller schools serving minoritized students via charter and magnet structures. However, we propose that CSRP requires precisely this kind of nonhomogenizing attention to local communities' expressed desires, resources, and needs. This responsiveness exemplifies community-based accountability.

The cases offer a glimpse into CSRP—its possibilities, tensions, and challenges. In each case the desire to heal forced linguistic wounds and convey important cultural knowledge to future generations anchors the school curriculum. This is a deeply felt responsibility on the part of these educators—in their words, a "tie back to [students'] homeland," a bond of "trust that [parents] have in us to . . . teach their children." Sustaining linguistic and cultural continuity and building relationships are central CSRP goals, premised on respect and reciprocity. The strategies for accomplishing these goals are locally defined: teaching five Native languages at NACA and offering multiple strands of bilingual education at PdH. The goal to support "both traditional and evolving ways of cultural connectedness" (Paris, 2012, p. 95) unites each school's efforts.

Through these cases we also emphasize the emotional dimensions inherent in these pedagogies. Love, loss, empathy, compassion, and pain run throughout teachers' accounts as they confront personal histories of linguistic exclusion, reconciling those histories with the aims of emancipatory practice. As one PdH teacher shared, "For most of us . . . we got beyond the shame and came to see our first language as a gift. I think that's why we're here."

Engaging the emotions that arise from and shape CSRP is integral to what Paris and Alim (2014) call an *inward gaze*—a loving but critical stance that counters colonization within and outside the school setting. Paris and Alim remind us that colonizing influences are often internalized by youth, whose understanding of their heritage may be shaped by lenses other than their own. For example, in the statewide research project of which NACA was part, one youth expressed dismay at not wanting to be regarded as a "fake Native" because of her limited Native-language abilities (Jojola et al., 2011). In her view, being Native required speaking her heritage language and knowing her people's history and culture.

The practice of CSRP has the potential to transform these expressions of Indigenous longing into powerful resources for language reclamation, thereby helping students connect meaningfully with their cultural communities (Lee, 2014; Wyman, McCarty, & Nicholas, 2014). Yet such expressions become problematic when they are essentialized. The youth statement above, for instance, may be uncritically interpreted as implying that one cannot be regarded as an "authentic" Native person without speaking a Native language or without knowledge of tribal history. Certainly these abilities and knowledge are important goals, and we have stressed how they might be achieved through CSRP. Yet we have observed many Native youth whose Indigeneity is denigrated within the larger society and even within the youth's communities if they do not possess that knowledge and skills.

Condemnation within the youth's community represents a form of lateral violence—damaging and destabilizing practices within communities that have experienced oppression, colonization, and marginalization—that community members inflict on one another (Wingard, 2010). As the youth's statement above shows, this comes at the expense of youth's cultural identity and sense of belonging. The common discursive markers of "speaker/nonspeaker" fortify these injustices, while pitting monolithic notions of urbanity and modernity against rurality and reservation life. From this view, one cannot be simultaneously "urban" and "Native."

By employing a decolonizing critique to deconstruct essentialisms that reduce the multidimensionality of human experience, CSRP fosters and reflects an inward gaze that confronts those practices as part of the language and culture reclamation project. Enos (2002) characterizes this as the exercise of "deep" sovereignty, in which Indigenous communities protect core values, knowledges, and ways of being. Deep sovereignty connotes engaging in relationships rooted in Indigenous practices and worldviews, and in this respect halts horizontal violence. When viewing what it means to be Indigenous and engaging in Indigenous education through frameworks of Indigenous philosophies, deep sovereignty is an active form of being. As Cajete (1998, p. 189) remarked, "Being Indigenous is a verb!"

For example, the mural at the entryway of PdH (Figure 4.4) depicts the extended family's support of *Kinaaldá*, the young girl's entry into womanhood. As suggested by the mural, this 4-day ceremony requires early morning running, all-day cooking, grinding corn, chopping wood, and prayers; in short, it requires the family to be disciplined, responsible, and supportive of one another. This embodies *k'é*—the Navajo concept that a PdH teacher, in an excerpted quote above, described as anchoring the Diné curriculum's family and community theme—and expresses active support, love, and caring for family and community. The work under way at NACA and PdH emanates from such a perspective—a place of deep sovereignty, which "is where education is then grounded" (Enos, 2002, p. 9).

CRITICAL CSRP, COMMUNITY-BASED ACCOUNTABILITY, AND INDIGENOUS EDUCATION SOVEREIGNTY

How can CSRP work in service to the goals of Indigenous education sovereignty implied by Paris's (2012) conception of the "democratic project of schooling"? We note first that no sovereignty is limitless; Indigenous sovereignties operate in interaction with the overlapping sovereignties of states, provinces, national governments, and international entities (Lomawaima & McCarty, 2006). The efforts by NACA and PdH to balance state and federal requirements with accountability to local Indigenous nations are evidence of this interaction.

In their meta-analysis of research on culturally responsive schooling, Brayboy and Castagno (2009) find "no evidence that [Native] parents and communities do not want their children to be able to read and write [in English] or do mathematics, science, etc." (p. 31). Instead, parents rightly insist "that children's learning to 'do' school should not be an assimilative process" but "should happen by engaging culture" (p. 31). Similarly, in an examination of language and tribal sovereignty among the New Mexico

Pueblos, Blum Martinez (2000) points out that the fact that Native parents want their children to do well in school does not negate the fact that they "also recognize that their children will need to lead their communities" in the future (p. 217). This requires that children have access to local knowledges, including the language(s) through which those knowledges are acquired. Schools can play a crucial role in fostering these multiple community-desired competencies.

The educators in our two cases recognize that balancing academic, linguistic, and cultural interests requires accountability to Indigenous communities. This approach stands in contrast to accountability policies that privilege a single monolingual, monocultural standard. As a consequence, CSRP can become a perilous balancing act that operates, in the words of one PdH educator, "under the radar screen" of state surveillance.

As with many schools serving minoritized youth, this remains an unsettled and well-recognized tension that educators at these schools negotiate every day, placing schools like PdH and NACA on the front lines of the fight for "the democratic project of schooling." Yet the fact that the fight has not yet been won does not mean it should be abandoned. The testimony of Indigenous educators, parents, and youth demands relentless commitment to community-based accountability. This is the heart of Indigenous education sovereignty, and the promise of critical CSRP.[3]

NOTES

This chapter is adapted with permission from Teresa L. McCarty and Tiffany S. Lee, "Critical Culturally Sustaining/Revitalizing Pedagogy and Indigenous Education Sovereignty," *Harvard Educational Review,* 84(1, Spring 2014), pp. 101–124. Copyright © 2014 by President and Fellows of Harvard College. All rights reserved. For more information, please visit http://hepg.org/her-home/issues/harvard-educational-review-volume-84-number-1/herarticle/critical-culturally-sustaining-revitalizing-pedago.

1. Each site gave permission to use its actual name. All names of research participants are pseudonyms.

2. The national research project of which the Puente de Hózhǫ case study was part was led by Bryan McKinley Jones Brayboy of Arizona State University.

3. We express sincere appreciation to the Native American Community Academy and Puente de Hózhǫ Trilingual Magnet School for their support of this research. Tiffany Lee thanks Kara Bobroff (executive director), Anpao Duta Flying Earth (head of the school), and NACA's language teachers for their help in preparing this manuscript and their support of its publication. Teresa McCarty thanks PdH founder Michael Fillerup, former principal

Dawn Trubakoff, current principal Robert Kelty, district superintendent Barbara Hickman, and the Diné teachers who participated in the study.

REFERENCES

Arviso, M., & Holm, W. (2001). Tséhootsooídí Ólta'gi Diné bizaad bíhoo'aah: A Navajo immersion program at Fort Defiance, Arizona. In L. Hinton & K. Hale (Eds.), *The green book of language revitalization in practice* (pp. 203–215). San Diego, CA: Academic Press.

Beaulieu, D. (2006). A survey and assessment of culturally based education programs for Native American students in the United States. *Journal of American Indian Education, 45*(2), 50–61.

Blum Martinez, R. (2000). Languages and tribal sovereignty: Whose language is it anyway? *Theory into Practice, 39*(4), 211–219.

Brayboy, B. M. J. (2005). Toward a tribal critical race theory in education. *Urban Review, 37*(5), 425–446.

Brayboy, B. M. J. (2010, October 8). *Promising practices and partnerships in Indian education: An overview of an Office of Indian Education study.* Paper presented at the Annual Meeting of the National Indian Education Association, San Diego, CA.

Brayboy, B. M. J., & Castagno, A. (2009). Self-determination through self-education: Culturally responsive schooling for Indigenous students in the USA. *Teaching Education, 20*(1), 31–53.

Brayboy, B. M. J., Faircloth, S. C., Lee, T. S., Maaka, M. J., & Richardson, T. (Guest Eds.) (2015). *Sovereignty and education* [Special issue]. *Journal of American Indian Education, 54.*

Brayboy, B. M. J., Gough, H. R., Leonard, B., Roehl II, R. F., & Solyom, J. A. (2012). Reclaiming scholarship: Critical Indigenous research methodologies. In S. D. Lapan, M. T. Quartaroli, & F. J. Reimer (Eds.), *Qualitative research: An introduction to methods and design* (pp. 423–450). San Francisco, CA: John Wiley.

Brayboy, B. M. J., & Maaka, M. J. (2015). K–12 Achievement for Indigenous Students. *Journal of American Indian Education, 54*(1), 63–98.

Cajete, G. (1998). Reclaiming biophilia: Lessons from Indigenous peoples. In G. A. Smith & D. R. William (Eds.), *Ecological education in action: On weaving education, culture, and the environment* (pp. 189–206). New York, NY: State University of New York Press.

Cajete, G. (2000). *Native science: Natural laws of interdependence.* Santa Fe, NM: Clear Light Books.

Castagno, A., & Brayboy, B. M. J. (2008). Culturally responsive schooling for Indigenous youth: A review of the literature. *Review of Educational Research, 78*(4), 941–993.

Cazden, C. B., & Leggett, E. L. (1978). *Culturally responsive education: A discussion of Lau Remedies II.* Los Angeles, CA: National Dissemination and Assessment Center.

Demmert, W., McCardle, P., Mele-McCarthy, J., & Leos, K. (2006). Preparing Native American children for academic success: A blueprint for research. *Journal of American Indian Education, 45*(3), 92–106.

Enos, A. D. (2002, November 4). *Deep sovereignty: Education in Pueblo Indian communities.* Paper presented at the Annual Meeting of the National Indian Education Association, Albuquerque, NM.

Ewing, E., & Ferrick, M. (2012). *For this place, for these people: An exploration of best practices among charter schools serving Native students.* Washington, DC: National Indian Education Association. Retrieved from http://www.niea.org

Fillerup, M. (2005). Keeping up with the Yazzies: The impact of high stakes testing on Indigenous language programs. *Language Learner,* September/October, 14–16.

Fillerup, M. (2008). *Building bridges of beauty between the rich languages and cultures of the American Southwest: Puente de Hózhǫ́ Trilingual Magnet School.* Retrieved from http://www.fusd1.org/Page/1942

Fillerup, M. (2011). Building a "bridge of beauty": A preliminary report on promising practices in Native language and culture teaching at Puente de Hózhǫ́ Trilingual Magnet School. In M. E. Romero-Little, S. J. Ortiz, T. L. McCarty, & R. Chen (Eds.), *Indigenous languages across the generations—Strengthening families and communities* (pp. 145–164). Tempe, AZ: Arizona State University Center for Indian Education.

Grande, S. (2004). *Red pedagogy: Native American social and political thought.* Lanham, MD: Rowman and Littlefield.

Hermes, M., Bang, M., & Marin, A. (2012). Designing Indigenous language revitalization. *Harvard Educational Review, 82*(3), 281–402.

Hill, R., & May, S. (2011). Exploring biliteracy in Māori-medium education: An ethnographic perspective. In T. L. McCarty (Ed.), *Ethnography and language policy* (pp. 161–183). New York, NY: Routledge.

Hinton, L. (Ed). (2013). *Bringing our languages home—Language revitalization for families.* Berkeley, CA: Heyday Books.

Hixson, L., Hepler, B. B., & Kim, M. O. (2012). *The Native Hawaiian and other Pacific Islander population: 2010* (2010 Census Briefs). Washington, DC: U.S. Census Bureau.

Holm, W., Silentman, I., & Wallace, L. (2003). Situational Navajo: A school-based, verb-centered way of teaching Navajo. In J. Reyhner, O. Trujillo, R. L. Carrasco, & L. Lockard (Eds.), *Nurturing Native languages* (pp. 25–52). Flagstaff, AZ: Northern Arizona University Center for Excellence in Education.

Jojola, T., Lee, T. S., Alacantara, A. M., Belgarde, M., Bird, C. P., Lopez, N., & Singer, B. (2011). *Indian education in New Mexico, 2025.* Santa Fe, NM: Public Education Department.

Ladson-Billings, G. (1995). Toward a theory of culturally relevant pedagogy. *American Educational Research Journal, 32*(3), 465–491.

Lee, T. S. (2014). Critical language awareness among Native youth in New Mexico. In L. T. Wyman, T. L. McCarty, & S. E. Nicholas (Eds.), *Indigenous youth and multilingualism: Language identity, ideology, and practice in dynamic cultural worlds* (pp. 130–148). New York, NY: Routledge.

Lomawaima, K. T. (2015). Education. In R. Warrior (Ed.), *The world of Indigenous North America* (pp. 365–387). New York, NY: Routledge.

Lomawaima, K. T., & McCarty, T. L. (2006). *"To remain an Indian": Lessons in democracy from a century of Native American schooling.* New York, NY: Teachers College Press.

McCarty, T. L. (2012). Indigenous languages and cultures in Native American student achievement: Promising practices and cautionary findings. In B. Klug (Ed.), *Standing together: American Indian education as culturally responsive pedagogy* (pp. 97–119). Lanham, MD: Rowman and Littlefield.

McCarty, T. L., & Lee, T. S. (2014). Critically culturally sustaining/revitalizing pedagogy and Indigenous education sovereignty. *Harvard Educational Review, 84*(1), 101–124.

Native American Community Academy [NACA]. (2012a). *Mission and vision.* Retrieved from http://nacaschool.org/about/mission-and-vision/

Native American Community Academy [NACA]. (2012b). *2011–2012 NACA class proficiency changes by subject and grade narrative.* Unpublished NACA document, Albuquerque, NM.

Native American Community Academy [NACA]. (2012c). *Native American Community Academy announces first graduation ceremony after six years of community support* [Press release], May 15, 2012.

Native American Community Academy [NACA]. (2013). *360 Survey for NACA students, teachers, staff, and community members.* Unpublished NACA document, Albuquerque, NM.

Norris, T., Vines, P. L., & Hoeffel, E. M. (2012). *The American Indian and Alaska Native population: 2010* (2010 Census Briefs). Washington, DC: U.S. Census Bureau.

Paris, D. (2012). Culturally sustaining pedagogy: A needed change in stance, terminology, and practice. *Educational Researcher, 41*(3), 93–97.

Paris, D., & Alim, H. S. (2014). What are we seeking to sustain through culturally sustaining pedagogy?: A loving critique forward. *Harvard Educational Review, 84*(1), 85–100.

Siebens, J., & Julian, T. (2011). *Native North American languages spoken at home in the United States and Puerto Rico: 2006–2010* (American Community Survey Briefs). Washington, DC: U.S. Census Bureau.

Valenzuela, A., Prieto, L., & Hamilton, M. P. (Guest Eds.). (2007). No Child Left Behind (NCLB) and minority youth: What the qualitative evidence suggests [Special issue]. *Anthropology and Education Quarterly, 38*(1), 1–96.

Wilkins, D. E., & Lomawaima, K. T. (2001). *Uneven ground: American Indian sovereignty and federal law.* Norman, OK: University of Oklahoma Press.

Wilson, W. H., & Kamanā, K. (2011). Insights from Indigenous language immersion in Hawai'i. In D. J. Tedick, D. Christian, & T. W. Fortune (Eds.), *Immersion education: Practices, policies, possibilities* (pp. 36–57). Bristol, UK: Multilingual Matters.

Wingard, B. (2010). A conversation with lateral violence. *International Journal of Narrative Therapy and Community Work, 1,* 13–17.

Wyman, L. T., McCarty, T. L., & Nicholas, S. E. (Eds). (2014). *Indigenous youth and multilingualism: Language identity, ideology, and practice in dynamic cultural worlds.* New York, NY: Routledge.

CHAPTER 5

"For Us, By Us"

A Vision for Culturally Sustaining Pedagogies Forwarded by Latinx Youth

Jason G. Irizarry
University of Connecticut

Over the past two decades a host of empirical studies have established a solid foundation for research regarding the potential utility of asset-based approaches to education that center students' cultural identities. Most often forwarded as a "bridge" between minoritized students and the culture of school, asset-based approaches have given less attention to helping students develop their cultural identities and a positive sense of self while critically engaging in the systems in which they are being educated. The concept of culturally sustaining pedagogies, as theorized initially by Paris (2012), later by Paris and Alim (2014), and extended throughout this book, fills important gaps by underscoring the fluid, multidimensional nature of culture, and emphasizing the potential of young people to challenge and change the systems of oppression in which they are embedded. As the body of literature regarding culturally sustaining pedagogies evolves, several questions remain: How might understandings of culturally sustaining pedagogies be enhanced if they were informed by teaching practices developed, implemented, and refined by students themselves? As the largest and fastest-growing group of minoritized students and a community that disproportionately experiences academic underachievement, what can Latinx students teach us about developing teaching strategies that have the potential to improve their educational experiences and outcomes? In other words, if Latinx youth were empowered to create sustaining classroom environments for themselves and other Latinx students, what would that look like? What elements and approaches would they employ? Crucially for the present volume, in what ways might answers to these questions inform conceptions and enactments of culturally sustaining pedagogy? In this chapter, I draw from a two-year ethnographic study of Latinx high school students in a participatory action research collaborative to answer these questions and raise others.

PROMISE AND POSSIBILITY: THE EDUCATION OF LATINX YOUTH

The population of Latinx people in the United States has increased dramatically over the last decade. Now numbering more than 55 million people, Latinx people represent approximately 17% of the population of the United States (U.S. Census Bureau, 2015). Because they are the nation's youngest major racial or ethnic group, they are a significant force in the rapidly changing racial/ethnic and linguistic landscape of schools. Currently, one in every four students in U.S. schools is Latinx (Excelencia in Education, 2015), and Latinx people already represent the majority of students in many districts across the country, ranging from cities like Los Angeles, California, with a Latinx presence that dates back centuries, to communities such as Windham, Connecticut, where Latinx people have settled in large numbers only recently. The "latinization" of U.S. schools (Irizarry, 2011)—where a growing population of Latinx students try to successfully navigate educational institutions that often exalt cultural assimilation over a culturally sustaining education while simultaneously trying to develop and maintain a positive sense of self—presents significant implications for educators and the country as a whole.

Despite their growing numbers, Latinx people remain one of the least formally educated groups in the United States (Gándara & Contreras, 2008) and are the focus of efforts to close the so-called "achievement gap" in school districts across the country. Although indicators of educational attainment have improved in recent years, data suggest that Latinx people continue to lag behind other groups on key educational indicators such as high school graduation (approximately 14% of Latinx students ages 16–24 were classified as dropouts/pushouts, as compared to only 5% of White students), enrollment in four-year colleges (56% versus 72%), and completion of bachelor's degrees (National Center for Education Statistics, 2012). Despite alarming educational indicators, Latinx students across the country have persevered and achieved academic success. Their accomplishments suggest that, contrary to popular deficit-based school reform discourses, the students are not the problem. The educational trajectories for large portions of the Latinx population have been adversely impacted by educational neglect (MacDonald, 2004) and insufficient attention given to how students' cultural frames of reference influence teaching and learning, particularly in educational settings serving communities that have been historically underserved by schools (Gutiérrez, Morales, & Martinez, 2009).

As researchers, policymakers, and educators search for remedies to improve the educational experiences and outcomes for Latinx youth, they often ignore the perspectives of those most directly impacted by the problem—namely, the students themselves. In what follows, I document the methods used to critically analyze features of students' teaching practices when they are positioned as teachers and given the power to develop curricula and deliver instruction. The findings of the study forward a vision for culturally sustaining pedagogies that honor and seek to sustain the diverse and complex linguistic repertoires of Latinx youth, underscore the need for curriculum that is connected to the histories and present sociocultural realities of students, and provides students with opportunities for civic engagement.

LEARNING FROM LATINX YOUTH IN PROJECT FUERTE

Data for this chapter were collected as part of a larger project that examined the experiences of seven Latinx youth engaged in a multigenerational participatory action research collaborative called Project FUERTE (Future Urban Educators conducting Research to transform Teacher Education). As part of the project, students enrolled in a course on action research offered by the author at their high school. The goal of Project FUERTE was to critically examine the educational experiences of and outcomes for Latinx youth and to develop empirically based recommendations to influence the preparation of preservice and inservice teachers to work with Latinx students (see Irizarry, 2011).

A primary goal of the study was to understand how Latinx youth experienced school within the contexts of Latinization and increased pressures on schools to meet accountability standards. Comments offered through formal interviews, class discussions, written assignments, and research presentations addressed an array of issues impacting the educational experiences and outcomes for Latinx youth (see Irizarry, 2011, for a thorough discussion of the methodology).

Because of the nature of participatory action research, students in Project FUERTE had significant control over the research and the content of our biweekly classes. As the youth became increasingly more comfortable with their role as researchers, they began to assert control over not only the material that was included in the course but also how that information was delivered. Over the two years, there were several prominent features of the students' approaches to teaching and learning within the research collaborative. These findings easily fit within the broad framework of culturally sustaining pedagogies, forcing us to complicate static notions of culture and how language is often used as a vehicle through which students perform their shifting cultural identities. Consistent with culturally sustaining approaches, the complex linguistic repertoires that students in the study brought with them to the classroom were honored and leveraged not only as a pedagogical tool to help students master the curriculum, which often omits or marginalizes the experiences and accomplishments of people of color, but as a sign of respect and affirmation of students' cultural identities. That is, students' cultures and cultural practices have value in and of themselves. Because students controlled much of the content of the course and were responsible for facilitating learning among the group members, the findings illustrate the concepts in which students were most interested and how these were connected to their cultural histories and present sociopolitical realities. Finally, a significant focus of students' work was an advocacy stance, exploring how the curriculum, and their learning experiences more broadly, can be used not only for personal success, such as graduating from high school, attending an institution of higher education, or securing what students referred to as a "good job," but also for communal goals. Their approach, consistent with the goals of culturally sustaining pedagogies, call for a heightened appreciation of cultural hybridity and more seamlessly speak to the academic and social needs of youth in an increasingly global society. This shift in stance and practice, reflected in the students' approaches to teaching and theorized in this chapter, can best be described as culturally sustaining pedagogies (Paris, 2012). The students' voices, highlighted in what follows, underscore the value, as well as absolute necessity, for culturally sustaining approaches to working with Latinx youth that reflect a more nuanced, contextualized approach to teaching and learning that speaks to the immediate material conditions of students' lives.

Languages and Literacies: The Emergence of Spangbonics

The United States has always been a multilingual country. The Indigenous peoples of the Americas spoke more than 1,000 different languages prior to the European settler colonial project (Zepeda & Hill, 1991). While many tribal communities of Indigenous peoples have continued across the centuries to speak and revitalize their languages (Chapters 4 and 12, this volume), settler colonial ideologies and policies have had devastating effects on Native languages. It is also worth mentioning that even as they participated in this devastating linguicide, ironically, the European immigrants' efforts to establish a new government on Native land were multilingual. Their founding documents, including the Articles of Confederation, which was a precursor to the Constitution of the United States, were written and distributed in multiple languages (Cockcroft, 1995).

Although more than 300 languages are spoken in the United States today, there seems to be a national backlash against speaking languages other than the dominant form of Dominant American English, especially in the public sphere. Within the context of RHS, there was a de facto rule, perpetuated by some teachers and administrators, that students could not speak languages other than American English, and harsh penalties were applied when they deviated from the language expectations of school officials. In contrast, the Action Research and Social Change class, and the larger collaborative research project in which we engaged, created an alternative space where students could use multiple languages. The students saw the classroom space as a reprieve from harsh restrictions on using their "native" languages—that is, languages emerging from their communities that students engaged in which can include but are not limited to heritage languages connected to their cultures. Interestingly, the students did not solely speak one language or another during class meetings but, rather, moved fluidly between multiple languages within one conversation, intermingling minoritized dialects and World Englishes with Dominant American English (Young & Martinez, 2011; see also Chapter 3, this volume). In the following excerpt from my fieldnotes a student in the class, Taína, illuminates students' emerging metacognitive understanding of the role of language in the learning process and the potential utility of supporting diverse language practices in the classroom.

> This [class] works better because in here we like talk how we talk out there (pointing to the window). This is like real talk. I know how [teachers] want us to sound, and if I go to a job [interview] I know what they want me to sound like. That's fine. I can do that. No problem. But sometimes you just want to relax and be you[rself] in school. I learn more this way, you know using the languages I know. You feel me? It is not just English, or just Spanish, or just Ebonics, it is like a mix of them with some other stuff . . . like Spangbonics. (Classmates start to laugh and several chime in to the conversation.) That's what's up. Spangbonics. Yup!

According to the participants, the spontaneous *code-meshing* (Young & Martinez, 2011), creatively labeled as Spangbonics, allowed for them to engage more deeply in classroom conversations and enhanced their learning experience. As Taína notes above, students understand the centrality of Dominant American English and its relationship to the "codes of power," ways of speaking that carry cultural capital in particular contexts (Delpit, 1995). Nevertheless, when empowered to shape the linguistic texture of the classroom, students seemed to move effortlessly within and across languages, often drawing from multiple languages to maximize meaning-making. As linguistic diversity and dexterity in the United States continues to increase, fueled largely by population growth among people of color, which language practices have "power" will continue to shift, and the current language hierarchy, which positions certain languages and linguistic practices above others, must continue to be interrogated (Paris & Alim, 2014).

Because of the restrictive language policies subordinating the use of languages other than Dominant American English in the school, the students often felt alienated from teachers and the content they needed to learn in order to meet their personal and educational goals. In addition to academic benefits associated with increased engagement and using diverse languages to promote a deeper understanding of material through connection to their everyday lives, code-meshing in this context also allowed for the affirmation of the hybrid identities students had developed as a result of interactions with peers across lines of cultural, racial, ethnic, and linguistic difference. Through the affirmation of the languages and literacies of the members of the class, the students created a liberatory space within the otherwise hostile context of the school.

Identities, including racial and ethnic identities, are performed, in large part, through language (Alim, Rickford, & Ball, 2016; see also Chapter 3, this volume). Subordination of one's language(s) is tantamount to the subordination of one's identity, as language, literacy, and culture are inextricably linked. In this way, uses of language within the classroom sustained students and their sense of selves. Within RHS, students of color were constantly surveilled and their language practices restricted, while, conversely, White students were praised for attempting to learn new languages and encouraged to communicate in them throughout the school day. As one student noted, "When we speak Spanish we get punished for it, sent to the principal's office, but when White kids do it, there isn't a problem." The racial undertones of the language policy speak to one of the ways institutional racism was manifested in the setting (see Chapter 10, this volume).

Within the confines of the Action Research and Social Change class, students were able to assert agency and take ownership over their educational experiences. When positioned as teachers and allowed to create to the culture of the classroom and norms that would govern classroom behaviors, students' practices underscore the importance of supporting ethnolinguistic communication. However, their ethnocentricity, or focus on their cultures and cultural frames of reference, was not conceptualized solely in terms of "native" or "home" language. Rather, the communication styles in which students engaged and featured in their pedagogical strategies were reflective of the rich linguistic repertoires students possessed that included Dominant American English, Spanish, and African American English and the multiple variations within each. The recombinations (Paris & Alim, 2014) were used intentionally and in context to convey meanings that would not have been adequately conveyed if confined to one language.

Importantly, contrary to the perception of students of color lacking the savvy to use language contextually, students in the research collaborative made deliberate choices about language use and were cognizant of the relationship between power and language. During the question-and-answer portion of a conference presentation, for example, one audience member, somewhat paternalistically, noted how impressed he was by the students' communication skills, noting how they didn't speak "street talk." In a sharp response, Christina replied:

> What do you mean street talk? You expected us to talk a particular way because of the way that we look? Think about that. Language is about sharing information in a way people understand it. Yes, I speak "street" as you say, when I am talking to friends and stuff. But frankly you

wouldn't understand me if I talked like that. So I talk like this so you all can understand. It doesn't mean one language is better than another like some of ya'll think. It's just knowing your audience.

In short, the students recognized the value of Dominant American English and used it effectively, but they rejected the notion that their learning experiences should be confined to one language. In this way, they sought to be part of changing linguistic norms in the classroom as a means of engaging academic material as they sustained themselves. Their commitment to multilingualism speaks to challenging the status of minoritized languages and the value of ethnolinguistic communication as a central feature of culturally sustaining pedagogies.

Culture and Content: "We Have a History"

The overwhelming majority of the students' time in school was spent learning discrete facts that might be referenced on standardized tests but were rarely applicable to their lives. It was seldom that students were encouraged or assisted in making connections between the content they learned in schools and their lived experiences or future goals. Reflecting on the Eurocentricity and marginalization of People of Color within the school curriculum, Alberto, a senior at RHS at the time, shared the following during a class discussion stemming from the students' analysis of the mandated curriculum and texts used in their courses:

> Now that we like really look at what we are learning . . . like think about it more, you can see what they [teachers and school administrators] think is important. I don't see nothing about Latinos, Black People, you know, in there. ¿Me entiendes? [Do you understand me?] I just assumed Latinos didn't do nothing, like nada, nothing. In this class we read so much written by Latinos, but in the rest of the school nothing. It is all focused on White history and books. What about Mexican history? What about the Puerto Ricans? Other people? We have a history. We have stories. In the book it is just like one little page, la última [the last page]. Merecemos mejor [we deserve better].

In contrast to their school curriculum, the content the students selected to include as part of the class demonstrated a commitment to moving the exploration of the experiences of marginalized peoples from the periphery of the curriculum to the center of their work. At the inception of the course, most of the students were apprehensive about applying themselves to academic tasks, and they were skeptical about investing in the class and larger research collaborative. They were largely unaware of Latinx participation in the struggle for civil rights, and few had read literature written by Latinx authors or that featured Latinx protagonists. Because of their long histories of academic neglect and marginalization within schools, including the subordination of their languages and language practices (as noted above) and omission of the communities with which they identified from the curriculum, the students were, understandably, reluctant to take the reins and create a curriculum that foregrounded their communities, histories, literatures, and languages. The shift in students' engagement in academic tasks, as evidenced by the following conversation documented in my fieldnotes, speaks to the potential of culturally sustaining approaches that center students' cultural frames of reference to create engaging, quality learning experiences.

> *Irizarry:* What will you take away from this year?
>
> **Carmen:** That we did all this work, but we liked it. It was about us, so you know we were wit' it.
>
> **Alberto:** It was the first time I learned anything about Latinos. I feel like *más inteligente* [smarter] now.
>
> **Taína:** I don't know. Like the whole thing. . . . Feel me? I thought Latinos were dumb, that we were not smart. That's probably the biggest thing. I see that we are [smart] now. I thought that because of what they teach us and how they treat us [in school]. But now when we have the power in this class, to like learn stuff, hard stuff, but stuff that we like are connected to, we do the work. The presentations were big . . .
>
> *Jasmine:* For me, too. The presentations, that's wassup. We were up there and people were actually listening to us, to what we had to say. That's what I'm talkin' bout.
>
> **Ramon:** I like that this is the beginning. I don't know how to say it, but the beginning for me. I want to keep learning like this. If I'm a teacher, this is how I am gonna roll, how I'm gonna do it. Project FUERTE *por vida* [for life]. [Smiles across the room]

The students' experiences in school were bleak, and their work on the research collaborative revealed the multiple ways in which educational institutions marginalized them. Nevertheless, the students did not lose hope in the potential for personal and communal transformation that can accompany approaches to teaching and learning that include students and their communities as meaningful partners in the process. At first they were critical of the texts that were assigned as required reading in their classes. However, their analysis stopped there because they were largely unaware of any titles written by or about Latinx people.

> *Irizarry:* So if these books aren't what you want to read, what are the books you would like to read?
>
> *Jasmine:* I don't know . . . Like books about us.
>
> *Irizarry:* Can you name any? [The class fell silent.]

After that conversation, the students decided to research titles that would interest them. Several of the students, on their own, started to read those novels, even though they were not assigned as part of the Action Research and Social Change class. Acknowledging that many teachers might be unfamiliar with the some of the books they selected, they developed a list of recommended titles that they would share with teachers who attended the various professional conferences at which they presented.

To be clear, it wasn't this simple: Books written by and about Latinx people will be of interest to Latinx students. Students resisted. Several students were apprehensive about embarking on reading long books or articles with challenging academic jargon. Like other high school students, they juggled schoolwork with co- and extracurricular activities, and their investment in the class sometimes waned. Despite these challenges, without exception the content students expressed a desire to learn, and the learning experiences that they co-constructed to share with the class all centered the experiences of People of Color and/or the experiences of urban youth, and the students in the project responded favorably to learning experiences that they believed were connected to their cultural identities, histories, and lived experiences.

The deepening racial and linguistic texture of the United States, and K–12 schools more specifically, stands in contrast to the "whitewashed" curriculum that is implemented in many schools, including RHS. Perhaps unintentionally, the school implemented a curriculum that none of the students found to be culturally sustaining. The participants took the omission of Latinx people from the curriculum to implicitly suggest that Latinx people didn't have a history worth mentioning, and developed a sense of race- and culture-based internalized oppression. When given free rein to inform the direction of a class, students worked to fill that void in their education and develop a deeper understanding of themselves through learning more about the experiences of Latinx people through literature and participation on a research project examining the education of Latinx students in urban schools. Their shift in engagement, from students with minimal investment in schooling (not to be confused with a lack of interest in education) to scholars with a passion for learning, was facilitated by an engagement with content that was connected to students' lives and interests, a core aspect of culturally sustaining approaches to teaching and learning.

Advocacy and Action: "We Can Do This"

Culturally sustaining pedagogies are approaches to teaching and learning with the potential to improve academic outcomes among students, particularly those who have been underserved by schools. Transforming the curriculum and building on students' cultural frames of reference, while important, are in and of themselves insufficient for transforming the educational experiences and outcomes for students embedded in school systems that seek to reproduce race- and class-based stratification (see Bowles & Gintis, 1976; MacLeod, 2008). RHS had a history of producing underachievement among Latino students, and many of the faculty and staff were reticent, and some even hostile, to the suggestion that the school should affirm the cultural identities of Latinx students, who accounted for approximately half of the student body. The students were aware that they were being tracked into the non-college-prep courses with little academic rigor and were cognizant of the omission of Latinx people and other People of Color from the curriculum. They saw themselves as passive recipients of an oppressive education with little sense of agency, other than engaging in self-defeating resistance (Solórzano & Delgado Bernal, 2001) in the form of cutting class or being disruptive. Offering an outlet and potential for transformational resistance (Solórzano & Delgado Bernal, 2001)—that is, forms of resistance that lead to personal and communal transformation—the class became not only a site for critiquing manifestations of institutional oppression, but also a space for coalition-building and collective action to transform their school and inform reform efforts in other districts through their presentations and publications.

At the inception of the class, the students didn't believe that they could do anything to change the culture and climate of their school, improve their educational experiences, and increase the likelihood of improved educational outcomes for themselves and future generations. Through participation in the research project, and more specifically through their experiences taking responsibility for the direction of the class in which the project was embedded, students began to feel empowered to challenge and attempt to transform the oppressive nature of their schooling experiences. As one student put it, "We can do this!"

The movement from apathy to agency began with a heightened awareness of the sociopolitical contexts in which they were being educated. Students knew that their experiences in schools were largely negative, and often pointed to strained relationships between themselves and individual teachers or administrators. However, they were less cognizant about how their experiences compared to other Latinx students at RHS and across the country. The systematic nature of their marginalization and the social reproductive function of schooling remained largely opaque. Once made more visible through their research, the tenor and direction of the class, informed by students' choices of texts to read, questions to ask in interviews conducted as part of their research, and their interests in learning more about the education of Latinx youth more broadly, shifted more squarely onto understanding systems of oppression. Articulating a vision of what a culturally sustaining approach to education means to her, Carmen offered the following in an interview:

> I used to like think that it was just me. Like I was just a bad kid, bad student. Then I was like, oh it is just me and a few other kids. Now I see,

it affects all of us. Latinos in this school, like we all get treated badly. Even if a teacher isn't always on you or you always in ISS [in-school suspension], the curriculum doesn't include us, and teachers don't think about that. Plus, we are not just students here. We are part of a larger community and world. We don't . . . like, I want to see how what I am learning connects to that, to the larger world, to other Latinos out there, to other people out there. That's what education should be about. It should include us and help us understand and push for our place in the world.

The students quickly grew frustrated with merely naming forms of oppression that were manifested in school and negatively impacting their lives; they wanted to transform them. Influenced by their reading of excerpts of Paulo Freire's *Pedagogy of the Oppressed* (1970) and motivated by a sense of urgency to improve their current circumstances, they saw education, and this class and research project more specifically, as an opportunity to assert agency and transform the system so that it would operate in the best interests of all students, including Latinx people. Locating their individual experiences within a larger sociopolitical context motivated students to develop a social justice orientation and work for educational equity within their school. Alberto spoke to the possibilities of a culturally sustaining approach rooted in critical pedagogy:

This class is about us. That's why it is good. We don't have anything that is here to help us. But it is different because we have to do it ourselves. We have say in what we do, what we are learning. At first all of us were like this is wack. This isn't going to be fun. Then we started working together and trying to help each other and trying to help other students. That's when this got good for me—when we started using the work we do to help other students, especially Latinos, because you know how they treat us. That is what was missing from our learning and education. If things are bad you have to fix them. You can learn while trying to make bad things good. We learned a lot and helped a lot of people with our presentations and stuff. That's what education needs to be.

As reflected in the students' comments above, using their platform to take action was central to the participants' vision of a culturally sustaining approach to teaching. For the students, education is most valuable when there is practical application to what they are learning, particularly opportunities that allow them to improve themselves as individuals and the communities in which they live. They acknowledge the pervasiveness of racism and other forms of oppression they experience as Latinx youth, and see how schools can and often do perpetuate the status quo by closing them off from future opportunities. Although they have been woefully underserved by schools, the students in this study, nevertheless, remained committed to the ideal that schools can be the "great equalizer," as once envisioned. Through their active participation in the class, they offered a vision for more race- and culture-conscious approaches to teaching and learning that not only acknowledge the pervasive nature of racism but also offer potential for challenging and dismantling systems of oppression. This commitment to social justice and educational equity corresponded with the students coming together as a research collective, comprised largely of Latinx students trying to navigate a system that they believed was designed to limit their options and ensure their failure.

FOR US, BY US: TOWARD A GROUNDED THEORY
OF CULTURALLY SUSTAINING PEDAGOGIES

When positioned as teachers and allowed to shape the classroom culture and climate, develop curricula, and take responsibility for its implementation, the students offered a vision for what culturally sustaining pedagogies can be. This vision is highly contextual, meaning that there is no one-size-fits-all, cookie-cutter model that can be implemented in any setting. Rather, their approach to culturally sustaining pedagogies spoke to the specific needs of students within that setting and allowed for students to make connections between their lives and what they were learning. The central features of their approach, thematically organized as *Language and Literacies, Culture and Content,* and *Advocacy and Action*, offered a framework that allows for a grounded theory of culturally sustaining pedagogies that was born out of their social marginalization and collective action to overcome it.

The students' approaches to teaching and learning did not map onto the myth of rugged individualism, which is often exalted within the narrative of "the American Dream" and central to most models of schooling. In contrast, theirs was a collective effort, where students worked collaboratively for communal success and not just individual achievement. They offered a vision for schooling that combines learning and academic achievement with social justice and educational equity. The students in this study, aware that the needs of Latinx youth like themselves were not being adequately addressed in school, decided to use the opportunities afforded them in the research collaborative to address the glaring disparities in educational opportunities at their school and beyond. Drawing from the name of a 1990s African American clothing company, which sought to fight exclusion in the clothing market by designing apparel that would be appealing to urban communities, FUBU™ (For Us, By Us) became an apt metaphor for the students' research. Building upon the cultural frames of reference of urban youth, FUBU became a unifying factor among students, allowing for the development of bonds of solidarity across lines of difference. It also speaks to the need for the development of more organic implementations of culturally sustaining pedagogies that emerge to meet the needs of students navigating particular contexts (see Chapter 9 in this volume on organic forms of CSP). The embodiment of FUBU within the students' work in this research collaborative maps onto the tenets of LatCrit theory that inform this analysis.

First, the students recognized the centrality of race and racism in their lives. The "us" in FUBU resulted from the racialized "othering" they had experienced because they were Latinx students in a community that they believed to be hostile to the recent surge in the population of Latinx people. Although Latinx people can be of any race, their experiences in the United States have undoubtedly been racialized, and they have been the target of individual as well as institutional manifestations of racism. In this case, racism intersects with language use, as demonstrated through the suppression of students' language practices, as well as immigrant status and other identity categories.

Gloria Anzaldúa's concept of *nos-otras,* literally translated as "we, the others," speaks to the divide that exists between many educational institutions and the students they are supposed to serve. Explaining the notion in an interview, Anzaldúa (1999, p. 243), in an interview with Karin Ikas, noted, "I have a term that is called nos-otras, and I put a dash between the nos and otras. The nos is the subject 'we,' that is the people who were in power and the colonized others. The otras is the 'other,' the colonized group. Then there is also the dash, the divide between us." While Anzaldúa accounts for interactions across the hyphen and the fluidity that can and does exist across the categories of colonizer and colonized, she also highlights the impact of oppression in creating division along lines of difference. For the students in Project FUERTE, their collective experience with racialized colonization embedded in their educational experiences in schools resulted in an "othering," or separation between them and many school employees. The students embraced the collective identity that emerged through their shared marginalization while simultaneously trying to build bridges through their teaching and research to connect with other students, teachers, and administrators in order to inform the work of those on the other side of the proverbial divide.

FUBU as a metaphor also represented a challenge to the dominant ideology of schooling as a color- and culture-blind process aimed at meeting the needs of "all" students. Students not only exposed the racialized differences in access to quality educational experiences within their school, but they also created a counterhegemonic space within the confines of the class and larger research collaborative where they were able to critically examine and challenge restrictive school policies and practices. Opportunities to learn at RHS were not distributed in a race-neutral manner, nor were they based on a system of meritocracy. Consequently, students sought to create a learning environment that integrated academic rigor with a race- and culture-conscious approach to teaching and learning.

Perhaps most notably, FUBU reflected a commitment to honoring and leveraging the experiential knowledge of students in the research collaborative and the communities of color with whom they interacted. Latinx youth at RHS were often rendered voiceless at the school, pushed to the periphery of the school community and encouraged to be passive recipients of education. Beyond the school, Latinx youth are rarely, if ever, meaningfully included in education policy debates or curriculum development efforts. In contrast, within Project FUERTE, students were positioned as experts of their own lives with invaluable insights into the education of Latinx youth. Who better, then, to develop recommendations on how to improve the quality of education offered to this community?

Finally, FUBU as a metaphor reflects LatCrit's commitment to cross-disciplinary boundaries and privileges perspectives that have been silenced or maligned within academic research, and in this case within school improvement efforts. Attending a high school in a district that was under the microscope for their lack of academic achievement meant that school administrators and teachers were in a state of panic, developing action plans to rectify the situation. According to the participants, students were never consulted in this process, even though they are well-positioned to offer important insights. Within the research collaborative, students' perspectives and knowledges were privileged, and they had the opportunity to raise their previously silenced voices to assert agency over their own educational trajectories—and the trajectories of those beyond the confines of their school.

TOWARD MORE STUDENT-CENTERED APPROACHES

When given an opportunity to teach, Latinx students' approach to educating themselves and their peers offers a framework with the potential to inform culturally sustaining teaching across contexts. Their commitment to honoring students' diverse linguistic repertoires, transforming the curriculum so that it is more inclusive and connected to the lives of students from marginalized communities, and using education as a vehicle to promote social and educational justice was both noteworthy and inspirational. Their approach was not informed by reading theories about effective teaching practices or taking courses focusing on teaching methods, although these resources certainly have value. Rather, their teaching methods were born out of necessity, a response to being ignored, neglected, and at times maligned within school.

Students' pedagogical practices were informed by what I have referred to in previous work as *barrio-based epistemologies and ontologies*—ways of being and knowing informed by sustained immersion in and connection to Latinx communities (Irizarry & Raible, 2011). In this case, the students' experiential knowledge served as a valuable form of capital that informed their teaching, making it culturally sustaining for the members of the classroom community. Obviously, the specific content and methods will likely vary across settings, as the experiences of students will likely vary (this is why a grounded theory of CSP is necessary). However, themes emerging from analyzing the students' approaches to teaching and learning suggest that if schooling is ever going to speak to the academic and social needs of Latinx youth, educational opportunities must be grounded in students' lived experiences, build on their systems of meaning-making, and provide students with the skills and confidence to advocate for themselves—indeed, to sustain themselves and their communities.

REFERENCES

Alim, H. S., Rickford, J., & Ball, A. (Eds.) (2016). *Raciolinguistics: How language shapes our ideas about race*. New York, NY: Oxford University Press.

Anzaldúa, G. E. (1999). Writing: A way of life. In A. Keating (Ed.), *Interviews/ Entrevistas*. New York, NY: Routledge.

Bowles, S., & Gintis, H. (1976). *Schooling in capitalist America*. London, UK: Routledge.

Cockcroft, J. D. (1995). *Latinos in the struggle of equal education*. New York, NY: Franklin Watts.

Delpit, L. (1995). *Other people's children: Cultural conflict in the classroom*. New York, NY: New Press.

Excelencia in Education. (2015). *The condition of Latinos in education: 2015 factbook*. Washington, DC: Excelencia in Education.

Gándara, P. C., & Contreras, F. (2008). *The Latino education crisis: The consequences of failed social policies*. Cambridge, MA: Harvard University Press, 2010.

Gutiérrez, K., Morales, P. Z., & Martinez, D. C. (2009). Re-mediating literacy: Culture, difference, and learning for students. *Review of Research in Education, 33*, 212–245.

Irizarry, J. G. (2011). *The latinization of U.S. schools: Successful teaching and learning in shifting cultural contexts*. Boulder, CO: Paradigm Publishing.

Irizarry, J. G., & Raible, J. (2011). Beginning with *El Barrio*: Learning from exemplary teachers of Latino students. *Journal of Latinos and Education, 10*(3), 1–18.

MacDonald, V. M. (2004). *Latino education in the United States: A narrated history from 1513–2000*. New York, NY: Palgrave.

MacLeod, J. (2008). *Ain't no makin' it: Aspirations and attainment in a low-income neighborhood* (3rd ed.). Boulder, CO: Westview Press.

National Center for Education Statistics. (2012). *Digest of educational statistics 2012*. Washington, DC: U.S. Department of Education.

Paris, D. (2012). Culturally sustaining pedagogy: A needed change in stance, terminology, and practice. *Educational Researcher, 41*(3), 93–97.

Paris, D., & Alim, H. S. (2014). What are we seeking to sustain through culturally sustaining pedagogy? A loving critique forward. *Harvard Educational Review, 84*(1), 85–100.

Solórzano, D. G., & Delgado Bernal, D. (2001). Examining transformational resistance through a critical race and LatCrit theory framework: Chicana and Chicano students in an urban context. *Urban Education, 3*, 308–342.

U.S. Census Bureau. (2015). *Hispanic roots: Breakdown of U.S. Hispanic population, by specific origin 2014*. Washington, DC: U.S. Department of Commerce.

Young, V. A., & Martinez, A.Y. (2011). *Code-meshing as World English: Pedagogy policy, performance*. Urbana, IL: National Council of Teachers of English.

Zepeda, O., & Hill, J. H. (1991). The condition of Native American languages in the United States. *Diogenes, 39*(153), 45–65.

CHAPTER 6

"This Stuff Interests Me"

Re-Centering Indigenous Paradigms in Colonizing Schooling Spaces

Timothy J. San Pedro
The Ohio State University

We must first "know the stories of our people" and then "make our own story too" . . . we must "be aware of the way they change the stories we already know" for only with that awareness can we protect the integrity of the Native American story.

—Kimberly Blaeser

Nearly every day, James[1] drives across the border between his reservation and the city. He sees the line in the sand, a wall constructed by the city's residential neighborhood. On one side: wall-to-wall housing, apartments stacked on top of one another. On the other: open fields, crops, houses separated by miles, not inches. He travels across this border to attend Desert View High School (DVHS), which has the largest population of Native American students in an off-reservation school in the city. It's a two-minute drive to get from this border to the school's parking lot. As he enters the barred and gated campus through a narrow passageway where security officers (and sometimes policemen) greet him, he flashes his school ID card attached to a shoelace necklace. Above, a faint roar comes from an airplane on its final descent to the city's major airport miles away.

James is surprised he's here, not just today, but this academic year, his senior year. He's surprised because the last few weeks of his junior year, he made the decision to drop out of school, a decision made easy because nothing taught at Desert View High School reflected his knowledges, his truths, or his beliefs; he could not see himself in the curriculum and saw little purpose in attending. Such invalidation and misrepresentation of his knowledges and truths was something he could no longer tolerate.

He had made his decision.

It was final . . .

Until he heard the news:

A brand-new course—an ethnic studies course—was beginning next year.

That course was called Native American Literature.

He said that it was more than just another class for him: "This [Native American Literature classroom] is the only reason I came to school for the first two weeks actually. Cuz I was gonna drop out, but I wanted to come to this class. And by luck I happened to stay in school."

According to James, who self-identifies as being from the Ute and Pima tribes, the anticipation of what this 12th-grade English elective course might be, could be, ought to be, made school worthy of his continued presence. By seeing this course through, he was able to help co-construct a space with students and the teacher that helped him see the worth in his education once again. Such spaces where students continue their development as critical members of society are referred to by Garcia and Shirley (2012) as *sacred spaces*. Sacred spaces are places within schools for students like James to "be vocal, active, and reflective about ways to counter inequality in their communities instead of passively accepting such circumstances" (pp. 83–84). Having one sacred space within school to develop and sustain James's critical Indigenous consciousness (Lee, 2006; Smith, 2003; Wane, 2009) was enough for him to deal with other schooling spaces that continued to invalidate and story over his knowledges, and graduate:

> . . . just the fact that I'm Native. Just the fact that we're talking about things [in the Native American Literature classroom] that I'm familiar with, ya know? Kinda like the ceremony and stuff. The different tribes and stuff and that's where I feel comfortable, you know? I think it's better that we learn about Native American stuff other than the stuff like in my history classes. Whatever they learn about: Columbus or whatever. That stuff don't interest me, ya know? This stuff—*this stuff*—interests me.

As he says "*this stuff*" the second time, he points to his heart.

At the time, he may not have known how revolutionary an action it was for him to graduate—to rebel and resist by succeeding academically (see Cammarota, 2004). He probably didn't know the exact statistics that he was almost part of: Native American students "are 237% more likely to drop out of school and 207% more likely to be expelled than white students" (National Caucus of Native American State Legislators, 2008, p. 5). What he did know was that graduating was an important accomplishment for himself and his family and a testament to what one ethnic studies course like this might be for other students like him.

His story wasn't the only one.[2]

Research on ethnic studies courses has shown that when curriculum affirms the identities of students through the development of critical intellectualism, students increase their motivation and engagement in schooling contexts (Banks, 2008; Cammarota & Romero, 2009; Sleeter, 2014). More recent studies have shown that participation in even one ethnic studies classroom—which works to foster critical thinking and engagement—positively impacts students' academic success (Cabrera, Milem, Jacquette, & Marx, 2014; Dee & Penner, 2016), although, as Paris (2016) points out, such "successes" are still based on dominant norms and beliefs that ought to be challenged. In questioning what we hope to attain through education in a pluralistic society, Paris and Alim ask: "What if, indeed, the goal of teaching and learning with youth of color was not ultimately to see how closely students could perform White middle-class norms but to explore, honor, extend, and, at times, problematize their heritage and community practices?" (2014, p. 86). For James (and many of the other 90-plus students I learned with over 3 years), he knew that having one classroom space that sought to sustain his cultural and linguistic pluralism (Paris, 2012) by centering his tribal histories and stories gave him greater opportunities to expand his critical consciousness and intellectualism. In the process, he was better equipped to comprehend and deal with other schooling spaces that continued to invalidate, story over, and erase his community's stories.

SACRED TRUTH SPACE AND CULTURALLY SUSTAINING PEDAGOGY

The stories shared in this chapter are part of a 3-year longitudinal classroom ethnography whereby I learned with students the ways an ethnic studies course (in the U.S. Southwest)—which actively worked to counter standard histories and literacies—impacted multitribal and multicultural students' motivation and engagement in schooling spaces (San Pedro, 2013). It is with the permission and support of students with whom I worked that I re-story one particular lesson plan taught early in the semester to illustrate one way to begin the crucial construction of what I have come to understand as sacred truth spaces. Such spaces build on Paris's (2012) culturally sustaining pedagogy (CSP), which is a call for educators, researchers, and community members to push beyond just responding to students' languages and cultures to make them relevant (while curricula continue to center White middle-class norms). In turn, CSP urges us to re-center "linguistic, literate, and cultural pluralism as part of the democratic project of schooling" (p. 95). This move calls for a crucial refusal: CSP must refuse static conceptualizations of cultures and languages as something locked in the past; rather, students' cultures and languages must be viewed as dynamic, shifting, and evolving. To clarify this theoretical shift, Paris and Alim (2014) ask themselves: "What are we seeking

to sustain through culturally sustaining pedagogy?" (p. 85). In this chapter, students reveal answers to this fundamental question by stating:
    We are seeking to:

- sustain the ways our cultures and languages are alive, in movement, and flowing.
- engage in reflexive practices that help us to question and problematize and sometimes change the way we live our cultures and languages.
- sustain opportunities to revitalize and reclaim that which has "been disrupted and displaced by colonization." (McCarty & Lee, 2014, p. 101)

This chapter takes readers into this Native American Literature classroom to "see" the ways culturally sustaining pedagogy works in conjunction with ethnic studies curriculum to aid in the co-creation of what I refer to as *sacred truth space* in schools. *Sacred truth space*—a weaving of Garcia and Shirley's (2012) "sacred space" and Patel's (2016) "truth space"—pushes the uncritical boundaries found when theorizing about the goals and outcomes of safe spaces in schools. Leigh Patel makes clear this push beyond "safety," saying:

... learning is not often safe as it involves such profound transformation. And what facilitates learning for one person is often unproductive or even harmful for another. The white centeredness of education is what has led to consistently harmful spaces for racially minoritized and Indigenous populations. Truth would involve reckoning with that history and the less than polite reality of learning. The danger with calls for safe spaces is that they are fueled more by logics of identity politics than learning and architectures of harm. (personal communication, 2016)

In building with Patel, if the goal is to create educational spaces that are "safe," one must ask: Safe for whom? Such pursuits of safety and feelings of comfort often leave Indigenous students and other students of color on the margins of classroom discourse, since dominant norms and standards are maintained in the pursuit of these so-called safe spaces (San Pedro, 2015a). If, however, the goal is to create spaces that are sacred and truth-seeking, then the development of critical listening and voicing (San Pedro, 2015b) engages students in dialogic conversations that might feel uncomfortable and unsafe, but have the potential to be affirming and life-changing for all involved. *Sacred truth space* centers students' ability to share their realities and experiences that counter/challenge/correct standard knowledge that leads to painful silencing experiences in schools. In sacred truth spaces, students are able to engage in the often vulnerable act of telling and hearing multiple truths. As such, safety is not necessarily the goal; the goal, rather, is creating a dialogic space to share our truths *and* to listen and learn the truths of others.

In this chapter, I argue that when relationships rooted in culturally situated respect, reciprocity, and responsibility are created, fostered, and nurtured, they lead to classroom discussions rooted not in academic debate, where conversations are won or lost; rather, it leads to the co-creation of sacred truth spaces rooted in humanizing dialogue, where meaning is made in the spaces between our stories because of—and not in spite of—our differences.

REMEMBERING/HONORING THE GENESIS OF THE NATIVE AMERICAN LITERATURE CLASS

To continue this storied journey, it is important to discuss the genesis of this Native American Literature classroom. This course began because concerned parents and students at DVHS voiced their frustration that at a school with the largest population of Native American students in an off-reservation school in this city (around 10% of the total student population), there was very little, if anything, that acknowledged their Indigenous knowledges and histories.

To heed these parents' and students' concerns, during the winter of 2007 the school district's diversity specialist—a position that has since been removed—sought the advice of a team of people to construct a curriculum that would validate, teach, and support the perspectives of the Native American peoples in the Southwest United States. Professors James Blasingame and Simon Ortiz led a group of educators and community representatives.[3] Blasingame said it was created for two reasons:

> One, Native American students are being harmed when none of the curriculum reflects their culture, their heritage, or their identity, and two, the other (non-Native) students are not getting the true picture when they're studying American literature devoid of any Native authors in North America. (personal communication, 2009)

Ortiz added that Indigenous knowledge in this metropolitan area has been "missing since the very beginning" and needs to be "recognized in the public school . . . because teaching knowledge is primary and fundamental to any society and nation" (personal communication, 2009). Despite this metropolitan area's location near numerous Native American nations, some that share borders with the city, this was the only classroom that emphasized Native American literature.

Such a class was an important accomplishment particularly because of the political climate in Arizona. Known for its conservatism, Arizona has been noted as having the harshest anti-immigrant laws in the United States, with legislation such as SB 1070 and HB 2281. The latter, which is often referred to as the Ethnic Studies Ban, prohibits schools from teaching courses that focus on perspectives, knowledges, and understandings that differ from a dominant Eurocentric one.[4] This understanding of knowledge is deeply problematic, as it does not consider the ways knowledge is living, in process, and co-constructed through the telling of and listening to stories that continue the forever construction of our being and becoming. Thinking of knowledge as living provides the context for the culturally sustaining, revitalizing, and humanizing pedagogies used by the classroom teacher, Ms. Bee. By engaging CSP, Ms. Bee made the radical move to co-construct the curriculum *with* students so as to center their emerging cultures and identities. In doing so, she moved beyond tired notions of culture as being trapped and isolated in the past, rather than constantly in process with family, with community, with language, and within our pluralistic society. The following lesson plan highlights this emphasis upon culture as lived and in process, as something worthy of sustaining and, at times, revitalizing (McCarty & Lee, 2014).

"I DON'T EXPECT YOU . . . TO OPEN UP UNLESS I DO THE SAME THING": HUMANIZING TEACHING

As an illustration of sacred truth spaces, I re-story the following lesson plan in which students created art pieces that represented their stories to others. They then wrote interpretations of their art that revealed their identities and cultures to one another. This highlights the importance of creating greater fertile spaces between storytellers and story hearers where our lives can be shared. Such storying creates trusting and caring relationships grounded in sacred truth spaces. In such spaces, our realities, our hearts, our knowledges can be shared and, if productive, reciprocated.

Two weeks into the semester, Ms. Bee leans on her podium. Students sit in desks that face the center of the room, leaving an aisle for Ms. Bee to walk up and down as she facilitates her lessons throughout the year. She tells students that over the next few days, they will be creating artistic representations of their stories. While handing out today's reading by G. Lynn Nelson, titled "Warrior with Words: Toward a Post-Columbine Curriculum," she says,

> I'm going to be sharing a lot of information about myself. I don't expect you guys to open up unless I do the same thing. Again, some of my colleagues are just like, "You share too much with your students." I respond to them and say, "If we're going to ask [our students] to share about themselves, I think it's only fair to share about ourselves."

A few students nod in silent agreement. The article is a call for writing teachers to understand that all students have stories to tell and that the power of stories is not only in the telling, but also in having someone to hear their words.

Ms. Bee makes her way back to her podium and begins reading a key quote from this article:

> . . . our stories sit in us, waiting to be told, to be acknowledged. Untold and un-acknowledged, they will eventually translate themselves into other languages—languages of abuse and addiction, of suicide and violence. In such a society and in such schools we are literally dying to tell our stories. (Nelson, 2000, p. 14)

In reading it, students soon realize that this article is in reference to the Columbine High School shootings in Colorado and how that specific story was told through gun barrels. Ms. Bee continues reading:

> Story is a "second look at personal history" that can transform a person from one who is "trapped in [their] past" to one who is "freed by it." But . . . the telling is not all. "Along the way, on [their] pilgrimage, each [person] must have a chance to tell [their] tale, there must be someone there to listen." (Kopp cited in Nelson, 2000, p. 15)

She then organizes four stacks of papers, each with a different symbol, while asking, "If you had a logo that represents who you are, what would it be?"

There is silence as they think about the question.

Damon breaks the silence: "That's a good question. No one's ever asked me that before."

She holds up the outlines of four symbols that students in prior classes stated were important in many Native American communities—a shield, drum, traditional housing (as represented by a tipi), and pottery—and explains the significance of the symbols (see Figure 6.1).[5]

She asks students to choose one that best represents them. Within the symbol, students are asked to create a piece of art that reveals who they are, where they come from, and who their families and communities are. She asks them to think about their family, friends, cultures, tribes, celebrations, and sorrows that, together, make them who they are today: "How would you put all that is in your heart and head and soul into a picture?"

The second part of the assignment is to take something that emerges out of their logo and put it in the form of a story, that is, whatever and however their stories need to be told.

"Will it be an essay? A poem? A song? Find the story behind your logo and put it down on paper. Use your best words," Ms. Bee says.

She gives them the rest of the period to work on their drafts and asks that they have something written about their logos to share during the writing groups tomorrow.

Figure 6.1. Four symbols to construct self logo.

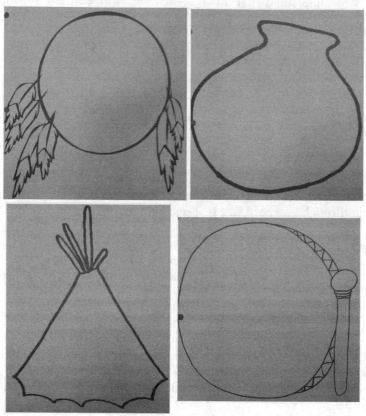

Ms. Bee handed these four symbols to students within which they drew pictures, scenes, and objects that reflected their identities.

The next day, Ms. Bee continues the lesson from yesterday, saying:

I am so excited to hear what you . . . [created] yesterday. Thank you, thank you, thank you for your honesty. Some of you wrote two pages, some of you wrote one sentence. Some of you guys said, "Ms. Bee, this is me; this is what I've done; these are some of the sorrows in my heart. Some of you guys are like, 'ya know, I'm okay for now.' And you guys come at this however you are comfortable with it. I'm not going to force you guys to share; I'm not going to ask you guys to do something you're not ready to do, so for some of us it takes a while to earn that trust and I totally, totally respect that."

Before students get into small groups to share the stories and art they've created, Ms. Bee makes herself vulnerable as she reads her poem and shows her art (see Figure 6.2). She titled her piece "My Publishing."

"Our stories get published, one way or another."

—Lynn Nelson

My once-crimson scar / has finally turned into a gentle, flesh-colored reminder / of my stories that needed/to be published / My right wrist tells the story/of a survivor / of my anger against myself / A story within a story within a story . . . / They never end / My past started at age 6 / I was abused in the darkness / of an abandoned cave / deep in the heart of North Carolina / 3 months of silent torture/swept into the cobwebs of innocence / My past continued at age 10 / I was abused in the darkness / of my own room / deep in the heart of an ignorant house / 12 months of unacknowledged torture / swept into the cobwebs of unwanted memories / My past haunted me at age 30 / I picked up my rusty, blue-handled scissors / and began carving my stories/into myself / smearing my blood / along the bathroom mirrors / and looking at my reflection / through red-tinted satisfaction / I was a newlywed / with an old soul / I could either save myself / or save my marriage / but not both / My first marriage / never even stood a chance / But the hawk of my heart refused / to let me die / Even today, she perches vigilantly above me / my animal spirit / my protector / myself / She lets me tell my stories / out of infinite pain / while she gives me the strength/to find tomorrow's stories / under the shadow of her wings / I am healed.

As Ms. Bee concludes the reading, she walks behind her podium while the students applaud and snap their fingers.

"Damn, that was good," Vince says.

"I'm not going to ask you to do anything that I'm not willing to do," Ms. Bee says.

Impacted, changed, I think about what must happen in the space between us for our conversations and stories to continue, to thrive, to grow. Here, Ms. Bee, who identifies as having Opata and Mayan ancestry, but was raised in a White culture, has shown the most vulnerable side of herself. She has revealed to them the pain of learning to become who she is and her growth in the process. She has modeled that all stories are okay in this classroom, even painful ones, ones that reveal the hurt and the hope.

She then asks students to form three groups of 10 as she makes nine copies of each of their writings, so that everyone in their group has a copy. After providing copies of their stories to each student, she asks them to share their stories with one another. Nisha takes the feather first. There is much hesitancy before she begins speaking, but after 5 seconds, she holds up her symbol and explains the large crack that separates the circle (see Figure 6.3). On one side of the circle is the border of one of her reservations, Zuni, and on the other is her other reservation, Jicarilla Apache. She says the crack represents the split her family has had to endure and how this splitting has

Figure 6.2. Ms. Bee's visual representation of her identity.

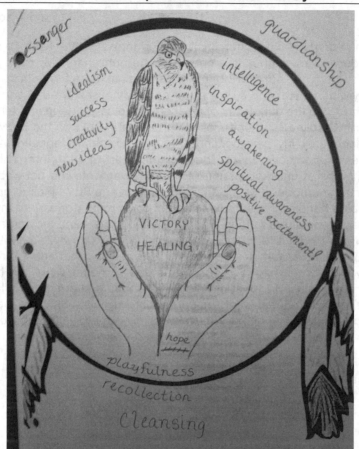

severed her two worlds. Her eyes look only to the back of the paper; they don't try to find anyone else's.

Beatriz goes next. She shares her story of her family living in two countries, Mexico and the United States, and the divide that a border has created for her, especially most recently. Students ask her to slow down and to speak more clearly, as they can't fully hear her story through her nervous giggles and quickened speech. She makes it through and passes the feather.

Abby, who self-identifies as Caucasian, receives the feather and holds up her symbol of a tiger and a dove: The tiger is her angry side, while the dove is her compassionate side. She says that she lost a great friend because of her inability to adapt to her friend's needs. She explains: "I strongly believe there is not a lot of hope for me to ever change, but I will strive to for the

Figure 6.3. Nisha's Symbol/Logo

rest of my life. I know I shouldn't change myself, that I should be true to who I really am, but I don't ever want to lose another important person."

Neena, who self-identifies as Pima, appears as if she will talk, but nothing emerges, not at this time. Just minutes prior, though, her story did emerge. She told her friends the significance of the three chicks walking in front of the mother duck. The three chicks symbolized her and her siblings and the duck in the back of the line symbolized her mother. The order was crucial to her story: Her mother (the duck) was being led by Neena and her siblings (the chicks) because of a painful situation that her mother had to endure and has not yet been able to overcome. Neena and her siblings have had to take the lead in her family until their mother is ready to lead again.[6] Although she shared this in her group of friends (which I was invited into), her story is not voiced in this larger group. She looks a little longer at the feather, then at her art. Without a word, she passes the feather to the next student.

The group asks her to share.

She shakes her head no.

They don't press.

"IF PEOPLE SHARE WITH ME AND CRY WITH ME . . .
THEN I CAN SHARE MY STORY WITH THEM":
CONSTRUCTING THE DIALOGIC SPIRAL IN TRUST

In the telling of story, we engage in a level of vulnerability, which may or may not be worth sharing depending on the trust we have (or don't have) with one another (see *dialogic spiral*, San Pedro, 2013). For Nisha, the impact was felt in a large way. She said,

> [When sharing our stories] we were able to hear people's stories . . . [and] it felt like, in a way, we were connected because certain things some of us would go through or certain things would represent a person and most people don't understand that, but to have people who have been there, it's really cool.

She was seeing the connections in other's stories with her own. She was making the connections in emotions, in feelings, in their realities and identities, which allowed her to see the commonalities of their collective lived experiences. In seeing this, she was willing to share her story: "I have trust in people. If people share with me and cry with me and if I know I can help them, then I can share my story with them."

However, for Neena, she did not share her story and, in a later interview, I asked her why. She said that her story was

> . . . too emotional, and I didn't wanna talk about it. I was like "nah, I must be getting weak." Being weak's like a real big thing for me. I don't like seeing weak at all. I don't wanna seem like that. Even for myself like when I'm at home if I'm going through something, I try not to share it with others. It's a sign of weakness.

For Neena, strength was in her ability to not show weakness. Perhaps it's connected to her story of having to lead her mother as her mother finds herself. Strength is in hiding story, in internalizing the emotions.

I asked Neena a follow-up question: "You don't like to show it, but did you see other students kinda showing emotion during that . . ." I begin to ask, but she knows where the question is going.

" . . . That was crazy [when Stacy shared her story]. I was like 'Oh, that's—that was really good.' After I heard her talk, I was like, 'Hmm, maybe I should share,' but then I was like, 'No, 'cause my story's too hard-core for it,'" she says.

In this instance, Stacy's willingness to reveal a painful moment in her life made Neena think, for a moment at least, that perhaps she should share her own. In the end, Neena did not tell her story, but hearing the power in Stacy's story[7] made her second-guess that decision, which made her own story one step closer to being told.

THANK YOU CARDS: VALIDATING THE WORDS OF OTHERS

After everyone had the option of sharing their stories, Ms. Bee hands them orange folded note cards. She asks them to write at least two thank you cards to someone in the group whose story impacted them.

Neena asks, "What if we want to write more than two?"

Ms. Bee responds, "Write as many as you'd like."

"I'm gonna write one for everyone," Nisha says.

As Ms. Bee passes them out, she skips me, and I ask if I could have a few cards as well. She smiles and says, "Of course." I end up writing six thank-yous to the students. I thank them for sharing their stories and listening to others. As I'm writing on these cards, I realize I missed an important moment. Ms. Bee's lesson begins to make its way into my consciousness. I think back to her statement that started this lesson plan: "I don't expect you guys to open up unless I do the same thing." I think about this in relation to the research process, which often asks of our participants: Who are you in the absence of me? rather than, Who are we in *relation* to each other (Grande, San Pedro, & Windchief, 2015)?

Why didn't I construct a piece of art that symbolized who I am? Why didn't I share a story and enact the level of vulnerability and trust-building that was happening all around me? In not doing so, how was I positioning myself to them (or separate from them), and how were they positioning me if I'm not willing to open up and reveal my stories with them?

An important shift occurred in me that I have enacted from that moment forward: If asked and when invited (which occurred often), I offer my stories in relation to their own. I explain my still-in-process understanding of my identity. I share with them a portion of my story: I am a Filipino American who grew up on the Flathead Indian Reservation in Western Montana. Through many conversations with friends and families from there, they positioned me as FilipIndian—one who was born with Filipino ethnicity, but has been shaped, impacted, and taught cultural ways of being Indigenous. They helped me realize that long-term participation, socialization, love, and the continued development of trust *is* who I am and forever striving to become. As students in this Native American Literature classroom engage in the lessons and teachings of this course, I think back to my own K–12 educational experiences, longing to be in a class like this one that never came to be while I lived near the geographic center of the reservation. I think about my friends and their families from the Salish, Kootenai, and Pond d'Oreille tribes who took me in as their own, who taught me lessons, who included me in their lives. I think about the stories I would have shared back then, and about the stories I now get to share—when asked, when prompted—as we construct new sacred truth spaces.

As this lesson settles, I hand the six thank-you notes I wrote to students and notice that the students who were the most vulnerable, who revealed the most in their stories, were the ones who received the most thank-you cards. Stacy's desk was covered in orange cards, and she read each one carefully. The bell rings, and I hear "Awwws" from students not ready or wanting to leave just yet. Ms. Bee says she'll give them time on Monday to finish writing these cards.

LESSONS LEARNED

Through this lesson, students came to understand the following underlying focus:

1. Culture is not static, nor is it trapped in the past: It is constantly in process as we engage in the process of being and becoming with those peoples and communities that are important to us, who shape us, and us them (Brayboy, 2005; Grande et al., 2015; Paris, 2012).
2. Our internal identities are multiple and varied depending upon the environments we enter (San Pedro, 2014).
3. The development of trust impacts the stories we are willing to share (or not share). As such, "Respect, reciprocity, responsibility, and the importance of caring relationships" (Brayboy, Gough, Leonard, Roehl, & Solyom, 2012, p. 436) impact who we are and how we reveal that authentic self to and with others (Kovach, 2005; Wilson, 2008).
4. Hearing, seeing, and feeling the visual and verbal stories of others—and having their stories valued and validated by another—fosters a classroom community in which future discussions of race, colonization, and oppression can be discussed meaningfully and dialogically.[8]

> "This stuff—"
> then points to his heart,
> "this stuff—interests me."

I think back to what may have helped James and others see the worth in their education once again and what occurred in this one ethnic studies classroom to help them "succeed" according to the narrow definitions we've set for students in academic settings. I wonder if what he meant when he pointed to his heart and said "*this stuff* interests me" was knowing that his story *was* the curriculum, that he had an opportunity to reflect on his reality and envision his futurity by making changes in his present actions. When educators and researchers move beyond making culture relevant or responsive to students, and make that radical move to create classroom spaces and curricula that are built upon and co-constructed *with* students evolving and developing cultural knowledges through stories, students' become central in their own education. In such a move to re-center students' experiences and realities that may counter standard curricula, students who were once marginalized by monocultural and monolingual curricula can begin to reinvest in their education because they can see themselves and their stories in ethnic studies classrooms like this one.

The lesson that Ms. Bee delivered began out of vulnerability, where even colleagues questioned her purposes in sharing such personal stories. By revealing her story within her poetry and her artwork, students became vulnerable as well to create and share their knowledge. Their collective stories helped me see the crucial importance of art and the ways it can unleash our stories through visual literacies. Through students' powerful stories, both in the visual and written stories shared, they helped me see the important contributions art can have in relation to culturally sustaining and revitalizing pedagogies.

And finally, I learned with students and with Ms. Bee that our stories—when given the opportunity to be drawn and written in educational spaces—validate who we are and who we are becoming. Our stories reflect the communities we belong to and the cultures we are shaping and creating through our living and remembering, and move beyond the continued teaching of curricula that centers White middle-class norms (Paris, 2012). When those stories are heard with our ears and hearts, they create something sacred in the spaces between us; it creates something truthful within those moments we co-construct together not in spite of our differences, but because of them. Being able to see and hear that our stories and our lives resonate and impact others provides the confidence to share the ways we are coming to view the world and how others view the world. In this way, students' cultures and languages shared through stories are not trivialized, minimized, or locked in the past; they are dynamic, shifting, and evolving in healing and revitalizing ways. Their stories herein provide a glimpse into the ways culturally sustaining pedagogies can unleash the power held in the space between the telling and hearing of stories through pens, pencils, and paintbrushes. To sustain our selves and the cultures that we are constantly shaping, creating, and impacting, there must be opportunities—particularly in schooling spaces—to be heard in meaningful ways that have the chance to be reciprocated in sacred truth spaces.

NOTES

1. Names of schools and participants are pseudonyms to protect anonymity.

2. In an effort *not* to disconnect the stories that were shared with me from those who created them—the students from Native American literature—I engage in *storying-as-literacy*. Storying-as-literacy is the intentional act of writing and re-storying to provide more fertile spaces for larger audiences, including those with whom we've worked, to share in the power of story *with* those who created them. Within this literacy, the power of stories—

the emotions, feelings, inclusion of self and relationships—fuels the writing so as to attempt greater connections with a more encompassing audience beyond an academic one.

3. The team of educators, by name, was: Kyle Wilson, Victor Begay, Natalie Tsinnijinnie, Laura Walsh, and Denise Olivas. They, along with Blasingame and Ortiz, held a total of 12 meetings and submeetings with 10 school district partners (including DVHS's principal, language arts coordinator, social studies specialist, director of curriculum and instruction, director of Native American education, and others), and two education and community representatives from two area Native American nations.

4. Two articles that discuss the root cause and issue of this legislation can be found at http://articles.latimes.com/2010/may/08/nation/la-na-ethnic-studies-20100508 and http://www.motherjones.com/mojo/2010/05/ethnic-studies-banned-arizona.

5. In the first year, Ms. Bee only gave them one option, the shield. In the second year, on the advice from Native American parents and community members, she gave them four options.

6. Having remained friends through Facebook, I reached out to Neena while writing this piece and asked permission to share this story with a larger audience, since it was only shared in a group of friends and I did not want to share that story without her permission. She eagerly agreed and stated that she hoped it would help others share.

7. Stacy's story:

> What is love without strength? Strength without love? One thing I know for sure is that together they can help you overcome anything. I was in 10th grade, like any teenage girl, I fell in love. I fell in love, but with the wrong guy. Rather than being in a happy, stable relationship, it seemed that love was what hurt me the most, I was weak. I admit, I was whooped. I couldn't even step up. I would only cry my heart out. My mind told me to leave him, but my heart could never do it until one day I found the strength. I finally told myself I had enough of him. Yes, it was hard, very. Up to this day, I still have mixed emotions. But thanks to my strength, I am happy. Happier then I have ever been before. I feel free. Unstoppable. Reading to overcome anything and anyone that gets in my way. That's why, thanks to love, I am stronger. Thanks to love, I think differently & I want to share this story because I know I am not the only person out there whether a girl or guy that has been through what I been through. (Written document, August 18, 2011)

8. Ohio State University PhD students Ah Ran Koo and Madith Barton have helped in theorizing this fourth concept as *visual storying*.

REFERENCES

Banks, J. A. (2008). Diversity, Group Identity, and Citizenship Education in a Global Age. *Educational Researcher, 37*(3), 129–139.

Brayboy, B. (2005). Toward a tribal critical race theory in education. *Urban Review, 37*(5), 425–446.

Brayboy, B. M. J., Gough, H. R., Leonard, B., Roehl II, R. F., & Solyom, J. A. (2012). Reclaiming scholarship: Critical Indigenous research methodologies. In S. D. Lapan, M. T. Quartaroli, & F. J. Reimer (Eds.), *Qualitative research: An introduction to methods and design* (pp. 423–450). San Francisco, CA: John Wiley.

Cabrera, N. L., Milem, J. F., Jaquette, O., & Marx, R. W. (2014). Missing the (student achievement) forest for all the (political) trees: Empiricism and the Mexican American studies controversy in Tucson. *American Educational Research Journal, 51*(6), 1084–1118.

Calefati, J. (2010, May 12). Arizona Bans Ethnic Studies. *Mother Jones.* Retrieved from http://www.motherjones.com/mojo/2010/05/ethnic-studies-banned-arizona

Cammarota, J. (2004). The gendered and racialized pathways of Latina and Latino youth: Different resistances in the urban context. *Anthropology and Education Quarterly, 35*(1), 53–74.

Cammarota, J., & Romero, A. F. (2009). A social justice epistemology and pedagogy for Latina/o students: Transforming public education with participatory action research. *New Directions for Youth Development, 2009*(123), 53–65.

Dee, T., & Penner, E. (2016). The causal effects of cultural relevance: Evidence from an ethnic studies curriculum. Working paper, *The National Bureau of Economic Research.* Cambridge, Massachusetts.

Esquivel, P., & Cruz, N. S. (2010, May 8). Arizona bill takes aim at ethnic studies classes. *Los Angeles Times.* Retrieved from http://articles.latimes.com/2010/may/08/nation/la-na-ethnic-studies-20100508

Freire, P. (1970). *Pedagogy of the Oppressed.* New York, NY: Continuum.

Garcia, J., & Shirley, V. (2012). Performing decolonization: Lessons learned from indigenous youth, teachers and leaders' engagement with critical indigenous pedagogy. *Journal of Curriculum Theorizing, 28*(2), 76–91.

Grande, S., San Pedro, T., & Windchief, S. (2015). 21st century indigenous identity location: Remembrance, reclamation, and regeneration. In D. Koslow & L. Salett (Eds.), *Multicultural perspectives on race, ethnicity, and identity* (pp. 105–122). Washington, D.C.: NASW Press.

Kovach, M. (2005). Emerging from the margins: Indigenous methodologies. In L. Brown & S. Strega (Eds.), *Research and resistance: Critical, indigenous, and anti-oppressive approaches* (pp. 19–36). Toronto, ON: Canadian Scholars' Press/Women's Press.

Lee, T. (2006). "I came here to learn how to be a leader": An intersection of critical pedagogy and Indigenous education. *InterActions: UCLA Journal of Education and Information Studies,* 2(1). Retrieved from http://escholarship.org/uc/item/92m798m0

McCarty, T., & Lee, T. (2014). Critical culturally sustaining/revitalizing pedagogy and indigenous education sovereignty. *Harvard Educational Review,* 84(1), 101–124.

National Caucus of Native American State Legislators. (2008). *Striving to achieve: Helping Native American students succeed.* Denver, CO: National Caucus of Native American State Legislators.

Nelson, L. (2000). Warriors with words: Toward a post-Columbine writing curriculum. *English Journal,* 89(5), 42–46.

Paris, D. (2012). Culturally sustaining pedagogy: A needed change in stance, terminology, and practice. *Educational Researcher,* 41(3), 93–97.

Paris, D. (2016). *On educating culturally sustaining teachers.* TeachingWorks working papers. Retrieved from http://www.teachingworks.org/images/files/TeachingWorks_Paris.pdf

Paris, D., & Alim, S. (2014). What are we seeking to sustain through culturally sustaining pedagogy? A loving critique forward. *Harvard Educational Review,* 84(1), 85–100.

Patel, L. (2016, April). In E. Tuck & R. Gaztambide-Fernández (Chairs), *Grounding red pedagogy: De-centering settler-logics in education.* Symposium conducted at the American Educational Research Association Conference, Washington, DC.

San Pedro, T. (2013). *Understanding youth cultures, stories, and resistances in the urban Southwest: Innovations and implications of a Native American Literature classroom.* (Doctoral dissertation). Retrieved from ProQuest Digital Dissertations (3558673).

San Pedro, T. (2014). Internal and environmental safety zones: Navigating expansions and contractions of identity between indigenous and colonial paradigms, pedagogies and classrooms. *Journal of American Indian Education,* 53(3), 42–62.

San Pedro, T. (2015a). Silence as shields: Agency and resistances among Native American students in the urban Southwest. *Research in the Teaching of English,* 50(2), 132–153.

San Pedro, T. (2015b). Silence as weapons: Transformative praxis among Native American students in the urban Southwest. *Equity & Excellence in Education,* 48(4), 511–528.

Sleeter, C. E. (2014). Multiculturalism and education for citizenship in a context of neoliberalism. *Intercultural Education,* 25(2), 85–94.

Smith, G. (2003). *Indigenous struggles for the transformation of education and schooling* [pdf document]. Retrieved from Keynote Address to the Alaskan Federation of Natives Convention online website: ankn.uaf.edu/curriculum/Articles/GrahamSmith/index.html

Wane, N. N. (2009). Indigenous education and cultural resistance: A decolonizing project. *Curriculum Inquiry,* 39(1), 159–178.

Wilson, S. (2008). *Research is ceremony: Indigenous research methods.* Black Point, Canada: Fernwood.

CHAPTER 7

Policing and Performing Culture

Rethinking "Culture" and the Role of the Arts in Culturally Sustaining Pedagogies

Casey Wong and *Courtney Peña*
Stanford University

The high school theater is pitch-black. Lights from above shine on six young Black, Latinx, and Polynesian students standing on the stage. A Latinx student is bent over a brown wooden cane at stage center. He is dressed in raggedy jeans, a worn plaid shirt, and a tattered camouflage headband. He gazes intently across the audience and carefully recites the ending of his monologue: "Giving money is not going to solve all our problems. What we really need to do is spare change, make change, wake change, create change." He finishes by gently prodding the audience, "Can you help us? Can you spare some change?" Suddenly there are red and blue lights, and a police siren echoes across the theater. An adult White man enters from stage right; he is dressed as a police officer. "What's going on here? We're having complaints about you. Let me see some ID." When the student feigns resistance, the police officer yells, "All right, that's enough outta you. I'm tired of your crap!" The police officer grabs the arm of the student and throws him facedown on the ground. The Polynesian student onstage calmly walks toward the police officer with his hands up. He cautiously challenges the officer, "Hey! All that ain't necessary!" Then the lights abruptly shut off, leaving the audience in darkness. Simulated gunshots loudly play over the theater speakers. The lights come back on, and the Polynesian student stands stage center, choreographing shock—he's been shot.

We open this chapter with a narrative about a student performance that, sadly, depicts a situation that is all too real for far too many U.S. students who live in communities that are highly policed. In fact, the year before this performance (2015), police forces killed well over 1,000 Americans, the majority of whom were People of Color, many unarmed.[1] This year (2016) looks no better. The twin arms of the carceral state—police brutality and mass incarceration—are common enough to have been normalized by students of color who live in communities like Bay Grove in northern California. Further, the metaphorical school-to-prison pipeline—where unequal education and racially-biased patterns of disciplining lead to diminished life chances for students of color, and eventually ensnarement by the criminal justice system—has become quite literal, as schools in poor communities of color are now also heavily policed.

What does culturally sustaining pedagogy (CSP) have to offer students living and learning under conditions of near-constant surveillance, aggressive policing, and mass incarceration? How does CSP's notion of culture take these oppressive conditions into account, particularly when we are teaching students whose families have fallen victim to overreaching and increasingly militarized state violence? For us, we take for granted that our pedagogies should, as Paris and Alim (2014) state, "explore, honor, extend and, at times, problematize" youth and community cultural practices, such as the Hip Hop, spoken word, or *El Teatro Campesino* (Farm Workers' Theater) performed by our students below. But how can we expand our notion of culture in CSP beyond cultural and linguistic practices by critically examining the everyday conditions under which those practices are lived? Further, in taking the immediate sociopolitical circumstances of our students into account, how do we do so in ways that do not reinforce racist, classist, "culture of poverty" arguments (Avineri & Johnson, 2015; Ladson-Billings, 2006; Paris, 2012) that can only seem to view our youth and their communities through the lenses of deficiency and pathology?

Beyond victimhood, do our notions of culture allow for the many cultures of resistance and reimagination that have sustained communities of color surviving in these oppressive contexts over the centuries? In the midst of so much pain and suffering, how can we help students reimagine these traditions of resistance in ways that include joy and happiness as well? In her theorization of a "Politics of Pleasure," Joan Morgan (2015) reminds us that we are often less *literate* in reading desire than pain. As CSP scholars and educators pursuing justice and equity, when we fail to support a *literacy* of pleasure and joy, we risk overlooking and undervaluing cultures and traditions of beatitude that are just as in need of being sustained, extended, and complicated in the interest of moving toward wholeness. As Alim and Paris write in the introduction to this volume, "CSP calls for sustaining and revitalizing that which has over the centuries sustained *us* as communities of color struggling to 'make it'—to resist, revitalize and reimagine—under enduring colonial conditions that constantly diminish our intellectual capacities, cultures, languages, and yes, our very lives." Current conceptualizations of CSP, they write, are informed by the activist work of many young people, such as the Movement for Black Lives, who are "calling out systemic racism across institutions, including schools." These social justice movements have raised their voices against the criminal justice system but have also "transformed our thinking about the need for CSP as being literally about sustaining our minds and bodies as communities of color within a schooling system that has often had the exact opposite goals."

In this chapter, we use our teaching and ethnographic research at Bay Grove High School—a school serving a multiracial, predominantly working-class student body in northern California—and Liberation Academy—a high school serving predominantly working-class, Latinx students (over 90% of the student body), also in northern California—to inform a meditation on the critical question raised by Paris and Alim (2014): What are we seeking to sustain through culturally sustaining pedagogy? One of the crucial issues that we have grappled with in exploring these contexts is the blurry line that rests between sustaining *survival* and sustaining *liberation*. For students who wake up in a country with a criminal justice system that continues to honor and extend the White Supremacist tradition of extrajudicially killing unarmed People of Color, just living can be construed as radical. That said, we are interested in sustaining cultures of liberation, that is, the shared aesthetic and material strategies—or what Carol Lee, in Chapter 15 of this volume, refers to as "intergenerational cultural practices" —that continue to be passed down and developed to further the hope that every human life has value.

At both Bay Grove and Liberation Academy, some teachers are seeking to take up these intergenerational cultural practices in order to enact Ladson-Billings's (1994, 1995) goal to develop and support students' sociopolitical consciousness. The following sections briefly explore the transformative work of two of those teachers—a White male performing arts teacher named Mr. Just at Bay Grove, and a Latinx English teacher at Liberation Academy named Mrs. B. We use our exploration of these teachers' practice to critically rethink culture and the role of the arts in CSP.

ACT 1: MR. JUST AND THE
COURAGEOUS WRITERS OF BAY GROVE HIGH SCHOOL

On April 30 and 31, 2016, 10 student performers premiered a play titled *Break the Cage.* These 10 student performers, known as the Courageous Writers, came together each week after school to write poetry and raps that were brought together to form a plot, which became a scripted play. The Courageous Writers program is the inspiration of the school's White performing arts teacher, Mr. Just, who directs, edits, and teaches the skills needed to put on the production. On both nights of the play, nearly every seat of the 194-seat theater was filled with young people and teachers from Bay Grove High School, the families of the performers, community organizers, professors and students from the local elite university, school board officials, and representatives of the local city government. In many ways, the biannual premier of the Courageous Writer's production has become a part of the culture of the city of Bay Grove.

The story of the city of Bay Grove—a 2.5-square-mile suburban city of roughly 30,000 working-class People of Color—is one that is familiar to many poor, working-class People of Color in the United States. On a typical evening in Bay Grove, it is not a surprise to see a pack of police cars haphazardly parked in front of one of the tiny single-story houses lining Bay Grove's labyrinth of worn roads. Many of the young people who live in Bay Grove struggle to find areas to study in overcrowded houses and apartments, some now sheltering generations of families. It is even more difficult for young people who have to care for their younger siblings as their parents increasingly work longer hours, more jobs, and for smaller wages. Bay Grove is widely considered a *food desert*—there is only one large supermarket, but dozens of liquor stores and fast food restaurants. In the midst of Bay Grove—affectionately known by residents as "the town"—sits a small public charter high school, Bay Grove High School. Enrolling 243 students, the demographics of Bay Grove High School align with the demographics of the city: 79% Hispanic, 8% Black, 7% Pacific Islander, and 6% "two or more" races. Unlike the larger and more affluent high school on the opposite side of the freeway, which has 7% students who participate in the free or reduced lunch program, 91% of Bay Grove High School's students qualify for free or reduced lunch.

When Mr. Just first began teaching, he saw ample evidence that marginalized young people were participating in various visual, writing, and performing arts traditions. In many ways, CSP relies upon teachers having a sincere interest and in-depth knowledge of their respective students' engagement in these various artistic traditions. Mahiri and Sablo's (1996) research examines two such teachers—Ms. Parks and Ms. Brown—who are not only aware that their students do voluntary writing, but are experts on how their respective students are "writing for their lives" and engaging in out-of-school literacy practices. As Valerie Kinloch points out in Chapter 2 of this volume, CSP depends upon teachers rejecting deficit-oriented perspectives and consciously considering the layers, intricacies, and meanings that underlie students' "performances of resistance" and relationships to literacy. Mr. Just follows in this tradition. He saw that many of his students were already actively participating in visual, writing, and performing arts traditions that were helping them survive their day-to-day lives and, beyond that, uplifting their communities. Mr. Just observed that these artistic practices often became key sites of inspiration for young people because they were linked to verbal artistic traditions that were as poetic as they were political. Hip Hop and spoken word, for example, encouraged students to obtain "knowledge of self" and to link their contemporary struggles to historic movements for freedom. As a teacher who himself was not a Person of Color and grew up in predominantly middle-class communities, it was especially crucial for Mr. Just to invest in listening and learning about what he would eventually join youth in seeking to sustain through the performing arts.

Based upon his early observations, Mr. Just now teaches introductory and advanced performing arts classes where students learn about local and global struggles for freedom through the investigation and practice of the performing arts, a departure from most traditional performing arts courses across the country, but in alignment with radical Hip Hop, spoken word, and performing arts classes that have always found their way into schools and out-of-school spaces (Alim, 2004; Dimitriadis, 2001; Fisher, 2003; Hill, 2009; Winn, 2011). At the onset of each academic school year, Mr. Just consults his students. He considers both what is familiar and unfamiliar to them and then decides which performing arts he will teach. Some of the traditions that Mr. Just has taught include Hip Hop (e.g., Jasiri X and Kendrick Lamar), the *haka* (e.g., All Blacks' ritual performance before rugby games and Polynesian war dances), Latinx theater (e.g., Josefina Lopez's *Real Women Have Curves* and Luis Valdez's *Zoot Suit*), prison writings (e.g., Malcolm X, Rubin "Hurricane" Carter, and Leonard Peltier), and freedom songs (e.g., songs composed by the African National Congress during South African apartheid, Black freedom fighters during the civil rights movement, and Native Americans during the American Indian Movement). Despite the impact of his classes, during those early years Mr. Just saw that there were often some students in his classes who wanted *more*. Inspired by his own awakening in high school, as well as his participation in a theatrical writers' collective when he was in college, he formed the Courageous Writers to meet the students' demand. Mr. Just's formation of the Courageous Writers falls within a tradition of educators who have made use of performance work for justice, as in the case of Joe and the Power Writers (Fisher, 2007), as well as Tim, Rashidah, and Bronwen with their Advanced Poetry ("AP") class (Low, 2011), among other examples. The Courageous Writers is now a biannual after-school program that culminates in a live production that is free and open to the public.

"All These Shootings Makes Us Feel Like a Target": Solomon's Rap

One of the veteran students in the Courageous Writers program this year was Solomon.[2] Solomon admits that despite his best efforts to avoid thinking about how he is racialized, he is well aware of what it means to walk through Bay Grove as a short but heavy-set, dark-skinned Polynesian ("Poly," as he and other Polynesian students self-identify) young man. Doing his best to encapsulate that understanding in one word, Solomon came up with—"edgy." Solomon maintains popularity among his peers and teachers alike by delicately balancing his Christian values with a *keepin' it real* approach to life—that is, Solomon makes it a point to be as truthful, authentic, and honest about his feelings and emotions as possible. Much of Solomon's reputation emerges from his well-respected participation in the performing arts. Solomon is a talented performer in the Polynesian tradition, and has sung, danced, and played the ukulele ("the uke") at a number of school assemblies. Anyone who knows Solomon well also knows that one of his deep passions is Hip Hop music.

Solomon cannot recall the first time he heard Hip Hop, but he knew Hip Hop was "in his blood" the moment he heard Tupac Shakur's "Changes." Solomon remembers how in 8th grade he began thinking about moving from being a passive listener to an active performer. He often recalls how sessions with his older cousin inspired him to think about rapping as a medium to share his struggles and joys. In my interviews with Solomon, he further attributes the development of his critical consciousness to the many intimate conversations that he had with his grandmother. He notes how difficult it has been for him since her tragic passing, but he tries to "hold her heart" close to his own as he makes decisions about his life. Solomon navigates school by leaning on many of the values that sustained his grandmother throughout her harsh life as a part of the Polynesian diaspora. Often described as "soft-spoken" and "easygoing"—and given the stereotype about Hip Hop culture as inherently violent—some teachers might easily miss Solomon's serious investment in Hip Hop culture and music. Because Solomon is Polynesian, not African American, other teachers who race Hip Hop as exclusively Black might also miss Solomon's passion for this art form. Mr. Just, however, did not make either of those mistakes.

Much of Mr. Just's aptitude for navigating the racial and ethnic pluralism of Bay Grove High School comes from his attention to human detail. Each year Mr. Just spends the first few months getting to know students—learning their favorite songs, who counts as family, what type of stories they like to tell, who's their best friend, what makes them sad, and what inspires or motivates them to come back to school each day. While not without missteps, Mr. Just continues to garner a deep respect among many students for the lengths he goes to in order to connect with them. He also makes great efforts to grapple with and be reflexive about the stereotypes and ideas that he brings into his classroom. Mr. Just's multiracial extended family and his brief but impressionable time attending school in London have opened him up to ways of viewing the world outside of the lens of monocultural, monolingual whiteness. However, he is also aware that he has benefited from many of the comforts and privileges that come with being raised in predominantly White, middle-class and affluent, suburban and urban communities.

While providing space in school events for Solomon to perform the Polynesian traditions close to his heart, Mr. Just sensed that Solomon was seeking to find a way to share his vision for what was right and just through Hip Hop. By Solomon's junior year, Mr. Just found that, much like for some of the Polynesian students in Paris's (2011) study of the same community, Hip Hop had become a primary way that Solomon was grappling with living as a racialized other in a highly policed, working-class community. Similar to Hill's (2009) observations of his students in Philadelphia, Mr. Just knew that Hip Hop had also become a medium through which Solomon was grappling with his introduction to love as a teenage boy. Rather than insist that Solomon adapt his writing to fit conventional, Eurocentric notions of theater or spoken word, Mr. Just challenged Solomon to use his skills in rapping on the stage to paint an intimate portrait of his life.

The scene that opened the chapter is framed around a rap that Solomon created during the Courageous Writers after-school program. In that scene, Solomon is shot as he tries to help an older homeless Latinx man who is being brutalized by police. In one of the most dramatic moments of the production, the other young people on the stage freeze as a light shines down on Solomon, who raps the following lines:

> Got my mother / my father / my sisters / my brother / my aunties / my uncles / my nieces / my nephew / my cousins / my grandma / my papa / who's gonna miss me / but now let me come back / to reality / life just ain't that easy / all these shootings makes us feel like a target / why do we feel like a target / target / if the popo / goin loco / with all of us locals / they just nu'n but murderers / comin at me foul / and I never heard of ya / now before you take my life / just know it ain't so right / to kill an innocent / because he ain't white / now let me take my last breath / looking up to the sky / cause I'm about to fly high / with the angels in the sky

In his rap Solomon grapples with an ongoing concern for him and other Polynesian youth in Bay Grove: Polynesian young people are frequently the target of abusive policing, though this is rarely, if ever, acknowledged by outsiders to Bay Grove. Like many youth of color in Bay Grove, Solomon navigates his community with a fear that he "could be next." By supporting Solomon's engagement with rapping and encouraging him to share his fears about police on a larger stage in front of the school and Bay Grove community, Mr. Just sustained Solomon's disruption of the dominant carceral narrative that portrays People of Color as less than human, and as worthy and deserving of being murdered by police. Solomon's rap sustained Hip

Hop as a medium with the potential for social justice work and challenged the dominant narrative that situates police as rational agents of justice and order, and People of Color as "super-predators,"[3] immoral criminals, and monsters without families who love them. On a more personal level for Solomon, Mr. Just's use of CSP offered him a temporal space of relief and release from the pressures of navigating the streets of Bay Grove as a target of near-constant police surveillance. The Courageous Writers could have been powerful as just an after-school program where students were given the opportunity to get relief from sharing their stories, but Mr. Just demanded more from his students as he saw them making broader connections to large-scale social injustices.

Weeks before the production, Mr. Just guided the Courageous Writers on how to use the after-school program to make connections about the inequities that they were facing. The above scene emerged as they reflected on their shared fears and experiences encountering the police as Black and Brown youth living in Bay Grove. As the conversation unfolded, Mr. Just not only shared stories of other young people across the United States who were having similar experiences, but showed how young people across the country were using the performing arts to confront their fears and work toward social justice. He showcased how young people were producing art that was almost always rooted in tradition(s) that emerged from neighborhoods and communities like their own. During moments like these, young people in the Courageous Writers often felt compelled to share art that they had previously produced that was inspired by artists in their lives and from their communities. In other words, Mr. Just was sustaining the same practices of solidarity and sharing that scholars such as Paris (2011) have noted flow through multiethnic school yards as students share art from one another's notebooks, from hidden phones by means of social media, or through impromptu dances between classes. However, Mr. Just did the added CSP work of complicating the sharing of this art in ways that helped students realize when, why, and how a particular piece of art might be hurtful to others, or on the flip side, helpful toward collectively thinking through or addressing an issue facing their community. In this way, the Courageous Writers' play came to expose and help students think through many of the adversities they were each facing in their racialized, classed, and gendered lives, as well as to provide an additional space for collaboratively and individually envisioning social change. Simply put, these facets of students' culturally situated lives, those aspects of their lives that they cherished and those parts of their lives thrust upon them by the carceral state, were critically engaged through art in a way that created a schooling space that sustained them. Following Solomon's rap, two Black students stepped forward to recite poetry that spoke to how they were experiencing hardship as young Black women, and shared their visions for liberation.

Judith and Amber's Spoken Word Poetry

One of the students, Judith, began writing her lines inspired by a workshop Mr. Just offered on policing. Moved by their collective conversation, Judith decided to finish the work with her friend Amber. As a junior at the school, Judith had become a part of the Courageous Writers. Amber, who was only a freshman, had experienced trauma in her life that had disrupted her plans to apply to the group. Rather than have Judith find a way to recite just her portion of their collaborative piece, Mr. Just invited Amber to join the production.

Both young women had long been writing poetry, but their joint piece came together as they sought to respond to the extrajudicial killings of Black and Brown people—men, women, children, immigrant, poor, queer, and trans—that were entering the national discourse during the spring of 2016. Part of the research work at Bay Grove became offering lunch to these young women so they could have one more weekly time period and space to share their poetry with other like-minded young women at their school. Before reading their poetry aloud, Judith and Amber often described how they had used their phones to write as they walked back from school, sat by their beds at night, attended a school event, or just chilled with their friends on the block. While an educator could easily create an intervention or lesson for students like Judith and Amber to extend their engagement in poetry as a practice of literacy, Mr. Just provided a schooling space where the young women could sustain the cultural concerns indelibly inflected and embedded in their poetry—the extrajudicial killing of Black and Brown people. As a critical pedagogy, educators using CSP cannot and should not sustain only the aspects of students' lives that are safe or easily addressable in schooling spaces. As Ladson-Billings points out in Chapter 8 of this volume, CSP is about complicating, sustaining, and extending what is important to students and their lives, not just what is important to educators and their agendas, whether their agendas are social justice–driven or not. During the performance, as Solomon lay on the ground onstage, the students playing Solomon's love interest, mother, and onlookers rushed to his side as he acted out the last moments of his life. Judith and Amber emotionally moved to the front of the stage to recite the following lines:

J: Gunned down because he matched a description / we're not all the
   same, but we're all a threat in 5-0's vision
Together: We can no longer pray for change
A: How many of us have to die before justice is finally served? / Justice
   is now a bittersweet word that rolls into the back of the throat / The
   word is no longer needed / for there is no such thing as justice

J: Being put in danger by the men that are supposed to protect us / How threatening is a 6 foot tall black man / standing on a corner . . .

A: Minding his own business?

J: Forced to the ground . . . he's screaming

A: "I can't breathe! I can't breathe! I can't breathe!"

J: Thoughts on his mind

A: "Why can't you hear me? / Why won't they release me?"

J: Those guns give them power / they're made superior

Together: Silence in our community

J: They made us inferior . . . in fear we are / to speak up against them / our minds . . .

A: our voices . . .

Together: are locked up . . . imprisoned

A: We can only stand tall and go about in peace / stop breaking into riots and causing more violence

Together: We come in peace

A: How many more marches?

J: How many more protests?

A: How many more letters?

J: How many more songs?

A: Do we have to create before change happens?

J: Dr. King said, "In the end we will remember not the words of our enemies, but the silence of our friends." / Hearing gunshots . . .

A: night after night . . .

J: again and again / perpetrators pleading not guilty because it was "self defense" / If you won't speak for us now . . .

A: you won't speak for us then

Together: Will my children's children go through this?

A: Or will the trigger be pulled before they can even step out the door? / Will they become trending hashtags on Twitter?

J: Our minds . . .

A: our voices . . .

Together: are locked up . . .

J: imprisoned

A: Is this the ending or the beginning?

Together: Let's begin.

Bay Grove young people are not strangers to death or police brutality. In many ways the headlines about the many tragic deaths of People of Color at the hands of police in 2015 and 2016 produced a disheartening affirmation of what they already knew. Just as important, these headlines were also met with a hope among youth—like Judith and Amber—that poor communities of color will continue to come together to counter ideas about the "disposability" of their bodies (Garza, 2014; Lamont-Hill, 2016). During the production the audience loudly snapped, clapped, and shouted their support. For many of the peers of the 10 student performers, it was the first opportunity they had to hear and realize that they were not alone, that others around them were experiencing similar or related injustices. The audience was electrified.

ACT 2: MRS. B AND LIBERATION ACADEMY

On a cold Thursday night, a room full of eager parents and tired high school students gather into a portable classroom. The attendees share a meal of tacos, rice, and beans. Anxious little ones squirm and run playfully around the room. The high school principal, Mr. C., has invited the attendees to learn about the research project being proposed at the high school by a group of researchers from a local university. "*Es una emergencia,*" exclaims Mr. C. "We are in an emergency in the state of California. The demographics of the country are shifting and schools are not responding to the needs of Latino students and their families." Parents cautiously listen to the words of the passionate principal, who switches from Spanish to English in an effort to accommodate the bilingual parent population. "Latino students are not going to college. They are being fed into the school to prison pipeline[4]," he explains. The consensus in the room is clear: Something needs to be done. That something is exactly what this small charter school (Liberation Academy) is intending to accomplish.

Liberation Academy is located in a racially, ethnically, and linguistically diverse, working-class, city in northern California that has a longstanding Mexican American population. Historically, the east side of the city has been racially segregated and is where Mexican and other agricultural workers were forced to reside. This involuntary segregation resulted in the city becoming one of the country's most significant sites of Mexican and Mexican American cultural production (Regua & Villareal, 2009). The neighborhood where the school is located is also home to a significant Vietnamese population, which comprises approximately 10% of the city's overall population. More recently, the city has been experiencing rapid transformation due to a major tech industry boom seen throughout the greater valley.

Liberation Academy is a small charter school now in its third year of operation and has a student body of approximately 300. Over 90% of the student population is Latinx (mostly of Mexican descent), while the rest of the population is African American, Asian, and White. The school has a largely Spanish–English bilingual student body with a significant number of English language learners. A small portion of students speak indigenous

Mexican languages, and a few are Vietnamese–English bilingual. Approximately 70% of students qualify for free or reduced lunch. Like Bay Grove and other high-poverty areas in the United States, police and crime narratives figure centrally in any description of the city by those living in the wealthier and Whiter surrounding areas.

Within this neighborhood context, Liberation Academy is determined to send as many of its predominantly Latinx students to college as it possibly can. While both Bay Grove and Liberation Academy support students' artistic expression, one difference from Bay Grove is that Liberation Academy has an explicit and intentional commitment to CSP. The school places an emphasis on empowering students to build their critical capacities and repertoires so that they may return to their communities to make positive changes. A unique feature of Liberation Academy is its commitment to the performing arts, which is a central component of the school, and to developing their contextualized enactments of CSP. The school also has a required course that incorporates technology and the Chicano theater tradition of *teatro*, a medium used throughout the Farm Workers' Movement,[5] demonstrating that culture and social justice are important foci for the school (see also Chapter 13, this volume). The spirit of Liberation Academy acknowledges a long history of Mexican American activism, and Mexican American History is a required course for first-year students. Most of the classes inform students of historical movements for human rights that have sustained their communities and, importantly for this chapter, reserve a space for students to recognize contemporary issues as a reflection of those ongoing struggles.

For the purposes of this chapter, we narrow our focus to one English language arts classroom where social justice materials are used as course content. The instructor, Mrs. B., was born in Michoacán, México, and identifies as generation 1.5. Her interest in social justice stems from her firsthand experience with prejudicial and systemic injustices in California's educational pipeline—one that she exited and returned to at different stages in her life.

Upon graduating college, she knew she wanted to become an English language arts teacher and enrolled in a graduate program that she believes was not properly preparing teachers for the Latinx population of California. She expressed frustration with her program, as she felt the faculty constantly framed Latinx students in terms of deficiency. She recalls a class where the professor was teaching a unit on how to recognize gang paraphernalia; to her surprise, the professor equated the Mexican flag with other signs of gang membership. Brown and Kraehe's (2010) research on teacher education programs stresses the need for teacher educators to "recognize the power of the pedagogical and curriculum choices," highlighting the importance of addressing the complexities of sociocultural knowledge that prepares teachers to address the needs of their students competently and equitably. Now in her third year of credentialed teaching at Liberation Academy, she has a vested interest in preventing the systemic injustices that pushed her out of school from doing the same to her students.

Mrs. B. does not use a textbook in her course; rather, she includes a variety of short stories, poems, plays, fiction, and nonfiction, in addition to her focus on preparing for Common Core–based tests.[6] An example of CSP as seen in Mrs. B.'s classroom is her inclusion of texts that explore dynamic views of culture and language. A prime example come from her freshman English course, where students read *Zoot Suit* (Valdez, 1992), one of Luis Valdez's most critically acclaimed works, which explores the complicated identities of Chicanas/os as well as the historical discrimination against people of color by law enforcement. Mrs. B used *Zoot Suit* as a tool to teach students about the complexities of oppression. In class, she had students analyze characters from the play using a Freirian lens as they identified horizontal/vertical oppression[7] and the "sub-oppressors" in the story. They later wrote about this and identified different types of oppression they see in their lives.

Much like the student response to Mr. Just's class in Bay Grove, one result of this method of teaching was increased student interest in civic engagement and social activism. This social justice component of Mrs. B.'s culturally sustaining practice was rooted in the legacy of such work in Latinx communities and resulted in students finding belonging in their learning process and feeling the need to move their learning beyond the classroom toward social action, an indicator of successful critical reflection in social justice education (Brown, 2004) as theorized by Freire (2000). Evidence of such civic engagement was found in the students' final projects, in which they chose such topics as environmental justice, invisible poverty, undocumented students, the War on Drugs, arts and activism, history of police in the United States, Black Lives Matter, and the school-to-prison pipeline. The groups were allowed creative freedom in how they would present their projects, and this ranged from multimedia presentations to informative theatrical performances.

One particularly notable example occurred during group presentations after the end of a unit. It was during this unit where students were assigned what Mrs. B. referred to as "heavy topics," which they worked on in small groups. At the end of most days, Mrs. B. gives prompts to students for their metacognitive journals, where they are given time to critically reflect on what they are learning. During this particular week, their prompt was, "What did you learn from your research? What caught your eye or stood out to you? How did that information make you feel?" One group of students had a particularly moving dedication to their topic, the school-to-prison pipeline. Their research investigated the ways that schools reproduce a culture of policing and punishment. The students in this group were noticeably dedicated to this topic. They used their skills from their digital media and theater class to produce a YouTube video where they acted out different scenarios of young students of color being criminalized in schools and how they are treated by the adults in the school system. They also performed this theatrical piece during a town hall meeting in order to raise awareness about the devastating impact of the school-to-prison pipeline on communities like theirs and Bay Grove.

Another group presented on the history of police and cited Michelle Alexander's *The New Jim Crow* (2012), reading material that has been used at the university level. Students connected issues of state-sanctioned violence and the responses to them, such as the Black Lives Matter movement and the ongoing protests for rural communities in southern Mexico to organize labor unions for teachers. Students observed and discussed commonalities in separate instances of injustice and pushed one another to think critically about the sociopolitical and historical contexts that created them. The most striking moment of the presentations, however, came when a student was wrapping up and said in front of his peers, "For us, this is more than just a PowerPoint." As with the students in Bay Grove, they understood that it is their peers—they *themselves*—who would be targeted by these systems of punishment and policing. Further, it would also be up to them to change these oppressive systems.

THE JOY AND PAIN OF CULTURALLY SUSTAINING PEDAGOGIES

In an educational system that generally does not respond well to students of color, Mr. Just and Mrs. B's classrooms are giving students a place to engage and belong. At the beginning of this chapter, we offered a series of questions to frame our observations of Bay Grove High School and Liberation Academy. CSP has provided a new lens for teachers looking to center and sustain their students' languages, literatures, cultures, and histories. Importantly, CSP has at its core a commitment to sustain that which sustains us, that is, sustaining the lives of our students is paramount. CSP, then, moves beyond sustaining languages and cultures, to sustaining the people who speak and enact those languages and cultures.

In raising our initial questions, we focused primarily on expanding our notions of what constitutes "culture" in CSP. In addition to language practices and culturally situated ways of knowing and being, how are our students' experiences of growing up in communities that suffer from nearly debilitating race–class oppression taken into account? Indeed, how are students and teachers using those very languages and ways of being as tools to disrupt and dismantle those conditions of oppression in community-rooted and ever-shifting ways? Moreover, for students living and learning in poor communities of color, how do we consider their race–class positions as part of the cultural ways of knowing and being without further stereotyping our students? In many ways, these conditions lead to experiences of pain.

Teachers like Mr. Just and Mrs. B. provide critical spaces for their students to express, work through, and intellectualize this pain, something that is rarely done effectively in schools.

While difficult to address, this pain, we argue, constitutes an important part of how young people experience the world, and therefore it cannot be ignored in our conceptualizations of CSP. But how do we meaningfully consider this pain, this oppression, as Mr. Just and Mrs. B. have, without defining our students solely by their suffering, what Eve Tuck (2009) calls *damage-centered narratives*? How can we provide spaces for students to be critical of society, yet also imagine and enact a world of joy beyond the intersecting oppressions that attempt to circumscribe their lives? In many ways this need to confront pain and enact and work toward joy has always been at the heart of critical pedagogy and research, but too often the pain is centered without an equal centering on joy. As we continue to theorize CSP as a collective, our work moving young people toward liberation requires us to pay equal attention to pain *and* joy.

In her open letter to educational researchers and practitioners, Tuck calls for a move from a *damage-centered* framework that considers our communities as "*only* damaged, as *only* broken," to a *desire-based* framework that is based in a complex personhood that sustains a sense of collective balance and celebrates survivance (2009, p. 421). Tuck responds to the work of Gerald Vizenor, who defines survivance as "not just survival but also resistance, not heroic or tragic, but the tease of tradition" that "outwits dominance and victimry" (1998, p. 93). In this way, Tuck reminds us that "even when communities are broken and conquered, they are so much more than that—so much more that this *incomplete* story is an act of aggression [emphasis added]" (p. 416). In considering how we sustain the culture of students—whether by means of performing arts, visual arts, research, public speaking, or writing—CSPs need to ensure that the *complete* stories of young people and their communities are told. CSPs need to move toward the "thirdspace" where the cultures of students and their communities are sustained, extended, and complicated outside of a dichotomy of reproduction and resistance, where human agency, complicity, and resistance live together in pedagogies toward liberation (Tuck, 2009, p. 420).

The role of the arts is paramount here. Returning to the student performances at Bay Grove, once the energy of the evening had dissipated, we were left with a strong feeling of hope that change was possible, but also a lingering heaviness: Where was the joy in this powerful piece of student-written theater? How can we ensure that there is space for youth to theorize and sustain joy as a part of their artistic productions of liberation? There is a brief scene where the Courageous Writers and extras from their class dance and act out a house party, but that scene quickly follows with young people expressing the difficulties they face trying to find and feel loved. There is a moving interlude where a Latinx female student briefly escapes her marginalization for loving a girl as she dances and theorizes joy, but that ecstasy is a liminal escape as the play moves forward with more grief and more pain. Brief moments of happiness are abruptly halted and overwhelmingly dominated by students grappling with the most difficult and trying parts of their lives—from police brutality to sexual violence to dealing with issues arising from poverty and Eurocentric standards of beauty and respectability.

Leaving Liberation Academy, we were left with more questions: What is the cost of always thinking of students and their communities as marginalized or oppressed, even in efforts centered on empowerment? Without a doubt, Mrs. B. had her students doing liberatory work, learning about their personal agency in dealing with a number of issues that became apparent in the topics appearing in work, presentations, and daily discussions: the history of policing, the Movement for Black Lives, the school-to-prison pipeline, the protests over missing students in Ayotzinapa, Mexico, and so on. Nonetheless, these were all heavy topics fixated on problems and issues, and the resistance with which people in these communities were powerfully engaging. Without intending it, the stories of these "marginalized" peoples were left incomplete. As culturally sustaining educators, how can we provide spaces for young people where they are not defined solely, or overwhelmingly, by their marginalization? How can we provide spaces for young people to extend and imagine joy—to experience and theorize happiness for the sake of happiness, not happiness only as a means of relief and release from their struggles? In many ways, these questions have been central concerns to struggles for freedom. We know many other programs across the country face the same questions as they offer incredible opportunities for young people to grapple with the injustices facing themselves and their communities. We also know that this is a general problem for many Hip Hop and spoken word programs as well.

At Bay Grove High School and Liberation Academy, there are so many young people looking for answers to why they and their loved ones are being systematically targeted by police, or why their communities have less material resources than surrounding wealthy White neighborhoods, or why they suffer exclusion as people who might love in ways that offend heteropatriarchal values. We know this is a weight on Mr. Just's and Mrs. B.'s consciences as they work incredibly hard to provide students the space to work through the injustices in their lives. These teachers both know that they can really only responsibly and lovingly handle a certain amount of students due to limitations on their time and emotional bandwidth. Much of the work at Bay Grove High School has been spent trying to assist Mr. Just and other educators in the school with the seemingly impossible task of grappling with all of the pain with which youth are contending.

We are aware that we raise these questions in times when Black and Brown young people, like students at Bay Grove and Liberation Academy (and even younger), continue to be assaulted and killed as they try to engage in joy and happiness—killed with toys in their hands (12-year-old Black boy Tamir Rice and 13-year-old Latinx boy Andy Lopez), killed while playing loud music in their car (17-year-old Black boy Jordan Davis), and assaulted by police officers at a pool party (15-year-old Black girl in McKinney, Texas) and even in school (a 16-year-old Black girl known simply as "Shakara" in media reports, who was flipped out of her desk by a school police officer, and 18-year-old young Black woman Niya Kenny was arrested for videotaping the brutal incident).

We also know that focusing on only the pain experienced by students of color does not reflect these teachers' personal visions of freedom, which we know includes joy. In fact, among students Mr. Just is celebrated for his sense of humor, as is Mrs. B. During most of the Courageous Writers' after-school sessions it was not unusual to hear the eruption of laughter, no matter how serious the topic of that day. This was the same during daytime classes, where it was not unusual for students like Solomon to engage in verbal play, which was sustained and often extended by Mr. Just. One reason Mr. Just gives for extending the length of the Courageous Writers program was to make room for moments of lightness. He always tries to find a moment for students if they want to "turn up" or "have fun for the sake of fun." This is also the case with Mrs. B., whose classroom is felt as a joyous space. As one student notes, "Most of us, like teenagers, we like making jokes in class and all that. Like when we're reading and something funny pops up or something immature, she'll like make a joke about it and we laugh. We like to have fun." Where some educators might see outbursts of laughter as a loss of control, Mrs. B. and Mr. Just remind us that we should adjust the White gaze to recognize the humanization that occurs in joy by means of collective laughter. Mr. Just and Mrs. B. give space for the jocular nature of youth, giving students props in recognizing the creativity required to craft on-the-spot puns and jokes when they arise.

Of course, as Tuck (2009) reminds us, it is important to remember that the notion of laughing to keep from crying predates both Mr. Just and Mrs. B.'s classrooms—this notion is at the heart of a desire-based narrative of students and their communities. When we are faced with the difficult challenge of trying to figure out how to provide space for the "turn-up" spirit in artistic productions that center struggle and liberation, educators should not carry the burden of complicating students and their communities alone. We must remember that these current manifestations of nation-state violence are not new and that our communities have long engaged in survivance. As educators making use of CSP, we need to turn toward our students and leave space to consider how joy is living beside pain, as it always has, even in the midst of the most somber and painful moments of our history. We need to work toward developing a literacy of joy and pleasure that lives beside a proactive attentiveness to discomfort and pain. Exploring narratives of American slavery, Stephanie Camp critiques the dominant narrative that has almost always framed enslaved African peoples—particularly enslaved

African women—as only experiencers of violence and victimhood. She reminds us that this particularly horrific moment of history was much more
complex than dominant narratives testify, as enslaved peoples evaded slave
patrols and engaged in "outlaw slave parties" (2002, p. 534). Not only were
these simply just moments of pleasure; Camp notes that outlaw parties were
well-planned events that became spaces where enslaved peoples innovated
aesthetics and performed music and movement that have been passed on
across generations:

> Dances included "set de flo'" (partners began by bowing to each other at the
> waist, with hands on the waist, then the dancers tap-danced, patting the floor
> firmly, "jus' like dey was puttin' it in place"), "dancin' on de spot" (the same
> as "set de flo'" except that dancers had to remain within the circumference of
> a circle drawn in the ground), "wringin' and twistin'" (the early basis of the
> "twist"), the "buzzard lope," "snake hips," and the "breakdown" . . . Compe-
> tition was a common form of amusement at outlaw dances, one that sometimes
> forged camaraderie among equals. To win a dance competition required the
> combination of expertly executing complex dance moves while maintaining an
> outward demeanor of "control and coolness" . . . (2002, p. 557)

In a similar way, under what many would consider oppressive circumstances, we know that most students in Bay Grove High School and Liberation Academy have active out-of-school lives that are rich in social gatherings,
church outings and other religious commitments, cultural events, reunions,
and other celebrations of life. We know that many of our most popular dances and music that are played on television and nationally syndicated radio, or
have gone viral over YouTube, began at family barbecues and *carne asadas*,
birthday parties and neighborhood fairs, where our students spend their time
out of school. Students come from rich histories and traditions, which have
always found moments to produce art that celebrates life in the face of terror
and death. Perhaps this is best exemplified in the well-known Mexican tradition of the *Día de los Muertos*, or Day of the Dead, where both pain and joy
are taken up simultaneously: pain in mourning the loss of a loved one, and
joy in celebrating life.

We raise these questions not as critiques of these teachers' and schools'
wonderful efforts, but as a meditation on what we need in ever more rich
enactments of CSP. In fact, students in both school contexts experience moments of joy throughout their school days—many enjoy schooling as a social
and intellectual experience. Given that we both are exploring contexts that
support student expression through the arts and other community-rooted
forms of creative expression, our insights here are shared with the spirit of
complicating our notion of culture to include complex and nuanced understandings of students' everyday experiences with the injustices of policing,
mass incarceration, and racist, capitalist oppression. Further, in focusing on

the arts, we are seeking more sophisticated ways that our pedagogies can engage our students' daily realities in healthy, life-affirming ways that do more than sustain their cultures, but sustain their lives as well.

NOTES

1. *The Guardian*'s (2016) article "The Counted" listed 1,146 people killed by police in 2015. As of December 5, 2016, 986 people have been killed by the police, almost keeping pace with the previous year.

2. Part of this data about Solomon comes from an interview performed by student researcher Janei Maynard. A shout-out to Janei and the incredible work she has done to support and document the work of Mr. Just and the Courageous Writers.

3. In the 2016 U.S. presidential election, the public was reminded of Hillary Clinton's use of the term "super-predators," a term almost always associated with young Black Americans. In her 1994 speech supporting then-President Bill Clinton's "crime bill," she stated: "They are often the kinds of kids that are called super-predators—no conscience, no empathy. We can talk about why they ended up that way, but first we have to bring them to heel." Watch the speech here: https://www.youtube.com/watch?v=8k4nmRZx9nc. Also read Michelle Alexander's article about Hillary Clinton's "racially coded rhetoric" in *The Nation*, "Why Hillary Clinton Doesn't Deserve the Black Vote" (February 10, 2016): https://www.thenation.com/article/hillary-clinton-does-not-deserve-black-peoples-votes/.

4. Also known as the cradle-to-prison pipeline, the process includes practices such as "diploma denial" (Fine & Ruglis, 2009), routine miseducation, and zero tolerance policies such as detentions and expulsions (Curtis, 2013; Smith, 2015; Winn & Behizadeh, 2011) that disproportionately affect youth of color (Hirschfield, 2008; Schiff, 2013). Other contributions to the pipeline are disparities in special education classifications, resource disparities, and unequal access of opportunity (Kim, Losen, & Hewitt, 2010; Meiners, 2011).

5. The Farm Workers' Movement began as a response to the ongoing abuse and injustices experienced by agricultural field workers and coincided with other movements of the Civil Rights Era (Regua & Villareal, 2009). The Farm Workers' Movement is often credited as being initiated by Cesar Chavez and the United Farm Workers of America (UFW) in the early 1960s (Ferriss, Sandoval, & Hembree, 1997; Pawel, 2009).

6. In 2010, California adopted the Common Core State Standards (CCSS) for Mathematics and English Language Arts.

7. According to Freire (2000), oppression can exist through top-down hierarchical means of subordination, or horizontal oppression, as well as oppression that is enacted by peers of a similar social group or status, which

he describes as vertical oppression. *Sub-oppressors* is the term Freire uses for the oppressed who become oppressors in the early stages of a struggle.

REFERENCES

Alexander, M. (2012). *The new Jim Crow: Mass incarceration in the age of colorblindness.* New York, NY: The New Press.

Alexander, M. (2016, Feb 10). Why Hillary Clinton doesn't deserve the Black vote. *The Nation.* Retrieved from https://www.thenation.com/article/hillary-clinton-does-not-deserve-black-peoples-votes/

Alim, H. S. (2004). *You know my steez: An ethnographic and sociolinguistic study of styleshifting in a Black American speech community.* Durham, NC: Duke University Press.

Avineri, N., & Johnson, E. (Eds.). (2015). Invited forum: Bridging the "language gap." *Journal of Linguistic Anthropology, 25*(1), 66–86.

Brown, K. M. (2004). Leadership for Social Justice and Equity: Weaving a Transformative Framework and Pedagogy. *Educational Administration Quarterly, 40*(1) 77–108. doi:10.1177/0013161X03259147.

Brown, K. D., & Kraehe, A. M. (2010). The complexities of teaching the complex: Examining how future educators construct understandings of sociocultural knowledge and schooling. *Educational Studies, 46*(1), 91–115.

Camp, S. M. (2002). The pleasures of resistance: Enslaved women and body politics in the plantation south, 1830–1861. *Journal of Southern History,* 533–572.

The counted: People killed by police in the US. *The Guardian.* Retrieved September 3, 2016, from: http://www.theguardian.com/us-news/ng-interactive/2015/jun/01/the-counted-police-killings-us-database

Curtis, A. J. (2013). Tracing the school-to-prison pipeline from zero-tolerance policies to juvenile justice dispositions. *Georgetown Law Journal, 102,* 1251.

Dimitriadis, G. (2001). *Performing identity/performing culture: Hip hop as text, pedagogy, and lived practice.* New York, NY: Peter Lang.

Ferriss, S., Sandoval, R., & Hembree, D. (1997). *The fight in the fields: Cesar Chavez and the farmworkers movement.* New York, NY: Houghton Mifflin Harcourt.

Fine, M., & Ruglis, J. (2009). Circuits and consequences of dispossession: The racialized realignment of the public sphere for U.S. youth. *Transforming anthropology, 17*(1), 20–33.

Fisher, M. (2003). Open mics and open minds: Spoken word poetry in African diaspora participatory literacy communities. *Harvard Educational Review, 73*(3), 362–389.

Fisher, M. T. (2007). *Writing in rhythm: Spoken word poetry in urban classrooms.* New York, NY: Teachers College Press.

Freire, P. (2000). *Pedagogy of the oppressed.* New York, NY: Bloomsbury Publishing.

Garza, A. (2014). A herstory of the #blacklivesmatter movement. *The Feminist Wire.* Available at http://www.thefeministwire.com/2014/10/blacklivesmatter-2/

Hill, M. L. (2009). *Beats, rhymes, and classroom life: Hip Hop pedagogy and the politics of identity.* New York, NY: Teachers College Press.

Hill, M. L. (2016). *Nobody: Casualties of America's war on the vulnerable, from Ferguson to Flint and beyond.* New York, NY: Atria Books.

Hirschfield, P. J. (2008). Preparing for prison? The criminalization of school discipline in the USA. *Theoretical Criminology, 12*(1), 79–101.

Kim, C. Y., Losen, D. J., & Hewitt, D. T. (2010). *The school-to-prison pipeline: Structuring legal reform.* New York, NY: NYU Press.

Ladson-Billings, G. (1994). *The dreamkeepers: Successful teachers of African American children.* San Francisco, CA: Jossey-Bass.

Ladson-Billings, G. (1995). Toward a theory of culturally relevant pedagogy. *American Educational Research Journal, 32*(3), 465–491.

Ladson-Billings, G. (2006). It's not the culture of poverty, it's the poverty of culture: The problem with teacher education. *Anthropology & Education Quarterly, 37*(2), 104–109.

Low, B. (2011). *Slam school: Learning through conflict in the Hip Hop and spoken word classroom.* Stanford, CA: Stanford University Press.

Mahiri, J., & Sablo, S. (1996). Writing for their lives: The non-school literacy of California's urban African American youth. *Journal of Negro Education,* 164–180.

Meiners, E. R. (2011). Ending the school-to-prison pipeline/building abolition futures. *The Urban Review, 43*(4), 547–565. doi: http://dx.doi.org/10.1007/s11256-011-0187-9

Morgan, J. (2015). Why we get off: Moving towards a Black feminist politics of pleasure. *The Black Scholar, 45*(4), 36–46.

Paris, D. (2011). *Language across difference: Ethnicity, communication, and youth identities in changing urban schools.* New York, NY: Cambridge University Press.

Paris, D. (2012). Culturally sustaining pedagogy: A needed change in stance, terminology, and practice. *Educational Researcher, 41*(3), 93–97.

Paris, D., & Alim, H. S. (2014). What are we seeking to sustain through culturally sustaining pedagogy? A loving critique forward. *Harvard Educational Review, 84*(1), 85–100.

Pawel, M. (2009). *The union of their dreams: Power, hope, and struggle in Cesar Chavez's farm worker movement.* New York, NY: Bloomsbury Publishing.

Regua, N., & Villarreal, A. (2009). *Mexicans in San José.* Mount Pleasant, SC: Arcadia Publishing.

Schiff, M. (2013). Dignity, disparity and desistance: Effective restorative justice strategies to plug the "school-to-prison pipeline." In *Center for Civil Rights Remedies National Conference. Closing the School to Research Gap: Research to Remedies Conference.* Washington, DC.

Smith, M. L. (2015). A generation at risk: The ties between zero tolerance policies and the school-to-prison pipeline. *McNair Scholars Research Journal, 8*(1), 10.

Tuck, E. (2009). Suspending damage: A letter to communities. *Harvard Educational Review*, 79(3), 409–428.

[The Young Turks]. (2016, Feb 15). *This video SHOULD cost Hillary Clinton the Black vote* [Video File]. Retrieved from https://www.youtube.com/watch?v=8k4nmRZx9nc.

Valdez, L. (1992). *Zoot suit & other plays*. Houston, TX: Arte Público Press.

Vizenor, G. (1998). Fugitive poses. In M. Katakis (Ed.), *Excavating voices: Listening to photographs of Native Americans* (pp. 7–17). Philadelphia, PA: University of Pennsylvania Museum of Archaeology and Anthropology.

Winn, M. T. (2011). *Girl time: Literacy, justice, and the school-to-prison pipeline*. New York, NY: Teachers College Press.

Winn, M. T., & Behizadeh, N. (2011). The right to be literate: Literacy, education, and the school-to-prison pipeline. *Review of Research in Education*, 35(1), 147–173.

ENVISIONING CSP FORWARD THROUGH THEORIES OF PRACTICE

CHAPTER 8

The (R)Evolution Will Not Be Standardized

Teacher Education, Hip Hop Pedagogy, and Culturally Relevant Pedagogy 2.0

Gloria Ladson-Billings
University of Wisconsin, Madison

I will admit that I am an odd choice to be found in the middle of the pedagogical revolution that Hip Hop education is producing. Indeed, when the Sugarhill Gang released the iconic "Rapper's Delight," I had already graduated from college, earned a master's degree, taught for 10 years in a big urban school district, and was sitting in graduate school pursuing a PhD. I was more Motown than Master P, more Mary Wells than Mary J, and more O'Jays than Jay Z. But somehow Hip Hop—the vibrant, dynamic culture born out of the inventiveness and sheer strength of will of our youth—has captivated me in ways that have forced me to reevaluate my work and how I relate to students.

I am known as a "pedagogical theorist," which is a sophisticated way of saying that I think deeply and seriously about the art and craft of teaching. I research teaching. I study teaching. I experiment with teaching in an attempt to improve my own teaching and the teaching that occurs in classrooms everywhere, especially in classrooms serving African American students. My specific focus on African American students has to do with the ways that our youth have been so marginalized and disrespected in schools and classrooms. In this chapter I attempt to explain exactly how I defined culturally relevant pedagogy, what I now believe is missing from those initial conceptualizations and is amenable to culturally sustaining pedagogies, and what this work means for teacher education.

Over 25 years ago I began researching the pedagogical practices of teachers who were successful with African American children. I chose this issue because after five years of graduate study at one of the nation's most prestigious universities I kept hearing how "nobody" had demonstrated academic success with Black children. So ingrained was this notion that all of the literature

I searched reinforced it. My first electronic searches using descriptors like "Black Education" and "African American Education" quickly defaulted to cross-references that read, "see culturally deprived," or "see cultural deficits." The language of academic excellence was absent when it came to considering African American children. Thus, my work became more than locating what I would later call "existence proofs"—evidence that there were teachers capable of fostering academic success among African American students. In addition, I focused on crafting a theoretical platform on which to build this kind of expertise so that it would become more widely distributed and appreciated. I developed a theory I called "culturally relevant pedagogy" (Ladson-Billings, 1995a/2009; 1995b).

Today, I hear the term "culturally relevant pedagogy" everywhere I go; it is ubiquitous. Unfortunately, the practices that I see rarely represent the practice that I described when I had the opportunity to spend three years with eight outstanding teachers. So I will begin by briefly describing what I meant by culturally relevant pedagogy (CRP) when I began to explicate these successful teachers' work. CRP involves three main components: (a) a focus on student learning, (b) developing students' cultural competence, and (c) supporting their critical consciousness. And every one of these key components is corrupted in most applications of CRP: Student learning is translated as assimilation and narrow forms of success, and cultural competence as "We did or read something Black"; and the goal of supporting students' critical consciousness is either distorted (viewed, as it often is, through the prism of whiteness) at best, or conveniently left out altogether at worst.

Student learning may seem an obvious component or, more specifically, outcome of teaching, but here I am referring to the intellectual growth that students experience as a result of the experiences they have in the school, community, and classroom, especially with the help of a skilled teacher. I am not merely referencing "gain scores" on standardized measures that are typically separate and disconnected from the curriculum. A teacher capable of fostering student learning makes a careful assessment of what knowledge and skills students begin with and builds from there. Thus, one might be a 4th-grade teacher who has a student who reads at a 1st-grade level. By the end of the school year that teacher may have brought the student to a 3rd-grade reading level. Based on a standardized test score, the teacher "failed" to have the student reading at grade level. However, in actuality the teacher helped the student improve two grade levels in one year. This is clear evidence of student learning despite what the standardized test records show. I want to be careful to note that I am not suggesting that standardized tests do not tell us anything. They can be instructive regarding curriculum misalignment—what is taught versus what is tested. They can be informative regarding where students stand vis-á-vis other students in their same age–grade cohort. They can also provide some insight into how students compare with their own growth and academic development, providing a look at year-to-year progress—at least a notion of progress along a Eurocentric curriculum norm. But my reference to student learning is much broader and deeper than a test score. To begin with, educational research has shown that standardized tests are narrowly normed along White, middle-class, monolingual measures of achievement. Relatedly, and critical to my conceptualization of CRP, culturally relevant teachers are interested in differences in students' reasoning ability, problem-solving skills, and moral development—things that are not so easily measured by standardized tests. The student who began the year attempting to solve every problem by punching another student but who ends the year talking out his concerns has clearly learned something important that will not show up on a test. The student who moves from non- or limited participation in a group to leadership and full participation has learned something not evident on a standardized test but important for further school and life success.

The second component of culturally relevant pedagogy is cultural competence. I think of this as the "misunderstood" aspect of CRP. As someone trained in anthropology, I have a deep sense of what is meant by the term *culture*. It involves every aspect of human endeavor, including thought, perceptions, feelings, and attitudes. It is not merely the visible and tangible components of a community such as artifacts, foods, and customs, although those things are indeed a part of culture. However, it is important to emphasize the dynamic and fluid nature of culture that is much more than lists of "central tendencies" or worse, "cultural stereotypes." From an anthropological perspective, culture encompasses worldview, thought patterns, epistemological stances, ethics, and ways of being along with the tangible and readily identifiable components of human groups.

A young "progressive" teacher with a more informal demeanor entering an urban classroom serving African American students suggesting that students call him or her "Wendy" or "Phil" may be unwittingly setting up a cultural conflict. In communities where I grew up and later worked, ALL adults, regardless of official status, were spoken to and about with a title— Miss, Mrs., Mr., Auntie, Uncle, Rev. Doc., or some form of differentiated status. This is considered a form of respect, and "children" are not permitted to violate that norm. I recall that when I was growing up there was a man in the neighborhood whose nickname was "Baby." As children we referred to him as "Mr. Baby!" The titles helped to delineate social distance. It told us what level of respect was due to people. Telling children they can call you by your first name lowered their respect for you, and I have seen many a classroom devolve into chaos in part because it was not clear who was the adult and with what authority people operated.

Learning these nuances of culture takes deliberate study. No teacher education course can ever cover every potential cultural conflict. Thus, culturally relevant teachers take the initiative to learn about the communities where they work. They may read larger cultural histories, but they can also attend cultural events and institutions. In one of my courses I invite students to visit community settings: grocery stores, health facilities, after-school programs, and especially churches. The traditional two-hour Black church service is always an eye-opening experience for my students. Those not socialized in these cultural spaces are often shocked by the degree of responsibility that children (even very young children) have. Some are ushers, others may be choir members, and still others may be in charge of making church announcements. The very children that many school personnel argue have ADHD (Attention Deficit Hyperactivity Disorder) or some other emotional malady can be seen sitting for long stretches of time and participating appropriately in the service. In those instances I ask students to think about the nature of the service and how it might contrast with the school setting. Typically the students point out the interactive nature of the church service. Traditional Black preaching is a dialogue where congregants are not expected to sit silently and listen. No, a good sermon is one where the congregation "talks back." When the preacher says something with which they strongly agree, it is not unusual for people to stand up as an expression of their approval. And if they don't, it's not uncommon to hear the preacher exclaim, "I wish I had a witness!"

As previously stated, my students also note the increased responsibility the children have. Small children may be ushering adults to their seats and passing the collection plate. This kind of behavior is unusual in school, and students who engage in these kinds of interactions (e.g., calling out an answer, "talking back," or leaving one's seat to assist another student) are regularly sanctioned. While we cannot expect the school to totally revamp its cultural style in the short term, culturally relevant teachers find ways of incorporating more familiar cultural forms in the classroom and provide clear explanations for why some things remain culturally different in school—not better, but different. Ideally, these explanations go far beyond quips like "that's the way the world works" (which are uncritical mandates that lack explanatory power) and take into account social power dynamics (which offer critical perspectives on normative expectations).

In many of today's human services, professionals use the term "cultural competence." Thus, we hear of culturally competent nursing, culturally competent counseling, or culturally competent policing. Unfortunately, much of what I have read and seen of these practices consists of using a list of "do's and don'ts" in dealing with clients who belong to racial, ethnic, or linguistic groups different from "the mainstream," which in the U.S. context is normed on White, middle-class culture and language. Further, this limited perspective on culture almost always conceives of culture as static, unchanging sets of actions or behaviors. In the context of CRP, cultural competence refers to the skill and facility to help students recognize and appreciate their culture of origin while also learning to develop fluency in at least one other culture. The goal of cultural competence is to ensure that students remain firmly grounded in their culture of origin (and learn it well) while acquiring knowledge and skill in at least one additional culture. For most marginalized students, the additional culture is typically the mainstream one, since it is typically the culture of commerce and social advancement. But the skilled pedagogue understands the value of keeping students grounded in the culture that represents their home, family, and loved ones. Developing a multicultural, multilingual perspective or competence means that all students (including White, middle-class students) broaden their cultural repertoires so that they can operate more easily in a world that is globally interconnected.

This definition of cultural competence has several important dimensions. First, it implies that all students have culture (whether they are aware of it or not) and that their culture is a valuable, indeed necessary, starting point for learning. Cognitive psychologists insist that prior knowledge is crucial for learning (see Chapters 14 and 15 in this volume). Those linguistic tools, thoughts, and ways of being that students come to school with are foundational for their learning. Second, as previously mentioned, this definition of cultural competence points out that *all* students should be able to develop fluency in at least one other culture—even those who are members of the dominant culture. What is often missing among teachers is their limited understanding of their own culture. Because I work in a university serving a large number of White, middle-class students, I regularly hear statements about their "not having a culture." Helping these young people do a bit of cultural excavation is one of the major challenges I face as a teacher educator. Accepting the fact that they too have "a culture" (even as we complicate the notion of culture) is often a major revelation for them. I often explain to them that due to social power dynamics that define whiteness as the unmarked, invisible norm, they are like fish who have trouble seeing the water that they swim in—and that extends to many others who have grown up in a homogenous environment.

While I described cultural competence as the "misunderstood" component of CRP, I describe the third component—supporting students' sociopolitical (or critical) consciousness—as the neglected dimension of CRP. Indeed, this component is the most often ignored element of CRP. In plain English, it might be thought of as the "so what" factor. Year after year our students ask us why they have to learn certain things. They want to know the purpose or use of the school knowledge they are subjected to each year. Unfortunately, as teachers we typically offer weak responses such as, "You're going to need this information next year!" Most students recognize early on that that answer is not true. Some will be compliant because they recognize the credentialing value of schooling, but far too many dismiss school as irrelevant and disengage to their own detriment.

Culturally relevant teachers work hard to help students engage in meaningful projects that solve problems that matter in their lives. They also work to help students develop a critical consciousness that allows them to question the veracity of what they read in classrooms and pose powerful questions about social, cultural, economic, political, and other problems of living in a democracy that attempts to serve a diverse populace. In one of the classrooms I visited, the teacher was frustrated with the increased violence that was plaguing the community. An influx of cheap rock cocaine (known familiarly as "crack") meant higher rates of addiction, increased gang activity, and rising violence. Every week another community member was assaulted and/or killed. The teacher recognized the way this shift in community behavior seemed to be desensitizing her students. Students were coming to expect funerals of young people, and some expressed an almost nonchalant attitude toward their own mortality. Rather than attempting to lecture students about drug use, she organized a service-learning project that helped connect her students with disabled veterans at a nearby VA hospital.

The students' task was to create a book that contained the life histories of the veterans. In return for sharing their stories, the students would do simple tasks for the vets such as calling the Veterans Administration to straighten out a claim or contacting the vets' family members. The students loved having the responsibility of making the calls and reading the prepared scripts. They never tired of being placed on hold and winding their way through the bureaucracy. When a colleague questioned the teacher as to why she was having her students interact with "those old people," the teacher pointed out that she wanted her students to develop relationships with the vets—to get to know their stories and tell the stories with fidelity. When the colleague replied, "But those people are dying," the teacher responded, "Yes, and with all the death and dying in this community I am noticing my students have come to accept it as normal. When they sit and talk with someone who has lived seventy-five or eighty years they come to understand that life should be longer. And when those people die they are saddened. Those deaths tap into their emotions and help them reconnect with the humanity that all this violence is stealing from them!"

The sociopolitical consciousness aspect of CRP must link to the challenges the students are confronting. Far too often, teachers choose a "problem" that interests *them*. Projects like "saving the rainforest," "recycling," or "animal rights" may emerge because the teacher has a deep passion for them. However, racial profiling, mass incarceration, or inequity in suspension may be impacting students directly. These more politically volatile topics are ones that teachers may want to hold at arm's length. But failure to engage them is exactly why students do not trust schools to be places that deal honestly and forthrightly with the issues of their lives.

THE R(E)VOLUTION OF CULTURALLY RELEVANT PEDAGOGY

Over 25 years ago, when I began researching the practice of exemplary teachers of African American students, I had no idea that this work would consume my scholarly life. But the road I traveled down a quarter of a century ago has taken me to an exciting and surprising point. I began to realize that the way many of the teachers I worked with deployed culture in their classrooms was to pull upon the established, historic aspects of students' culture. The teachers were concerned that conventional textbooks and mandated curriculum rarely included the histories and experiences of students who were not a part of the dominant culture. And I must say that the CRP teachers I first documented did a marvelous job of increasing students' knowledge of and pride in their history, heritage, and culture.

However, what I began to recognize was missing from the work was any attention to youth culture. Almost everyone who was working on youth culture at the time was working in out-of-school and community-based settings (Lopez, 2015). I realized that I was missing an important part of what mattered to students—their own, organic, self-generated culture. And what a culture it was! Students' expression of their identities showed up in their dress, their language, their dance, their art, their fascination and facility with technology, and above all their music (Nilan & Feixa, 2006). The melding and mixing of strong backbeats with incredible lyrics delivered at staccato, rapid-fire rates signified a new way of thinking about and conceiving music— and schools and classrooms were missing out on all of this ingenuity.

Of course, as these new youth cultural forms were developing, I was living in the academy. I worked with students who had already demonstrated their ability to master the standard curriculum. For the most part, that mastery is what got them into the university. However, it was clear as I worked to prepare the next generation of teachers that our teacher preparation program had some serious shortcomings. Despite being heralded as a top program, we struggled to attract racially and culturally diverse prospective teacher cohorts, and nothing in our program was addressing the way new forms of youth culture could influence and promote student learning.

Coincident with learning more about youth culture, I also learned that students from our campus's award-winning First Wave Hip Hop and Urban Arts Learning Community (see https://omai.wisc.edu/) often started our teacher education program but rarely completed it. The First Wave students felt that sitting in classes with 24 White, middle-income mostly females from suburban or rural Wisconsin or some other Midwestern state was not the best way to learn to teach in the urban centers they wanted to return to and impact. First Wave students typically came from Milwaukee, Chicago, New York, Detroit, and other major urban centers. They were students who survived schools, communities, and circumstances that were difficult but taught them resilience and perseverance. They were not merely survivors; they were thrivers. And many of them were determined to go back into their home communities and work as educators to ensure that more students like themselves would have a fair shot at getting a real education and being productive in their communities and beyond.

First Wave director Willie Ney and I sat down to talk about possible solutions to the students' concerns. My first strategy was to help the students develop what our campus calls "independent majors," where we could hand-pick a suite of courses that better suited their needs. However, what I learned was that many of the students continued to pursue their dream of teaching despite not earning teacher certification. Thus, many of the students ended up in alternative teacher certification programs like Teach for America or Teach for New York (or some variant based on the city or school district). Because I knew that these programs rarely prepare young people to work effectively in the challenging environments in which they are placed, I agreed to design a course that would provide some rudimentary preparation for thinking about teaching and merging youth culture.

The first course I developed was titled "Pedagogy, Performance, and Culture." It was designed as an introduction to education course that looked at the social foundations of education and the social foundations of Hip Hop. With the aid of a little money from our Equity and Diversity office and our Office of Multicultural Arts Initiatives (OMAI), we were able to pair the course with a public lecture series where we would invite scholars, artists, and activists to give a lecture to the larger campus community and spend time interacting more intimately with the students enrolled in the course. We were careful not to make it just a First Wave course by holding half of the seats for students who were not a part of their urban arts community. For one thing, I wanted to be careful not to "ghettoize" the experience, and for another, I wanted the nonartists/performers to experience what it meant to learn with and from students whose experiences were vastly different from their own. In a typical course at the University of Wisconsin, Madison, there are usually no more than one or two students of color or students from an urban community. Their voices are muted and sometimes discounted, and their experiences are rarely integrated into the class discourse. Half of the students in this course were students of color from our Hip Hop arts scholarship program.

I began the first session with an activity called "Where I'm From," which is a takeoff of a poem by George Ella Lyon. I gave each student a few minutes to create a spoken word piece in order to introduce themselves to the rest of the class. True to my usual way of teaching, I too created a piece. In my piece I included a hook that goes, "You know me, I'm GLB; you know me, I'm GLB." From that moment, that's who I became to the students—GLB. The work we did together helped me to embrace this new identity. Could I literally function as an MC in this new teaching format? Could a "Big Homie" and "OG" become "GLB"? Notice how terms like "OG" and "Big Homie" were applied to me by my students of color to denote the kind of respect that I referred to earlier in the chapter, but this time from a Hip Hop–centered epistemology.

We called the public lecture series "Getting Real 2" to keep it consistent with a previous series the Office of Multicultural Arts Initiatives had hosted. Our guests included Hip Hop filmmaker Eli Jacobs-Fantauzzi, whose films *Inventos: Hip Hop Cubanos* and *Homegrown: Hip Life in Ghana* explore the global spread and influence of Hip Hop. We later had cultural studies scholar Mark Anthony Neal of Duke University, who talked about Hip Hop, wealth, and social justice. This talk challenged us to think about whether moguls and stars like Jay Z and Kanye West actually were engaged in some form of social justice. We followed up with lectures by Dawn-Elissa Fisher, the "Def Professor," from San Francisco State University, and her colleague and co-teacher, the infamous "Davey D," who shared what it meant to do community-based teaching as well as some of the behind-the-scenes machinations of the commercial radio business. Our next guest was Professor Elaine Richardson, aka "Docta E," from Ohio State University. She was the first of our guest lecturers to actually perform along with sharing her research interests of working with middle school girls in out-of-school contexts. We then welcomed Anna West, a youth spoken word organizer who many of the Chicago-based students knew from the Louder Than a Bomb poetry slam competition. In our next week we heard from linguist H. Samy Alim of Stanford University via Skype to discuss the linguistic inventiveness of Hip Hop youth around the world and the challenges that these linguistic practices pose to educators and policymakers. We were also fortunate enough to be able to host Christopher Emdin of Teachers College, Columbia University, whose exploration of Hip Hop and urban science was a fabulous presentation that culminated with a mini-freestyle battle between Chris and three of the First Wave students. In the remaining weeks we hosted Marc Lamont Hill of Morehouse, CNN, Huffington Post Live, and BET; Martha Diaz and Eddie Fergus of NYU; David Stovall of the University of Illinois at Chicago; and Chris Walker of the University of Wisconsin, Madison), who serves as the artistic director for First Wave.

In the culminating activity for the students, I had originally planned for the First Wave students to develop performance pieces and the non–First Wave students to develop some type of curriculum project. However, about a third of the way through the semester I determined that it would be a more challenging and satisfying learning experience for all of the students to participate in the performance. All students would be a part of a small group that would conceptualize, write, and perform a piece onstage before an audience. I offered the students the option of having me assign the group membership or doing it themselves. My only stipulation was that every group had to be comprised of both First Wave and non–First Wave students. The students wanted to select their own groups, and they did a fair and equitable job of balancing the composition of the groups.

On the evening of the final cypher (which is how I referred to my class meetings, using Hip Hop terminology), the students presented five pieces that integrated the educational research we studied with spoken word, dance, and Hip Hop. Some of the skits employed humor, and some focused on very serious themes of disparity, inequity, injustice, education, and pedagogy. The students synthesized the research and the art in powerful ways. It was exciting to see the nonperformers push themselves beyond their comfort zones and feel that giddy nervousness and adrenaline rush of standing before an audience. Their comments afterward were, "I've never been so scared in my whole life, but I've never felt more alive!"

One of the students was a White woman from a suburban Milwaukee community, and I confess that I always had an eye out for her because I assumed she would be crushed by the fact that her experiences and knowledge were so limited compared to many of the other students. But I also saw her working hard to understand and learn. She probably had the steepest mountain to climb in the course, but climb it she did. Today she is a teacher in a nearby community, but I notice that she regularly attends First Wave events and Hip Hop performances. She talks easily and readily about how Hip Hop informs her teaching and has opened her up to new ways of thinking.

But truth be told, I was the person who learned the most from this experience. I was forced to read, study, and work to learn about the way aspects of Hip Hop fit this theoretical concept I termed culturally relevant pedagogy. I learned that the work of learning culture applied to me also. I had to learn how to reinvent my practice in the context of new cultural forms and cultural practices. I had to be willing to r(e)volutionize CRP, to breathe into it new life, to keep it fresh, to represent culture in new and evolving ways.

In order to teach this course, I had to study up.[1] As previously noted, I was already an adult when Hip Hop emerged in popular culture. I grew up as a soul, rhythm and blues, and jazz aficionado. I studied music and grew up in a household where music was omnipresent. I was a part of the Motown generation and, of course, as a Philadelphian, "the sound of Philadelphia." I went to school with Dee Dee Sharp, who would become the first wife of Kenny Gamble of Gamble & Huff. The original *American Bandstand* program was produced in my neighborhood at 46th and Market Streets before it migrated to the West Coast. When the Sugarhill Gang released "Rapper's Delight" I was a teacher and a parent. My experience with spoken word came from the militant voices of the 1960s, especially "The Last Poets," Amiri Baraka, Haki Madhubuti (then known as Don L. Lee), Sonia Sanchez, and June Jordan. To me, Hip Hop was a part of what we would now call "house music," not to be sold or consumed commercially, but a vehicle for releasing the hostility and tension that built up in our communities. Hip Hop was something you went to the streets or dance parties to hear, not buy in a record store.

My initial text was Jeff Chang's *Can't Stop Won't Stop: A History of the Hip Hop Generation* (2006). The history teacher in me liked that I could put my hands on a reliable and long-range view of the art form. Chang starts in Jamaica and links Hip Hop to its Rastafarian roots. Here I came to understand the political underpinnings of the movement that was much more than shouting, "hotel, motel, Holiday Inn!" It was a way to restore the spoken word, always sacred in the Black community. Our heroes have always been wordsmiths—Frederick Douglass, Sojourner Truth, Martin Luther King Jr., Fannie Lou Hamer, Malcolm (El Hajj Malik Shabazz) X, Stokely Carmichael, Audre Lorde, Toni Morrison, and Barack Obama, to name a few. This thing called Hip Hop was just the latest iteration of what had been present in our communities for centuries. One of its innovations was in the crafting of powerful beats to accompany the rhymes. But it also brought an assertive and provocative critique of the society and the structural inequality that oppressed people faced at every turn.

From Chang's text I explored Jay Z's *Decoded* (2011), along with Tupac Shakur's *The Rose That Grew from Concrete* (2009) and Forman and Neal's (2011) Hip Hop studies reader, *That's the Joint!* In addition to the texts that celebrated Hip Hop, I knew it was important to read work that offered critique. I read Charnas's *The Big Payback: The History of the Business of Hip Hop* (2011) to look at the money trail that emerged when Hip Hop moved from an accessible street art form where artists performed, mixed, and dubbed their own CDs and sold them from the back of their car trunks to a multimillion dollar enterprise. I knew enough about the history of the entertainment business to know that many extremely successful Black artists ended up penniless and destitute. Capitalism would do to Hip Hop what it did to all original art forms—rip it off, repackage it, and resell it to a community as if they had not created it in the first place.

Also, I thought it was important to read the ideological and political critiques that developed around Hip Hop. I turned to Tricia Rose's *The Hip Hop Wars: What We Talk About When We Talk About Hip Hop—And Why It Matters* (2008). Here Rose lays out the basic public arguments, pro and con, about Hip Hop and challenges them. A few of those pro and con arguments include a focus on violence, demeaning women, keeping it real, and the absence of the discussion of what some designate as conscious or positive Hip Hop.

The point of my course was not to have students sitting around listening to their favorite Hip Hop songs, but rather to engage Hip Hop as a way to think about how popular art forms shaped students' thinking and worldviews. Hip Hop would be both a vehicle and a pedagogical strategy.

For me, it would be a way to help CRP evolve for 21st-century teachers and students. I learned a tremendous amount by becoming Hip Hop that has less to do with the specific music, art, dance, or fashion than it does with what it means to place students' needs first.

I believe it is important to include this section on my own learning to illustrate the need for teachers who choose to incorporate culture—linguistic, ethnic, regional, generational, and so forth—to do the serious and necessary study of those cultures. It is important to treat cultures with integrity and work to avoid misappropriation by trivializing commercial iterations of those cultures. Over and over I see young, White teachers on YouTube doing routines with their urban, mostly Black students to popular songs like Pharrell's "Happy" or Silentó's "Watch Me Whip (Watch Me Nae Nae)" as proxies for cultural knowledge and competence. Instead of actually reading, observing, and engaging in conversation with people who are a part of a culture they are learning, far too many teachers are selecting the most trivial aspects of the culture in an attempt to entice students into learning some of the same old information they have been teaching for years. No. Just no.

Later I offered a second course titled "Pedagogical Flows: Hip Hop in the K–12 Classroom." While the first course (Pedagogy, Performance, and Culture) was more appropriately a foundational course, this second course was more focused toward methods. In addition to providing some historical and sociological background, we used this course to look at the curriculum and how Hip Hop could be used to teach various subjects. Again we paired the course with a public lecture series with the caveat that all speakers would spend time with our students. In this series we included Ebro Darden, who was program director for New York City's Hot 103 radio; Baba Israel, artist, producer, and educator; Brittney Cooper, known as the Crunk Feminist and professor at Rutgers University; Mama C, an activist from the 1960s who has been living and working with her husband in Tanzania; Colman Domingo, actor on stage and screen; and H. Samy Alim, linguist and professor at Stanford University.

In this class at least half of the students had plans to go into teaching via an alternative route. Four seniors had already accepted positions in cities such as Chicago, Denver, Washington, DC, and rural Louisiana. Some of the underclassmen/women have also now graduated and taken teaching positions in Boston, New York, and Milwaukee. One of the students was a freshman who enrolled in the campus teacher education program but regularly talked to me about how different the program was compared to the issues and methods we were exploring in this course. Several of the other students have become campus activists who have led the Black Lives Matter movement on campus and protests to bring more awareness to sexual violence against college women. By incorporating youth culture into the course, we were able to dig deeply into issues that mattered in students' lives.

WHAT THIS MEANS FOR TEACHER EDUCATION

One of my main interests in Hip Hop pedagogy lies in its implications for teacher education. Unfortunately, increasing numbers of prospective teachers who might choose to teach in urban settings are not enthusiastic about pursuing teacher certification through traditional teacher education pathways. And they have good reasons for looking elsewhere for preparation, because although most of the discourse about diversity and teaching focuses on the demographic mismatch between pre-K–12 teachers and their students, one of the most critical, underexamined issues is the "incredible whiteness of (being) teacher educators."

The overwhelming proportion of university-based teacher educators is White (Ducharme & Agnes, 1982). Over the last two decades this population has shifted from mostly male to mostly female, so White women dominate the ranks of both pre-K–12 teaching and those who prepare people to teach. Some of the same problems endemic to teaching at the pre-K–12 level are evident at the college and university levels. Teachers with limited perspectives are being asked to teach (or prepare people to teach) students from backgrounds very different from their own.

Despite the large number of teacher education programs across the country, there is more uniformity than one might expect in these programs. In undergraduate programs students enter teacher education programs in their junior year and complete four or five semesters of professional preparation. In graduate or postbaccalaureate programs, prospective teachers can take between one to two years of professional education courses. Some of the similarities of the programs are the inclusion of foundations courses (in history, sociology, or psychology of education), methods courses (how to teach specific subject areas), and clinical practice (student teaching and other fieldwork).

Because of these similarities, I recognize what I call "leverage points" that teacher educators can use to ensure that prospective teachers of students in urban (and also rural) classrooms are fully prepared to do the work. The first leverage point is admissions. Who we admit into teacher education is one of the more crucial decisions teacher educators can make. Many institutions of higher education have changed their overall demographic profiles by seeing diversity as a value-added factor. Elite universities like Harvard, Yale, Penn, and Stanford have relatively high numbers of students of color. They maintain those numbers by actively recruiting students of color. Most of these elite universities are private and do not have to adhere to state regulations and scrutiny regarding admissions, but most teachers are prepared in state universities.

In undergraduate teacher education, we are limited to the students who are already admitted to the university as our universe. Thus, if we want to diversify the teacher candidate pool, we have to aggressively recruit those students we want to see in teacher education. We need to urge admission offices to seek out and admit diverse students so that we can have a more diverse pool from which to select potential teacher candidates. The other important aspect of the admissions process is determining what we want to use as admission criteria. Typically, teacher education programs rely heavily on students' grade point averages and test performance on standardized preprofessional tests. This reliance on grades and test scores means we typically admit students with similar backgrounds and profiles (see national statistics of 80-plus percent White women teachers). If we are serious about revolutionizing teaching, we have to have new criteria by which to select prospective teachers.

The second leverage point is prior to student teaching. Since student teaching is a legal designation (i.e., student teachers can be sued), it is important that we more carefully scrutinize teacher education students before we place them in the classroom. Merely having completed the coursework is not sufficient for putting someone in classrooms with students. We need a higher standard before we allow students to engage in clinical practice. However, if we do not pay close enough attention to students before we declare them ready for student teaching, we have little evidence on which to base a decision. What are we looking for that tells us that our students are ready to take on the responsibility of student teaching? Why do we assume that student teaching should just naturally follow coursework without a deeper evaluation of a prospective teacher's readiness?

The third leverage point we have as teacher educators is certification. Far too many students mistakenly believe that their teacher education program certifies them to teach. In actuality, the state certifies teachers. The teacher education program recommends prospective teachers to the state. Just because a student has completed all aspects of the prescribed course, we cannot assume that we should recommend them to the state for certification. It is possible to complete the program and not receive certification. We should be willing to make clear to prospective teachers that finishing coursework and completing student teaching are no guarantee of certification.

My own contribution to teacher education is firmly grounded in the long-term work I have done in culturally relevant pedagogy. Today, that work is undergoing important and exciting change as younger scholars such as those included in this volume (e.g., Alim, Haupt, Paris, San Pedro, etc.) help to remake and reshape culturally relevant pedagogy into what we now call culturally sustaining pedagogy. In my earlier *Harvard Educational Review* article on this topic (Ladson-Billings, 2014), I argued,

> In developing this theory, culturally sustaining pedagogy (Paris, 2012), these authors use culturally relevant pedagogy as the place where the "beat drops" and then layer the multiple ways that this notion of pedagogy shifts, changes, adapts, recycles, and recreates instructional spaces to ensure that consistently

marginalized students are repositioned into a place of normativity—that is, that they become subjects in the instructional process, not mere objects. Indeed, in response to my earlier work (Ladson-Billings, 1995a/2009), people regularly asked me why I chose to focus on African American students as subjects for developing a pedagogical theory. While tempted to respond, "Why not use African American students as subjects (rather than objects) of study?" I generally took the time to point out that our work to examine success among the students who had been least successful was likely to reveal important pedagogical principles for achieving success for all students. A literature that tells us what works for middle-class, advantaged students typically fails to reveal the social and cultural advantages that make their success possible. But success among the "least of these" tells us more about what pedagogical choices can support success. (p. 76)

Similarly, for me the need to reposition students of color in the space of normality in our teacher education programs is also critical. We cannot keep admitting teacher candidates who see students of color, students whose first language is not English, and/or who are recent immigrants as defective and whose major need is to become some version of White, middle-class students. We cannot continue to run teacher education programs that create fear and trepidation in the minds of teacher candidates about the students for whom they have responsibility. Thus, the culturally sustaining pedagogy we are championing in our K–12 classrooms has an important and central role to play in the higher education classrooms where we prepare our teachers. No amount of teacher tests, screening devices, or selecting for high grade point averages will help us transform teacher education. Indeed, the teacher education revolution will not be standardized!

NOTE

1. This section of the chapter on my own learning about hip-hop is adapted from another work in progress, Ladson-Billings, "Beyond beats, rhymes, and Beyoncé: Hip Hop, Hip Hop education, and culturally relevant pedagogy." In G. Sirrakos & C. Emdin (Eds.), *What the world can teach us about urban education*. Rotterdam, The Netherlands: Sense Publishers.

REFERENCES

Chang, J. (2006). *Can't stop won't stop: A history of the Hip Hop generation*. New York, NY: Picador.

Charnas, D. (2011). *The big payback: The history of the business of Hip Hop*. New York: New American Library.

Ducharme, E. R., & Agnes, R. M. (1982). The education professoriate: A research based perspective. *Journal of Teacher Education, 33*(6), 30–36.

Forman, M., & Neal, M. A. (Eds.). (2011). *That's the joint: The Hip Hop studies reader* (2nd ed.). New York, NY: Routledge.

Jay Z. (2011). *Decoded.* New York, NY: Spiegel & Grau.

Ladson-Billings, G. (1995a/2009). *The dreamkeepers: Successful teachers of African American children.* San Francisco, CA: Jossey Bass.

Ladson-Billings, G. (1995b). Toward a theory of culturally relevant pedagogy. *American Educational Research Journal, 32,* 465–491.

Ladson-Billings, G. (2014). Culturally relevant pedagogy 2.0: a.k.a. the re-mix. *Harvard Educational Review, 84,* 74–84.

Lopez, M. E. (2015, May). *Leave them wanting more!: Engaging youth in afterschool.* Cambridge, MA: Harvard Family Research Project.

Nilan, P., & Feixa, C. (Eds.). (2006). *Global youth? Hybrid identities, plural worlds.* New York, NY: Routledge.

Paris, D. (2012). Culturally sustaining pedagogy: A needed change in stance, terminology, and practice. *Educational Researcher, 41*(3), 93–97.

Rose, T. (2008). *The Hip Hop wars: What we talk about when we talk about Hip Hop—and why it matters.* New York, NY: Basic Civitas Books.

Shakur, T. (2009). *The rose that grew from concrete.* New York, NY: MTV Books.

CHAPTER 9

Reviving Soul(s) with Afrikaaps
Hip Hop as Culturally Sustaining Pedagogy in South Africa

H. Samy Alim
University of California, Los Angeles

Adam Haupt
University of Cape Town

When [these Hip Hop artists] speak, you just see the children's faces light up and they come alive in school like never before. Someone knows who they are, speaks their language (and how they actually *say* it, you know), treats them like human beings and doesn't put them down. But they're not just teaching or connecting with the students . . . they are reviving souls, do you know what I mean?

—Shihaam Domingo, organizer and promoter of Afrikaans-
language festivals and theater productions, Cape Town,
March, 2015, interview with Alim

Writing over a decade ago, Alim (2007, p. 27) made an ideological distinction between pedagogies that center the cultural and linguistic realities of students on one the hand, and ones described as *culturally appropriate*, *culturally responsive*, and *culturally relevant* on the other. Pedagogical theorists had produced these terms to describe classroom practices that utilized the linguistic and cultural resources of students as a "bridge" to cross the cultural "mismatch" that made it difficult for teachers to teach prescribed academic knowledge and skills to students of color. But relegating students' cultural and linguistic resources to being tools for advancing the learning of an "acceptable" curricular canon, a "standard" variety of language, or other "academic" skill had some unintended consequences.

As predominantly White teachers and teacher education programs began (mis)interpreting culturally relevant pedagogies (CRPs) through the lens of hegemonic whiteness, they often unwittingly devalued students of colors' cultural and linguistic practices (Ladson-Billings, 2014). Intentionally or not, whiteness was frequently and uncritically positioned as the unmarked norm by which all others are measured. Further, as Ladson-Billings notes, teachers and teacher education programs often neglected the aspect of CRP that supported the development of students' sociopolitical consciousness (in all fairness, how can teachers support what they themselves often don't possess?). Teachers "rarely pushed students to consider critical perspectives on policies and practices that may have direct impact on their lives and communities" (Ladson-Billings, 2014, p. 78) (think racism, police brutality, rising incarceration rates, income inequality, etc.).

Alim (2007, p. 28) worried that *curriculum* would continue to be disconnected from *community* and *culture*, that educators might be offering pedagogies that function as "a strawberry-flavored, culturally sensitive pill for our children to swallow," the result of which would ultimately be the same illness: the uncritical devaluation of students' languages, cultures, and experiences. What was needed was a paradigm shift, one that centered "our students' abilities and experiences as the sources of knowledge and learning" (p. 28). Paris (2012, p. 93) offered that paradigm shift by proposing a bold terminological and theoretical move from CRPs to CSPs—culturally sustaining pedagogies—"as an alternative that . . . embodies some of the best research and practice in the resource pedagogy tradition and as a term that supports the value of our multiethnic and multilingual present and future."

CSPs demand explicitly pluralist outcomes that are not centered on dominant White, middle-class, monolingual/monocultural norms of educational achievement (Alim & Paris, 2015; Paris & Alim, 2014). Whereas previous approaches sought to build upon the cultural and linguistic practices of students to support academic learning, CSPs, to quote Carol Lee (Chapter 15), have expanded these ideas to argue that "diverse funds of knowledge and culturally inherited ways of navigating the world need to be sustained as goods unto themselves." This fundamental shift argues that the cultural and linguistic practices and knowledges of communities of color are of value in their own right, and should be creatively foregrounded rather than merely viewed as resources to take students (almost always unidirectionally) from "where they are at" to some presumably "better" place, or ignored altogether. As Paris and Alim (2014) argue, the goal of teaching and learning with youth of color must move beyond seeing how closely students can perform White, middle-class norms of language and culture; the practices and knowledges of communities of color, including youth culture, are valuable resources in and of themselves to be cultivated, sustained, and revitalized.

ORGANIC FORMS OF CULTURALLY SUSTAINING PEDAGOGIES

In this chapter, we draw from years of ethnographic research with Hip Hop communities in Cape Town, South Africa, and seek to theorize from the ground up, so to speak, by engaging the concept of CSPs from the vantage point of youth culture. What can we learn from *organic forms of culturally sustaining pedagogies* and from the techniques used by cultural actors to develop, sustain, re-create, and reinterpret linguistic and cultural traditions? How have Hip Hop artist-pedagogues, in particular, resisted often overwhelming dominant ideologies of language (which are almost always racist, classist, and discriminatory) and imagined new pedagogical possibilities that center our communities' cultural and linguistic practices? In contexts that are aggressively anti-Black, how do the Hip Hop arts—and the expressive arts more generally—do more than teach content knowledge but also critically provide ways for Black/Coloured youth in South Africa to sustain their humanity?

In much of our work to date (Alim, 2006; Alim, Ibrahim, & Pennycook, 2009; Haupt, 2008, 2012), we highlight the function of the Hip Hop arts in providing marginalized youth with the means to reclaim, reimagine, and reconstruct themselves and their histories, cultures, and languages. In this chapter, we begin by suggesting that Hip Hop functions always/already as an organic form of CSP in at least three important ways. First, both implicitly and explicitly, much of U.S. and South African Hip Hop has historically foregrounded "Knowledge of Self" as a consciousness-raising ideology and as political, pedagogical practice (as Big Daddy Kane famously rapped, "Knowledge of Self broke every shackle and chain," and as Prophets of da City proclaimed, "Knowledge of Self is gonna make us strong"). Second, in addition to the explicit political, pedagogical function of Hip Hop, the art form itself, in terms of aesthetics, functions as an organic form of CSP through the practice of sampling, which archives and revives valued musical, cultural, and verbal artistic traditions. Last, and most importantly, in considering Hip Hop cultural and linguistic practice as organic forms of CSP, we argue that Hip Hop provides pedagogical theorists with ways to consider how education can sustain and revive the souls of students who, far too often, experience schooling as a soul-deadening process where the very things that they hold dear—their languages, cultures, families, identities, and histories—are absent at best, or overtly stigmatized, marginalized, and excluded at worst.

Beginning with the Hip Hop art of sampling, we theorize Hip Hop as a project of revisionist historiography that draws centrally upon the remixing and reclamation of language and other cultural symbols to revive what Gates (1988) refers to as "the negated signs of Blackness." In our larger collaborative project, we consider three cases—(1) Critical Hip Hop Language Pedagogies in the United States, (2) the Afrikaans language movement by South African artist Hemelbesem, and (3) the Hip Hop theatrical production and documentary *Afrikaaps*—as examples of organic projects of linguistic remixing and reclamation through Hip Hop cultural practice. For this chapter, we will focus on the practice of sampling in Hip Hop and the Hip Hop theatrical production and documentary *Afrikaaps,* the anticolonial, raciolinguistic project of South African Hip Hop artists in Cape Town. We conclude by considering the implications of these organic, community-based efforts for theories of pedagogy in the increasingly diverse (across race, gender, sexuality, etc.) and currently volatile contexts of the United States and South Africa, where youth of color and their communities are currently engaged in sustained protests about racial justice and equity. In these sometimes dehumanizing contexts, how can our pedagogies be about more than "just teaching" content knowledge or "connecting with students," but rather, as Shihaam Domingo observed in the opening of this chapter, the necessary act of "reviving souls"?

THE HIP HOP ART OF SAMPLING AS CSP

Much has been written about the Hip Hop art of sampling, "the digital recording and manipulation of sound that forms the foundation of Hip Hop production" (Schloss, 2004, p. 79). As Schloss points out, the artistic practice of sampling is also pedagogical in that DJs educate themselves and others by "diggin' in the crates," or searching for rare records and unique sounds, in order to display and pass on knowledge of various musical and literary traditions. In fact, literary scholars have long posited that Hip Hop music's techniques were not simply ones of selective extension and modification. As Baker (1993, p. 89) has argued, "They also included massive archiving. Black sound (African drums, bebop melodies, James Brown shouts, jazz improvs, Ellington riffs, blues innuendos, doo-wop croons, reggae words, calypso rhythms) were gathered into a reservoir of threads that DJs wove into intriguing tapestries of anxiety and influence."

In a society where culture—and Black culture in particular—is bought and sold as intellectual property, these aesthetic, pedagogical practices have created challenges for the music industry, to say the least. The legal response to Hip Hop sampling, as Haupt (2008, 2014) has pointed out, provides a helpful point of entry into the hegemonic ways in which Black cultural expression has been framed. Sampling involves the use of various media sources to produce new music texts, whether they are loops of musical instruments or snippets from news broadcasts or film soundtracks. As such, Hip Hop sampling can be productively viewed as "alternative history lessons about Black cultural achievement that compete with dominant representations about Black subjectivity" (Haupt, 2008, p. 73).

Early Hip Hop, especially, largely sampled the work of African American artists in order to produce new, layered music performances that challenged listeners to explore the sources from which the Hip Hop texts were produced. Hip Hop texts are thus intertextual in terms of the multiple literary references they may contain as well as the multiple media sources upon which the music is constructed (Alim, 2006; Perry, 2004). Writing about Hip Hop in the late 1980s and early 1990s, Tricia Rose contends that sampling "in rap is a process of cultural literacy and intertextual reference." In addition to the musical layering and engineering strategies involved in these soul resurrections, these samples are "highlighted, functioning as a challenge to know these sounds, to make connections between the lyrical and musical texts. It affirms Black musical history and locates these 'past' sounds in the 'present'" (Rose, 1994, p. 89).

Hip Hop therefore plays an important role in developing cultural literacy in a context that undervalues Black cultural expression. Hip Hop music, quite literally, as Rose observed, revives Soul music. Stevie Wonder lives through the Wu-Tang Clan; Nina Simone lives through Lauryn Hill. Importantly, the revival of soul music is also paired with the concept of reviving, to sample W. E. B. Du Bois, the souls of Black folk. As Banks (2011, pp. 3–4) writes, in spinning, stream-of-consciousness, Hip Hop– and Soul-inspired prose, the Hip Hop DJ is a "digital griot" that stands

> between tradition and future . . . always searching always questioning always researching digging in the crates looking for that cut that break that connection nobody else has found, nobody else has used quite that way. practicing her craft constantly. bearer of history, memory, and rememory, able to turn on the planetary or intergalactic time space transporter within seconds . . . *but still escape with our souls* . . . [emphasis ours]

Whether it's through pedagogical forms of consciousness-raising, or through the sheer joy and ecstasy that we feel when we hop on "the planetary or intergalactic time space transporter" that is Hip Hop music, the Hip Hop arts do more than revive Soul, they revive souls. Following Ibrahim's (2009, p. 240) description of Hip Hop as "a cultural space of affective and identity investment," this transformative experience is precisely the kind of affective and intellectual work that we should expect of our pedagogies. Below, we describe how the Hip Hop theater production *Afrikaaps* attempts to do just that—to provide transformative, culturally sustaining pedagogy— through an explicit focus on the remixing and reclaiming of their racial and linguistic history.

AFRIKAAPS: A PEDAGOGICAL PROJECT OF LINGUISTIC RECLAMATION

Afrikaaps is a Hip Hop–based theater production that explicitly revises hegemonic understandings of Afrikaans. Specifically, it offers a creative re-examination of the language variety they refer to as *Afrikaaps* (a neologism that combines the term *Afrikaans* with the term *Kaaps*, meaning "from the Cape" or "Capetonian"). This project of historical linguistic revisionism boldly and creatively contests traditional, static, colonial definitions of Afrikaans as "the language of the Dutch settlers" in Cape Town, for example, as well as traditional resistance narratives of Afrikaans as "the language of the colonizer." Through a clever, politicized orthographic maneuver, Afrikaans is rendered Afrikaaps, calling upon the reader/listener to question the taken-for-granted assumptions about this language variety, its history, and the people who speak it (see Figure 9.1).

One of the production's key assertions is that Afrikaans is a creole language, drawing on the history of slavery in the Cape and linguistic contributions of Muslims from Southeast Asia to Afrikaans, an argument that is corroborated by the research of Achmat Davids in his book *The Afrikaans of the Cape Muslims* (2011). Revising the work of Dutch scholar Adrianus van Selms, Davids aims to "evoke an awareness of the existence of Cape Muslim Afrikaans as a useful source for broadening the linguistic nature of Cape Afrikaans and to provide the basis to facilitate the pursuit of intensive philological studies in both Cape Muslim and Cape Afrikaans" (2011, p. 16). Davids's research on the Arabic-Afrikaans literary tradition is important because evidence suggests that Afrikaans was written in Arabic script from the early 19th century and that research in this regard "was generally avoided by Afrikaans academics," probably because many of them did not "read or understand the Arabic script" (Davids, 2011, p. 15).

Figure 9.1. Poster of Afrikaaps theatre production scheduled at Die Afrikaanse Taalmonument (or the Afrikaans Language Monument), a contested site of Afrikaner nationalism. The performance was ultimately cancelled.

Photo by H. Samy Alim.

Our view is that the net effect of this gap in research on the history of Afrikaans allowed the language's Dutch "origins" to be foregrounded, which facilitated its cooptation by White Afrikaner nationalists after 1948 when the National Party came into power and implemented legislated apartheid. A further effect is that varieties, such as Kaaps or Afrikaaps, became viewed through a normative, racialized Afrikaner lens; Afrikaans varieties associated with White speakers became standardized and elevated, while varieties associated with Coloured speakers (as apartheid-era lexicon would have it) were marginalized and constructed as "nonstandard." While "White" Afrikaans became the language of the educated, the upwardly mobile, and the orderly, "Coloured" Afrikaans became the language of the ignorant, the lazy, and the disorderly. The criminalization of Coloured bodies during (and after) apartheid applied to their languages as well. In response to these discriminatory, raciolinguistic ideologies, artists on the soundtrack for the theater show asserted, "Afrikaaps is legal!" (Afrikaaps, 2011).

These artists echo a viewpoint expressed by the late Mr. Fat of Brasse vannie Kaap (BVK), the first Capetonian Hip Hop crew to record a Hip Hop album exclusively in Afrikaaps, when he indicated that the crew's aim was to prove that "*gamtaal* is legal" (Haupt, 2001). The term *gamtaal* refers to the language of Coloured people, who were described derogatorily as "gam"—a reference to the biblical son Ham that signified the so-called shame of Coloured people being the products of miscegenation (Haupt, 2001). In the song "Afrikaaps Is Legal," Bliksemstraal (Lightning Bolt), aka Charl van der Westhuizen, raps:

Baie mense strui en praat van legalise jou taal
Mix it op in Engels binne 'n hele klomp styles
Rep it met die waarheid, druk it vas met confidence . . .
Wat 'n guy
Hy vra nog wat is daai
Hy vat my taal *maar kannie my siel vattie,* die blêddie spy
Binne die hof ek verwoordig ek net myself
Maar aanhou as ek rep dan wil ek klink ek soos someone else

[Many people argue and talk about legalizing your language
Mix it up in English in many styles
Rap with truth and confidence
What a guy
He questions what it is
He takes my language, *but he can't take my soul,* the bloody spy
In court, I represent myself, but when I rap I want to sound like someone else]
(Afrikaaps, 2011; emphasis ours)

The opening verse of "Afrikaaps Is Legal" speaks to the ways in which Black modes of speech are marginalized. Bliksemstraal calls for Afrikaaps to be legalized through remixing (or translanguaging, in sociolinguistic terms) and for the truth to be articulated with confidence. Afrikaaps speakers' souls cannot be taken despite the fact that their linguistic practices are both appropriated and denigrated. It is in this sense that they are validating negated signs of Blackness; they are reviving Black modes of expression and, therefore, reviving soul(s). The last line in the excerpt speaks to specific negated signs of Blackness in Cape Town (South African Black linguistic signs), where, ironically, speakers feel confident representing themselves in legal matters, but are less bold when representing their art on their own terms in a context where a different set of Black signs (Black American linguistic signs) are viewed as pervasive and hegemonic (Haupt, 2012, p. 2001).

As a complement to the culturally and linguistically sustaining ideas in "Afrikaaps Is Legal," Bliksemstraal tells the story of a girl who "finds herself" while conducting research about her cultural history (as he raps in Monox aka Moenier Adams's "Kyk Na Die Maan" ["Look at the Moon"]):

Yo, yo, een dag was daar gewies 'n klein meisie
Nêrens waar sy gaan voel sy pleisie
Niks wat die girl doen is in place'ie
Die groot baas sê sy'tie taal, sy'tie race'ie
Toe vat die girl trop met haar ancestors
Leer sy om te gaan soek waar die les is
Doen wat jou ma gedoen het toe sy klein was, toe sy rein was
Nog nuut in die Mitchells Plein was
Mense soek waarheid van hier tot in die Kaap
Is ek wat praat, Doman Namoah!
Die soldier van die Kaapse Vlakte, ou ja
Hemel op die aarde van met a tou, ja

[Yo, yo, one day there was a little girl
She didn't fit in anywhere
Nothing she did was in place
The big boss told her that she doesn't have a language or a race
Then the girl took a trip with her ancestors
Learned to search for the lesson
Do what your mother did when she was little
Still new in Mitchells Plain
People search for truth from here to the Cape
It's me talking, Doman Namoah!
The soldier from the Cape Flats, oh yeah
Heaven on earth secured with a rope, yeah]
(Afrikaaps, 2011)

The protagonist in the verse overcomes her sense of dislocation and alienation by doing research on her ancestors, thereby countering hegemonic claims that she has no race or language. Research on the example of her ancestors is presented as the route to reviving her soul, or to rediscovering herself as a person with a sense of belonging. The young girl's soul is revived through her intellectual quest for Knowledge of Self; her motivation for learning, and living, is revived through the creation of a counternarrative that pushes back against the colonial narratives of inferiority, lack, and shame by explicitly highlighting and valuing her cultural and linguistic identities. Both "Afrikaaps Is Legal" and "Kyk Na Die Maan" are performed in Afrikaaps—the medium *is* the message. In addition to the cast's use of Afrikaaps in their live performances, both songs' efforts to sustain the language variety are affirmed by narratives that center Black/Indigenous cultural histories and modes of expression.

COMBATING THE STANDARD LANGUAGE MYTH THROUGH AFRIKAAPS

These organic forms of CSPs are not uncontroversial when enacted in school settings. Hip Hop activist Emile YX (Emile Jansen) posted an amusing narrative and a set of photographs (in which he tagged the authors on a social media platform) about a school workshop at Muizenberg High School in Cape Town. The first photograph revealed a wide shot of the uniformed school pupils seated in a school hall. The second shot revealed a Muizenberg High School detention slip, which indicated that Emile Jansen had been booked in detention for "swearing at school" (Jansen Facebook post, March 17, 2015). Jansen's narrative frames the images by explaining how he, an adult visitor to the school, ended up in detention due to a misinterpretation of his use of an Afrikaans word:

> Today I did a workshop at Muizenberg High about Afrikaaps, Our-story and language and used the word "BEFOK" to explain how amazing something was and got detention from the teacher . . . but my BEFOK meant it was KWAAI, JITS, DUIDELIK, YSTER, LEKKER, AMAZING and not whatever they thought it meant. Just wondered how many other kids from the Cape Flats who are learners, end up in detention for people not overstanding AFRIKAAPS or KAAPS. Hahaha. (Jansen Facebook post, March 17, 2015)

Needless to say, detention only applies to students and not visitors. No doubt, the detention slip was given to Jansen as a tongue-in-cheek gesture, but the symbolic censure of his choice of words stands. The Afrikaans adjective "befok" can mean "amazing," "cool," or "nice," as Jansen argues.

It can also mean "fucked up" or refer to a crazy, demented state of mind. The word "fok" literally means "fuck" in Afrikaans. Therefore, regardless of which set of connotations are evoked by the speaker, the word "fuck" is being used and this probably elicited the symbolic censure from the school-teacher. In effect, we see evidence of the double-coded ways (cf. Gates, 1988) in which meaning is conveyed in Afrikaaps. The post received a number of amused replies from friends, but one commentator summarized a hegemonic view of language quite succinctly, repeating the oft-heard hegemonic script of "standard language ideology" (U.S. readers will recognize the immediate similarities with debates about African American Language and the imposition of "standard" English):

> That's fine if you're planning to live the rest of your life on the Cape Flats [or, in the United States, in the hood]. We should be equipping the children with the tools to expand their horizons. Encouraging language like this does nothing for them. It's slang, nothing more, it's not another language. (Comment on Facebook post by Jansen, March 17, 2015)

Setting aside for the moment that the field of sociolinguistics holds the notion of a "standard" language as a myth (stating that all language varieties are systematic and rule-governed), this comment captures the key dilemma that Jansen and the cast of *Afrikaaps* have been trying to address. We do not believe that the above comment was made from a position of judgment. The view reflects the concerns of many parents and teachers who want to prepare students for the world of work and tertiary education beyond the township schooling context. Historically, this context placed a higher premium on standardized varieties of English and Afrikaans, while dominant and discriminatory raciolinguistic ideologies (see Chapter 10, this volume) positioned Cape Flats speakers in ways that limited their agency and their possibilities. As in any society, parents and teachers would be keen for pupils to learn the standardized varieties because they have greater social capital; the belief is that these varieties will ensure pupils' success in the workplace and in their pursuit of higher education.

The documentary *Afrikaaps*, which focuses on the process of producing the theater show and unpacks language and identity politics via the director's own language history, speaks to this issue in a scene where the cast conducts a workshop at Lavender Hill High School in the Cape Flats. A school pupil reflects on the ways in which his Cape Flats variety will be interpreted in mainstream institutions that valorize standardized forms of Afrikaans:

> If someone interviewed me and I'm talking and I didn't hear them properly, then I'll say [in the variety of Afrikaaps], "Sorry, brother, what did you just say?" Then immediately he's going to get the impression that I'm a gangster.

> Regardless of whether I have a degree or how intelligent I am. He's going to judge me by the language I used. For one question he's going to judge me for that job, which could impact on my life. (English translation in Valley, 2010)

The insight reveals that the pupil is conscious of the ways in which his speech will be used as a measure of his competence and ability. His reflection therefore allows us to think of the ways in which Fanonian (1967) racial interpellation operates through language practices and the extent to which the Du Boisian (1963) concept of double consciousness operates in the Cape context (Haupt, 2012). The pupil is aware of the ways in which his language use will be read along with his phenotypic features in order to locate him in terms of his race and class positions, thereby limiting his agency. On the other hand, the fact that he expresses this consciousness demonstrates that he is able to exercise some agency by styleshifting depending on the context in which he finds himself. A counter to this argument is that he has internalized the way in which he has been interpellated (cf. Fanon, 1967; Foucault, 1980) and that hegemonic understandings of race, class, and language remain unchallenged, as is also reflected by the critical comment on Jansen's Facebook post about detention. No alternative is offered.

In many ways, CSPs provide this much-needed alternative not only because they create spaces for students and teachers to reject the assimilationist drive of hegemonic institutions, but they also center organic cultural and linguistic forms in inorganic spaces, linking the social world beyond the school walls to the practices of teaching and learning, wherever they occur.

A HIP HOP ALTERNATIVE TO ASSIMILATIONIST EDUCATION

Afrikaaps is one such alternative to these (sometimes internalized) dominant raciolinguistic ideologies that link language, race, and phenotype in ways that subjugate people of color. Not only does the production affirm Black/Indigenous cultural histories and modes of expression, it opens up the debate by highlighting the important role of multilingualism and indigenous languages in education. Heugh's (2012, p. 11) research in "The Case Against Bilingual and Multilingual Education in South Africa" identifies fives myths about languages and education in the South African context:

> *Myth 1: There is little or no indigenous South African research on language in education to show what is wrong or what could work well. This myth is used to discredit international research as being not appropriate to our circumstances, and it ignores very fine and important work done here.*

Myth 2: Parents want straight for English—and in a democracy it is our duty to give people what they want, without question or the need for (responsible) intervention.

Myth 3: In South Africa English is the only language which has the capacity to deliver quality education to the majority; African languages do not and cannot.

Myth 4: African language speaking children are multilingual and therefore do not need mother tongue education. South African children are unique; they are unlike children in other parts of the mainly multilingual world. Our children's multilinguality means, according to the myth, that they do not have a mother tongue, and therefore have no need of mother tongue education.

Myth 5: Bilingual or multilingual education is too expensive and we have only one option: English only (or mainly) [sic].

According to Heugh, then, the hegemony of English is therefore maintained by the academy itself, which often frames education in learners' mother tongue as difficult and multilingual/bilingual approaches to education as impossible. Writing two decades "after" apartheid, Makoe and McKinney (2014) confirmed that the standardized variety of English continues to be hegemonic in the school context. They contended, "As was the case in the past, post-apartheid policies continue to advance and invest in monoglot ideologies that legitimise and give authority to standard English language at the expense of pluralism and diversity" (pp. 670–671).

While traditional approaches to language learning reinforce linguistic imperialism, the work of Hip Hop activist-pedagogues, such as the cast of *Afrikaaps*, "seek[s] to perpetuate and foster—to sustain" the kind of "linguistic, literate, and cultural pluralism" argued for in work on CSPs (Paris & Alim, 2014, p. 88). Following the groundbreaking work of McKinney (2007), Makoe and McKinney (2014) conclude: "For some of these linguistic imbalances to be addressed, it will be crucial for policymakers (and relevant stakeholders) to critically interrogate deeply entrenched historical ideologies that seem to persist in our language policies today with the aim of 'crafting' a new order of ideologies: with multilingualism understood as the ability to use a range of linguistic resources, at the centre rather than at the periphery" (2014, p. 671). This position resonates with the goal of CSPs to develop practices and policies that foster a pluralist future, moving beyond practices and policies that uphold and reproduce assimilationist, monolingual, monocultural, and antidemocratic futures.

As is the case with our discussion of sampling in the previous section, we see a tension between the will of Black subjects to represent themselves on their own terms and the overriding hegemonic context that is still largely consistent with the apartheid-era educational context that places a higher premium on standardized/hegemonic English. It is from this perspective that the remarks made by the critical commentator on Emile Jansen's social media post begin to make sense. In both the case of Hip Hop sampling and the language education of our youth, we find that both the legal and educational mechanisms currently in place effectively negate Black cultural and linguistic expressions that aim to respect and promote pluralist values. The efforts of Hip Hop artist-pedagogues, therefore, provide a necessary challenge to a legal and educational context that is consistent with that of the apartheid era. These challenges seek to affirm Black/Indigenous cultural modes of discourse/expression and ways of knowing/being that promote a democratic, pluralist future where people of color are full participants in society, on their own terms.

CONCLUSION: A LOVING CRITIQUE OF OUR COLLECTIVE WORK

To begin with, we are convinced that *Afrikaaps*, and the culturally sustaining artist-pedagogues involved in its production, are doing much-needed, revolutionary work in the area of language, race, and education. *Afrikaaps* can be viewed as revolutionary not only because it challenges standard language ideologies; the production goes a step further by rewriting the history of the variety claimed by White Afrikaner nationalists as "Afrikaans." The artists do not straightforwardly ask for inclusion *into* Afrikaans, but rather, for an anticolonial reinterpration of how the history of that language is even understood. In the production, Afrikaaps is not merely a variety to be accepted; Afrikaaps is, in fact, the appropriate name by which we can refer to a language variety that *began with* and *belongs to* indigenous Africans of the Cape. The variety constructed by White Afrikaner nationalists as Afri kaans, then, grew out of Afrikaaps, not the other way around ("That's how we created Afrikaaps," raps Emile YX, and Jitsvinger reminds the audience, "We are the descendants of those who built the language"). This is what we mean when we consider *Afrikaaps* as a transformative project of revisionist historiography; its power, like much of Hip Hop, lies in the remixing and reclaiming of history, language, and other cultural symbols to invert and subvert oppressive, colonial narratives.

Further, not only are these artists challenging long-held, regressive ideologies about Black and Coloured South Africans—and how they speak—but they are doing so in a context where people of color continue to suffer from White Supremacist ideologies and racialized systems of global, capitalist oppression. Indeed, they have upended establishment discourses (flipped the script) in literary production and theatrical performance, challenging some of the nation's most established Afrikaans-language conventions as well as language learning, interrogating decades of linguistic profiling and marginalization in South Africa's classrooms.

Their community outreach has extended across dozens of schools, reaching hundreds of young boys and girls with a message of linguistic reclamation that has countered so much of the linguistic shame within the community of speakers. As we have seen in our work, the response by young South African learners has been astounding. After attending an *Afrikaaps* performance, one young boy exclaimed, quite literally overcome with emotion: "I feel, *OHHH!* It was *mind* blowing! I never knew my forefathers speak through me." A young girl commented confidently, "I won't be shy to speak the way I do anymore. I won't compromise on my language for other people" (Valley, 2010). Students also show a deep sociopolitical consciousness of how language is linked to power, and even teachers and principals are moved to reflect upon their pedagogical orientation to their students' language. As Bliksemstraal raps in the production, "os kan count op osse taal osse siel te liberate" ("we can count on our language to liberate our souls."). In all of these ways, *Afrikaaps* is a model of dope, necessary, organic forms of CSP, offering much to scholars theorizing what CSPs might look like in the classroom.

However, as Paris and Alim (2014, p. 94) argue, CSPs must create generative spaces for learning that support and sustain the practices of youth and communities of color while maintaining a critical lens vis-à-vis these practices. CSP, as a pedagogical stance, "should also help youth, teachers, and researchers expose those practices that must be revised in the project of cultural justice" (p. 94). In the same spirit that Paris and Alim refer to as "a loving critique," we offer some final thoughts in an effort to advance the work of Hip Hop artists, pedagogues, and scholars alike, including our own work.

In our previous work, we have cautioned educators against making overdeterministic links between race and language. Can the same be said of the *Afrikaaps* project? What kinds of links are being made between Coloured populations and language, particularly when Afrikaaps, as some have argued, is perhaps too often framed as the language variety spoken by Coloured folks on the Cape Flats? What about those who identify as Coloured, but speak varieties of Afrikaans not associated with the Cape Flats? Or those Coloured populations in the northern suburbs beyond Cape Town who also speak marginalized varieties of Afrikaans, but where, as Hip Hop artist-pedagogue Hemelbesem has argued, region becomes at least as important as race? In foregrounding Afrikaaps as a project of linguistic reclamation tied to racial self-determination, are urban/rural divides being ignored at the expense of already marginalized Coloured Afrikaans speakers beyond the city? CSPs foster linguistic and cultural flexibility while, at the same time, resisting static, isomorphic notions of race/culture/language that reinforce traditional versions of difference without attending to shifting, evolving, and contested definitions of culture. Given that, can we imagine a project that puts speakers of the various and differentially marginalized varieties in conversation, so to speak, with urban, Cape Flats–focused Afrikaaps?

Beyond rural speakers of marginalized varieties and those beyond the Western Cape, how does *Afrikaaps* attend to the gendered dynamics and indexicalities associated with speaking Afrikaaps? In many ways, this is a question beyond *Afrikaaps* and for Hip Hop education more generally. Often, as Hip Hop education projects move from the streets to the schools, we are inevitably confronted with problematic practices within Hip Hop culture, specifically in relation to gender and sexuality (Alim et al., 2010, 2011; Haupt, 2001, 2008). Hip Hop is an important cultural and community practice that we must seek to sustain, but that we must also love enough to critique; the same goes for Hip Hop education. The vast majority of Hip Hop education research and pedagogy continues to focus on the many progressive and politically conscious aspects of Hip Hop, while ignoring the regressive elements of youth culture (and all culture), not to mention how those elements will be dealt with upon implementation in classrooms where young women and queer youth have an equal right to learn.

Despite our best intentions, patriarchal, heterosexist currents within Hip Hop culture (and dominant culture, more generally) will leak into the classroom space and be refracted upon students' learning experiences, and therefore must be dealt with directly. For *Afrikaaps*, would incorporating emerging queer-identified South African Hip Hop artists like Dope Saint Jude open up a space for discussing intersectional oppression and freedom? For Hip Hop education scholars, how might our work benefit by including a gendered analysis of classroom participation when using Hip Hop? What would our pedagogies look like if we acknowledged that Hip Hop can sometimes be a space for the expression of toxic masculinities, a site of exclusion and hurt for young women and queer youth, or a space where youth of color who do not identify as Black feel marginalized or silenced? In our own scholarship, including this chapter, what if we refrained from using the generic terms "youth" and "youth culture" and offered feminist perspectives that centered young girls in the research process?

When we began this chapter, we emphasized the important social and pedagogical roles of the arts in communities of color; we suggested that practitioners and theorists of CSPs, ourselves included, can learn from explorations of the arts in our communities; and we made explicit our belief that education, above all else, should provide us the tools we need to sustain our humanity, particularly for those of us living under dire, exploitative conditions of racialized, neoliberal, capitalist oppression and extreme inequality. Our questions, then, are not meant to derail the necessary and dynamic project of Hip Hop education. As many scholars have shown, Hip Hop continues to be one of the most powerful pedagogical approaches for teaching and learning with youth of color (Dimitriadis, 2001; Emdin, 2010; Hill, 2009; Low, 2011; Love, 2012; Petchauer & Hill, 2013). Rather, our "loving critique" can be read as a Hip Hop–inspired call to "represent," that is, to bring all of our skills to this pedagogical cipher in ways that constantly challenge ourselves and others to "show and prove," to do pedagogical work that allows us to escape with our souls—because, as Bliksemstraal reminded us in "Afrikaaps Is Legal," *hy vat my taal maar kannie my siel vattie.*

REFERENCES

Afrikaaps. (2011). *Afrikaaps*. The Glasshouse. Capetown, South Africa.

Alim, H. S. (2006). *Roc the mic right: The language of Hip Hop culture.* New York, NY: Routledge.

Alim, H. S. (2007). "The Whig party don't exist in my hood": Knowledge, reality, and education in the Hip Hop Nation. In H. S. Alim & J. Baugh (Eds.), *Talkin Black talk: Language, education, and social change* (pp. 15–29). New York, NY: Teachers College Press.

Alim, H. S., Ibrahim, A., & Pennycook, A. (Eds.). (2009). *Global linguistic flows: Hip Hop cultures, youth identities, and the politics of language.* London, UK: Routledge.

Alim, H. S., Lee, J., & Mason Carris, L. (2010). "Short, fried-rice-eating Chinese emcees and good-hair havin Uncle Tom niggas": Performing race and ethnicity in freestyle rap battles. *Journal of Linguistic Anthropology, 20*(1), 116–133.

Alim, H. S., Lee, J., & Mason Carris, L. (2011). Moving the crowd, 'crowding' the emcee: The coproduction and constestation of Black normativity in freestyle rap battles. *Discourse & Society, 22*(4), pp. 422–439.

Alim, H. S., & Paris, D. (2015). Whose language gap? Critical and culturally sustaining pedagogies as necessary challenges to racializing hegemony. *Journal of Linguistic Anthropology, 25*(1) [Invited forum, "Bridging 'the Language Gap'"], pp. 66–86.

Baker, H. (1993). *Black studies, rap, and the academy.* Chicago, IL: University of Chicago Press.

Banks, A. (2011). *Digital griots: African American rhetoric in a multimedia age.* Chicago, IL: NCTE/CCCC and Southern Illinois University Press.

Davids, Achmat. (2011). *The Afrikaans of the Cape Muslims.* Pretoria, South Africa: Protea Book House.

Dimitriadis, G. (2001). *Performing identity/performing culture: Hip Hop as text, pedagogy, and lived practice.* New York, NY: Peter Lang.

Du Bois, W. E. B. (1963, 2009 [ebook]). The souls of black folk. *Journal of Pan African Studies.*

Emdin, C. (2010). *Urban science education for the hip-hop generation.* New York, NY: Sense Publishers.

Fanon, F. (1967). *Black skins, white masks.* London, UK: Pluto Press.

Foucault, M. (1980). What is an author? In D. Bouchard (Ed.), *Language, Counter-Memory, Practice: Selected Essays and Interviews* (D. Bouchard & S. Simon, trans.). Oxford, UK: Basil Blackwell.

Gates, H. L. (1988). *The signifying monkey: A theory of African-American literary criticism.* Oxford, UK, & New York, NY: Oxford University Press.

Haupt, A. (2001). Black thing: Hip Hop nationalism, "race" and gender in Prophets of da City and Brasse vannie Kaap. In Zimitri Erasmus (Ed.), *Coloured by History, Shaped by Place.* Cape Town, South Africa: Kwela Books & SA History Online.

Haupt, A. (2008). *Stealing empire: P2P, intellectual property and Hip Hop subversion.* Cape Town, South Africa: HSRC Press.

Haupt, A. (2012). *Static: Race & representation in post-apartheid music, media & film.* Cape Town, South Africa: HSRC Press.

Haupt, A. (2014). Interrogating piracy: Race, colonialism and ownership. In L. Eckstein and A. Schwarz (Eds.), *Postcolonial piracy: Media distribution and cultural production in the global south.* London, UK: Bloomsbury.

Heugh, K. (2012). The case against bilingual and multilingual education in South Africa. *PRAESA Occasional Papers* No. 6. Retrieved from http://www.praesa.org.za/files/2012/07/Paper6.pdf

Hill, M. L. (2009). *Beats, rhymes and classroom life: Hip Hop pedagogy and the politics of identity.* New York, NY: Teachers College Press.

Ibrahim, A. (2009). Takin Hip Hop to a whole nother level: Métissage, affect, and pedagogy in a global Hip Hop nation. In H. S. Alim, A. Ibrahim, & A. Pennycook (Eds.), *Global linguistic flows: Hip hop cultures, youth identities, and the politics of language.* New York, NY: Routledge.

Ladson-Billings, G. (2014). Culturally relevant pedagogy 2.0: a.k.a. the remix. *Harvard Educational Review, 84*(1), 74–84.

Love, B. (2012). *Hip Hop's Li'l Sistas speak: Negotiating identities and politics in the New South.* New York, NY: Peter Lang.

Low, B. E. (2011). *Slam school: Learning through conflict in the Hip Hop and spoken word classroom.* Stanford, CA: Stanford University Press.

Makoe, P., & McKinney, C. (2014). Linguistic ideologies in multilingual South African suburban schools. *Journal of Multilingual and Multicultural Development, 35*(7), 658–673.

McKinney, C. (2007). "If I speak English, does it make me less black anyway?" Race and English in South African desegregated schools." *English Academy Review, 24*(2), 6–24.

Paris, D. (2012). Culturally sustaining pedagogy: A needed change in stance, terminology, and practice. *Educational Researcher, 41*(3), 93–97.

Paris, D., & Alim, H. S. (2014). What are we seeking to sustain through culturally sustaining pedagogy? A loving critique forward. *Harvard Educational Review, 84*(1), 85–100.

Perry, I. (2004). *Prophets of the hood: Politics and poetics in Hip Hop.* Durham, NC: Duke University Press.

Petchauer, E., & Hill, M. L. (Eds.). (2013). *Schooling Hip Hop: Expanding Hip Hop based education across the curriculum.* New York, NY: Teachers College Press.

Rose, T. (1994). *Black noise: Rap music and black culture in contemporary America.* Hanover, PA, and London, UK: Wesleyan University Press.

Schloss, J. G. (2004). *Making beats: The art of sample-based Hip Hop.* Hanover, CT: Wesleyan University Press.

Valley, D. (Director). (2010). *Afrikaaps* [Motion picture]. Plexus Films: South Africa.

CHAPTER 10

Do You Hear What I Hear?

Raciolinguistic Ideologies and Culturally Sustaining Pedagogies

Jonathan Rosa
Stanford University

Nelson Flores
University of Pennsylvania

Scholars calling for the development of culturally sustaining pedagogies often point to the need for new educational approaches in response to dramatic demographic shifts that have transformed the nation's ethnoracial makeup (Paris, 2012; Paris & Alim, 2014). Now that students of color predominate within U.S. public schools, the marginalization of the linguistic and cultural practices of these students can no longer be attributed to their "minority" status. The rapidly rising U.S. Latinx[1] population is central to this changing cultural, linguistic, and ethnoracial terrain. In this chapter, we focus on the ways that culturally sustaining pedagogies can reframe our thinking about language learning among Latinx students—"heritage Spanish learners" and "English language learners" alike. Specifically, we show how "asset-based pedagogies," which seek to position Latinx students' linguistic practices as resources rather than deficits by building on them to facilitate standardized language learning, can inadvertently contribute to the reproduction of the very forms of stigmatization that they seek to overcome. By embracing Latinx students' cultural and linguistic practices only insofar as they contribute to the learning of "academic language," asset-based pedagogies are often rooted in the notion that "home languages" and "academic languages" are empirically discrete categories rather than ideological constructions. These asset-based pedagogies are based on the presumption that students of color will become academically successful when they learn to produce the appropriate academic codes. However, we demonstrate the ways that the linguistic practices of students of color are systematically misheard and devalued regardless of the extent to which they might seem to correspond to standardized academic language. These mishearings and devaluations are linked to forms of linguistic profiling (Alim, 2004; Baugh, 2007; Zentella, 2014) that people of color face when communicating in "White public space" (Hill, 1998).[2] Jane Hill defines "White public space" as "a morally significant set of contexts that are the most important sites of the practices of a racializing hegemony, in which Whites are invisibly normal, and in which racialized populations are visibily marginal and the objects of monitoring ranging from individual judgment to Official English legislation" (1998, p. 682). Building on these analyses of race and language, we suggest that perceptions of different populations' language use as "academic" or "unacademic" should be understood in relation to "raciolinguistic ideologies," which conflate certain racialized bodies with linguistic deficiency unrelated to any objective linguistic practices, and highlight the ways in which culturally sustaining pedagogies can challenge the educational inequalities that these ideologies (re)produce.

In this chapter we seek to contribute to the emergent literature on culturally sustaining pedagogies by entering into critical dialogue with advocates of asset-based approaches to language education. We stand in solidarity with the view that deficit-based approaches to language diversity are stigmatizing and contribute to the reproduction of educational inequality. However, we question some of the underlying assumptions in many asset-based approaches—specifically, the discourses of "appropriateness" that lie at their core, and the ways that such discourses devalue Latinx students' linguistic practices. Discourses of appropriateness are tied to respectability politics. For people of color, respectability politics often frame racial inequality as the product of individual behaviors rather than structural processes (Harris, 2014). The implication is that if marginalized populations would engage in adequately respectable or appropriate behaviors, they would avoid stigmatization. However, as we have seen with countless cases, including President Barack Obama (Alim & Smitherman, 2012), racialized populations can be stigmatized regardless of their behavior. When it comes to language, these discourses of appropriateness, we argue, involve the conceptualization of standardized linguistic practices as a discrete set of linguistic forms that are understood to be appropriate for academic settings. Examples of discourses of linguistic appropriateness include the notion that for students of color, the goal of language education is the mastery of mainstream spoken and written language norms. This is one of the ways in which the thinking that students of color "should conform to White, middle-class social norms and identity representations persists" (Ladson-Billings, 1999, p. 196). Such "one-way" or "assimilate into Whiteness" thinking continually places the onus on students of color to modify their behavior so that they embody appropriateness (Paris, 2016, p. 5).

In contrast, we seek to highlight the racialized ideas about language through which different racialized persons come to be constructed as engaging in appropriately academic linguistic practices. Specifically, we suggest that the ideological construction and value of standardized linguistic practices are anchored in what we term *raciolinguistic ideologies*—ideologies that conflate certain racialized persons with linguistic deficiency irrespective of their empirical linguistic practices. That is, raciolinguistic ideologies produce racialized language users who are constructed as linguistically deviant even when engaging in linguistic practices positioned as normative or innovative when produced by privileged White language users.[3]

This raciolinguistic perspective builds on the critique of the White gaze—a perspective that privileges dominant White perspectives on the linguistic and cultural practices of racialized communities—that is central to calls for enacting culturally sustaining pedagogies (Paris & Alim, 2014). We, too, seek to reframe racialized populations outside of this White gaze and hope to answer the question of what pedagogical innovations are possible if "the goal of teaching and learning with youth of color was not ultimately to see how closely students could perform White middle-class norms but to explore, honor, extend, and problematize their heritage and community practices" (Paris & Alim, 2014, p. 86). The framework of raciolinguistic ideologies allows us to examine not only the "eyes" of Whiteness but also its "mouth" and "ears." Specifically, a raciolinguistic perspective seeks to understand how the White gaze is attached both to a speaking subject who engages in the idealized linguistic practices of Whiteness and to a listening subject who hears and interprets the linguistic practices of Latinx students as deviant. This "deviance" is based on the racial positioning of Latinxs in society as opposed to empirical characteristics of their language use.[4] As with the White gaze, the White speaking and listening subject should be understood not as a biographical individual but rather as an ideological position and mode of perception that shapes our racialized society. In this sense, White listening subjectivities are inhabited and enacted not simply by individual White people, but also potentially people of color, as well as seemingly inanimate objects such as institutions and assessments. Thus, it is crucial to analyze the ways that a range of actors and entities privilege hegemonic Whiteness as it pertains to language and other social practices.

Here we explore the ways that raciolinguistic ideologies affect the education of Latinx students designated as long-term English learners (i.e., students who have been designated as English language learners for 7 or more years) and heritage Spanish language learners (i.e., students who have learned Spanish primarily at home or in other settings outside of school). These educational categories are typically thought to classify distinct populations and linguistic practices and are thus conventionally analyzed separately. However, by theorizing raciolinguistic ideologies, we offer a perspective from which long-term English learners and heritage Spanish language learners can be understood to inhabit a shared position as raciolinguistic Others vis-à-vis the White listening subject. Throughout the chapter, we illustrate how asset-based approaches to language education, which might appear to embrace Latinx students' linguistic practices as valuable resources rather than handicaps, in fact reproduce inequality by positioning their linguistic practices as less "appropriate" for academic settings than others. These asset-based pedagogies are particularly deceptive because they appear to value linguistic diversity, yet they are ultimately anchored in the notion that only particular groups need to change their linguistic practices in order to experience educational achievement. Asset-based pedagogies often require Latinx students to model their linguistic practices after the White speaking subject despite the fact that the White listening subject continues to perceive these students' language use in stigmatizing ways. In contrast, culturally sustaining pedagogies can help us to reimagine the linguistic practices of Latinx students not simply as starting points from which to learn appropriate academic language, but as legitimate practices in their own right.

RACIOLINGUISTIC IDEOLOGIES AND LONG-TERM ENGLISH LEARNERS

Long-term English learners have been defined in the literature as students designated as English learners for 7 or more years (Menken & Kleyn, 2010). Scholars have argued that subtractive language education that has failed to build on the home linguistic practices of long-term English learners has led to a situation in which their "native languages have not been fully developed in school and instead have been largely replaced by English" (Menken & Kleyn, 2010, pp. 399–400). Based on this framing, Menken and Kleyn (2010) argue that "the education of these students must be additive, particularly in the area of academic literacy, so that we provide students with a strong foundation as they move to higher grades" (p. 414).

This exemplifies a typical asset-based approach, which attempts to value minoritized linguistic practices as starting points to build on, as opposed to a culturally sustaining pedagogies approach, which attempts to reimagine minoritized linguistic practices not simply as starting points but rather as central components of all stages of learning across contexts. We understand from personal experience the appealing nature of such an asset-based approach to working with this population of students, as Nelson worked closely with Menken and Kleyn in developing the original asset-based framework in response to deficit framings of this student population. Yet, as the work was taken up in ways that will be examined below, we began to identify limitations to the framework. Though we continue to support the idea of building on, rather than replacing, the home linguistic practices of students who are categorized as long-term English learners, we realized that such framing places the brunt of the responsibility on these students to mimic the linguistic practices of the White speaking subject while reifying the White listening subject's racialization of these students' linguistic practices (Flores, Kleyn, & Menken, 2015).

This racialization of language can be found in deficit perspectives that are often used to describe the linguistic practices of students categorized as long-term English learners. In a widely circulated policy report on long-term English learners, Olsen (2010) describes these students as having "high functioning social language, very weak academic language, and significant deficits in reading and writing skills" (p. 2). She also describes them as lacking "rich oral language and literacy skills in scholastic English needed to participate and succeed in academic work" and exhibiting "little to no literacy skills in either language and often only a skeleton academic vocabulary in their home language" (p. 23). In short, long-term English learners are seen as deficient in the academic language that is appropriate for a school context and necessary for academic success.

The solutions Olsen (2010) offers for confronting the challenges faced by long-term English learners focus exclusively on changing their linguistic practices. One recommendation calls for long-term English learners to master the language deemed appropriate for school by placing them in "Academic Language Development" classes that focus "on powerful oral language, explicit literacy development, instruction in the academic uses of English, high quality writing, extensive reading of relevant texts, and an emphasis on academic language and complex vocabulary" (p. 33). Another calls for long-term English learners to receive additive instruction that develops their home language through placement in "native speakers classes" that are "designed for native speakers, and include explicit literacy instruction aligned to the literacy standards in English and designed for skill transfer across languages" (p. 35). In both of these recommendations, the solution to the problem posed by long-term English learners is squarely focused on molding them into White speaking subjects who have mastered the empirical linguistic practices deemed appropriate for a school context.

This appropriateness discourse overlooks the ways that the very construction of a linguistic category such as long-term English learner is produced by the White listening subject and is not based on discrete linguistic practices. In fact, if we look at their complete linguistic repertoires across languages and varieties, we find that these so-called long-term English learners are adept at using their bilingualism in strategic and innovative ways—indeed, in ways that might be considered quite appropriate and desirable were they animated by a privileged White student (Flores et al., 2015).

An example from an interview with Tamara,[5] a Latina New York City high school student classified as a long-term English learner, illustrates this point (Menken & Kleyn, 2010). This interview was conducted as part of the aforementioned study examining the schooling experiences of long-term English learners in which Nelson participated (Menken & Kleyn, 2010). At the time of the interview Tamara was a sophomore who was classified as a long-term English learner because she had failed to pass the state English language proficiency exam throughout her schooling career. Her parents were both born in Mexico, but Tamara was born in the Bronx. Tamara and her parents communicate primarily in Spanish, though Tamara claimed to sometimes "mix English with Spanish." Like Tamara, her siblings are bilingual, and she reported frequently moving back and forth between the languages in her interactions with them. She also reported texting and emailing in both languages, depending on the person with whom she was communicating. During an interview, she described the ways she strategically uses her English and Spanish to communicate:

> *Researcher:* So you mix English and Spanish a lot? A little?
> *Tamara:* It depends, 'cause some people they know English and Spanish, but not a lot of Spanish. And sometimes they don't know Spanish at all. I'll have to talk to them in English. Well everybody I know speaks English.
> *Researcher:* Anyone you know who speaks Spanish, is there usually some mixing?
> *Tamara:* Yeah, like I have these friends downstairs. There's some that speak English, but it's less than 50 percent that they speak English, so I have to speak Spanish. And there's some that I speak English, English only.

Were Tamara a privileged White student engaging in English linguistic practices in the ways that she did in this interview, her linguistic practices would likely be perceived differently. In fact, were she a privileged White student who was able to engage in the bilingual language practices that she described, she might even be perceived as linguistically gifted and as a talented cultural broker more broadly. Tamara not only showed her competence in English during the interview (which was conducted entirely in English), but she also demonstrated her understanding of appropriateness—namely, that she should use English, Spanish, or a combination thereof in ways that accommodate her interlocutor. She understands the necessity of adapting her speech to the situation in which she finds herself. Yet the language proficiency exam continues to "hear" Tamara as an English language learner. In this sense, the state language proficiency exam operates as a particular form of the White listening subject by classifying students like Tamara as linguistically deficient despite evidence that illustrates their linguistic dexterity.

Tamara faces stigmatization based on ideological perspectives from which students designated as long-term English learners may be recognized as engaging in English language practices that are appropriate outside of an academic context, yet are unable to master English language practices that are necessary for success in school. Indeed, Olsen (2010) articulates a dichotomous framing of home and school linguistic practices when she describes the home language of long-term English learners "as commonly referred to with terms such as 'Spanglish' or 'Chinglish,' and while it is expressive and functional in many social situations, it is not a strong foundation for the language demands of academic work in Standard English" (p. 23). In other words, the home linguistic practices of long-term English learners are seen as appropriate outside of school but inappropriate inside school. In addition, their home linguistic practices are seen as contributing little to the development of the linguistic practices deemed appropriate in a school context. Valdés (2015) argues that these strict distinctions between home and school linguistic practices inform mainstream educational approaches to language learning that undermine and stigmatize Latinxs' bilingual "multicompetencies" across generations.

Another excerpt from the interview with Tamara also complicates this dichotomous framing of home and school language proficiencies. This is best illustrated by her response to a question about how she felt taking a "Spanish for Native Speakers" class that was explicitly designed to teach her and other long-term English learners the Spanish deemed appropriate for school:

> I felt like it was good. I thought that I was actually learning more about my original language that I have at home, and I think it was very helpful because I had to do some speech in church, so actually working in this class actually helped me with that speech. It was good.

In contrast to Olsen's assertion that the home linguistic practices of long-term English learners are not a strong foundation for academic work, Tamara articulated the ways that the linguistic practices in which she engages at church and at school complement one another. Tamara is able to build bidirectional relationships between home and school that transcend the crude dichotomy of academic versus nonacademic that lies at the core of the long-term English learner label. Tamara's case dovetails with Brooks's (2016) analysis of long-term English learners' literacy practices, which highlights the ways in which these students' English language abilities are systematically overlooked or erased by researchers, policymakers, and educators. Were Tamara a privileged White student, questions would never be raised as to whether her home linguistic practices provide a strong foundation for what she does in school. Instead, these connections would be seen as a natural outcome of the education process—a natural outcome denied to Tamara because of her racial positioning in U.S. society.

Tamara's experiences demonstrate how asset-based pedagogies that seek to build on the home linguistic practices of Latinx students designated as long-term English learners are fundamentally limited in that they reproduce the notion that only particular practices are legitimate or appropriate for academic settings. A culturally sustaining pedagogies approach would allow us to see how Tamara's home linguistic practices are not simply starting points from which to learn academic language, but rather how Tamara is already engaging in similar linguistic practices at home and in school despite how raciolinguistic ideologies make it difficult to hear her in this way. The next section explores the ways in which Latinx students designated as heritage Spanish learners are faced with similar raciolinguistic ideologies that continually mishear their linguistic practices as inappropriate, incorrect, or inadequate.

RACIOLINGUISTIC IDEOLOGIES AND
HERITAGE LANGUAGE LEARNERS

Heritage language learning is often framed as addressing issues of language loss and/or recovery, or of language shift away from one's "native language" to state-sponsored languages. Indeed, there are "problems of definition" (Valdés, 2005, p. 411) in determining what constitutes a heritage language and its speakers. Definitions range in focus from membership in a particular community and personal connection through family background, on the one hand, to particular kinds of linguistic proficiency, on the other (Carreira, 2004). Fishman (2001) notes that based on this range of definitions, "heritage language" can be used in the United States to alternately refer to languages of peoples indigenous to the Americas (e.g., Navajo), languages used by the European groups that colonized the Americas (e.g., German), and languages used by immigrants arriving in the United States after it became a nation-state (e.g., Korean). Many languages fit into more than one of these groups (e.g., Spanish, which was a colonial heritage language before it was an immigrant heritage language). Focusing on applied perspectives, Valdés (2001) points out that "foreign language educators use the term [heritage language learner] to refer to a language student who is raised in a home where a non-English language is spoken, who speaks or at least understands the language, and who is to some degree bilingual in that language and in English" (p. 38).

Similar to the interventions proposed for long-term English learners, many heritage language programs distinguish between the acquisition of language skills that are relevant only to restricted domains outside of school settings (e.g., homes and communities) and skills that are associated with success in mainstream educational institutions. From these perspectives, the goal of heritage language learning is to build academic language proficiency in one's "native language." These programs seek to value the skills students bring to the classroom while expanding their "academic" language repertoires in their "native" language. At the same time, they often reproduce standard language ideologies that draw rigid distinctions between appropriate "academic" and "social" language use. This constructed distinction between appropriate academic and social language obscures the ways that academic language is effectively used outside of formal school contexts and social language is effectively used in conventional classroom settings. Despite the constructed nature of this distinction, only some groups are stigmatized for using so-called social practices in academic settings. As with the case of long-term English learners, the discourse of appropriateness here serves as a vehicle for the White listening subject to position heritage learners as deficient for engaging in practices that would likely be seen as dexterous for privileged White students.

It is clear that advocates and theorists of appropriateness-based models of heritage language education seek to value the linguistic and cultural practices of language-minoritized students. For example, Valdés (2001) calls into question the notion of the "mythical" bilingual with equal proficiencies in two languages. She also emphasizes the arbitrary nature of characterizing "prestige" varieties of linguistic practice as inherently more sophisticated than "nonprestige" varieties. This distinction is based on the sociolinguistic concept of diglossia (Fishman, 1967), which refers to the ways that language varieties are positioned as formal or "high" (i.e., prestige) and informal or "low" (i.e., nonprestige). Highlighting the ideological nature of this distinction, Valdés (2001) notes that there are features of language that are familiar to nonprestige speakers yet unfamiliar to prestige speakers and vice versa. In this formulation, the problem is not that nonprestige speakers possess "a somewhat narrower range of lexical and syntactic alternatives" (p. 46), but that they do not use the prestige variety. We extend this argument to suggest that the notion of prestige language reflects a form of linguistic normativity anchored in raciolinguistic ideologies and serves as a coded way of describing racialized populations that is unrelated to empirical linguistic practices. We suggest that people are positioned as speakers of prestige or nonprestige language varieties based not on what they actually do with language but, rather, how they are heard by the White listening subject.

Valdés and Geoffrion-Vinci (1998) provide us with a point of entry into illustrating this claim through their description of Estela, a second-generation Chicana from Texas who grew up speaking English and Spanish, has a BA in Spanish, and is a "doctoral student in a Spanish literature department at a prestigious university" (p. 473). Despite these bilingual experiences and academic credentials, some of Estela's professors described her Spanish as "limited" and questioned the legitimacy of her admission to the doctoral program. Meanwhile, some of her fellow students laughed when she spoke Spanish in class. Valdés and Geoffrion-Vinci face significant difficulty when they seek to identify the specific linguistic issues involved in the stigmatization of Estela's Spanish:

> When pressed to describe what they perceive to be her limitations, Estela's professors can give few details. . . . Most of the faculty agree that Estela's written work . . . is quite competent. Still, there is something about her speech that strikes members of the Spanish department faculty as not quite adequate and causes them to rank her competence even below that of Anglophones who have acquired Spanish as a second language. (p. 473)

Estela has clearly enjoyed a great deal of academic success, and yet her professors continue to "hear" her as having linguistic deficits that they cannot quite identify. Taking a raciolinguistic perspective allows us to situate this hearing within the racial hierarchies of U.S. society. As a second-generation Chicana, Estela's Spanish language use is stigmatized vis-à-vis European and Latin American varieties of Spanish, which are privileged in mainstream Spanish language learning at the university level in the United States. This stigmatization is based on the notion that U.S. Latinxs are not socialized to correct Spanish or English linguistic practices by their families and communities. This reflects the deficit-based perspectives from which their bilingualism is viewed as a problem rather than a strength (Rosa, 2014; Zentella, 2005). What if the problem is not Estela's limited communicative repertoire but the racialization of her language use and the inability of the White listening subject to hear her racialized body speaking appropriately? The notion that there is something unidentifiable, yet inferior, about Estela's speech—so much so that it is viewed as less proficient than that of students who learned Spanish as a second language—suggests that raciolinguistic ideologies are at play in shaping perceptions of her language use as somehow insufficiently academic. These ideologies lead to situations in which racialized students such as Estela, whose lived experiences of bilingualism could be interpreted as significantly more sociolinguistically dexterous than her classmates and even many of her professors, are perceived as linguistically inferior and in need of remediation.

Valdés (2001) analyzes these contradictions, noting that heritage learners often possess the ability to "carry out conversations on everyday topics with ease and confidence and may even be able to understand rapidly spoken language that includes the subtle use of humor" and goes on to state that "in comparison to students who have acquired the language exclusively in the classroom, the heritage language student may seem quite superior in some respects and quite limited in others" (p. 47). For many heritage language education advocates, the solution to this contradiction is to embrace an asset-based approach where heritage language learners must build from proficiencies developed outside of the classroom in order to master the language that is appropriate in an academic setting. However, from a raciolinguistic perspective, heritage language learners' linguistic practices are devalued not because they fail to meet a particular linguistic standard, but because they are spoken by racialized bodies and thus heard as illegitimate by the White listening subject. That heritage speakers with highly nuanced language skills are positioned as less skillful than their counterparts "who have acquired the language exclusively in the classroom" is precisely the power of raciolinguistic ideologies as they apply to conceptions of heritage language issues. More recently, Valdés (2015) has shown how the "curricularization of language" stems from and contributes to problematic language ideologies that arbitrarily associate some language practices with school uses and others with social uses. This insight is connected to our critique of asset-based approaches to heritage language education, which are often rooted in arbitrary distinctions between linguistic practices that are appropriate for academic and social uses. These asset-based approaches do not sufficiently address the ways that the language practices of students of color are systematically heard as nonacademic based on raciolinguistic ideologies enacted by White listening subjects.

By approaching heritage language learning with the understanding that the social positions of different language users, rather than simply their linguistic repertoires, impact how their linguistic practices are heard, we can move beyond the idea that establishing the legitimacy of all linguistic practices will somehow lead to the eradication of linguistic stigmatization. This involves shifting the focus of both research and practice in language education from analyzing linguistic forms to analyzing positions of enunciation and reception; such a shift makes it possible to see how different linguistic practices can be stigmatized in strikingly similar ways based on marginalized speakers' shared, racialized positions of enunciation and particular listeners' hegemonic positions of reception. Conversely, similar linguistic practices can be valued in strikingly different ways based on raciolinguistic ideologies. For example, Hill's (2008) analysis of "Mock Spanish" practices (e.g., "no problemo," "el cheap-o," etc.) shows how "language mixing" can be celebrated for White monolingual English speakers and yet stigmatized for Latinxs positioned as heritage speakers. When U.S. Latinxs engage in similar practices, such as using *rufo* instead of *techo* for "roof" or *parqueando* instead of *estacionando* for "parking," they are often chastised for using inferior Spanglish forms as opposed to "pure" Spanish. In fact, heritage language learning is often regarded as an effort toward cleansing particular populations of these so-called impurities. Linguistic purity—like racial purity—is a powerful ideological construct. We should seek to understand the perspectives from which such forms of purity and impurity are constructed and perceived rather than focusing on the forms themselves. Thus, we must redirect attention away from empirical linguistic practices and toward raciolinguistic ideologies that overdetermine people as particular kinds of language users.

For Latinx heritage language learners such as Estela, culturally sustaining pedagogies present the possibility of a radically different set of educational experiences from those described above. How might Estela's language be heard differently by a Chicanx professor or a professor well versed in the ways that Chicanx Spanish has been used across a range of spoken and written contexts, encompassing the so-called academic Spanish language skills embraced in university classrooms? What if culturally specific Spanish language use in everyday Latinx communities were incorporated into all aspects of the curriculum? These shifts would allow us to reimagine the Spanish language skills Estela learned at home and in the community as central to her educational success rather than as starting points from which to learn "legitimate" Spanish.

NEW WAYS OF HEARING IN LANGUAGE EDUCATION

In this chapter we have sought to contribute to efforts toward imagining culturally sustaining pedagogies by introducing a critical raciolinguistic perspective. We use this perspective to examine the ways that discourses of appropriateness, which permeate asset-based approaches to language education, are complicit in normalizing the reproduction of the White gaze by marginalizing the linguistic practices of language-minoritized populations in U.S. society. Specifically, we analyze the raciolinguistic ideologies that connect asset-based educational approaches to teaching Latinx students designated as long-term English learners and heritage Spanish learners. We argue that what links members of these different (though often overlapping) groups is not their lack of linguistic proficiency but their racial positioning in society and how this position affects the ways their linguistic practices are heard.

Therefore, the solution to the marginalization of language-minoritized students cannot be to add linguistic practices to their repertoires—as many asset-based approaches to language education suggest—but instead to engage with, confront, and ultimately dismantle the racialized hierarchy of U.S. society. This effort, we argue, must be central to the vision for and implementation of culturally sustaining pedagogies. Simply adding "appropriate" forms of language to the linguistic repertoires of language-minoritized students will not lead to social transformation. As our examples show, even when Latinx long-term English learners and heritage Spanish learners adopt idealized linguistic practices, they are still heard as deficient language users. Attempting to teach Latinx students to engage in the idealized linguistic practices of the White speaking subject does nothing to challenge the underlying racism of the White listening subject. Asset-based approaches to language education inadvertently legitimate and strengthen, rather than challenge, the marginalization of language-minoritized Latinx students.

We are not suggesting that people from racialized or language-minoritized communities should not seek to engage in linguistic practices deemed appropriate by mainstream society. However, we contend that the question of whether members of racialized communities are accepted as appropriately engaging in these linguistic practices continues to be determined by the White listening subject, not by the speakers' actual practices. Therefore, antiracist social transformation cannot be based solely on teaching Latinx students to engage in the linguistic practices of the White speaking subject, but must also work actively to dismantle the hierarchies that produce the White listening subject. We are also not suggesting that advocates of asset-based approaches to language education should abandon all of their efforts to legitimize the linguistic practices of their language-minoritized Latinx students. Instead, we suggest that shifting the focus to scrutiny of the White listening subject may open up possibilities for reconceptualizing language education in ways that move beyond appropriateness-based approaches.

Culturally sustaining pedagogies that engage with the dynamic linguistic practices of language-minoritized Latinx students and raises questions about issues of language and power mark an important starting point for developing this alternative approach. We suggest that a careful consideration of raciolinguistic ideologies and the White listening subject that produces them adds an important element to this framework. Specifically, it allows for the development of pedagogies that move away from a sole focus on the speaking subject and examines the role of the listening subject in producing "competent" and "incompetent" language users. This shifts the conversation from trying to improve the linguistic practices of language-minoritized Latinx students toward challenging the ways that their linguistic practices are taken up and interpreted by the White listening subject.

Were this approach applied in the educational contexts analyzed in this chapter, the challenges faced by Latinx long-term English learners and heritage Spanish learners could be reconceptualized not as problems produced by linguistic deficits but as products of racial and linguistic hierarchies. This approach would also empower teachers to move beyond pedagogies geared toward responding to students' purported linguistic deficiencies or "gaps" and to develop a more robust vision of how language-minoritized Latinx students' educational experiences could combat raciolinguistic ideologies. These insights open up the possibility of theorizing the education of language-minoritized Latinx students as part of broader conflicts and struggles that provide these students with tools to challenge the forms of marginalization with which they are faced. This is a powerful shift from teaching students to follow rules of appropriateness to working with them as they struggle to imagine and enact alternative, more radically inclusive realities.

The critical perspectives discussed in this chapter point to the benefits of reframing language education from an asset-based approach embedded within a discourse of appropriateness toward a culturally sustaining pedagogies approach that seeks to denaturalize standardized linguistic categories. This offers the possibility of shifting language education from inadvertently perpetuating the racial status quo to participating in struggles against the ideological processes associated with the White speaking and White listening subject. While this approach to language education cannot singularly eradicate the forms of marginalization students of color face in mainstream schools, it can powerfully disrupt appropriateness-based approaches to language education in ways that might link to larger social movements that challenge the racial status quo.

NOTES

This chapter is an adapted version of Flores, N., & Rosa, J. (2015). Undoing appropriateness: Raciolinguistic ideologies and language diversity in education. *Harvard Educational Review, 85*(2), 149–171.

1. We use "Latinx" as a gender nonbinary label for U.S.–based populations of Latin American descent. It serves as an alternative to "Latina/o" or "Latin@" as male/female gender-inclusive labels, as well as labels such as "Hispanic" and "Latino." We use "Latina" or "Latino" when referring to self-identified females or males, respectively.

2. In Flores and Rosa (2015), we build on the work of Alim (2004) to compare the racialized ways in which Latinx and African American students' language practices are systematically misheard in mainstream educational settings.

3. Importantly, the normative forms of Whiteness associated with these raciolinguistic ideologies intertwine race, class, and language. Thus, we are not claiming that all White people benefit from these ideologies in the same ways, nor that all people of color are stigmatized by them in the same ways. Instead, we seek to highlight how imagined, idealized forms of class-privileged Whiteness position particular linguistic and cultural practices as more or less educationally legitimate, and how these ideologies shape the ways that different groups' practices are interpreted.

4. For an analysis of the ways that raciolinguistic ideologies stigmatize not just Latinx students, but racialized and language-minoritized populations in general, see Flores and Rosa (2015).

5. All participant names are pseudonyms.

REFERENCES

Alim, H. S. (2004). Hearing what's not said and missing what is: Black language in white public space. In S. Kiesling & C. B. Paulson (Eds.), *Intercultural discourse and communication: The essential readings* (pp. 180–197). Malden, MA: Blackwell Publishing.

Alim, H. S., & Smitherman, G. (2012). *Articulate while black: Barack Obama, language, and race in the U.S.* New York, NY: Oxford.

Baugh, J. (2007). Linguistic contributions to the advancement of racial justice within and beyond the African diaspora. *Language and Linguistics Compass, 1*(4), 331–349.

Brooks, M. (2016). "Tell me what you are thinking": An investigation of five Latina LTELs constructing meaning with academic texts. *Linguistics & Education, 35,* 1–14.

Carreira, M. (2004). Seeking explanatory adequacy: A dual approach to understanding the term "heritage language learner." *Heritage Language Journal, 2*(1), 1–25.

Fishman, J. (1967). Bilingualism with and without diglossia: Diglossia with and without bilingualism. *Journal of Social Issues, 23*(2), 29–38.

Fishman, J. (2001). 300-plus years of heritage language education in the United States. In J. Kreeft Peyton, D. Ranard, & S. McGinnis (Eds.), *Heritage languages in America: Preserving a national resource* (pp. 81–99). Washington, DC: Center for Applied Linguistics.

Flores, N., Kleyn, T., & Menken, K. (2015). Looking holistically in a climate of partiality: Identities of students labeled "long-term English language learners." *Journal of Language, Identity, and Education, 14*(2), 113–132.

Flores, N., & Rosa, J. (2015). Undoing appropriateness: Raciolinguistic ideologies and language diversity in education. *Harvard Educational Review, 85*(2), 149–171.

Harris, F. C. (2014). The rise of respectability politics. *Dissent, 61*(1), 33–37.

Hill, J. H. (1998). Language, race, and white public space. *American Anthropologist, 100*(3), 680–689.

Hill, J. H. (2008). *The everyday language of white racism.* Malden, MA: Wiley-Blackwell.

Ladson-Billings, G. (1999). Preparing teachers for diversity: Historical perspectives, current trends, and future directions. In L. Darling-Hammond & G. Sykes (Eds.), *Teaching as the learning profession: Handbook of policy and practice* (pp. 86–125). San Francisco, CA: Jossey-Bass Publishers.

Menken, K., & Kleyn, T. (2010). The long-term impact of subtractive schooling in the educational experiences of secondary English language learners. *International Journal of Bilingual Education and Bilingualism, 13*(4), 399–417.

Olsen, L. (2010). *Reparable harm: Fulfilling the unkept promise of educational opportunity for California's long term English learners.* Long Beach, CA: Californians Together.

Paris, D. (2012). Culturally sustaining pedagogy: A needed change in stance, terminology, and practice. *Educational Researcher, 41*(3), 93–97.

Paris, D. (2016). On educating culturally sustaining teachers. *TeachingWorks Working Papers.* Retrieved from http://www.teachingworks.org/images/files/TeachingWorks_Paris.pdf.

Paris, D., & Alim, H. S. (2014). What are we seeking to sustain through culturally sustaining pedagogy? A loving critique forward. *Harvard Educational Review, 84*(1), 85–100.

Rosa, J. (2014). Learning ethnolinguistic borders: Language and the socialization of U.S. Latinas/os. In R. Rolón-Dow & J. G. Irizarry (Eds.), *Diaspora studies in education: Toward a framework for understanding the experiences of transnational communities* (pp. 39–60). New York, NY: Peter Lang.

Valdés, G. (2001). Heritage language students: Profiles and possibilities. In J. Kreeft Peyton, D. Ranard, & S. McGinnis (Eds.), *Heritage languages in America: Preserving a national resource* (pp. 37–80). Washington, DC: Center for Applied Linguistics.

Valdés, G. (2005). Bilingualism, heritage language learners, and SLA research: Opportunities lost or seized? *Modern Language Journal, 89*(3), 410–426.

Valdés, G. (2015). Latin@s and the intergenerational continuity of Spanish: The challenges of curricularizing language. *International Multilingual Research Journal, 9*(4), 253–273.

Valdés, G., & Geoffrion-Vinci, M. (1998). Chicano Spanish: The problem of "underdeveloped code" in bilingual repertoires. *Modern Language Journal, 82*(4), 473–501.

Zentella, A. C. (Ed.). (2005). *Building on strength: Language and literacy in Latino families and communities.* New York, NY: Teachers College Press.

Zentella, A. C. (2014). TWB (Talking while bilingual): Linguistic profiling of Latinxs, and other linguistic torquemadas. *Latino Studies, 12,* 620–635.

CHAPTER 11

Socially Just, Culturally Sustaining Pedagogy for Diverse Immigrant Youth

Possibilities, Challenges, and Directions

Stacey J. Lee
University of Wisconsin, Madison

Daniel Walsh
New York City Department of Education

The number of youth from immigrant families is growing in schools across the United States, but too often schools fail to welcome and prepare immigrant students to participate as equal members of society; in the words of Nancy Fraser (2003), institutions limit young people's ability to participate in society "on par with" their peers. Despite the nearly ubiquitous rhetoric around diversity, multiculturalism, and culturally relevant pedagogy, immigrant youth today, like those from previous generations, continue to encounter assimilative policies and practices that are premised on deficit perspectives of immigrant cultures and languages. As many scholars have argued, deficit perspectives marginalize youth and communities from schooling and limit opportunities. Immigrant youth who are English language learners (ELLs) are frequently tracked into ESL classes that focus solely on instrumental English acquisition at the expense of academic content (Callahan, 2005; Callahan, Wilkinson, & Muller, 2008; Valenzuela, 1999). Furthermore, such pedagogical practices do not equip young people with the critical literacy skills they need to decipher the myriad of images and sound bites with which they are daily bombarded. Current educational policies have further increased challenges for immigrant students who are ELLs and for schools working with ELLs (Menken, 2008). As a result of these policies, ELLs score lower on standardized tests, graduate from high school at lower rates, and are pushed out at higher rates than their native English-speaking peers (Fine, Stoudt, & Futch, 2005; Menken, 2008). These practices and policies lead to the subtraction of cultural resources (misrecognition), have possible long-term material consequences (maldistribution), and challenge immigrants' sense of belonging in the United States (Fraser, 1997).

In our previous collaborations, we (Danny, a high school educator, and Stacey, a university educator) worked to articulate the possibilities and challenges of a social justice education for low-income immigrant youth who are English language learners. As a white man from four generations of the New York City working class and a third-generation Chinese American woman from a middle-class family, we were acutely aware of how our identities primarily diverged from, yet at times converged with, those young people whom we studied and learned alongside. We were aware that immigrant youth who are ELLs and from low-income families faced a host of injustices inside and outside of schools, including deficit attitudes regarding their cultural and linguistic backgrounds, Eurocentric curricula, high-stakes testing, anti-immigrant policies and attitudes, racism, poverty, and limited economic opportunities.

Building on the work of political philosopher Nancy Fraser (1997, 2003, 2009), we argued that a social justice education for immigrant youth must *recognize* their diverse identities and experiences and simultaneously engage in the act of *redistribution* by giving students the tools to navigate and challenge existing material inequalities (Lee & Walsh, 2012, 2015). Furthermore, we supported an education that motivated immigrant students to work for a more just society for all, one that moves beyond liberal whitewashed notions of diversity and inclusion, postraciality, and "soft" multiculturalism. As this description suggests, our thinking was influenced by insights from culturally relevant pedagogy, critical multicultural education, and critical pedagogy. Here, we extend our work by engaging with Paris and Alim's latest conceptualization of culturally sustaining pedagogy. In particular, we are motivated by Paris and Alim's (2014) assertion regarding the centrality of cultural and linguistic flexibility in our globalized world and their idea that education must support students' evolving identities. Immigrant youth are embodiments of globalization and as such express amazing cultural and linguistic flexibility, and as young people living and learning across and beyond borders, they are constantly engaging in creative identity work.

In this chapter, we argue for a socially just, culturally sustaining pedagogy that builds on students' evolving identities and simultaneously prepares youth to challenge social injustices in "our demographically changing U.S. and global schools and communities" (Paris, 2012, p. 95). But what does the practice of a socially just, culturally sustaining pedagogy for diverse immigrant youth look like? What are the possibilities and challenges of a socially just, cultural sustaining pedagogy for immigrant youth?

To explore these questions, we draw primarily from our collaborative research, which focused on how Danny and his colleagues negotiated their commitment to social justice education for immigrant youth in an era of high-stakes testing at a high school in the Internationals Network for Public Schools. The 19 schools in the network are designed to serve the unique academic and socioemotional needs of recently arrived immigrant youth who are English language learners. In addition to schools in NYC, the network has helped to open schools in California and the DC area. Students attending schools in the Internationals Network come from over 100 countries, speak over 90 languages, and are primarily from working poor families; they come from diverse educational backgrounds, and their English literacy skills range from early elementary to approaching grade level. A significant number of students have limited and/or interrupted schooling, either in their countries of origin or in the United States. Compared to most urban public high schools, those in the Internationals Network have a strong record of successfully educating newcomer immigrant youth who are ELLs. In explaining the relative success of the Internationals, scholars have pointed to the Internationals' commitment to valuing the cultural and linguistic diversity of its students, the small size of the schools, the interdisciplinary project-based curriculum that incorporates language development, the collaborative team-based teaching, and performance-based assessment (Darling-Hammond, 1997; Jaffe-Walter, 2008; Jaffe-Walter & Lee, 2011). Additionally, many of the schools in the network employ teachers and other staff members who themselves have immigrated to the United States and/ or have lived and worked abroad and experienced cultural and linguistic dissonance. These adults draw on these experiences to inform their work with the students.

Our collaboration was motivated by an assumption that breaking down the traditional boundaries between researcher and participant would allow new perspectives to emerge (Erickson, 2006; Hawkins & Legler, 2004; Irizarry & Brown, 2014; Kinloch & San Pedro, 2014). We worked collaboratively to articulate the evolving research questions, analyze the data, and write up the results. Over the span of three semesters (November 2007–December 2008), Stacey observed Danny's classes with a focus on his practice (e.g., curriculum and pedagogical decisions) and on the students' class participation. In addition to data from Stacey's classroom observations and observations of teacher team meetings, our data include notes and transcriptions from Danny and Stacey's ongoing dialogues (face-to-face and via email) about Danny's teaching. At the time of our research collaboration, Danny had a master's degree in TESOL, taught 11th-grade English, and served as an instructional coach for language and literacy development and as the academic and personal advisor to a group of 13 students. As a founding faculty member of his high school, he had a deep understanding of the school from an insider's perspective and looked to the collaborative work as a way to get an outsider's perspective in the hopes that this would further improve his work with immigrant youth. Stacey came to the collaboration as an ethnographer who had focused on the challenges faced by immigrant youth. She was initially drawn to conducting research at the Internationals because she was interested in investigating school contexts that encourage a social justice approach to educating immigrant youth.

THE AMERICAN STUDIES CURRICULUM AND THE CONTEXT OF HIGH-STAKES TESTING

While immigrant youth personify the very cultural flexibility needed in a globalized world, educational policies continue to judge immigrant students against the standards of whiteness still dominant in the United States. When we began our research in 2007, Danny and the other members of the 11th-grade team at his school were grappling with the onslaught of high-stakes testing policies. In 2000 the state of New York mandated that all students, including newcomer English language learners, had to pass five Regents exams in order to earn a high school diploma. Since the implementation of this mandate, ELLs have struggled to pass the exams, and dropout rates among these students have increased (Menken, 2008).

In response to the concerns raised by the Regents exams requirement, Danny and his colleagues created an interdisciplinary American Studies curriculum, which aimed to draw on students' identities and encourage critical dispositions about social inequalities while also preparing students for the exams. During the 2007–2008 academic year, the American Studies curriculum included three units—Native American experiences, African American experiences and U.S. immigration—and in the 2008–2009 academic year it also included a unit on globalization. Each unit was designed to introduce students to critical understandings of the United States and to prepare students for the English and U.S. History Regents exams. While the team selected topics strategically based on what was likely to be covered on the exams, they presented the material in counterhegemonic perspectives, challenging dominant narratives about the United States.

DANNY'S PRACTICE: DRAWING ON STUDENTS' BACKGROUNDS AND CHALLENGING HEGEMONY

One of the first things that Stacey noticed when she began coding the fieldnotes from the observations of Danny's classes was that Danny engaged students' cultural backgrounds in every class she observed over the course of three semesters. In one of our early dialogues, Danny explained that he believed that it was important to connect to students' experiences and cultures, which required that he know something about where his students were from, including the historical and contemporary contexts of their countries of origin. He also noted that it was important to understand what life was like for them as immigrants, particularly the realities of living in New York City. Although Danny was clear that he didn't think it was realistic for teachers with students from diverse cultural and national and regional backgrounds to have deep knowledge about each student's backgrounds and/or to know the specific issues facing their neighborhoods, he asserted that the youth "are sources of knowledge." Indeed, the idea of learning from students was central to Danny's practice and to the practice of many of his colleagues at the Internationals. In the words of Ladson-Billings (2014), teachers in the network have a greater tendency to construct students as " . . . subjects in the instructional process, not mere objects" (p. 76).

Danny regularly drew on students' backgrounds in teaching concepts and vocabulary, and students responded enthusiastically by sharing their knowledge in large- and small-group discussions. In one class, for example, Danny, in preparing students for a reading about Native American perspectives on Thanksgiving, asked why some might consider the holiday a national day of mourning. When it became clear that students were confusing "morning" with "mourning," Danny offered a definition of "mourning" and then asked students to share examples of how people mourn in their native countries. Through this exercise, he engaged with students' previous knowledge and encouraged cultural exchange. Additionally, Danny would often ask students to write key curricular concepts on the whiteboard in their home languages. In this way, he sought to build their linguistic and cultural flexibility, as he recognized the link that such flexibility has "to access and power in U.S. and global contexts" (Paris & Alim, 2014, p. 87). Ultimately, the unit emphasized Native Americans' material and cultural dispossession, their resistance to it, and the need to repair both the cultural recognition and distribution of land/capital.

In the unit on immigration, Danny encouraged students to reflect on their family's immigration experiences as a way of making sense of current immigration policies. In classes, students talked about their commitments to both their homelands and the United States in ways that challenged the idea of the citizen within a single bounded nation-state. Not insignificantly, as immigrants from low-income families, students often referred to the economic challenges faced by their families. During a class on human rights, Danny asked students to work in groups to create a poster on which they identified "problems or needs faced by your community" on the outside of a circle and "by you and your families" on the inside. Students in all of the groups identified economic challenges as being the most central in their lives. Specifically, they identified landlord–tenant issues, safe/affordable housing, access to health care, gang violence, drugs, and other issues associated with living in poverty (Lee & Walsh, 2015). The students were keenly aware of the misrecognition of their cultural and linguistic repertoires and the need for the redistribution of material resources, yet they did not appear to recognize the ways in which these experiences were racialized.

Danny's goals for the immigration unit went beyond a simple desire to connect to students' experiences. Reflecting the influence of critical pedagogy, Danny wanted his students to see the ways that power and inequality have been imbricated in U.S. immigration policies throughout history. He recognized that many students had experienced and/or were still experiencing the effects of restrictive immigration policies on their families, and he planned assignments and selected readings that revealed the ways in which inclusion/exclusion in the United States have always been related to racial identities. In an interview with Stacey, Danny explained that his goals for the unit were for students to see the way U.S. immigration history has been marred by racist policies and ideologies that continue today (Lee & Walsh, 2012). In class discussions of current immigration policies, the experiences of undocumented immigrants were a recurring theme (Lee & Walsh, 2015). Students spoke about undocumented immigrants as real people—neighbors, family members, friends—and were openly sympathetic to the barriers faced by those "without papers." In observing these class discussions, Stacey noted how different these conversations were from those observed by scholars conducting research in schools serving primarily U.S.-born white students, where discourses of illegality and criminality go unchallenged (North, 2009). Danny's curricular and pedagogical choices often reflected not only his own sociopolitical consciousness, but also the social justice consciousness he desired for his students. His curriculum and pedagogy contained a "forward-looking third space" (Paris, 2012) and were grounded "in the historical and current particulars of students' everyday lives, while at the same time oriented toward an imagined possible future" (Gutierrez, 2008, as cited in Paris, 2012, p. 94).

During the unit on globalization, Danny built upon the fact that immigrant youth embody globalization. More than a theoretical or abstract concept for immigrant youth, globalization is reflected in their use of language, clothing styles, and consumption of popular culture, among other things. Reflecting his concerns regarding material inequality and the politics of redistribution, Danny encouraged students to grapple with how consumerism fuels unequal labor conditions and economic inequality around the world. In one exercise, Danny had students identify where their clothes and other products they owned were made. In response to a film on global sweatshops, students talked about labor conditions in the garment industry around the world and in New York City's Chinatown, where some students lived. The cultural sustenance here emanates from the fact that students knew of such working conditions in their countries of origin and, in some cases, through the daily work experiences of their immediate and extended family in the United States. Furthermore, the pedagogy provided students with an understanding of the global forces behind such working conditions, that is, unfettered capital accumulation requires relative profit maximization and wage reduction.

In addition to encouraging students to draw on their cultural knowledge to make sense of material, Danny and his colleagues scaffolded material to help ELLs access rigorous academic content. Danny, for example, often gave students opportunities to act out scenes or to make visual representations of their ideas before beginning the writing process. Importantly, the practice of simultaneously drawing on students' identities and offering rigorous academic content was common among teachers in schools in the network. In contrast to most high schools, where immigrant youth who are English language learners are silent and silenced in classes, students at the Internationals claim space in their classrooms and corridors. Danny has a clear memory of a student at his school claiming to "own these hallways" in response to the interactions that occur between classes. This is, in its own right, a pedagogy of reclamation and revitalization (McCarty & Lee, 2014). In schools in the Internationals Network, students can be heard speaking in English and in their native languages, as well as in other students' native languages.

Through the process of sharing stories about their experiences in their native countries, the students learned about other cultures; at times, they experiment with, "try on," and perform one another's cultural and linguistic repertoires. By talking about their immigration experiences and their evolving identities as immigrants, they developed a shared identity as immigrants (Lee & Walsh, 2015). In short, in the Internationals, both teachers and students demonstrate " . . . a fluid understanding of culture, and a teaching practice that explicitly engages questions of equity and justice" (Ladson-Billings, 2014, p. 74); they also see identity as "hybridity, fluidity and complexity" (p. 82).

FROM SOCIAL JUSTICE TO SOCIALLY JUST, CULTURALLY SUSTAINING PEDAGOGY

As we have reflected on expanding our understandings of social justice education for immigrant youth to include insights from culturally sustaining pedagogy, we have asked ourselves the following questions: What does it mean to engage in an education that sustains immigrant youth, that provides cultural and linguistic sustenance akin to the sustenance provided by consumed food and drink? What does it mean to recognize that immigrant youths' identities are flexible and evolving? Our work together points to three crucial facets of SJCSP for immigrant youth: (1) the importance of fostering a justice-oriented citizenship that encourages youth to be active agents in the political process, (2) encouraging critical dialogues around race, and (3) recognizing the evolving and hybrid nature of immigrant youths' identities.

Our attention to citizenship grew out of Danny's concerns that his teaching had focused on helping students make sense of inequalities without adequately delving into how students might challenge existing inequalities. Thus, he fears he may have inadvertently given students the impression that they are helpless in the face of inequities. For example, while Danny offered students a space to critique immigration policies, he typically did not engage in explicit discussions with his students about how they might challenge inequalities through political participation and social action. Danny's experiences working with undocumented immigrant students raise particularly important questions for SJCSP. Researchers estimate that there are 1.8 million undocumented immigrant youth in the United States. Danny estimates that between 20% and 30% of the students at schools in the Internationals Network are undocumented, and that many more students are from families with mixed documentation status. From a cultural, political, and economic standpoint, the policies and practices around those without papers represent a nadir of dispossession. As high school students prepare to leave the relatively protected space of high schools, they must cope with the reality that their futures will not be the same as their peers "with papers" (Gonzalez, 2011). And this difference precludes them from true participation in a democratic, pluralistic, and egalitarian society.

Most efforts at citizenship education in the United States focus on integrating youth into the existing society, developing patriotism, and transmitting majoritarian perspectives on political participation (Abowitz & Harnish, 2006). Mainstream approaches to civics and citizenship education, which focus on voting as the single most important form of political participation, fail to adequately address issues of power and inequality and entirely exclude undocumented youth. Drawing on insights from the scholarship on cultural citizenship and justice-oriented citizenship, we support an approach to citizenship that embraces immigrants' cultural and linguistic diversity and gives them the tools to be change agents (Abu El-Haj, 2009; Watts & Flanagan, 2007; Westheimer & Kahne, 2004). Specifically, such an approach would equip immigrant youth with the critical reflexivity needed "to critique regressive practices (e.g., homophobia, misogyny, racism) and raise critical consciousness . . . challenging hegemonic ideas and outcomes" (Paris & Alim, 2014, p. 92).

Youth participatory action research (YPAR) offers the possibility for encouraging action-oriented citizenship alongside rigorous academic development. It does so by challenging the epistemological assumptions of where knowledge lies and who can create it, and by recognizing that those who have lived inequity and injustice have the greatest insight into their sources and impact (Cammarota & Fine, 2008; Irizarry & Brown, 2014). In his efforts to encourage engaged critical citizenship, Danny designed a dissertation research project with YPAR as its foundation. Youth co-researchers crafted questions, designed research methods, and analyzed data around an issue that they essentially embodied as immigrant youth of color learning English. Yvonne, for example, the U.S.-born child of undocumented parents, focused on the experiences of young people without papers. After living with her father's parents in Senegal for approximately 10 years and then returning to the United States to live with her mother, Yvonne discovered her mother's immigration status:

> What I didn't know about my mother, because I was only a young child when I left her, was that she counts herself among the millions of undocumented people in the U.S. How I came to understand this unfolded as I asked her questions that any teenager would ask a mother she hadn't seen in a decade: Why don't you work in the supermarket anymore? My mom told me she was fired, but never explained why. I saw that my mom was missing teeth and asked why she didn't have them fixed. She told me she doesn't have Medicare. I wondered why I had it and she didn't.

During the YPAR project, Yvonne repeatedly brought to the fore the need for the undocumented to have more equitable access to resources (Walsh, 2013). She contended that undocumented Americans need access to living-wage jobs and the benefits that accompany them, to higher education financial aid, and to social welfare programs. Yet their illegal status renders them voiceless—with the term "illegal" itself having a dehumanizing effect. Fueled by her comparison of her mother's life and her own, Yvonne calls into question the meaning of citizenship and belonging in the early 21st century. She begs us—on her mother's and undocumented young people's behalf—to move beyond legalistic notions of citizenship by considering the economic, cultural, or even emotional contributions and attachments that one has to and in a society. It is these lived understandings of citizenship that SJCSP must support Yvonne in engaging and sustaining.

Further, as we consider the evolving identities of immigrant youth and the development of justice-oriented citizenship, all of us as SJCSP educators need to pay attention to how immigrant youth are making sense of race and racism. Indeed, research shows that learning about race and undergoing racialization are central to the immigrant experience, and that schools play a central role in the process of racialization (Lee, 2005, 2009; Olsen, 1997). While immigrant students bring understandings of race and racialization with them to the United States, many have not had to grapple with being racialized subjects until their arrival in the United States. Thus, Chinese students learned that they are "Asian" and Haitian students learned they are "Black." Danny's students recognized the existence of a racial hierarchy in the United States that positions whites at the top, but they simultaneously held a belief in meritocracy and the "American Dream" (Lee & Walsh, 2015). While most of Danny's students and those in the Internationals are immigrants of color and have been subjected to racializing forces, they often downplayed racism as a matter of individual "prejudice" or "ignorance." When Danny presented them with evidence of the ongoing inequalities experienced by African Americans and other groups of color, students used the discourse of individualism and achievement to dismiss racism against African Americans, and even to blame African Americans for ongoing inequality. Indeed, diminishing the significance of racism and focusing on individual "prejudice" allowed students to maintain their belief in the American Dream in the face of racism. Furthermore, we found that Danny's students' pride about being immigrants was often expressed through troubling comparisons between immigrants and "Americans," particularly African Americans. Previous research has revealed that immigrant students often compare themselves and are compared by their teachers to African American students (Lee, 2009). The model minority stereotype, for example, is part of larger discourses of anti-Blackness and other damaging racializing ideologies.

Like many youth today, many students at Danny's school have embraced the rhetoric of color-blindness and postraciality, which suggests that institutional racism has been eliminated and that people of all races have equal opportunities (Bonilla-Silva, 2010). As immigrants coming of age in an era dominated by neoliberal discourses, which celebrate free markets, competition, individualism, and the idea of a postracial society, it really isn't surprising that many immigrant youth have adopted the discourse of meritocracy to make sense of social inequalities (Harvey, 2005; Kumashiro, 2008). Furthermore, like many immigrants, Danny's students possess an immigrant optimism that motivates them to persist in the face of the hardships they encounter in the United States. While it isn't particularly surprising that many immigrant youth struggle to grasp the nature of racial inequality in the United States, it is troubling and problematic. We believe it is important for our pedagogies to support immigrant youth, as new citizens of this country (once again, we are speaking about cultural and social citizenship rather than legal citizenship), in understanding that they have inherited the problems of race and racism embedded in the United States and thus can't escape or avoid them.

We are arguing that a SJCSP for immigrant youth must engage students in deep conversations about race, including the relationship between immigrant groups and long-term groups of color. Previous scholarship has identified tension between immigrants and U.S.-born People of Color, including African Americans and the children of Latino and Asian immigrants (Lee, 2009). These tensions reflect a complex intersection of cultural misunderstandings, different historical relationships to the United States, and different experiences with racism. In teaching about the history of immigration in the United States, educators need to move beyond dominant narratives of American immigration in order to highlight the racialized nature of immigration policies and requirements for citizenship. In his classes, for example, Danny presented his students with a timeline of voluntary and forced migration (slavery) throughout U.S. history. As we reflected on Danny's classes, we were struck by the fact that one of his Chinese students was shocked to learn about the Chinese Exclusion Act and a time when Chinese were singled out for nativist outrage. Our argument here is that immigrant youth need opportunities to examine the varying ways that immigration policies and immigrant experiences have been racialized throughout U.S. history. Additionally, the goal would be to demonstrate that while the experiences of African Americans and immigrants have been and are "different" from each other, they are related and linked (Cacho, 2012; Molina, 2014). In order to demonstrate the relational nature of race, a SJCSP could focus on the way racial scripts have been repeated and used against various groups throughout U.S. history (Molina, 2014). Ultimately, a SJCSP would help students grapple with the following questions: How are ideas about criminalization and illegality constructed and related? What is the relationship between the Ahmed Mohamed clock incident and the pool party incident in McKinney, Texas, where African American youth were subjected to police harassment?[1]

In order to illustrate the current relationship between racism and anti-immigrant policies and the intersecting interests of African Americans and immigrants, educators could point to the work of groups such as the Black Alliance for Just Immigration, which organizes African American and Black immigrant communities to advocate for racial justice. Not insignificantly, the tensions between African Americans and various immigrant groups are often fueled by dominant discourses that position the interests of African Americans and immigrants as being at odds. Equipping immigrant youth with accurate historical knowledge and critical lenses with which to analyze current events and their reporting by the conservative and liberal media is paramount.

For educators working with immigrant youth today, the Black Lives Matter movement provides fruitful opportunities for critical discussions regarding race (Garza, 2014). Though our research period preceded the explicit formation of this movement, our data suggest that immigrant youth might internalize and reproduce dominant discourses regarding police interactions: If the person has done nothing wrong, why doesn't s/he simply comply; police officers put their lives on the line daily and should be respected; and, perhaps the most ubiquitous, "all lives matter." Students need the historical and cultural knowledge of the role police play as a paramilitary organization in U.S. society—that is, their obligation to protect capital, whites, and their property—in order to critically deconstruct the discourse of "all lives matter." Providing a more accurate and nuanced representation of history would help young people to understand the degradation of Black bodies and the need to interrupt the liberal inclusion of "all" in lives that matter. The Black Lives Matter movement in fact draws attention to both recognition and redistribution. In fact, without simultaneous redress of both capital dispossession through enslaved labor and its legacy and the misrecognition of the historical and cultural relationship between Black lives and the state-sanctioned violence rendered by police officers, there will be no progress. A pedagogy that strives to engender such a justice orientation could potentially not only equip immigrant youth with antiracist ways to interpret the media images that bombard them, but also provide them with tools to understand how they themselves are racialized. As described above, YPAR has the potential to equip young people to critically analyze structure and lives (Cammarota & Fine, 2008) by engaging them in crafting research projects that emanate from observations of their own families, schools, and communities (Walsh, 2013).

A SJCSP for immigrant youth must also recognize that immigrant youths' identities are in constant motion as they move across borders (literally and figuratively) and encounter diverse cultures and languages. Although Danny's students and other students at the Internationals expressed a common discourse of "becoming Americanized," it would be inaccurate to think of them as "assimilating" into a single existing culture. Rather, they were creatively developing hybrid identities and cultures that reflected their immigrant experiences and contact with the superdiversity of NYC. They spoke about their identities as being transformed through interactions with their peers from around the world. In many cases, for example, they were not just becoming English speakers, but multilinguals. Through their peers they picked up phrases in different languages, learned about different cultural practices, and heard about political conditions in different countries. One particularly telling interaction involved a Russian student asking Stacey how many languages she spoke. When Stacey reported that she could speak elementary-level Chinese, the student giggled and reported that he spoke three languages and was learning Spanish from his classmates. This student embodies the very cultural and linguistic flexibility that schools should be promoting, and his response to Stacey's limited abilities in Chinese suggest that he understands the limitations of English-only perspectives better than many policymakers.

While Danny and many of his colleagues recognized immigrant youths' linguistic flexibility, current educational policies that privilege English acquisition above multilingualism and identify students by what they lack (i.e., English proficiency) are deeply problematic. A SJCSP must focus on youths' possibilities as emergent bilinguals and trilinguals (Garcia, 2009). Educators who embrace SJCSP must prepare students for high-stakes tests and simultaneously challenge the use of high-stakes tests that privilege monolingualism (Lee & Walsh, 2012).

TYING IT TOGETHER

Immigrant youth embody globalization, and a SJCSP should build on and recognize their experiences, attachments, and evolving identities as assets to build on and critically to sustain. A SJCSP must also include meaningful academic preparation that will enable immigrant youth to earn both the necessary credentials and the critical knowledge to resist being trapped in low-level service jobs. Furthermore, we assert that a SJCSP should promote a justice-oriented citizenship that underscores the importance of challenging social injustices in the service of broader community interests (Watts & Flanagan, 2007; Westheimer & Kahne, 2004). Importantly, we are arguing that academic rigor and the goals of cultural sustenance and justice-oriented citizenship can and should be pursued simultaneously. Given the tremendous diversity represented in the Internationals, it may be impossible for teachers to develop curriculum that deeply examines and reflects each and every student's cultural background, but Danny and his colleagues successfully incorporate students' backgrounds by drawing on the students as experts. Thus, a lesson on Native Americans can become a lesson on how various cultures express mourning. By building on students' cultural and linguistic flexibility, the schools in the Internationals give students a sense of belonging, encourage academic confidence and achievement, and foster cultural pluralism. In addition to building on immigrant students' strengths, we believe a SJCSP requires that teachers be aware of the challenges and barriers that immigrants face in the dominant society. As we've argued, issues and challenges surrounding race, racialization, and racism are central to the immigrant experience, and schools need to prepare immigrant youth to be active justice-oriented citizens who can negotiate and challenge racism and other inequalities locally, nationally, and globally. As Danny's own research suggests (Walsh, 2013), incorporating YPAR into curriculum for immigrant students is one promising practice that builds academic competence, is culturally sustaining, and promotes justice-oriented citizenship. In short, we are advocating for a SJCSP that supports immigrant youths to become active agents in their own lives and justice-oriented citizens in the United States and beyond. Moving toward social action is an inclusive pedagogy of solidarity and hope.

NOTE

1. In 2015, police in Irving, Texas, detained 14-year old Ahmed Mohamed when school officials accused him of making and bringing a fake bomb to school. The "bomb" was actually a clock that Mohamed had built from reassembled parts. The incident brought the issue of Islamophobia

to national attention. Also in 2015, police in McKinney, Texas, responded to calls regarding a disturbance at a pool party. When police arrived at the scene, one police officer drew his gun on the teens and then wrestled an unarmed 14-year-old girl dressed only in a bikini to the ground.

REFERENCES

Abowitz, K. K., & Harnish, J. (2006). Contemporary discourses of citizenship. *Review of Educational Research, 76*(4), 653–690.

Abu El-Haj, T. R. (2009). Becoming citizens in an era of globalization and transnational migration: Re-imagining citizenship as critical practice. *Theory into Practice, 48*(4), 274–282.

Bonilla-Silva, E. (2010). *Racism without racists: Color-blind racism and the persistence of racial inequality in the United States.* Washington, DC: Rowman & Littlefield.

Cacho, L. M. (2012). *Social death: Racialized rightlessness and the criminalization of the unprotected.* New York, NY: NYU Press.

Callahan, R. M. (2005). Tracking and high school English learners: Limiting opportunity to learn. *American Educational Research Journal, 42*(2), 305–328.

Callahan, R., Wilkinson, L., & Muller, C. (2008). School context and the effect of ESL placement on Mexican-origin adolescents' achievement. *Social Science Quarterly, 89*(1), 177–198.

Cammarota, J., & Fine, M. (2008) Youth participatory action research: A pedagogy for transformational resistance. In J. Cammarota & M. Fine. (Eds.). *Revolutionizing education: Youth participatory action research in motion.* New York, NY: Routledge.

Darling-Hammond, L. (1997). *The Right To Learn: A Blueprint for Creating Schools That Work.* The Jossey-Bass Education Series. San Francisco, CA: Jossey-Bass.

Erickson, F. (2006). Studying side by side: Collaborative action ethnography in educational research. In G. Spindler & L. Hammond (Eds.), *Innovations in educational ethnography: Theory, methods and results* (pp. 235–257). Mahwah, NJ: Lawrence Erlbaum Associates, Publishers

Fine, M., Stoudt, B., & Futch, V. (2005). *The Internationals Network for public schools: A quantitative and qualitative cohort analysis of graduation and dropout rates. Teaching and learning in a transcultural academic environment.* New York, NY: The Graduate Center, CUNY

Fraser, N. (1997). *Justice interruptus: Critical reflections on the "postsocialist" condition.* New York, NY: Routledge.

Fraser, N. (2009). *Scales of justice: Reimagining political space in a globalizing world.* New York, NY: Columbia University Press.

Fraser, N., & Honneth, A. (2003). *Redistribution or recognition?: A political-philosophical exchange.* London, UK: Verso.

García, O. (2009). Emergent bilinguals and TESOL: What's in a name? *Tesol Quarterly, 43*(2), 322–326.

Garza, A. (2014). A herstory of the #blacklivesmatter movement. *The Feminist Wire.* Retrieved from http://www.thefeministwire.com/2014/10/blacklivesmatter-2/

Gonzales, R. G. (2011). Learning to be illegal undocumented youth and shifting legal contexts in the transition to adulthood. *American Sociological Review, 76*(4), 602–619.

Gutiérrez, K. D. (2008). Developing a sociocritical literacy in the third space. *Reading research quarterly, 43*(2), 148–164.

Harvey, D. (2005). NeoLiberalism: A brief history. Oxford: Oxford University Press

Hawkins, M. R., & Legler, L. L. (2004). Reflections on the Impact of Teacher-Researcher Collaboration. *TESOL Quarterly, 38*(2), 339–343.

Irizarry, J., & Brown, T. (2014). Humanizing research in dehumanizing spaces: The challenges and opportunities of conducting participatory action research with youth in schools. In D. Paris and M. Winn (Eds.), *Humanizing research: Decolonizing qualitative inquiry with youth and communities* (pp. 63–80). Thousand Oaks, CA: SAGE.

Jaffe-Walter, R. (2008). Negotiating mandates and memory: Inside a small schools network for immigrant youth. *Teachers College Record, 110*(9), 2040–2066.

Jaffe-Walter, R., & Lee, S. (2011). "To trust in my root and to take that to go forward": Supporting college access for first generation immigrant youth. *Anthropology & Education Quarterly, 42*(3), 281–296.

Kinloch, V., & San Pedro, T. (2014). The space between listening and storying: Foundations for projects in humanization. In D. Paris and M. Winn (Eds.), *Humanizing research: Decolonizing qualitative inquiry with youth and communities* (pp. 21–42). Thousand Oaks, CA: SAGE.

Kumashiro, K. K. (2008). *The seduction of common sense: How the right has framed the debate on America's schools.* New York, NY: Teachers College Press.

Ladson-Billings, G. (2014). Culturally relevant pedagogy 2.0: aka the remix. *Harvard Educational Review, 84*(1), 74–84.

Lee, S. J. (2005). *Up against whiteness: Race, school, and immigrant youth.* New York, NY: Teachers College Press.

Lee, S. J. (2009). *Unraveling the model minority stereotype: Listening to Asian American youth* (2nd ed.). New York, NY: Teachers College Press.

Lee, S., & Walsh, D. (2012). Resistance and accommodation: Social justice education for immigrant youth in an era of high stakes testing. *Encyclopaideia: Journal of Phenomenology and Education, (34)*, 15–36.

Lee, S., & Walsh, D. (2015). Teaching (in)justice: One teacher's work with immigrant English learners. *Urban Review, 47*(1), 45–66.

McCarty, T., & Lee, T. (2014). Critical culturally sustaining/revitalizing pedagogy and Indigenous education sovereignty. *Harvard Educational Review, 84*(1), 101–124.

Menken, K. (2008). *English learners left behind: Standardized testing as language policy* (Vol. 65). Clevedon, UK: Multilingual Matters.

Molina, N. (2013). *How race is made in America: Immigration, citizenship, and the historical power of racial scripts* (Vol. 38). Berkely, CA: University of California Press.

North, C. E. (2009). The promise and perils of developing democratic literacy for social justice. *Curriculum Inquiry, 39*(4), 555–579.

Olsen, L. (1997). *Made in America: Immigrant students in our public schools.* New York, NY: The New Press.

Paris, D. (2012). Culturally sustaining pedagogy: A needed change in stance, terminology, and practice. *Educational Researcher, 41*(3), 93–97.

Paris, D., & Alim, H. S. (2014). What are we seeking to sustain through culturally sustaining pedagogy? A loving critique forward. *Harvard Educational Review, 84*(1), 85–100.

Valenzuela, A. (1999). *Subtractive schooling: US-Mexican youth and the politics of caring.* Albany, NY: SUNY Press.

Walsh, D. (2013). *In their own right: Immigrant adolescents research the global city.* (Unpublished doctoral dissertation). The Graduate Center, City University of New York.

Watts, R. J., & Flanagan, C. (2007). Pushing the envelope on youth civic engagement: A developmental and liberation psychology perspective. *Journal of community psychology, 35*(6), 779–792.

Weis, L., & Fine, M. (2012). Critical bifocality and circuits of privilege: Expanding critical ethnographic theory and design. *Harvard Educational Review, 82*(2), 173–201.

Westheimer, J., & Kahne, J. (2004). What kind of citizen? The politics of educating for democracy. *American Educational Research Journal, 41*(2), 237–269.

CHAPTER 12

Finding Sustenance

An Indigenous Relational Pedagogy

Amanda Holmes and *Norma González*
University of Arizona

> We can begin with the recognition that the fundamental reality in our physical world is a strange kind of energy that is found within everything—from stars to humans to stones to quantum energy fields. This energy is personal—or can be experienced personally. It is mysterious, and so potent and varied that it is useless to explore all the possible ways to define it. If we say anything about this power or energy, we can say that the world we live in, sustained by this power, is ultimately spiritual and not physical. . . . (Deloria, 2009, p. 184)

> There is a story I know. It's about the earth and how it floats in space on the back of a turtle. I've heard this story many times, and each time someone tells the story, it changes. . . . But in all the tellings of all the tellers, the world never leaves the turtle's back. And the turtle never swims away. (King, 2003, p.1)

"What are we seeking to sustain through culturally sustaining pedagogy?" ask Paris and Alim (2014) in their provocatively challenging essay that pushes us to the next edges of what it means to engage productively with asset-based pedagogies. How do we embrace dynamic flows of language and practices that cross communities in ways that do not essentialize or trivialize expansive pedagogical possibilities? How do we confront practices that emanate not from a celebratory stance toward community cultural resources, but are embedded in sometimes contentious sociopolitical contexts that arguably impact all knowledge production and learning? How does the sustainability of asset pedagogies lead us to consider complex ecologies of learning? And more importantly, how do we sustain those reservoirs of deeply felt but difficult-to-theorize sentiments and subjectivities that undergird historically constituted narratives and identities? How do we sustain, maintain, embrace, fortify, and extend the funds of knowledge of communities so that repositories of knowledge are not invalidated or lost?

This chapter itself has emerged from a place of loss. Our colleague, mentor, and friend, Richard Ruiz, was to be a co-author on this chapter. We mourn that we cannot write the chapter that can no longer be written.

Within this sense of loss we also find sustenance and sustaining possibilities. This chapter emerges as a dialogue that intertwines the textures and nuances of CSP, funds of knowledge, and Indigenous relational pedagogies. The dialogical space that interconnects these three positionings suggests affordances for unraveling persistent tensions about "resource orientations" (Ruiz, 1984) and how, when, by whom, and for what purpose community knowledge is alchemized into pedagogical possibilities. This chapter is populated by overlapping voices inhabiting the dialogical space. As we weave together the polyphony of expressions and standpoints, we struggle to engage a deeper awareness of "What are we seeking to sustain?"

ELDER PEDAGOGY: AN INDIGENOUS RELATIONAL, INTERGENERATIONAL PEDAGOGY

Amanda Holmes and *Rosalie Little Thunder*

Before beginning to talk about traditional Elder pedagogies and practice, it is critical to address a few things. First, it is necessary to discuss the concept of "Elders" as used in this chapter, which centers on Indigenous ways of knowing. While the term "Elder" varies across contexts, there is widespread Indigenous understanding of the meaning and significance of who Elders are and what it means to be an Elder. From traditional Indigenous standpoints, being an Elder is not defined by chronological age. The following quotes serve to explicate the concept of Indigenous Elder from within the academic literature: "In traditional Aboriginal societies Elders were and still are evolved beings who possess significant knowledge of the sacred and secular ways of their people, and who act as role models, often assuming leadership positions in their communities. They are highly respected by the people. They are the teachers, healers, and experts in survival. . . . Elders teach a world-view based on the knowledge that all things in life are related in a sacred manner and are governed by natural or cosmic laws" (Kulchyski, McCaskill, & Newhouse, 1999, p. xvi). Vine Deloria writes, " . . . elders are the best living examples of what the end product of education and life experiences should be. We sometimes forget that life is exceedingly hard and that none of us accomplishes everything we could possibly do. . . . The elder exemplifies both the good and the bad experiences of life, and in witnessing their failures as much as their successes we are cushioned in our despair of disappointment and bolstered in our exuberance of success" (Deloria, 2001, p. 45). Anishinaabe scholar

LeAnne Simpson reflects on the critical nature of Elders as, "[Elders'] ways of being in the world and their interpretations of our teachings were reflective of a philosophical state, a set of values and ethics and a way of being in the world where they didn't feel the need to employ exclusionary practices, authoritarian power and hierarchy. They 'protected' their interpretations by embodying them and by living them. They 'resisted' colonialism by living within Nishnaabeg contexts" (Simpson, 2011, p. 19).

And now I must acknowledge the place from which I write: I write this from a place of mourning. My Maske (no real English translation . . . "dear friend"), my Elder, Rosalie Little Thunder, walked on to spirit in August 2014, changing my life forever. I am trying to find the places in me that will allow me to write about what she wanted to do, the places of strength and resilience that might unlock my heart so that I might approach again what she asked me to do with her and, in her distinctive way, suggested gently but firmly to make a commitment to carrying out, whether she was here on this Earth or not.

I have written this as perhaps one small step in the direction of honoring her work and her life, and what she wanted to accomplish here. This is only a small step in finding ways to honor her, but as she gave me a responsibility to continue, I begin with these baby steps of remembering what she charged me to remember, and find ways to keep alive.

Rosalie Little Thunder animated what a traditional, self-determining, decolonizing Indigenous pedagogy looked like, deeply centered within an Indigenous consciousness. As I no longer have her in front of me, I only now begin to reflect on things that before I took for granted, that I did not see because it was part of my everyday. I realize now that we were not only doing "the work," the substance of what she wanted to get done, to nurture out of her mind and heart something that could be useful to her People once she passed. But so much of her teaching lay in the *way* she was—how she carried herself, what she said and didn't say and how she did both, her "practices" and manner, the protocols, values, and disciplines she spoke about—and was so keen to document, and that she *lived*. As a listener and learner, in deepening reflection now, it has been these things, these practices and ways, *as much as the teachings themselves*, that have affected my perception, behavior, mind, heart, and spirit. Now, into the rigor of subjectivity (Meyer, 2013, p. 254) and personal, interconnected patterns of relationship.

Rosalie Little Thunder was a Sicangu Lakota of the Little Thunder Tiospaye. She was raised up in her beloved Lakota language and cultural teachings, surrounded by her old people on the Rosebud reservation of South Dakota. She grew to be an Elder. She walked with the last remaining wild herd of Buffalo in this country from the sacred Paha Sapa (Black Hills) of South Dakota to Yellowstone National Park, to stop their slaughter by the National Park Service, Montana Department of Livestock, and other complicit federal and state agencies.

In standing up for these relatives, she helped reeducate her people and the non-Indian world about old Lakota ways of thinking and being. And she taught me, brought me into her Tiospaye, moving me in ways I will be understanding until I leave this Earth. She was just that powerful. In writing this I hope to honor her life and her work and her world, to share a small bit of who she was/is, the teachings and way of life she held so dear as she lived her life, to ensure that they were brought back, and to give thanks for such a strong and coherent Lakota presence.

Rosalie developed a process of cultural mapping to identify and deepen understanding of Lakota language, knowledge, and cultural values by charting the geography of age-old Lakota disciplines that reflect and construct Lakota values and meaning, working to illuminate ancestral knowledge/value systems revealed and animated through the Lakota language. Rosalie always talked about the ways in which the connection between knowledge, language, ethics, and action was continuous, that because of how she and other Elders were raised within this oral value system and practice, their Lakota ancestors were constantly alive and reinvigorated. She expressed it as being a mirror to her ancestors because of how she was taught through oral processes and protocols—and just as she was this reflection, so too were other Lakota Elders, all of whom form a collective genealogy of knowing reflective of their grandparents and their grandparents' grandparents, stretching across time and space. This is part of the power of oral intergenerational transmission. It is simultaneously a practical and spiritual process to be honored. The gifts we are given, that Elders have chosen to share with us, the wisdom of their lives, mirror and animate the wisdom and experience of *their* grandparents, ancestors all the way around. We have inherited the responsibility to continue on, that they might live even from the depths of our grieving and acknowledgment of the passing of each generation, transforming our grief into transformative possibilities of survival.

Rosalie was teaching not only the substance of what she wanted to get done—language and cultural mapping—but also the way to become . . . better. Grounded. More coherent. More human. A good relative. A good relative maintaining a relationship to the rest of the universe, a fundamental, orienting Lakota principle, consciousness, ethics, and way of being. By enacting Indigenous relational pedagogies, we realize and facilitate the growth of our gifts discovered through the unfolding of our relationships.

Sitting with this Elder's Lakota "theory" (the mapping of Lakota language, disciplines, value systems) and Lakota practice (actions and ways of being) guides the way knowledge develops out of the long interweaving of storying, experience, memory, interpretation, and language-become-teachings because they are *lived*, because they have been lived before by human and other-than-human beings and energies, because they are being lived again in the oral interaction between speaker, listener, and energies stirred with breath shared, because they are being enacted in the ways of being of an Elder at once living them and passing them along to a younger generation, in turn expected to live and create with them, to make them relevant and useful to each successive generation. An Indigenous sensibility, to enable and enhance survival into seven generations, before and to come, generations interacting in responsible, reciprocal relationship with the rest of the natural world. As I write this, something catches my eye and I realize I am being watched—the slight movement of a deer at the edge of the field, whose breath becomes visible in the early morning cold. The deer adds her breath to the story. Don't forget, she reminds me.

I have been thinking about how Rosalie did what she did, ways I now see as instructions that ignite in my memory so that I might share some of her ways of being that reflect Elder epistemologies and pedagogies. No matter where she had to go or who she had to talk to, she maintained a steady, deliberate pace that refused to be rushed—and as I was sometimes in the unenviable role of having to get her places "on time," I knew what it meant to try to sway her from her course. It simply wasn't going to happen. Whether getting to the United Nations, where she participated in leadership as part of the Permanent Forum on Indigenous Issues, or to an elite university where she was a keynote speaker, she took her time. It was not that she was unaware of time; she always noted it. But the other things around her—conversations and visiting, eating, browsing . . . *paying attention* to the details, the unfolding relationships around her—took precedence.

She was totally grounded in the now and in her ancestors' present and future. She made people crazy with this, people operating in the rushing around of schedules, meetings, appointments, deadlines. Reflecting more closely, putting her practice and words into the context of other Elders I have watched and listened to, she was actually embodying an *Elder praxis* of deliberation, slowness, persistence. She knew she would get there, but the *way* that you do things is as important as the getting there itself. This engaged not only the Lakota values of perception, presence, and purpose that happen when we slow down, but it enacted the deep Lakota value of *humility*, which recognized that neither was she so important as to be indispensable (and that if she happened *not* to make it, it would require the stepping-up of other people's skills), nor was it so important she get there on time that she upset the calm and deliberateness of her own mind (which would affect others), nor was any human endeavor so all-important as we make to believe it is: a reflection of the humility not to put humans and a human agenda, even (and perhaps especially) if she was at the center of it, first.

Another aspect of her pedagogy as Elder was the relational protocol, cultural value, and discipline of visiting. Again, time: "It takes *time* to visit," she would say, "to really sit down and be present. That's what I remember." She described how she grew up, when to visit meant that the person or family would come with their wagon full of tents and food, setting up camp for weeks or months on your land . . . which was required to have a good visit. When they were done, they would pack up and head on to the next person's place or back home. This protocol was something that I have to admit sometimes made me crazy when she was alive, because it is in fact one of the reasons we did not do nearly as much taping as we wanted to (that, and issues of deep reservation poverty), because by the time we finished visiting (over the phone or in person), something would invariably come up and she or I would have to go. We never just launched into "the work." We had to check in with each other to see where each of us was first, before we could get into whatever was in front of us to do. Following this traditional protocol could be seen in the West to have "gotten in the way of the work." But when your work is embedded within traditional ways of being and be-having, they are inseparable: The visiting, the attention, the relationship are embedded within the work. Knowing and behaving cannot be teased apart. So while I wanted to hear her talk about her knowledge and teachings, at the same time she was *living* the teachings about how to *be*, how to conduct oneself as a Lakota, value systems that emphasize care and attention to detail, participation, connection, respect, deliberateness, discernment, per-ception born out of relationship and reciprocity.

Even within my grieving about the losses and my failings over what I did not do, her teachings are emerging still, showing me what was actually going on, being lived in front of me—these very teachings we were working on, about how to be a human being, a respectful, humble, generous relative, were being unfolded in front of me. I was a part of it, it was happening out of our relationship, which strengthened that connection, so that when we talked together it was always with more trust, more safety, more ability to be authentic, to be able to address challenges or misunderstandings together, to feel free to talk deeply, to become more profoundly human, relatives. Of course, this affected the work in return and the *quality* of our talks. Quan-tity was not in her vocabulary, as it is not in the vocabulary of any Elders I have ever met, except in numbers of grandchildren. But her passing so early, with the hope for many years more, has me wishing for quantity. I remind myself that it is quality, the quality of the relationship, that was deepened and enriched by the doing of it, by the ways of being that Rosalie embodied.

Indigenous methodologies and pedagogies are embodied in the prac-tice of Elders. Rosalie's commonsense, action-oriented universe (in rela-tionship with the larger Universe) embodied Lakota ways of knowing/ being, reflecting, and bringing life to time-tested, time-honored Lakota values and disciplines in her everyday. These aspects of Lakota ways of knowing, ways of approaching knowledge, and Elder pedagogies reflect and mutually reinforce one another. These ways have been given so little space, afforded so little respect by non-Native society and particularly by Western academia, that they need some space of their own so that we might think more deeply and begin to dwell more profoundly within some of these critically relevant pedagogies of survival, ways that have created the possibilities for simultaneously ancient and contemporary meaning, coherence, and power. Here are some of those—I share them now because that is what Rosalie wanted—to make an impact so that human beings might reflect on and change their behavior, aligning themselves again, finally, with the rest of the natural world:

The value and discipline of *ethical usefulness* and the emphasis on *survival*, an ethical survival, as the ultimate test of knowledge;

The value and discipline of the *collective*, where the individual is located within the greater good, where one's actions reflect the awareness that the People must be considered in one's ways of thought and action, where the collective helps the individual to find and be sustained in the development of their life's purpose, and the individual's life purpose holds the People at its heart;

The value and discipline of *visiting*, having discernment and perception to make time within your life for others' lives, which is again a reflection of the individual-collective (I-We dialogic) and of relationality;

The value and discipline of *perception*, to be able to perceive without being asked or told what to do (which is a reflection of interlocking values of independence, interdependence, competence, sensitivity, generosity), developing the acuity to pick up on nuances and slight changes (in the weather, landscape, behavior of animals, climate, people, and ceremony), all of which in turn reinforce relationality and survival, a relationality of survival;

The value and discipline of *slowness* and *deliberateness*, where to go slowly means to go with care, perception, and discipline, where slowness encourages reflection, deliberation, and pause, in turn nurturing skills of critical thought, intuition, insight, and vision, which develop leadership and wisdom; deliberation cycles back into relationship, where to go slow and be thoughtful again encourages perception that looks more closely at the unfolding of the world; this is a practice very much embodied by Elders, a value that younger generations learn to understand by spending time watching how Elders approach *doing*. A person or culture in a rush, hurrying around, is suspect; it is seen as a reflection of disorientation, a profound lack of attention, perception, and respect, an avoidance of responsibility, exposing a people out of touch with the cyclical requirements of self, collective, and the natural world.

The value and discipline of *consistency* and *dependability*, where you can be counted on to come through, to keep your word, to honor commitments so that you can be depended upon, all of which feed into the survivability of the People; these are found in the values of relationship and honor;

The value and discipline of *honor, integrity,* and *honesty,* where words are chosen thoughtfully and with precision, because the language holds great power and speaking is an enactment of that power, where one's life is in alignment with spiritual teachings, where to do the *right* thing is called for, no matter the hardship, invoking deep relationality with self, community, and spirit;

The value and discipline of *noninterference*, where each person is recognized as an individual put here by the Creator, having their own set of gifts and the ability to make decisions free of interference from others, where there is strong respect for each human being, with each person expected to make their own decisions that are right for them from within their own context and their location within the collective. Self-determination emerges out of this ethics of noninterference, where recognition of the integrity, distinctiveness, and diversity of individuals, of Nations, and all of life is fundamental;

The value and discipline of *orality*, where clarity and coherence in listening, speaking, and memory are critical; where past, present, and future, ancestors and those yet unborn, physical, spiritual, mental, and emotional worlds are engaged at once; where practices of the spoken and unspoken word and corresponding practices of listening and discerning for language and for other languages of body, natural world, and spirit awaken protocols embedded in language and cultural values;

The value and discipline of *generosity*, where the greatest gift is to give, to let go, invoking the understanding that nothing is really ours in the first or last place, that everything has been given to us by the Creator and our Mother Earth, and that they have provided more than enough for all. It is a responsibility not only to recognize their gifts, but to ensure that they are shared with purpose, discernment, perception, and integrity for the good of the collective, a value tied deeply to relationship and humility, and to survival. Leaders of the People, in the old ways—and this is still seen today—have the least material possessions, for they give everything away. Accumulation, greed, and taking more than you need are cultural taboos—indeed, this one value in contact with settler capitalist society has wreaked havoc culturally;

The value and discipline of *humility* and *gentleness*, which circulate with generosity and within the collective, in recognition of the great value and meaning of all life, where each of us is but a small piece . . . this value recognizes our interconnectedness and how critical it is not to stand out as apart, but that to stand within the circle, with a generous heart and mind for the People and all our relations, holds the possibility for creating the greatest of human beings, the way human beings were put here to be. Humility and gentleness hold great strength and power, and are critical to keeping peace, to providing a check on the weakness of uncontrolled ego.

The value and discipline of *responsibility* and *reciprocity* have to do with the values of integrity and accountability to self and group, extending to perception and the discernment to be coherent to the interconnected web of the Universe; relations of interconnectedness require reciprocity and generosity to engage more than just harmonious co-existence—they nurture relationships of co-creation;

The ultimate value and discipline of *relationship* embodies the utmost respect, care, and consideration for the ways one carries oneself into relations with others, these others as integral to self, in a nonhierarchical circle of existence; this is a deep Lakota value, required in every action of your life to consider your relationship with the rest of Creation. The critical cultural ethics of Lakota relationality are reflected profoundly in language, and are often the final words spoken at the end of ceremony or gathering: *Mitakuye Oyasin* (All My Relations).

Bringing out these values and disciplines as I have reflected on them in a different way with Rosalie's passing, I see more clearly her everyday practices, the *ways* she lived and walked her life. My perception and discernment, my own *woableze,* is being developed with her passing in the unfolding of the generations, guided by Elders and by those Elders now ancestors, echoing their ancestors, in an ever-renewing cycling of these ancient value systems of respect, relationship, humility, generosity, consistency, vision, perception, and gentleness that may have more relevance than ever today.

Rosalie always made sure to emphasize that "Elders are the center. Because Elders are the mirrors of our ancestors" (Little Thunder, personal communications to Amanda). Rosalie Little Thunder embodied Elder epistemologies, methodologies, and pedagogies, and it is these that I look to center in ensuring my own critical practice of what it means to enact decolonizing, self-determining Indigenous approaches to and practices of knowledge and research. These are pedagogies of the center, of the roots, of the heart. They touch us deeply and move us to act in ways that are conscious and awake, deliberate, generous and coherent, because they reflect, enact, and reengage generations of wisdom before and to come. Elder pedagogies sit with you because they are real, because they are alive, and because they are becoming yours, in your own journey, as you listen into silences, ancestors, beauty, nature, sound, and the spinnings of the Universe. And are moved.

CULTURALLY SUSTAINING PEDAGOGIES, INDIGENOUS KNOWLEDGES, AND RELATIONAL PEDAGOGIES

These resurgences, multiplicities of thought and action, must be founded on Onkwehonwe philosophies and lead us to reconnect with respectful and natural ways of being in the world. (Alfred, 2005, p. 36)

Taiaiake Alfred and Jeff Corntassel (2005), in their critical work on the regeneration and resurgence of Indigenous communities, discuss the commonality and unique positionality of Indigenous peoples as ". . . the struggle to survive as distinct peoples on foundations constituted in their unique heritages, attachments to their homelands, and natural ways of life is what is shared by all Indigenous peoples, as well as the fact that their existence is in large part lived as determined acts of survival against colonizing states' efforts to eradicate them culturally, politically and physically" (p. 597). Indigenous communities hold different priorities and aspirations that arise out of this distinctness as Peoples, a context of enduring presence and relationship with homelands now occupied and colonized by settler societies.

Taking up Paris and Alim's (2014) offer of possibility and promise in pedagogical scholarship and practice, culturally sustaining pedagogy asks that "youth, educators, and researchers join us to take this struggle further, with love" (p. 96). To take this struggle further, the possibility and promise of CSP can suggest that Indigenous community perspectives and positionalities offer different vantage points from which to engage asset-based pedagogies, because their locations are different, distinct, and "hold a relationship to enduring patterns and languages that must be brought forward to be of service, again, to what is before us" (Meyer, 2013, p. 259).

Indigenous methodologies and pedagogies are informed by deep cultural memory and meaning-making, an ancestral collective value system springing from the wisdom of longevity and experience within places, carried by Elders. Relational consciousness and knowledge emerge out of Indigenous worldviews of interconnectedness, engaging responsible, respectful, and thankful ways of knowing all of life and practices of being a good relative. Native Hawaiian scholar Manulani Meyer (2013) describes an "epistemological hologram" of Indigenous knowledge where the wholeness of knowledge is contained in each of its parts (pp. 255–256). Honored Lakota scholar Vine Deloria Jr. talked about how we understand and make sense of the world, reminding us that the ancestors not only asked the questions of modern science "how does it work" and "what use is it" but " . . . always asked an additional question: what does it mean?" (Deloria, 1999, p. 134). Comprehending the meaning of knowledge from Indigenous worldviews makes all the difference as to whether it is appropriate, relevant, sustaining. Is knowledge useful? Does it enhance possibilities of survival, regeneration, and resurgence? This is an Indigenous bottom line.

Vine Deloria constantly reminds us that "all knowledge, if it is to be useful, was directed toward that goal" of "finding the proper moral and ethical road upon which human beings should walk" (Deloria, 1999, pp. 43–44). Knowledge must be useful, relevant, and contribute to the survival of the collective and individual, the People and their human and nonhuman relations. These responsibilities and commitments to ethical knowledge and value systems embedded within language, traditional teachings, and worldviews lie at the heart of Indigenous epistemologies, ways of being, pedagogies, and education.

In McCarty and Lee's (2014) discussion of sovereignty, revitalization, and the work of asset-based pedagogies, they maintain that "tribal sovereignty must include education sovereignty" (p. 102), requiring attention to "cultural and linguistic survival" (p. 103). By extending this idea of Indigenous education sovereignty to *center* traditional Indigenous pedagogies, knowledge, ethics, values, ways of knowing/being, philosophies, and worldviews, guided by Elders through oral intergenerational practices and lifeways, we are paying attention to, and privileging, those relationships that unfold and intertwine within the grass roots. These roots push deeply into waiting, fertile ground to create regenerational space for cultural and linguistic relational resurgence.

TRADITIONAL KNOWLEDGE AND SURVIVAL: COMPREHENDING TRADITIONAL KNOWLEDGE

The traditional way, when viewed as a methodology, could be the Native peoples' greatest asset. In fact, it could turn out to be the only way that communities of Native people can organize for their own survival. (Mohawk & Barreiro, 2010, p. 212)

The core of our existence as nations is in our traditional cultures. (Alfred, 2004, p. 95)

Traditional knowledges, epistemologies, and ways of being are central to Indigenous survival and coherence. Asset-based pedagogies that are relevant and sustaining to grassroots Indigenous communities will acknowledge that traditional knowledge and cultural ways have helped to maintain and will continue to provide for the endurance of Indigenous people as Peoples, as integral Nations. Dakota scholar Waziyatawin Angela Wilson (2004) emphasizes "the recovery of Indigenous knowledge as a decolonization strategy for the solving of contemporary issues facing Indigenous communities" (p. 362). Anishinaabeg scholar Leanne Simpson (2004) asserts,

Anticolonial strategies for the recovery of Traditional Indigenous Knowledge systems require a deconstruction of the colonial thinking and its relationship to [Indigenous Knowledge] . . . the recovery of Indigenous intellectual traditions, Indigenous control over Indigenous national territories, the protection of Indigenous lands from environmental destruction, and educational opportunities that are anticolonial in their political orientation and firmly rooted in traditions of their nations. (p. 381)

This chapter centers, highlights, and privileges Indigenous traditional locations, priorities, and ways while placing Western academic concerns at the periphery. That said, it is instructive to note the reluctant pause when academia as a Western institution is forced to acknowledge Indigenous peoples' centering of traditional cultural processes and practices as critical Indigenous locations of individual and collective coherence. This is a deep schism, and one that I assert is not the burden of Indigenous Peoples to heal. It is the responsibility of Western scholars and society to engage in decolonizing, anticolonial self-reflection and reorientation, to recognize that the very knowledge systems they may have perceived to be static, stuck, antimodern, and antiprogressive could be the very ways of knowing that hold the possibilities for collective human survival upon Iethi'nihstenha Onhwentsia (Our Mother the Earth).

Indigenous traditional ways of knowing/being provide a flexible framework and capacity for responding to intertwining layers simultaneously, within a spiraling understanding of time and space, as they have always done. The late beloved Seneca scholar and traditional Elder John Mohawk focused on the importance of traditional understandings and community cultural, political, spiritual, and economic self-development, maintaining that "Traditionalism is a form of social organization based on principles developed by Native peoples centuries ago. Its goal is the redevelopment of community life and the empowerment of land-based peoples in ways that promote the survival of cultures and provide a practice of social justice" (Mohawk & Barreiro, 2010, p. 203).

These "enduring patterns of knowing" (Meyer, 2013, p. 251) and experience that lie at the heart of an Indigenous collective consciousness of survival invigorate the capacity to at once continue and to transform. A challenge before us is to shake what has become habitual—the everyday of colonization—and, in the ways of old teachings, renew our relationship and reciprocal engagement with intergenerational processes, practices, and pedagogies. Can we comprehend now how profoundly recentering and renewal of ancestral centers and consciousness wakes us out of the stupor of colonization?

Indigenous communities are looking deeply within their own collective traditional cultural knowledges to *sustain* them, to the power that has sustained them through the intensity of colonization, occupation, and the constancy of aggression, interference, and violence. The sustaining power that keeps the spark of survival and regeneration alive is recognized as the ancestral collective knowledge systems of Indigenous communities, carried and continued by traditional Elders and Knowledge Keepers. Taiaiake Alfred asserts the urgency of this ancestral coherence. "These words are an attempt to bring forward an indigenously rooted voice of contention, unconstrained and uncompromised by colonial mentalities. A total commitment to the challenge of regenerating our indigeneity, to rootedness in indigenous cultures, to a fundamental commitment to the centrality of our truths . . . " (Alfred, 2005, p. 33). The seeds of this rootedness, the gathered viability of experiences, truths, and wisdoms of the People, are still alive, nurtured in local places, finding ways to grow so that they might once again feed the People into health, sustenance, and strength.

In his essay on traditionalism, John Mohawk asserts, "The self-development of peoples is a powerful set of politics. It is the wave of the future for Indian people, not the ghost of the past. It provides the politics from which will grow the efforts to develop the people's culture, to rejoin the people to the spiritual ways, to reenact the respect for the sacred web of life that will provide for the survival of the future generations" (Mohawk & Barreiro, 2010, p. 202). By centering grassroots, Elder-mediated ways of being, off the beaten path of Western academia, this chapter reflects on the nuanced complexities of traditional Indigenous education and relational pedagogies.

Relationality, or coming to know oneself through the contextual constellation of relationships, is a central sustaining value of Indigenous views and visions of the meaning of traditional education, practices, and pedagogies. Traditional education from Indigenous centers strives toward the whole and ethical development of the person situated within the collective, the human and other-than-human relatives, allowing these relational understandings to unfold within the collective so as to contribute to the well-being and ethical survival of the People, as distinct, as integral, as who they were meant to be.

Indigenous people know that the depths of their languages, ways of knowing, and conducting themselves as relatives within the living Universe actually *make sense*, resonating through deep and reverberating layers from within their places of power, homelands, languages, and ceremonial ways. We are not invoking a "return" to some mythic state of cultural purity of knowledge, language, and being. Ancestral knowledges are ways of knowing that have been gained out of persistent, long cycles of experience, perception, visioning, imagining, dreaming, and relating within the classroom of the ever-shifting expansiveness of the natural world. Powerfully, humbly, Vine Deloria expressed, "As Indians we know some things because we have the cumulative testimony of our people" (Deloria, 2001, p. 86). Indigenous people locate and sustain themselves within a traditional understanding of interconnected, intergenerational relationality as a means of surviving, of living in a good way, and of transformational, resurging continuance . . . and are fearlessly standing in that center.

RE-PLACING YOUTH INTO THE INTERGENERATIONAL CIRCLE

While acknowledging that the field of asset-based pedagogy has contributed greatly to positive outcomes for marginalized students and communities, traditional Indigenous understandings may help to deepen thinking and reflection so as to strengthen these critical pedagogies. Much of the asset-based peda-gogical work privileges youth. From traditional Indigenous perspectives on the education of younger people, these pedagogies need to be placed within the proper framework of intergenerational learning and teaching—that is to say, that in looking to places of Indigenous community coherence, Elders are the location of wisdom, knowledge, and instruction. To separate youth out of the relational, intergenerational circle by privileging their practices without deeply acknowledging the critical place of Elders in their education is simply not an Indigenous framework of knowledge or practice.

Indigenous youth have always been guided, challenged, and protected by Elders. Elders hold collected wisdom and instructions, practices by which the people will emerge and reemerge and emerge again into each successive gen-eration in a continuing cycle of pedagogy, practice, knowledge, experience, and language. These cycles of ways of knowing are embodied and held by Elders and the oral relational transmission of collective, ancestral knowledges experienced, expressed, and circulating deeply from within places and par-ticularities. Separating youth from the circle of other generations—*especially* Elders—is not an Indigenous practice, and ultimately hastens the demise of cultural protocols, processes, and ways of knowing.

Privileging youth agency without simultaneously putting them into con-tinuing and meaningful connection within locally defined protocols of re-lationship is incoherent within Indigenous ways of knowing and collective processes of knowledge production, which hold at their heart the survival and ethical continuance of the People. Isolated youth agentic empowerment, from an Indigenous standpoint, reinscribes colonial practices by continu-ing the disruption of Indigenous intergenerational processes, pedagogies, and protocols of knowledge transmission. Indigenous Elders consciously mirror ancestral pasts and futures—memory practices—a cycling, spiraling response of memory, without which the continuous formation and re-for-mation of the People into the future becomes diminished.

Instead, nesting, placing, and locating traditional Indigenous ways of knowing and being, languages, and oral practices of intergenerational trans-mission at the center of a movement of reawakening creates the possibility for contemporary reflexivity and responsiveness to the demands and immedi-acy of the times that are now presenting a vision of an earth straining under the unfolding grip of a worldview that is fundamentally and inherently un-sustainable over the long term. *All* generations are needed to be in relation-ship with one another. Traditional Indigenous education and pedagogical practice is sustaining, situating younger generations (babies, children, youth, and adults) in relationship with Elders so that in time they too will come to find their particular places and roles within the community, their individual gift and contribution that will help ensure collective survival, continuance, and transformation. Such is an Indigenous practice of education, one that has sustained the People over generations.

Indigenous Elders embody and give life to cultural ways and under-standings in a critical intergenerational space, closest to ancestor, situated between ancestors and younger generations, holding onto the continuity of persistence, change, and the possibility of transformation. Manulani Meyer (2008) reminds us that "our epistemology still differs from those who oc-cupy our shores, and as we awaken, a revolution of remembering will bring us back to what is valuable about life and living, knowledge and knowing" (Meyer, 2008, p. 218). This remembering is our center, and that memory is held by our Elders. Elders animate what Meyer calls a "radical remembering of our future" (Meyer, 2003, p. 54). Locally defined Elder protocols, prac-tices, and pedagogies embody a close and deep listening and wakefulness not only toward what Elders are *saying*, but their *ways of being*—the ways they pass on knowledge and enact ancestral knowledge systems they have been handed down to carry. It is time now to breathe in some commonsense everyday Indigenous thinking, the depth of Elders who do not so much respond or react to criticism, but instead continue on their path, knowing what is right for them and what they need to get done during the time they have been given here.

FINAL REFLECTIONS: CULTURALLY SUSTAINING PEDAGOGY AND TRADITIONAL INDIGENOUS COMMUNITY ASPIRATIONS

This chapter has suggested that calling out unique histories, colonizations, survivances, and sovereignties provides multiple pathways for engaging with culturally sustaining pedagogics, and that asset pedagogies in themselves are historically and contextually contingent. To the asset pedagogies that are re-viewed in Paris and Alim (2014), we can add May and Sleeter's (2010) critical multiculturalism, Yosso's (2005) community cultural wealth, Moje's (2007) social justice pedagogy, Cammarota's (2011) pedagogy of hope, and Martin's (2002) cultural wealth. The underlying commonality of these epistemolog-ical and pedagogical claims is that sustaining pedagogies seek teaching and learning outcomes that respectfully engage with community funds of knowl-edge and that acknowledge that while culture can be dynamic and processual, there are historically constituted reservoirs of knowledge from which com-munities draw (Gonzalez, 2005). More importantly, we have argued that, as the opening quote by Vine Deloria Jr. evocatively communicates, sustenance and sustainability are ineffable spiritual powers, and culturally sustaining pedagogies must look beyond the material, the artifact, and the concrete to renarrate stories of survivance. We must look beyond schools and classrooms as sites of deep learning and powerfully reject binaries that devalue "out-of-school" or nonacademic knowledge. What does it mean to really operate from an assets-based pedagogical stance when the lives of our students are complex (Gonzalez, 2016)? We cannot understand our students nor nurture their voices if the layered contingencies of their lives are invisiblized or erased.

In self-determining, endlessly distinct ways, looking toward ancestral possibilities and promise, Indigenous communities are locating who they are and the profound implications of this vision with coherence and power. Kiowa writer N. Scott Momaday says, "Our very existence consists in our imagination of ourselves. The greatest tragedy that can befall us is to go un-imagined" (Momaday, 1978, p. vi). They are enacting what the Lakota call *woableze*, a way of perceiving that creates the possibility for survival and continuance (Little Thunder, personal communication to Amanda).

Locating sustaining practice, pedagogy, knowledge, and language by going deeper into critical sustenance—self-determining ways of knowing and being—presents the challenge and call of developing (from a Lakota context, for example) collective, contextual woableze—perception, discipline, vision—with local cultural coherence. Culturally sustaining pedagogy envisions sustaining pedagogies, practice, and knowledge; thus, Indigenous grassroots community perspectives, enacting their own particular traditional ways of knowing (like woableze), extend the pedagogical and conceptual diversity and development of CSP into deepening engagement within the priorities of locally derived, sustaining, self-determining sense-making, meaning, relevance, and usefulness.

Indigenous pedagogies of the grass roots hold up this lens: that to engage and enact traditional values, disciplines, and practices embedded within the language (i.e., for the Lakota, woableze, as an example of one particular traditional location of sense and meaning) is to hold the transformational possibility of cultivating the local unfolding of that which is relevant, coherent, meaningful, and sustaining from within Indigenous ancestral knowledge systems. These pedagogies of the center carry the power to strengthen communities that are reawakening and revitalizing their own traditional, integral, distinct ancestral knowledge and value systems, languages, ways, and collective community aspirations.

Vine Deloria (2001) maintained that the "proper context of Indian education" should focus not only on the context of existing conditions, but on the "traditional manner in which the tribe has faced its difficulties" (p. 83). Traditional Indigenous perspectives on the necessity of considering current conditions through the vision of deep cultural context and traditional community response may be helpful to asset-based pedagogical frameworks in encouraging, strengthening, and deepening the conceptualization of its work by sharpening its vision of the particular places from which pedagogies emerge and unfold.

From outside academia, Indigenous grassroots community perspectives might in turn nurture and sustain CSP, deepening the contextual meanings of what sustaining practices and pedagogies look like from a different location, from within local traditional Indigenous ways of knowing and being. This chapter engages from a relational place with one Lakota Elder who lived traditional Lakota knowledge systems and pedagogies to support and encourage her People, and other Indigenous Peoples, to find their own places of meaning once again. As Rosalie Little Thunder so often explained, comprehending and cultivating the traditional practice of woableze develops the capacity and acuity for listening to and respecting the particularity of experience; and, with sensitivity, generosity, clarity, insight, and vision, enacting ways of knowing that emerge from oral traditions and relational practices (Little Thunder, personal communication to Amanda). As woableze deepens and the particular ways, needs, and aspirations of community are discerned and clarified, the possibility of survivance—"an active sense of presence, the continuance of native stories . . ." (Vizenor, 2009, p. 100)—is enhanced, made meaningful, sustained.

Delving into and engaging traditional knowledges, languages, and "collective narrative memory" (McLeod, 2007, p. 9), while "keeping the particular in mind as the ultimate reference point of Indian knowledge," as Vine Deloria (2001, p. 22) instructed us, are ways that traditional Indigenous perspectives contribute to an understanding of what culturally sustaining pedagogies might mean from their places embedded within context.

REFERENCES

Alfred, T. (2004). Warrior scholarship: Seeing the university as a ground of contention. In D. A. Mihesuah & A.C. Wilson (Eds.), *Indigenizing the academy: Transforming scholarship and empowering communities*, (pp. 88–99). Lincoln, NE: University of Nebraska Press.

Alfred, T. (2005). *Wasase: Indigenous pathways of action and freedom*. Peterborough, ON: Broadview Press.

Alfred, T., & Corntassel, J. (2005). Being indigenous: Resurgences against contemporary colonialism. *Government and Opposition, 40*(4), 597–614.

Cammarota, J. (2011). From hopelessness to hope: Social justice pedagogy in urban education and youth development. *Urban Education 46*(4), 828–844.

Deloria Jr., V. (1999). *Spirit & reason: The Vine Deloria Jr. reader*. Golden, CO: Fulcrum Publishing.

Deloria Jr., V. (2009). *C.G. Jung and the Sioux traditions: Dreams, visions, nature, and the primitive*. New Orleans, LA: Spring Journal Books.

Deloria Jr., V., & Wildcat, D. R. (2001). *Power and place: Indian education in America*. Golden, CO: Fulcrum Publishing.

González, N. (2005). The hybridity of funds of knowledge. In N. Gonzalez, L. Moll, & C. Amanti (Eds.), *Funds of knowledge: Theorizing practices in households, communities and classrooms*. Mahwah, NJ: Erlbaum.

González, N. (2016). Imagining literacy equity: Theorizing flows of community practices. *Literacy Research: Theory, Method and Practice 66*(1), 1–25. doi: 10.1177/2381336916661528

King, T. (2003). *The truth about stories: A native narrative*. Toronto, ON: House of Anansi Press.

Kulchyski, P., McCaskill, D., & Newhouse, D. (Eds.). (1999). *In the words of elders: Aboriginal cultures in transition.* Toronto, ON: University of Toronto Press.

Martin, J. R. (2002). *Cultural miseducation: In search of a democratic solution.* New York, NY: Teachers College Press.

May, S., & Sleeter, C. (Eds.). (2010). *Critical multiculturalism: Theory and praxis.* New York, NY: Routledge.

McCarty, T. L., & Lee, T. S. (2014). Critical culturally sustaining/revitalizing pedagogy and indigenous education sovereignty. *Harvard Educational Review, 84*(1), 101–124.

McLeod, N. (2007). *Cree narrative memory: From treaties to contemporary times.* Saskatoon, SK: Purich.

Meyer, M. A. (2003). Hawaiian hermeneutics and the triangualtion of meaning: Gross, subtle, causal. *Social Justice, 30*(4(94)), 54-63.

Meyer, M. A. (2008). Indigenous and authentic: Hawaiian epistemology and the triangulation of meaning. In N. K. Denzin, Y. S. Lincoln, & L. T. Smith (Eds.), *Handbook of critical and indigenous methodologies* (pp. 217–232). Los Angeles, CA: Sage.

Meyer, M. A. (2013). The context within: My journey into research. In D. M. Mertens, F. Cram, & B. Chilisa (Eds.), *Indigenous pathways into social research: Voices of a new generation* (pp. 249–260). Walnut Creek, CA: Left Coast Press.

Mohawk, J., & Barreiro, J. (2010). *Thinking in Indian: A John Mohawk reader.* Golden, CO: Fulcrum.

Moje, E. (2007). Developing socially just subject-matter instruction: A review of the literature on disciplinary literacy teaching. *Review of Research in Education, 31*, 1–44.

Momaday, N. S. (1978). Indian voices. In G. R. Vizenor, *Wordarrows: Indians and whites in the new fur trade* (p. vi). Minneapolis, MN: University of Minnesota Press.

Paris, D., & Alim, H. S. (2014). What are we seeking to sustain through culturally sustaining pedagogy? A loving critique forward. *Harvard Educational Review, 84*(1), 85–100.

Ruiz, R. (1984). Orientations in language planning. *NABE Journal, 8*(2), 15–34.

Simpson, L. (2004). Anticolonial strategies for the recovery and maintenance of indigenous knowledge. *American Indian Quarterly, 28*(3), 373–384.

Simpson, L. (2011). *Dancing on our turtle's back: Stories of Nishnaabeg re-creation, resurgence and a new emergence.* Winnipeg, MB: Arbeiter Ring.

Vizenor, G. R. (2009). *Native liberty: Natural reason and cultural survivance.* Lincoln, NE: University of Nebraska Press.

Wilson, A. C. (2004). Introduction: Indigenous knowledge recovery is indigenous empowerment. *American Indian Quarterly, 28*(3/4), 359–372.

Yosso, T. (2005). Whose culture has capital? A critical race theory discussion of community cultural wealth. *Race, Ethnicity and Education 8*(1), 69–91.

CHAPTER 13

"Se Hace Puentes al Andar"

Decolonial Teacher Education as a Needed Bridge to Culturally Sustaining and Revitalizing Pedagogies

Michael Domínguez
San Diego State University

Caminante, no hay puentes, se hace puentes al andar.

—Gloria Anzaldúa

"Traveler," Anzaldúa says, "there are no bridges, you make the bridges as you walk." These are beautiful words that I have always felt spoke to something sincere and meaningful in what it means to work toward justice. There is effort and imagination involved, and uncertainty to the enterprise as we set out into unknown terrain. And as I reflect here on the growing importance and significance of culturally sustaining/revitalizing pedagogy (CSRP)[1] (McCarty & Lee, 2014; Paris & Alim, 2014) as a paradigm shift in education, these words seem increasingly relevant. Anzaldúa's message resonates with the spirit of CSRP and its call for our pedagogy and praxis to sustain and revitalize heritage practices and deeply rooted community wisdom, while nurturing the dynamic, evolving identities, ingenuity, and practices of historically marginalized and culturally diverse youth. This CSRP spirit, of seeking to create in unknown terrain by bringing the past into conversation with the present and future, is both so fittingly Anzaldúan, and pedagogically exciting.

Yet as a Xicano teacher educator in increasingly contested times, I have lately been grappling with what seems to be a critical question to this movement: What will teacher education and learning need to look like to adequately reflect the same spirit of discovery, vulnerability, and growth we hope to provide to youth? Essentially, if CSRP is about sustaining, revitalizing, and nurturing the identities, linguistic skills, and practices of youth culture, our teacher education pedagogies must be capable of producing the types of *decolonizing* educators whose humanizing ideologies recognize the value in such things and allow CSRP to become permissible, and possible, in the classroom.

What I mean by this is that although teacher education is replete with "bridge" metaphors and discourses on equity and justice, there is work yet to do in encouraging teachers to engage in epistemic travel. Are we challenging our novice and practicing educators, and ourselves, to press into unknown terrain, beyond the old, worn, and faulty paths that lead inexorably on a dehumanizing march toward whiteness? CSRP has asked us to *do* something both revolutionary and new, and also rooted in the long histories of our continuing resistances (Chapter 1, this volume). We will need to revitalize community-rooted wisdom and nurture the dynamic practices of youth in order to create new, humanizing, and decolonial bridges in our own understandings and pedagogies as we move toward this new paradigm.

With this said, the aim of this chapter is to make a case for a decolonial teacher education, one that focuses on the development of teachers whose core interest is to sustain, revitalize, and nurture the identities, practices, ingenuity, agency, and humanity of youth of color, on their terms. I begin this process by reflecting on the intersection of *coloniality*, teacher education, and CSRP, before considering how *ontological distance*—a term I use to describe the dehumanizing distancing between subjects that emerges from uninterrogated coloniality—is central to any liberatory teacher education effort. From there I conclude by offering an outline—drawing on data from a teacher education effort aimed specifically at cultivating CSRP—of what a decolonizing teacher education might entail, as a starting point for defining and refining a paradigm that will produce CSRP-ready educators.

COLONIALITY AND ONTOLOGICAL DISTANCE IN SCHOOLING

Coloniality, and the related verb *decolonize* (as in, "to *decolonize* our pedagogy"), are the types of words that typically find little traction in spaces of teacher learning. They can feel like philosophical jargon, undefined, impractical, and irrelevant to novice and practicing teachers alike, not to mention some teacher educators. In a nation where colonialism has ostensibly ended, and the vast majority of our discourse and efforts in teacher education are supposedly oriented toward equity and social justice already, talk of decolonization can appear overly political, and uninviting. Yet understanding the idea of coloniality, and what decolonization really means to teachers and teacher educators, is critical to successfully enacting—and sustaining—any truly liberatory youth or teacher education pedagogy, CSRP included. Put another way, enacting CSRP is more than a new teaching toolkit; it requires a *decolonial* mindset that must be developed, cultivated, lived, and deeply felt. To make this clear, we can begin by examining coloniality as a concept in contemporary terms, demystifying the word, and putting it into conversation with the context of schooling, teacher education, and CSRP itself.

Drawing on the work of Mignolo (1995, 2003), Quijano (2000), and many others, Maldonado-Torres (2010, p. 97) explains that *coloniality*

> . . . refers to long-standing patterns of power that emerged as a result of colonialism, but that define culture, labor, intersubjective relations, and knowledge production well beyond the strict limits of colonial administrations. . . . It is maintained alive in books, in the criteria for academic performance, in cultural patterns, in common sense, in the self-image of peoples, in aspirations of self, and so many other aspects of our modern experience.

Colonization as an explicit de jure system of political domination has ended, yes. Yet bans on ethnic studies, the proliferation of reductive curricula, disproportionate suspension/expulsion rates for youth of color, the prevalence of the school-to-prison pipeline, increasing levels of school segregation, legislation and policymaking that target and privatize schools in communities of color, police brutality in and out of schools, and so many other policies, concerns, indignities, and assaults on agency, culture, language, and identity persist. These are the accruing injuries of coloniality that "we breathe . . . all the time and everyday" (Maldonado-Torres, 2010). They are constant reminders to youth, families, and communities of color that while we may be allowed to participate in U.S. schooling, we are far from welcome; something oppressive, *colonial*, survives about how we are treated and how we are valued.

Yet even as I list these disturbing tangible, material, and systemic injustices, I want to suggest that as we consider CSRP, these issues—daunting and troubling as they may be—are not our most pressing concerns in teacher education, at least not directly. Understanding both that such injustices exist and are incredibly urgent is crucial, but in teacher education contexts, a narrow focus on fixing observable systemic injustices—the symptoms—of coloniality is both limiting and misleading. Rather, as Bhabha (1994) tells us, the heart of coloniality is not individual, or even systemic, actions or knowledge and content; it is about how we see, understand, and value the humanity of others: "It is not the colonialist self or the colonized Other," Bhabha writes, "but the disturbing distance in-between that constitutes the figure of colonial otherness" (1994, p. 45). To decipher this, and frame it in terms of schooling, learning, and teaching, Bhabha's words draw attention to the *affective* dimensions of coloniality that pervade our daily lives, and shape our sociopolitical relationships in and beyond the classroom. Unjust policies and discriminatory practices exist, but it is the deep-seated, uninterrogated assumptions, values, and beliefs of cultural normativity that perpetuate coloniality. This is the process of *Othering*, through which the subjectivity, the humanity, the ways of being and knowing of non-White[2] individuals and cultures, is rendered "Other," and denied both agency and legitimacy. The result is an *ontological distance* between the colonizer and the colonized that makes school—and societal institutions in general—challenging for youth of color.

What I am getting at here is that CSRP requires *affective* change, a shift in ontology, in how teachers see and value the diversity of experiences, ways of being, and realities that exist in the world. In education, ontological distance refers to the vast, affective terrain—emerging centuries ago when European colonization first began to frame indigenous communities in the global south as subordinate—between the practices, knowledges, and goals that are recognized in schools and beyond as valid and normative on one hand, and an evolving multitude of others, deeply rooted in community histories, and present and vivid in the lives of youth of color, on the other, that, at least at present, continue to be denied institutional validity. And it is this distance that makes CSRP both so critical to prepare teachers to enact, and potentially difficult to prepare them to attain.

CSRP AND THE COLONIALITY OF TEACHER EDUCATION

At this point, we might pose the question: Why does all this reframing around coloniality relate to CSRP and teacher education? Why do I need to make sense of ontological distance to produce or develop CSRP-capable educators? These are reasonable questions, given that many teacher leaders and teacher educators are already conscious of the aforementioned unjust realities of schooling facing youth of color. They are concerned about social justice and systemic bias, and eager to engage with their novice or practicing educators or peers around these topics, and to support them as they learn to be antiracist, multicultural, culturally relevant, and asset-based in their pedagogies. However, as I have noted, CSRP asks for something new, a step beyond where teaching and teacher education have already been and what they have previously done to promote justice. This begs a different question as we reflect on the implications of CSRP to teacher education: On whose terms is this focus on equity and justice occurring?

To clarify this, it is worth turning to the core question that CSRP and other liberatory pedagogies are actually asking of us. As Paris and Alim (2014, p. 86) put it:

> What if . . . the goal of teaching and learning with youth of color was not ultimately to see how closely students could perform White middle-class norms but to explore, honor, extend, and, at times, problematize their heritage and community practices?

While Paris and Alim's question raises issues of what CSRP might look like in diverse classrooms, as teacher educators, it is perhaps most important to consider why the question has to be asked at all. Despite decades of efforts in teacher education focused on equity and social justice, little has changed in the schooling experiences of youth of color. Despite pervasive talk of social justice, multiculturalism, and evidence of the effectiveness of asset-based pedagogies, students of color are still being asked to assimilate to White, colonial norms. Equity has stalled and stagnated. The term "social justice" has become so ubiquitously appropriated—leveraged with equal abandon by progressives interested in civic engagement, as well as neoliberal reformers out to transform teaching into educational entrepreneurship—that for all intents and purposes, it has lost all meaning.

Responding substantively in our work (and so, by proxy, in the praxis of our novice and practicing teachers who will be the ones implementing CSRP with youth) to these uncomfortable realities requires that we wrestle with the fact that while there are many nuanced and complex reasons for the continued inequity of education beyond our control, teacher education has largely failed to be liberatory. Far too many of our tacit assumptions and approaches remain mired in the White gaze of coloniality. Far too often, our best intentions and goodwill act to dehumanize, diminish, and dismiss youth of color, positioning teachers at arm's length from the Othered subjectivity of these students. Teacher education continues to struggle at disrupting those White middle-class norms in our own prevailing discourses. We continue to promote systems that claim justice and equity, but remain firmly rooted in a framework of coloniality. As a result, our own ability to produce the types of teachers needed to enact CSRP has been, and remains, limited. To ground this argument, let us reflect on how coloniality shapes three prominent discourses related to social justice and equity in teacher education: diversification of content, high-leverage practices, and identity work with educators.

COLONIALITY AND MULTICULTURAL CONTENT

While conversations on increasing representation in curricula are of course important for teacher educators to have with novice and practicing educators, relevance, we have learned, is not enough. Better text choices, strategic uses of Spanish, lessons on Kendrick Lamar's newest album as a bridge to the canon, and proudly posting a BlackLivesMatter poster, may all be valuable, requisite, and affirming aspects of a culturally sustaining curriculum and pedagogy, but even in abundance, they are not necessarily so, nor adequate in and of themselves. Materials like these are equally, and easily, likely to be misused, creating a false veneer over a pedagogy that still curricularizes racism (Paris, 2016), and replicates colonial expectations and constructions of success, knowledge, and behavior. If taken up in ways that (regardless of intention) miss the fundamental need to rupture dominant ways of being in, and doing, schooling and learning, and redefine whose knowledge ultimately matters, even the most promising critical-multicultural content has no decolonial substance. Multicultural content, even critical-multicultural content, isolated from affective questions of coloniality, will ever so gradually (or rapidly) see all the community and cultural knowledge bases they purport to honor subsumed by dominant, privileged ones. Ironically, multiculturalism becomes antithetical to decolonization, positioning these profoundly meaningful cultural productions as the "extra" whose value remains contingent on its usefulness to spiral back toward the cultural normative canon of whiteness. If our discussions around diversifying content are not equally concerned with repositioning what valued knowledges and cultural patterns *are*, we continue to perpetuate coloniality.

COLONIALITY, ACHIEVEMENT GAPS, AND HIGH-LEVERAGE PRACTICE

Coloniality is also evident and pervasive in those approaches—much in vogue—that have focused on "achievement" and "opportunity" "gaps," and on cultivating discrete, "high-leverage" practices and teacher skill sets that will lead to remarkable academic growth. When we misconstrue a focus on closing "achievement/opportunity gaps" as the ends of social justice, we perpetuate and anchor ourselves to the very logic of coloniality. This move insists to teachers and youth alike that ultimately, agency will always necessarily remain dominated by a White gaze, "centered implicitly or explicitly around the question of how to get working-class students of color to speak and write more like middle-class White ones" (Paris & Alim, 2014, p. 87). Moreover, by equating these "gaps" with social justice, we allow for the simultaneous prioritizing of a particularly limited type of educator whose skill sets—oriented toward these colonial goals—are the only skills that can lead us to suitable, high-impact academic growth. It is a masterful colonial falsehood that has construed rigorous teaching practice as somehow mutually exclusive or antithetical to sustaining the cultural practices and humanity of youth of color. "Teaching like a champion"[3] may open some doors for youth, but the colonial logic, assimilate-or-fail ideology, narrow definitions of success, and oppressive behavioral norms it employs to do so means that any progress comes at incredible cost to youth identity, agency, and humanity (Mommandi, 2016). These related approaches to teacher learning do not just fail to challenge coloniality, or close ontological distance, but in their adherence and valorization to the "criteria for academic performance" and "intersubjective relations" of coloniality (regardless of secondary attention to joy or democracy or multiculturalism in curriculum and learning), they bolster the rest of the colonial system. The patterns of power, valued knowledge production, aspirations of self, cultural patterns: all these elements of coloniality remain intact even in the face of shrinking "gaps," and the teachers we have produced will merely be equipped to more efficiently demand assimilation of youth of color.

COLONIALITY AND WHITE INTELLECTUAL ALIBIS

Finally, coloniality continues to pervade the identity work that teacher education is replete with. Social justice efforts in teacher education have lately shown a great interest in service learning, action research field experiences, and reflection on personal racial identity and privilege, to ensure that novices have unpacked their own "invisible knapsacks," or had fleeting contact with youth of color before they begin teaching in these communities. While there is value and necessity to this intent, and importance to ensuring that educators have interrogated their own positionalities, these types of efforts too often begin by positioning colonial ways of being and whiteness as normative. Ultimately, they prioritize the needs and interests of the teacher/colonizer, continuing to Other the agency and humanity of the colonized/student and community by presupposing "damage" (Tuck, 2009) and a need for assistance. When achieving justice becomes a paternalistic task of service and self-reflection, its successful enactment becomes performative, not substantive. Equity-minded teachers and teacher educators (regardless of ethnicity) can grow to feel satisfied with their self-awareness of race and privilege, proud of their good intentions and time spent working with youth of color. Yet closing ontological distance, breaking down the ways colonial relations live in and through schooling, requires more than positive interpersonal relationships.

There are plenty of well-liked teachers who connect with their students of color on personal levels, yet remain participants—whether intentionally or not—in incredibly problematic, colonizing practices that deny or negate the practices, wisdom, and identities of these students. Such practices construct what Leonardo and Zembylas (2013) call "white-intellectual alibis" for educators, absolving individuals from any responsibility for disrupting the patterns of power and dehumanizing intersubjective relations—the Othering—at the heart of coloniality. Instead of producing decolonial educators and creating openings for CSRP, such approaches invite pedagogies of resentment (McCarthy & Dimitriadis, 2005), fueled by benevolent and color-blind racism (Bonilla-Silva, 2006), and predicated on correcting the "pathological" non-White identities, practices, and ways of being of students.

DECOLONIZING TEACHER EDUCATION

So why, returning to the question I posed earlier, do we need to make sense of ontological distance in order to produce or develop CSRP-capable educators? Because these critiques, and many more like them, of elements and discourses common in teacher education are not new. There is an extensive and well-documented history of critique on the ways teacher education has framed and engaged equity and social justice that goes well beyond these three limited examples (e.g. Darling-Hammond, 2010; Gay, 2002; Nieto, 2000, 2005). For too long, teacher education has failed to disrupt coloniality, or at least failed to play the transformative role in liberation that it might have, because it has taken place on the terms of the colonizer, and not the terms of the colonized. Rather than move us toward liberation, extant discourses of "diversity," "equity," and "social justice" in teacher education have failed to rupture the affective ways in which coloniality exacerbates ontological distance between teachers and students. Social justice as it is widely construed has remained colonial; it is justice only in that it seeks to make inequitable subjectivity (a colonized way of being, seeing the world, and defining success and value) available to all. That is not liberatory, revitalizing, nurturing, or sustaining, and it never has been. We need something more than this.

My intent here is not to dismiss very real logistical, policy, and educative concerns that teacher educators face (e.g., addressing opportunity gaps, the "demographic imperative" in teacher education, diversifying school content), or to devalue the equitable intentions and efforts of teacher educators. These are real and important concerns. But it is also the case that decades of research shows that liberatory, asset-based pedagogies, including, if not especially, CSRP, address all the concerns of rigor and academic growth that can be mustered (e.g., Cabrera et al., 2014; Dee & Penner, 2016), while also extending youth learning, social, and civic development in powerful, humanizing ways (e.g., Gutiérrez, 2008; Sanchez et al., 2015). Rather, the issue at hand is that it is all too easy to allow coloniality to dominate our teacher education efforts—our discourses, ideologies, and practice—when it need not do so, and when resistance to this coloniality might actually lead to more powerful outcomes by any definition.

Essentially, to make CSRP a permissible outcome for developing teachers, we are being called to help close ontological distance and humanize pedagogy from the inside out. If CSRP involves a new and different paradigm for praxis and curricular development in nation-state classrooms, then we need a new paradigm and pedagogy for cultivating liberatory educators as well; otherwise, they will never become the types of people who will be able to enact CSRP. An educator cannot *sustain* something in their curriculum or pedagogy (i.e., the evolving identities and emergent and heritage practices of youth of color), love it, nurture it, appreciate the humanity it represents, when that thing is continually rendered impermissible, Other, to them. Instead, CSRP demands that we cultivate educators who are able to see the promise and possibility in the subjectivity and agency of youth and communities of color without needing to orient themselves to some institutionally (read: colonial) acceptable object of schooling, society, or achievement.

Ultimately, we need a decolonizing teacher education pedagogy, one that centers itself—intentionally and intensely—on the humanity and possibility of students of color, and on dismantling the accepted logics and prevailing discourses of coloniality that only highlight their "otherness" and subordinate their wisdom. That is the challenge, and paradigm shift in teacher education, that CSRP calls us to: a pedagogy that helps educators learn to contest the ways coloniality lives in and through schooling. This does not mean failing to develop skill sets or practices, neglecting rigor, or ignoring demographic realities. Rather, a decolonial, culturally sustaining approach to teacher education asks for the simple, but also immensely difficult, move of shifting whose terms we strive for justice on, and situating the work of preparing teachers on the terms of the colonized, rather than allowing it to continue occurring on the terms of the colonizer.

CULTIVATING LIBERATORY EDUCATORS

In the remainder of this chapter, I want to turn my attention to how we might make this happen, and suggest five elements of what a decolonizing teacher education will need to entail to close ontological distance by cultivating dynamic educators for whom CSRP is central to their praxis. I situate my arguments here in relation to my own work designing for decolonial teacher learning. To that end, the evidence I draw on reflects my work with a diverse group of novice educators[4]—a group atypically composed mostly of Xicanx students of color—in the context of a pedagogical methods course that ran for one semester and one summer, operating in conjunction with the educators' participation in *Aquetza* (Romero Jr, Domínguez, Landa-Posas, Valadez-Fraire, & Gutiérrez, 2013), a summer enrichment program for high school youth of color. Keeping in mind that CSRP is dynamic and contextual by definition, my hope is to offer an initial outline of what teacher education will need to look like when we position it to start on someone else's terms and set off into the decolonial unknown, closing ontological distance and inviting culturally sustaining possibilities into existence.

1. Decolonial teacher education must displace colonial epistemologies, and foreground epistemologies reflective of youth and community wisdom. Perhaps the most foundational element of a decolonizing teacher education is to actively and intentionally disrupt and unsettle the epistemology—the norms, logic, values, and way of knowing—that guides our thinking about, and in, the process of pedagogical development. For far too long, the development of teachers has begun by assuming that knowledge should, and always does, follow from the same White, Western European origins that coloniality dictates. Teacher educators engaged in cultivating decolonized, CSRP-capable educators work to disrupt these staid and tired patterns. If we mean to close ontological distance and open the possibility for teachers to sustain other cultural practices and ways of being, then we must introduce and use other epistemologies as ways to think about and approach the work of teaching, and build new appreciations for the diversity of how cultures understand the world, in both heritage and emergent terms.

In the *Aquetza* program methods course, we began by actively framing our work and conception of teaching around the *Nahui Ollin*, a Mexica (Aztec) epistemic framework deeply rooted in the heritage, histories, and demographics of the complex, mestizo, Xicanx community we intended to serve. These principles became central to the way we framed and discussed pedagogy, as a bridge constructed with heritage wisdom to support the evolving identities of youth in our praxis. It was not uncommon to invoke, for instance, the concept of *Huitzilopochtli*—the will to take positive action in the world—to ask: "How is this teaching practice encouraging students to take positive action and take the lead? How is this supporting their agency?" The Nahui Ollin was infused across our development of praxis, shaping, on a foundational level, what we valued as knowledge and positioned as meaningful pedagogical outcomes.

These epistemologies should vary based on the perspectives of local youth and communities, and should avoid applying colonial standards to their comprehensiveness. First Nations communities retain unique, rich, and distinct epistemologies; Black and Chicana feminist epistemologies are robust and compelling; Hip Hop is also an epistemic framework. To expect these and other similar frameworks of cultural wisdom to be as comprehensive, prescriptive, and ready-made for all our needs as Eurocentric epistemologies might appear to be is to ignore the ways in which the epistemologies of the global south have been actively silenced and destroyed for over 500 years. Simultaneously, our efforts to engage alternative and heritage epistemologies should not assume that they are beyond reproach. Coloniality can be internalized[5], and even deeply rooted community and cultural wisdoms may themselves reflect and perpetuate unjust social relations (Castillo, 1994; Hill Collins, 2004). It would be an error to shy away from internal critique and problematizing elements of heritage epistemologies that have been mutated by coloniality. We will need to engage creatively to discover, apply, and critically develop alternative (perhaps multiple alternative) cultural epistemologies to meet the pedagogical needs in our communities.

Taking this work on might be uncomfortable for teacher educators who may themselves have little to no experience with such alternative epistemologies, but it is a vitally important task. Teacher educators committed to decolonization and CSRP must be willing to critically engage with these deeply rooted epistemologies and share them with teachers. Inviting the guidance and wisdom of local communities into the teacher education setting, and partnering with ethnic and cultural studies departments, are strongly recommended to help do this work of foregrounding new ways of seeing and being.

2. Decolonial teacher education must engage educators with frameworks of race that capture the dynamic ways in which youth racial and cultural identity is being produced and reimagined. The demographic imperative has long been a concern of teacher educators. Today, the majority of public school youth are children of color, and this percentage will only increase (Hussar & Bailey, 2014), while the majority of teachers and teacher educators remains White (Boser, 2011). This has meant that efforts to engage race have often started with a focus on whiteness, which, as noted earlier, is problematic. Equally problematic, however, are engagements with racial identity beyond whiteness that portray race and identity as static. Focusing on whiteness, privilege, psychological models of race, social construction, and even intersectionality can all obfuscate the complex ways youth experience their racial identities as both incredibly salient, and increasingly dynamic, and it is these identities that produce the dynamic practices and cultural innovations CSRP looks to nurture.

As such, a decolonizing teacher education pedagogy must push teachers to grapple, challenging as it may be, with complex notions of race as immanent, evolving, and salient—drawing from the diverse, deeply rooted epistemologies that are introduced, as well as the emergent practices of youth. Doing this opens up possibilities for engaging with the shifting, contingent nature of identities, and firmly acknowledges the historical and continued salience of racialized experience. With this said, it should also be noted that such frameworks are valuable to teachers of color as well, for it is likely that their experiences engaging with race and their own racial identities have been shaped through colonial lenses (Fanon, 1952).

These issues were tensions in our methods course and the *Aquetza* program as we sought to explore new ways to be and learn with youth. To address the dynamic appreciation for identity we hoped to see, we took time to explore and view race and identity through the lenses of *nepantla* (Anzaldúa, 1989, 1993), and *assemblage* (Puar, 2007). These complicated approaches were challenging at first, but allowed us to situate our thinking on the identities and needs of youth, rather than the identities and needs of us educators. This orientation was evident as Andrea, a Xicana novice educator, reflected on the contingency of identity, even within our Xicanx studies focus:

I think we have to keep in mind that for all these things, there's not one solid definition of these things, it's all dependent on the individual, in what context, in what communities. We can't say there's going to be one specific [identity] . . . because you can like see, everyone's individual way of seeing things, and then try collectively to come up with something . . . and I think that's one of the most unique parts of this, is because it is collective, we aren't only seeking to target one type of student, or one single identity, but all the complexity that just comes from being in this space.

Here, Andrea captured the tension and challenge we were embracing: that this process was less about prescribing a static Xicanx identity—even if that was meaningful to many of us—and instead about working to ensure that youth could embrace the complexity of decolonized ways of being, reveling in what resonated with them individually, and collectively.

While *nepantla* and *assemblage* were productive for our program, community, and youth, they reflected the heritage, epistemologies, and evolving needs of our context. Other dynamic frameworks of racial and cultural identity certainly exist that might be explored in different contexts and communities. What is clear, however, is the importance of engaging with more nuanced, decolonial conceptions of race in our teacher education pedagogy that disrupt static framings of identity and bring the past into conversation with the present.

3. Decolonial teacher education must rethink the ways that field experiences position the expertise of educators in relation to youth and community knowledge. Recently, calls for richer, more comprehensive field experiences (e.g., Ball & Forzani, 2009; Darling-Hammond, 2006) have gained traction. Yet, given the sorts of development needed for teachers to enact CSRP, too little attention has been given in these conversations to how we position the expertise of youth and teachers in relation to one another. Too often, field experiences (for both novice and practicing educators) at best expose educators only to schooling as they already know it, and to youth in superficial ways. At worst, these experiences lead to damage-centered (Tuck, 2009) or pathological views of youth and toward acceptance of deficit, command-and-control pedagogies. These types of generic experiences in schooling, or voyeuristic contact with youth of color, will not produce the educators we need.

Closing ontological distance requires enriching and intentional experiences that bolster teachers' appreciation for the ingenuity, knowledge, and deeply rooted wisdom youth and communities of color already possess. As such, field experiences in decolonial teacher education must disrupt illusions of expertise, helping teachers recognize the contingency of their own knowledge and perspective. Teachers can then defer to the expertise of youth, position themselves as learners, and center their work on students' wisdom, practices, and ingenuity. Leslie, a novice educator of mixed White and Mexican racial background, captured these goals as she reflected on the positionality that the CSRP praxis we were working toward in the methods course would need to entail:

> I was thinking about how necessary it's going to be for us to be vulnerable, and for us to be in positions that aren't comfortable, and to like, navigate that, and to like, you know, be able to be in that same place of learning as students, I don't know, like, we're all learning always. . . .

In the *Aquetza* program, our disruption of expertise—our drive to position teachers as Leslie says, as vulnerable learners—came in two ways. First, the program was constructed with what we called a transdisciplinary ethnic studies content. While many of our educators had rich, discipline-specific content knowledge in traditional subject areas, this institutionally affirmed expertise (and the security and ontological safety that came with it) was of little use here. Yet even our participants well-versed in ethnic/cultural studies as a discipline, like Leslie, were challenged to rethink their expertise, recognizing that youth experiences and reactions to these concepts would be different from their own. Effectively, the challenge became considering—and embracing—what it meant to teach when you were not master of the content.

Second, the residential nature of the summer program was itself incredibly beneficial and transformative. For all of our participants, even those who shared similar backgrounds and even came from the same communities and neighborhoods as our Xicanx youth participants, the process of living intimately with youth—spending time with them between course sessions, dining together, playing games, engaging in conversation—was eye-opening. Rather than simply positioning youth as neophytes, with trivial and passing fads and interests, our teachers came to appreciate and understand the variety and complexity of youth practices and interests and how these reflected, shaped, and extended their identities and ingenuity.

To decolonize teacher education, we need to reflect on how field experiences are achieving the dual goals of decentering expertise and appreciating youth ingenuity, for both novice and practicing teachers alike. Specifically, while opportunities to live as closely with youth as our novices in *Aquetza* did might be rare and logistically challenging, rethinking what "residential" could mean, and what it might involve to deeply embed teachers in community settings in appropriately humble ways, could be a key step in developing a successful decolonial teacher education, and cultivating decolonial teachers.

4. Decolonial teacher education must actively confront coloniality and create alternative frameworks and identities endowed with hope and possibility. I have already noted the ubiquity with which "diversity," "social justice," and "multiculturalism" have been used in teacher education discourses, with minimal impact or decolonial commitment. With this in mind, a liberatory teacher education must not be apprehensive about naming coloniality, pressing for the decolonial, and challenging fundamental assumptions of schooling, society, and power, even if these directions lead to uncomfortable self-reflection, or the unsettling of long-held ontological beliefs and values.

Understanding coloniality for what it *is* is critical to the task of liberation and moving beyond damage-centered, symptom-focused, narrow and shallow views of social justice education. Failing to name and unsettle coloniality in spaces of institutional power, including the teacher education or professional development classroom, means that the onus of change is forever on the colonized, and that success for youth of color will endlessly revolve around finding ways to conform and succeed on another's terms, rather than around sustaining and nurturing their own practices and criteria for success and achievement. To this end, we began our work in *Aquetza* by deconstructing what we collectively understood the parameters of colonized schooling to be from our own experiences and engagement with the concept across texts.

This process of engaging deeply with how coloniality worked in schools, and teasing out the ways it shaped learning into a repetitive, noncreative enterprise, privileging White cultural norms and limiting youth agency and possibility, proved revelatory to many of our educators. This was evident in the response Sandra—a Xicana novice educator who had attended a heavily underresourced urban high school—had to discussing coloniality and next-step assistance pedagogy:

> Ay! Wait, that is really . . . this is why, I, I suck at chemistry. Especially in lab, 'cause this week we have to develop our own scheme for our lab, and develop our whole lab by ourselves, with no guidance, and I'm just like, " . . . What am I supposed to do?" 'Cause usually it's like, "This is the right answer." So from here you go to this, and from here you go to that, and it's just . . . I'm mind-blown right now.

Yet decolonial teacher education needs to be infused with hope and possibility as well. Just as we must be deconstructive around coloniality, breaking down the ways colonial relations live in and through schooling, we must also be constructive around alternatives. Freire is a common reading in teacher education, but how often is his work used centrally to frame courses, rather than positioned as a romantic idea to be considered in passing? In the *Aquetza* methods course, approaches to critical and transformative pedagogy, guided by the epistemology of the Nahui Ollin, were the center of our work and discussion. We intently read Freire, Darder, hooks, Ladson-Billings, and others. We talked explicitly about CSRP, and worked purposefully to tease out the practices and dispositions that were embedded in these visions of teaching and pedagogy. In many ways, this was a methods course on how to reposition the Othered knowledge of marginalized youth, to live liberatory praxis, and close ontological distance.

That was by no means a straightforward or simple task. Actualizing powerful, liberatory ideas was a complicated process, and our discussions were infused with both consensus and contradiction. On one occasion, we deeply considered what it meant to be "knowledgeable" as a teacher, but placed this idea in conversation with maintaining "hubris" and the position of "learner" while teaching. We found intersubjectivity, but often without agreement (Matusov, 1996), which only made for richer engagement with what it meant to disrupt coloniality and live these ideas. Eventually these ongoing conversations coalesced into visions for instruction, an example of which is evident in Figure 13.1, which we charted out in our classroom space.

These frameworks and visions did not just live as archives, but remained live documents that served to drive and inform our pragmatic work both in and beyond the course. In participants' fieldwork and in the residential summer program, we continually returned to and referenced these artifacts as a staff to reflect on how courses were working in general, and how particularly challenging teaching moments might be handled.

A decolonial teacher education must engage in both the purposeful, uncomfortable work of naming and deconstructing coloniality in schooling as well as the intentional exploration of decolonial possibilities realized as pedagogical frameworks.

5. Decolonial teacher education must engage practices that unpack coloniality and explore liberation in the mundane, everyday work

Figure 13.1. Novice educators' conceptual map of culturally sustaining pedagogy.

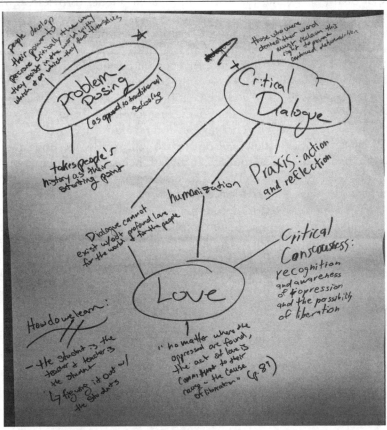

of teaching. As much as cultivating CSRP-capable educators requires the productive unsettling and disruption of colonial ways of schooling and exploring alternative, liberatory frameworks, it is critical to note that it also requires attention to the mundane ways that the effect of coloniality lives in schools. As metaphysical and far-reaching as coloniality is, we reproduce and perpetuate it through even our most routine actions. In other words, it is essential that a decolonial teacher education be as equally focused on practicing, developing, and rehearsing the skill sets of liberatory CSRP praxis as it is on developing the mindsets required to enact them.

What I mean, pragmatically, is not to occupy our time with rehearsal practices that replicate reductive or rote disciplinary teaching actions, or replicate and refine command-and-control responses to crisis role-plays. Rather, decolonial teacher education must look to leverage approximations of practice in purposeful, ideologically conscious ways that create opportunities to rehearse how new, more liberatory dispositions through which ontological distances can be closed, and CSRP realized, can be lived. In our methods course, we sought to do this by using *teatro del oprimido* practices—drawing on the work of Boal (1979), and the *Teatro Campesino* model (Broyles-González, 1994)—to reflect on and play with the ways everyday classroom choices can replicate or disrupt colonial patterns of power, and positively position and nurture youth practices, knowledge, and identity. Examples included enactments that led us into a 20-minute conversation on the affective impact and ethics of using the word "No" with youth; grappling with what types of questioning strategies were most conducive to fostering agency in a quiet group; and playing with ways to negotiate damaging ideologies being voiced in the classroom, and respond with compassion and revolutionary love.

To be clear, these instances of our *teatro* rehearsal work, and other activities to build pedagogical toolkits, in and of themselves did not amount to CSRP, nor were they ever construed as discrete practices. Similar activities could be done, with similar focal concerns and similarly reflective conclusions, but never deployed in decolonial ways. Yet in the broader context of the course and program, linked explicitly to discussions of liberatory epistemologies and critical pedagogies, these moments, and many others like them, provided small opportunities to engage concrete strategies and dispositions that reflected and extended what it would look like to teach while working to break down the colonial relations of the classroom and redress ontological distance.

In order for CSRP or any liberatory praxis to become tangible, it must be normalized, its feasibility assumed from the outset, without becoming entangled in colonial questions of whether such pedagogy is "realistic." Thus a decolonial teacher education must find ways, amidst its concerns for broader, conceptual growth, to entertain and play with enacting CSRP and grounding the lived nature of liberatory values.

LOOKING FORWARD

Right away, I should note that this outline is far from comprehensive. It is general, and specific efforts should take these principles as guides, while considering local context, grade level, and community needs. While I have drawn on my own work here, similar efforts that do just that, focused on cultivating CSRP-ready educators for their contexts, are at work elsewhere, among university-based teacher educators (e.g., Camangian, 2015; Gunnings-Moton & Flennaugh, 2016, cited in Paris, 2016) as well as in professional development contexts for experienced educators (e.g., XITO Collective—Acosta, Arce, Fernández, Gonzalez, & Gonzalez, 2016). CSRP, though progressing rapidly, remains a nascent process. We can hope that by continually sharing our successes and struggles, this outline of a decolonial teacher education will continue to evolve, becoming more refined and offering an ever-more generative path into the unknown.

And this returns us to Anzaldúa's words: *Se hace puentes al andar.*

We must make the bridges as we go. CSRP is not meant to be an incremental step. It is a paradigm shift, a resounding call to change tack and unsettle our practices. To make CSRP permissible, we must recognize that an educator coming to understand their work to be "responsive," or "equitable" in the colonial molds that now proliferate, is engaged in a wholly different task than an educator who is coming to see their work in decolonial terms, focused on sustaining, revitalizing, and nurturing culture and youth ingenuity. Our practices need to change as well, and if we are unwilling to do this, we risk losing CSRP to the same lethal pressures of coloniality that assimilated, co-opted, and consumed previous liberatory efforts.

I want to close here by sharing what Kirsten, a White educator who worked hard in *Aquetza* to discover and embrace a decolonial teaching identity, had to say as she reflected on the challenge of embodying and enacting CSRP as she moved into her own classroom:

> I . . . it's something I believe in so much. . . . I've seen it used so well by certain teachers, but at the same time, I've seen it not being used at all, but by people who think they are doing that, and, I don't want to be that person. . . . I dunno, that's a challenge for me, basically not fucking up!

Cultivating the types of educators for whom CSRP is possible is going to involve new, decolonial approaches to teacher education. We must set off into the unknown, and create new bridges across ontological distances, for the old ones, built on colonial logic, tired and well-worn with obligatory use, have failed us. "Fucking up" may be part of the CSRP process—both for our teachers and for us—but it is a process full of hope, rooted in resistance, leading us toward decolonization and liberation.

NOTES

1. Following from McCarty and Lee (2014), I use CSRP to acknowledge that particularly in indigenous communities, pedagogies that *sustain* emerging identities and practices and pedagogies that *revitalize* heritage practices that have been assailed and colonized, are both needed. Thus, a vision of CSRP—rather than CSP alone—is critical to the work of decolonization with historically marginalized youth and communities.

2. When considering Othering and ontological distance, it is important to note that race/ethnicity are highlighted here because in the history of colonization in the global south, these were, and remain, the most significant markers of difference. However, the hegemonic, colonial construction that is whiteness, also involves exclusionary patriarchal, heteronormative, classist, linguistic, and ableist discourses—all of which are important *distancing* factors to be considered as well.

3. This reference is of course to Doug Lemov's (2010) *Teach Like a Champion*, a how-to text on teaching that has become popular in neoliberal "high-performing" charter schools, as well as urban schools more generally. Despite embedded claims of simply focusing on "what works," Lemov's text begins with deeply colonial assumptions (e.g., these strategies "work" for whose interests, and for what outcomes?). As such, this text and the discrete practices it suggests embody colonial, assimilate-or-fail ideologies, and implicitly position non-White race and culture in deficit terms.

4. Of our cohort of novices, over half identified as students of color—primarily Latinx or Xicanx, with one Black educator—a demographic breakdown unusual to teacher education classrooms that certainly impacted the trajectory of our work together. As is common in teacher education, however, the majority remained women.

5. I am thinking here, for example, of the ways that misogyny has, over time, become embedded in the community practices and epistemologies of, for instance, the Chicano Movement and Hip Hop such that it appears natural to them, when in reality it is evidence of the ways in which coloniality has seeped into and distorted marginalized cultures. Internal critiques aimed at redressing internalized coloniality are vital to the success of CSRP.

REFERENCES

Acosta, C., Arce, S., Fernández, A., Gonzalez, J., & Gonzalez, N. (2016) *Xican@ Institute for Teaching and Organizing* [Professional development program]. Retrieved from http://www.xicanoinstitute.org/

Anzaldúa, G. (1989) *Borderlands/La frontera*. San Francisco, CA: Aunt Lute Books.

Anzaldúa, G. (1993). Border arte: Nepantla, el lugar de la frontera. In A. Keating (Ed.), *The Gloria Anzaldúa reader* (pp. 176–187). Durham, NC: Duke University Press.

Ball, D., & Forzani, F. (2009). The work of teaching and the challenge for teacher education. *Journal of Teacher Education, 60*(5), 497–511.

Bhabha, H. K. (1994). *The location of culture.* New York, NY: Routledge.

Boal, A. (1979). *Theatre of the oppressed.* New York, NY: Theatre Communications Group.

Bonilla-Silva, E. (2006). *Racism without racists: Color-blind racism and the persistence of racial inequality in the United States.* Lanham, MA: Rowman & Littlefield Publishers.

Boser, U. (2011). *Teacher diversity matters: A state-by-state analysis of teachers of color.* Washington, DC: Center for American Progress.

Broyles-González, Y. (1994). *El teatro campesino: Theater in the Chicano movement.* Austin, TX: University of Texas Press.

Cabrera, N. L., Milem, J. F., Jaquette, O., & Marx, R. W. (2014). Missing the (student achievement) forest for all the (political) trees: Empiricism and the Mexican American studies controversy in Tucson. *American Educational Research Journal, 51*(6), 1084–1118.

Camangian, P. (2015). Teaching like lives depend on it: Agitate, arouse, inspire. *Urban Education, 50*(4), 424–453.

Castillo, A. (1994). *Massacre of the reamers: Essays on Xicanisma.* New York, NY: Plume Publishing.

Darling-Hammond, L. (2006). Constructing 21st century teacher education. *Journal of Teacher Education, 57*(3), 300–314.

Darling-Hammond, L. (2010). *The flat world and education: How America's commitment to equity will determine our future.* New York, NY: Teachers College Press.

Dee, T., & Penner, E. (2016). *The causal effects of cultural relevance: Evidence from an ethnic studies curriculum.* Washington, DC: National Bureau of Economic Research.

Fanon, F. (1952). *Black skin, white masks.* New York, NY: Grove Press.

Gay, G. (2002). Preparing for culturally responsive teaching. *Journal of Teacher Education, 53*(2), 106–116.

Gunnings-Moton, S., & Flennaugh, T. (2006). *Michigan State University Urban Educators Cohort Program* [Teacher training program]. East Lansing, MI. Retrieved from http://education.msu.edu/teacher-preparation/urban/

Gutiérrez, K. (2008). Developing a sociocritical literacy in the third space. *Reading Research Quarterly, 43*(2), 148–164.

Hill Collins, P. (2004). *Black sexual politics: African Americans, gender, and the new racism.* New York, NY: Routledge.

Hussar, W., & Bailey, T. (2014). *Projections of education statistics to 2022* (41st ed., U.S. Department of Education Publication No. NCES 2014-051).

Washington, DC: Institute for Education Sciences—National Center for Education Statistics.

Lemov, D. (2010). *Teach like a champion: 49 Techniques that Put Students on the Path to College (K–12)*. New York, NY: John Wiley & Sons.

Leonardo, Z., & Zembylas, M. (2013). Whiteness as technology of affect: Implications for educational praxis. *Equity & Excellence in Education, 46*(1), 150–165.

Maldonado-Torres, N. (2010). On the coloniality of being: Contributions to the development of a concept. In W. Mignolo & A. Escobar (Eds.), *Globalization and the decolonial option* (pp. 94–124). New York, NY: Routledge.

Matusov, E. (1996). Intersubjectivity without agreement. *Mind, Culture, and Activity, 3*(1), 29–45.

McCarthy, C., & Dimitriadis, G. (2005). Governmentality and the sociology of education: Media, educational policy, and the politics of resentment. In C. McCarthy, W. Crichlow, G. Dimitriadis, & N. Dolby (Eds.), *Race, identity, and representation in education* (2nd ed., pp. 321–335). New York, NY: Routledge.

McCarty, T., & Lee, T. (2014). Critical culturally sustaining/revitalizing pedagogy and indigenous education sovereignty. *Harvard Educational Review, 84*(1), 101–124.

Mignolo, W. (1995). Decires fuera de lugar: Sujectos dicentes, roles sociales, y formas de inscripcion. *Revista de critica literaria latinoamerica, 11*, 9–32.

Mignolo, W. D. (2003). *The darker side of the renaissance: Literacy, territoriality, and colonization* (2nd ed.). Ann Arbor, MI: University of Michigan Press.

Mommandi, W. (2016, June). *The racial and political pedagogic project of Doug Lemov's* Teach Like a Champion. Paper presented at the Critical Race Studies in Education Conference, Denver, CO.

Nieto, S. (2000). Placing equity front and center: Some thoughts on transforming teacher education for a new century. *Journal of Teacher Education, 51*(3), 180–187.

Nieto, S. (2005). Schools for a new majority: The role of teacher education in hard times. *The New Educator, 1*(1), 27–43.

Paris, D. (2016). *On educating culturally sustaining teachers* [Working paper]. Teaching Works. Retreived from http://www.teachingworks.org/images/files/TeachingWorks_Paris.pdf

Paris, D., & Alim, H .S. (2014). What are we seeking to sustain through culturally sustaining pedagogy? A loving critique forward. *Harvard Educational Review, 84*(1), 85–100.

Puar, J. (2007). *Terrorist assemblages: Homonationalism in queer times*. Durham, NC: Duke University Press.

Quijano, A. (2000). Coloniality of power, eurocentrism, and Latin America. *Nepantla: Views from the south, 1*(3), 533–580.

Romero Jr., J., Domínguez, M., Landa-Posas, M., Valadez-Fraire, J., & Gutiérrez,

K. (2013). *UMAS y MEChA de CU Boulder—Aquetza: Youth and teacher leadership program* [Teacher training program]. Boulder, CO.

Sánchez, S., Domínguez, M., Greene, A. C., Mendoza, E., Fine, M., Neville, H., & Gutiérrez, K. (2015). Revisiting the collective in critical consciousness: Diverse sociopolitical wisdoms and ontological healing in sociopolitical development. *The Urban Review, 47*(5), 824–846.

Tuck, E. (2009). Suspending damage: A letter to communities. *Harvard Educational Review, 79*(3), 409–428.

CHAPTER 14

Understanding Identity Sampling and Cultural Repertoires

Advancing a Historicizing and Syncretic System of Teaching and Learning in Justice Pedagogies

Kris D. Gutiérrez and Patrick Johnson
University of California, Berkeley

We begin by briefly situating our discussion of the power and possibility of culturally sustaining pedagogy (CSP) in the long arc toward educational equity and dignity. We view CSP to be a robust approach to pedagogical justice, contributing to the "river of educational struggle" in the United States. Vincent Harding (1981) employed the metaphor of a river of struggle to capture the civil and human rights struggles of the 20th century in all their complexity, contribution, and enduring historical significance. It is an apt metaphor to discuss how critical pedagogies in general, and here CSP in particular, continue to play an important role in helping youth and adults leverage cultural histories as resources for consequential learning and social change.

The river of struggle has many vibrant tributaries that connect people, connect us, to the larger river of struggle. Culturally sustaining pedagogy is one such tributary in a family of pedagogies advanced as a means of foregrounding the plural and dynamic nature of youths' identity and cultural practices, while recognizing the agentic, linguistic, sociocultural, and sociopolitical moves and practices that youth develop and leverage. Of significance, CSP is attempting to forge new terrain and further theorize its various dimensions, attending to constraints of previous conceptions of culturally relevant and other pedagogies, both pushing against and forward toward new notions of access and equity and resulting pedagogical practices.

In this chapter, we have several aims. We hope to contribute to the ongoing theorization of CSP by addressing aspects of the three goals identified by Paris and Alim (2014) in their theory-building piece, "What Are

We Seeking to Sustain Through Culturally Sustaining Pedagogy? A Loving Critique Forward." In this piece, Paris and Alim set out to take stock of the histories and contributions of previous asset pedagogies, offering culturally sustaining pedagogy as an extending frame for justice pedagogies. We examine several tensions in CSP that Paris and Alim themselves pursue. We are particularly interested in two tensions with which they grapple, tensions that we, too, examine in our own work:

1. Asset pedagogies that foreground the heritage practices of communities of color without taking into account contemporary/evolving community practices.
2. Asset pedagogies that do not critically contend with problematic elements expressed in some youth cultural practices. (Paris & Alim, 2014, pp. 91–95)

With these in mind, we organize our discussion around the following questions as generative considerations for advancing our collective work:

1. How do we reconcile notions of cultural sustainability with cultural historical views of culture as dynamic and instrumental?
2. How can we develop pedagogies that support practices that honor and hold onto youths' valued cultural practices while also acknowledging and capturing tensions in practices, including the hybrid and syncretic nature of youth's repertoires?
3. How can equity-oriented pedagogies such as CSP leverage the internal contradictions in practices that youth may experience?

We engage these questions and focus on notions of culture, which are at the heart of different understandings and uses in pedagogical and learning practices. We address how reductive notions of culture can subvert the aims of justice-oriented pedagogies. We discuss misunderstandings of our own work on third space (Gutiérrez, 2008; Gutiérrez, Mendoza, & Paguyo, 2012; Gutiérrez, Rymes, & Larson, 1995) and advance the importance of situating justice pedagogies in larger activity systems that attend to constellations of mutually influencing dimensions, including people, tools, and practices. We proffer syncretic approaches to pedagogy that leverage practices that should be in tension but instead support cultural amplification (Cole & Griffin, 1980) and expansive forms of learning. Within this frame, we address the importance of acknowledging the ways youth live in and experience the internal contradictions that are part of their everyday practices. We argue that youth operate in the everyday tension of youth cultural practices with ambivalence, without resolution of the contradictions that are part of the various activity systems in which they participate. We exemplify this point by providing a salient example of living in the tension and contradictions of everyday practices, in this case, in the domain of Hip Hop. First, we return to a discussion of the concept of culture as it undergirds the larger discussion in this chapter.

WHAT COUNTS AS CULTURE?

Focusing on culture is central to equity-oriented pedagogies; however, how culture is conceptualized varies and is consequential to how the practices of nondominant communities are understood, and how learning and pedagogical practices are defined. In particular, its conceptualization implicates the nature of the mediating role of equity pedagogies. Celebrating, affirming, sustaining, and accounting for culture is the central object of pedagogies that seek to redress educational inequities and histories of curricular exclusion and pedagogical malpractice for youth from nondominant communities. Pedagogies that seek to sustain culture (Paris, 2012; Paris & Alim, 2014), for example, work toward reclamation of the histories, contribution, and possibilities of cultural communities, particularly those who have been and continue to be racially, linguistically, and otherwise marginalized.

Our own work is centrally interested both in how we theorize and study culture and the implications on youth from nondominant communities, pedagogically, sociopolitically, and sociohistorically. We have been particularly concerned with the role of culture in learning, as well as how notions of culture have both extended and constrained how we conceptualize cultural communities and their members and practices. There is a long history of research that has essentialized members of cultural communities by flattening or diminishing differences that are consequential to learning and to living resonantly, fully, and with dignity (Gutiérrez & Arzubiaga, 2012). As we have written elsewhere (Gutiérrez et al., in press), when writing about nondominant communities, the constructs used to describe, analyze, and make sense of communities' practices must be interrogated and examined against their history of use and the explanatory power they provide for understanding people-in-practice, both locally and historically. We ask: How can one *see* dignity in people's everyday lives when the operant analytical lens (e.g., urban, poor, English Learner, "gritless") has already defined the nature and possibility of people and their practices? Of relevance to this volume, we are concerned that such analytical frames find their way into curricula. A first-order question, then, asks: How has culture been conceptualized in equity- and culturally-oriented curricula and pedagogical practices?

Narrow understandings of culture contribute to narrow conceptions of learning, resulting in reductive frameworks evident across scholarship that grow out of very different sensibilities, intellectual traditions, and political aims; yet even pedagogies that have oppositional stances with one another can use culture reductively. In some pedagogical approaches, culture is understood to be a trait of individuals or of collections of people; such views assume that members of cultural communities possess sets of shared traits by virtue of their membership in cultural communities. A cultural-historical perspective challenges these understandings, defining a "cultural community" as

> a coordinated group of people with some traditions and understandings in common, extending across several generations, with varied roles and practices and continual change among participants as well as transformation in the community's practices (see Rogoff, 2003). For example, people draw on intergenerationally conveyed concepts, ways of talking, and belief systems that may be used and negotiated locally in communities that are often identified internally and by their neighbors in terms of ethnicity and race. (Gutiérrez & Rogoff, 2003, p. 21)

Here culture is not conflated with race and ethnicity, in which the characteristics of cultural groups become immutable and static. This view makes it more difficult to fall into the trap of one-size-fits-all pedagogical approaches that assume a kind of uniformity in cultural groups that simply does not exist. Consider, for example, that learning styles curricula that are organized around the idea that people who share a broad cultural history argue that people also share a uniform approach to learning. A culture-as-trait pedagogical approach minimizes people's experience in activities, treats contexts as if they exist independently of the people active in creating and maintaining them, and views individuals as though their characteristics are unrelated to the contexts in which they and their families have participated in recent generations (Gutiérrez, Asato, Santos, & Gotanda, 2002).

We argue that people participate in various ways, some overlapping, but in practices and ways that shift and change and are transformed over time (Gutiérrez & Rogoff, 2003). These shifts take place over lifetimes, including the historical change in a community's organization and relationships with other communities (Cole, 1998; Lave, 1996; Rogoff, 2003; Rogoff & Angelillo, 2002). Cole and Engeström (1993) underscore this point succinctly and help us understand the importance of cultural variability, asserting that culture "is experienced in local, face-to-face interactions that are locally constrained and heterogeneous with respect to both 'culture as a whole' and the parts of the entire toolkit experienced by any given individual" (p. 15). We elaborate this key cultural historical theoretical principle in forthcoming work in which we contend that employing a robust notion of culture is a theoretical, political, pedagogical, and methodological issue, since a failure to capture complexity, ingenuity, and the nuanced textures of community members' lives can contribute to flawed research and poor and ineffectual educational and social policies and practices (Gutiérrez et al., in press). So why does this matter, and what makes understanding what is truly cultural about an individual's practices important to consequential and equitable forms of learning?

Our nation's preoccupation with difference, notably racialized difference, and its inclination to fix perceived deficiencies is rooted in longstanding tendencies in education to categorize, describe, and make value judgments that suggest value hierarchies in cultural practices. The result is an epistemological form of segregation (Artiles, 2015; Bang, Faber, Gurneau, Marin, & Soto, 2015) in which the knowledge and repertoires of practice are not understood as foundational, or valued and fundamental, to learning. Too often the resulting default pedagogical script for youth from nondominant communities is to assume difference from the norm as deficit, and to attribute practices to individuals on the basis of race, ethnicity, or shared national origin. Instead, from a cultural historical theoretical view of learning and an equity-oriented pedagogical perspective, it is much more productive and accurate to focus on how people live culturally, to understand people's history in involvement in practices and the meaning and value attributed to them, and to account for the repertoires that people develop in socioculturally organized practices. Further, from a disciplinary learning perspective, making what youth do not know the primary focus of pedagogies is neither useful nor accurate in terms of assessing potential. Thus, a focus should be on people's repertoires of practice—that is, the ways of engaging in activities stemming from participation in a range of cultural practices, as well as the learning that occurs in the development of those repertoires (Gutiérrez & Rogoff, 2003). This view helps us understand the hybridity and shifts that occur in youths' movement within and across everyday practices.

Further, a notion of culture that expects regularity, variance, and change helps us resist the dichotomies that are too often employed in studying, teaching, and understanding the practices of cultural communities and their members. We call attention to dichotomies employed even in robust equity-oriented or "asset" pedagogies, traps that we also find ourselves in at times. Paris and Alim (2014) note the constraints of foregrounding "the heritage practices of communities of color without taking into account contemporary/evolving community practices" (p. 85) and offer the concepts of heritage and community practices (Paris, 2012). As Alim (2007) has argued, the heritage and contemporary practices of students and communities should be valued and leveraged, noting the importance of students' own everyday linguistic and cultural practices.

However, preserving enduring and stark binaries between such practices as heritage and community without acknowledging their mutual constitution over cultural historical time also makes it easier to ignore or minimize their relation, their inherent tensions, and their mutual possibilities, as well as their potential to co-exist with ambivalence (Johnson, 2017), as we will discuss shortly (see also Chapters 1 and 12, this volume). Paris and Alim acknowledge this tension and have noted that longstanding and contemporary practices are not discrete (See Chapter 1, this volume, and Paris & Alim, 2014).

SUSTAINING DYNAMIC NOTIONS OF CULTURAL PRACTICES AND CULTURAL COMMUNITIES

Understanding what counts as culture in theorizations of teaching and learning is particularly important, as culturally relevant and equity-oriented pedagogies are often misunderstood and taken up in ways that diverge from their original intent. In short, "bad things can happen to good ideas," limiting the potential to sustain robust pedagogical practices. Since their inception, these pedagogies have been distorted by prevailing ideologies and commonsense beliefs about race, intelligence, learning, language, and ability, for example, as well as theorizations of cultural practices and communities. Consider, for example, how a funds of knowledge framework (Gonzalez, Moll, & Amanti, 2005) has been reduced to static and generalized cultural practices, instead of its call for understanding the rich network of practices that are part of people's everyday lives. Within this interpretation, funds of knowledge are misunderstood as inert knowledge rather than networks of productive exchange and knowledge production. Of relevance to this chapter, we argue that the other widely taken up pedagogies—culturally relevant pedagogies (Ladson-Billings, 1995) cultural modeling (Lee, 1995), and culturally sustaining pedagogies (Paris, 2012; Paris & Alim, 2014)—have been instantiated in ways that are at odds with their conceptualizations and intent, with unintended consequences for youth from nondominant communities.

Even our own work on the concept of the third space (Gutiérrez, 2008) has been imagined by others as a pedagogy, that is, a third space pedagogy; as a teachable moment; or as the celebration of local literacies. Conceiving of third spaces as a pedagogical approach paves the way for unintended consequences for youth and their teachers and belies the important point that third spaces do not exist a priori, nor can they be willed into existence via curricular or pedagogical plans. Third spaces are about learning—expansive forms of learning that invoke particular pedagogies in which sociocritical literacies and sociocritical thought are desired objects of activity (Gutiérrez, 2008). However, it would be a narrow interpretation of learning to understand learning in third spaces as what students can do with assistance, or even what can happen in discrete literacy events with rich social and linguistic interactions. Instead, in the Vygotskian sense, third spaces are collective zones of proximal development (Gutiérrez, 2008). More accurately, third spaces are particular kinds of activity systems—functional systems whose division of labor, tools, and practices are oriented toward expansive forms of learning and powerful literacies and the development of "historical actors." As historical actors, youth can develop a new social imagination in which they can engage in historicized, sociocritical, and syncretic processes of reframing their cultural past as a resource in the present and a tool for future action. As syncretic processes—that is, the reorganization of two disparate practices, genres, and tools—the dynamic nature of cultural practices, with enduring and shifting dimensions, are acknowledged. Third spaces, then, are predicated on an understanding that cultural practices are both enabling and constraining, with inherent tensions within. Teaching and learning systems, then, are not unproblematic spaces, and youths' learning must necessarily involve the negotiation of systems' tensions and contradictions. In the following, we briefly discuss third space to contrast its fuller conceptualization with its misunderstandings and uptakes and use this discussion to set the ground for a final argument about the affordances of conceptualizing racial justice and equity-oriented pedagogies as part of robust learning ecologies where expansive learning, equity, and heteroglossic and syncretic practices are an explicit part of the design, implementation, assessment, and ongoing remediation of teaching and learning systems. Pedagogy is a tool that cannot be disembodied from practices and people in systems.

RETHINKING EQUITY-ORIENTED PEDAGOGIES AS ACTIVITY SYSTEMS

Third spaces are collective and dynamic spaces that emerge in developing functional systems characterized by forms of reclamation, the development of critical social thought, intra- and intercultural attention to historicity, and syncretic approaches to learning grounded in decolonizing pedagogies (Gutiérrez, 2008; Tejeda, Espinoza, & Gutiérrez, 2003). Espinoza (2009) elaborates a study of an instantiation of these collective third spaces, described as "educational sanctuaries," in which equitable learning, dignity, and educational rights are understood from a social interactional perspective. From this empirical frame, Espinoza and Vossoughi (2014) advance an understanding of learning as "dignity-conferring" and "rights-generative," as sociocultural accomplishments. Common across these conceptualizations is a dynamic and instrumental notion of culture that undergirds designs that highlight and leverage students' full linguistic and sociocultural repertoires toward newly imagined futures through social dreaming—a collective dream for a more just world (Gutiérrez, 2008).

Our own research on social design–based experiments with nondominant communities as co-participants focuses on remediating a history of inferior education by reframing what counts as education generally and literacy specifically. This approach to design employs a syncretic approach to learning and literacy as a central pedagogical piece, as it offers an approach to designing robust and equitable systems that are socioculturally organized and framed around a recognition of the unequal power relations that exist between dominant and nondominant communities, particularly around race, citizenship, and language. Thus, syncretic pedagogies seek to preserve the integrity of everyday practices, including their dynamic nature, by "foregrounding them so as to maintain the value and history of the everyday genre vis-à-vis the dominant form" (Gutiérrez, 2014, p. 57). In this way, syncretic approaches can offer a challenge to the reproduction of dominant views of knowledge in research, and pedagogies focused on marginalized communities. Because these designed interventions are grounded in community practices, their design and pedagogies have a greater likelihood of being embraced, sustained, and leveraged. Moreover, a syncretic approach works to resist the binaries of the everyday and school-based, the formal and informal, heritage and community, as well as static notions of cultural practices, which are ineffectual and produce inaccurate, incomplete, and reductive descriptions and conclusions of the nature, possibility, and potential of people's everyday practices (Gutiérrez, 2014; Gutiérrez & Jurow, 2016).

In the domain of literacy, "syncretic approaches to literacy are oriented toward the development of sociocritical literacies" (Gutiérrez, 2008), organized around an understanding of "practices" as sociocultural formations imbued with histories, local influences, and future orientations. As such, shifts and changes in practices, their reorganization, hybridization, re-mixing, overlaps, and tensions, are expected. Briefly, syncretic approaches to disciplinary learning involve the strategic reorganization of meaningful everyday and school-based practices in ways that neither romanticize everyday knowledge nor privilege school-based skills and dominant forms of knowledge; instead, from a learning perspective, a syncretic approach recognizes that expansive forms of learning involve the renegotiation and productive hybridization of valued cultural forms with the new.

POPULAR CULTURE, DIGITAL MEDIA, AND IDENTITY SAMPLING

Understanding culture also orients us to consider idiocultures (Fine, 1979), such as the worlds of new media. Fine defined idioculture as "a system of knowledge, beliefs, behaviors, and customs shared by members of an interacting group to which members can refer and employ as the basis of further interaction" (p. 734). We argue that the intersecting vectors of popular culture and digital media provide an ideal site for seeing the dynamic nature of syncretic approaches in action. As Morley (2006) reminds us, "in the age of the remote control device, [audiences] watch cannibalized schedules of their own construction, as they jump from one bit of programming to another" (p. 110).

While requiring consumers to sift through a barrage of information and images, digital media affords consumers the ability to actively craft their identities by leveraging ideas found across multiple mediums. Jenkins (2008) defines this process as convergence through which "each of us constructs our own personal mythology from bits and fragments of information extracted from the media flow and transformed into resources through which we make sense of our everyday lives" (pp. 3–4). This point is key to understanding identity sampling, which is fundamentally about extracting and rearranging fragments of sound to create a new composition. It is a selective process that requires accessing the utility of the source material and, to a degree, breaking the material into smaller units (Schloss, 2004). We engage in a similar process as media consumers. Following Jenkins (2008), what is particularly important to understand is that we use these fragments to help us understand ourselves and others, that is, how we live culturally.

Relatedly, Appadurai's (1990) notion of "mediascapes" helps describe the processes by which consumers must navigate as being largely "image-centered, narrative-based accounts of strips of reality" (p. 9)—strips of reality that are experienced and transformed into scripts of "imagined lives, their own as well as those of others living in other places" (p. 9). In this sense, we can imagine youth as constantly sampling fragments of reality, mixing and matching them as a way to make sense of their world, not unlike Hip Hop DJs and producers. Drawing on Freire's (1970) conception of consciousness, Karimi (2006) posits that youth who grow up involved in Hip Hop culture develop their identities by making sense of and sampling various ideas and experiences. He describes a sampled consciousness as

> a state of self (being) created by the act of sampling different experiences: education, stories, interactions, and observations. The individual takes these experiences, knowingly or unknowingly, and makes them part of their worldview, the way they create/interact. The consciousness is continually in flux, alternating, adding, subtracting, choosing. (p. 222)

A sampled consciousness often requires reading a text against the grain, or marking what is useful and what is expendable, thus producing readings that may diverge from dominant readings. The concept of sampled consciousness also reflects the intellectual work that Ladson-Billings (2000) contends is necessary to resist dominant worldviews perpetuated through institutions "designed to create individuals who internalize the dominant worldview and knowledge production and acquisition process" (p. 258). However, she acknowledges that ways of knowing that contrast with Eurocentric epistemologies are often unacknowledged through traditional research methodologies (Smith, 2012; Zuberi & Bonilla-Silva, 2008).

Acknowledging the pedagogical power inherent in youth cultural practices does not require muting critiques of how the practices may reify hegemonic discourses. However, it is important not to assume that youth are blind to problematic elements in their cultural practices. Instead, employing a syncretic approach also requires creating space for youth to wrestle with the multiple feelings about texts and practices they enjoy. We contend that we also should make these critiques the object of legitimate analysis and theorizing as part of teaching and learning (Gutiérrez, 2014; Chapter 1, this volume).

Hip Hop fans are often forced to negotiate conflicting affects about the music and other aspects of the culture. When asked how he reconciles his commitment to social justice with some of the problematic messages expressed in the culture, radio host and vlogger Jay Smooth helps us understand how adults negotiate the double bind.

> That's always sort of the tightrope walk of the adult Hip Hopper; having this bond with a community and an art-form that connects you to [it] for life, but having things going on and ideas being expressed that you vehemently disagree with . . . That's something that you have to learn how to do if you are going to remain within the Hip Hop community. You gotta learn how to challenge people for saying things that you are totally against while still honoring that bond you have as a fellow Hip Hopper, not just saying you know what I just don't respect you, I'm never talking to you again. You gotta figure out how to say the way you talk about women, that anti-gay stuff you're kicking right now, I can't rock with that at all but say it in a way that's respectful and is the way you speak to family about something that you disagree with. (Einenkel, 2015)

While Jay Smooth describes this balancing act as emblematic of being an adult Hip Hop–head, youth often navigate similar tensions in their relationships to Hip Hop culture. Understanding this work as performative provides a productive frame for considering how educators can help youth wrestle with the multiple feelings they may have about the cultures they belong to and the media texts they enjoy. This requires embracing the productive nature of ambivalence.

Merriam-Webster's dictionary defines ambivalence as "the simultaneous and contradictory attitudes or feelings (as attraction and repulsion) toward an object, person, or action." Banet-Weiser (2012) situates this term and identifies ambivalence as an organizing principle for brand cultures, noting that the meaning of a given brand or cultural product is never given but rather is open to a variety of meanings and interpretations. She observes that because ambivalence connotes inconsistency and uncertainty, it is often treated as an affect that is better avoided, as it is discomforting and produces unease. The concept of ambivalence is useful here, as it troubles our seemingly commonsense impulses toward certainty and reconciliation, while it furthers the potential and possibility of syncretic pedagogical approaches.

Consider an everyday example: If young adults are ambivalent about an idea or issue, they are often implored to make up their mind and pick a side. Ambivalence is often framed as the antithesis of critical thinking, with the belief that after embarking on a sufficient fact-finding mission or hashing out the requisite points, people will know exactly how they feel about a subject or issue. However, Banet-Weiser argues that understanding ambivalence solely as a problem fails "to take seriously the cultural value of emotion and affect and the potential of ambivalence. Its generative power, for it is within these spaces that hope and anxiety, pleasure and desire, fear and insecurity are nurtured and maintained" (p. 218). For Banet-Weiser, ambivalence has the potential to "disrupt the expected flow of consumption" (p. 218); it is a condition that opens the possibility for audiences to reject the hegemonic discourses encoded in a brand, product, or cultural text and allow audiences to occupy a negotiated or oppositional reading position (Hall, 2000).

We use this example to underscore the point that robust pedagogical practices must incorporate understandings of the complex nature of youths' cultural lives; that is, the way young people engage media is already a form of remixing. From this perspective, we could read contemporary media consumption as a syncretic practice. The culturally mediated world that youths inhabit is constantly changing and forces them to craft their identities from seemingly disparate parts. But as an extension of this understanding, while young people are already practicing holding multiple texts and ideas simultaneously, we could do a better job of acknowledging how they also hold multiple feelings about the cultures in which they participate. Holding those multiple feelings is actually a critical part of youths' intellectual development that educators and robust pedagogies can help facilitate (Johnson, 2017).

EXPANDING CONCEPTIONS OF JUSTICE PEDAGOGIES

In this chapter, we have argued the importance of situating justice and equity-oriented pedagogies in larger learning ecologies or activity systems that together help to constitute a social context of development for consequential learning and educational dignity. This is key, as pedagogies are tools and as such have enabling and constraining properties; but tools only become tools in sociocultural interaction, that is, in human cultural activity. What does this then mean for pedagogies that are bounded and firmly defined outside of praxis? We hope that our analysis and discussion have been directive in the ways we think about members of cultural communities and their normative, emergent, and syncretic practices, including how we conceive of and design appropriate and productive educational projects. However, the design of new pedagogies, in particular, involves a substantive shift from simply pointing out, labeling, and identifying the valuable practices and rich toolkits non-dominant youth bring to learning environments. As Brian Street (2004) has argued, "just getting such practices 'accepted' does not challenge the framing discourses that marginalize them in the first place" (p. 327). We, along with colleagues in this volume, call out research and pedagogies that romanticize or present uncomplicated understandings of the practices of youth from non-dominant communities—renderings, portraits, and analyses that are not embedded in more complex landscapes. We argue that narrow conceptions of what counts as culture and their attendant discourses and ideologies are particularly consequential for youth and the potential for understanding learning as the organization of possible futures (Gutiérrez, 2008).

REFERENCES

Alim, H. S. (2007). The Whig Party don't exist in my hood": Knowledge, reality, and education in the Hip Hop Nation. In H. S. Alim & J. Baugh (Eds.), *Talkin Black talk: Language, education, and social change* (pp. 15–29). New York, NY: Teachers College Press.

Appadurai, A. (1990). Disjuncture and difference in the global cultural economy. *Public Culture*, 2(2), 1–24.

Artiles, A. (2015). Beyond responsiveness to identity badges: Future research on culture in disability and implications for response to intervention. *Educational Review*, 67(1), 1–22.

Bang, M., Faber, L., Gurneau, J., Marin, A., & Soto, C. (2015). Community-based design research: Learning across generations and strategic transformations of institutional relations toward axiological innovations. *Mind, Culture, and Activity*, 23(1), 1–14.

Banet-Weiser, S. (2012). *Authentic TM: The politics of ambivalence in a brand culture*. New York, NY: New York University Press.

Cole, M. (1998). Can cultural psychology help us think about diversity? *Mind, Culture, and Activity*, 5(4), 291–304.

Cole, M., & Engeström, Y. (1993). A cultural-historical approach to distributed cognition. In G. Salomon (Ed.), *Distributed cognitions: Psychological and educational considerations* (pp. 1–46). Cambridge, UK: Cambridge University Press.

Cole, M., & Griffin, P. (1980). Cultural amplifiers reconsidered. In D. R. Olson (Ed.), *The social foundations of language and thought: Essays in honor of Jerome S. Bruner* (pp. 343–364). New York, NY: Norton.

Einenkel, T. (2015, October 6). *The library: Jay Smooth interview*. Retrieved from http://podtail.com/podcast/the-library-with-tim-einenkel/the-library-jay-smooth-interview/

Espinoza, M. (2009). A case study of the production of educational sanctuary in one migrant classroom. *Pedagogies: An International Journal*, 4(I), 44–62.

Espinoza, M., & Vossoughi, S. (2014). Perceiving learning anew: Social interaction, dignity, and educational rights. *Harvard Educational Review*, 84(3), 285–313.

Fine, G. A. (1979). Small groups and culture creation: The idioculture of Little League baseball teams. *American Sociological Review*, 44, 733–745.

Freire, P. (1970). Cultural action and conscientization. *Harvard Educational Review*, 40(3), 452–477.

Gonzalez, N., Moll, L., & Amanti, C. (2005). *Funds of knowledge: Theorizing practices in households, communities, and classrooms*. Mahwah, NJ: Erlbaum.

Gutiérrez, K. (2008). Developing a sociocritical literacy in the third space. *Reading Research Quarterly*, 43(2), 148–164.

Gutiérrez, K. (2014). Integrative research review: Syncretic approaches to literacy learning. In P. Dunston, L. Gambrell, K. Headley, S. Fullerton, & P. Stecker, (Eds.) *Leveraging horizontal knowledge and expertise: 63rd literacy Research Association yearbook* (pp. 48–61). Alamonte Springs, FL: Literacy Research Association.

Gutiérrez, K. D., Asato, J., Santos, M., & Gotanda, N. (2002). Backlash pedagogy: Language and culture and the politics of reform. *The Review of Education, Pedagogy & Cultural Studies*, 24(4), 335–351.

Gutiérrez, K., Cortes, K., Cortez, A., DiGiacomo, D., Higgs, J., Johnson, P., Lizárraga, J., Mendoza, E., Tien, J., & Vakil, S. (in press). Replacing representation with imagination: Finding ingenuity in everyday practices. *Review of Research in Education*.

Gutiérrez, K., & Jurow, S. (2016). Social design experiments: Toward equity by design. *Journal of Learning Sciences*, 1–36 (online first version). Retrieved from http://www.tandfonline.com/doi/full/10.1080/10508406.2016.1204548

Gutiérrez, K. D., & Arzubiaga, A. (2012). An ecological and activity theoretic approach to studying diasporic and nondominant communities. In F. Tate IV (Ed.), *Research on schools, neighborhoods, and communities: Toward civic responsibility* (pp. 203–216) Lanham, MD: Rowman & Littlefield.

Gutiérrez, K., Mendoza, L., & Paguyo, C. (2012). Third space and sociocritical literacy. In J. Banks (Ed)., *Encyclopedia of diversity in education* (pp. 2160–2163). Thousand Oaks, CA: Sage Publishers.

Gutiérrez, K., & Rogoff, B. (2003). Cultural ways of learning: Individual traits or repertoires of practice. *Educational Researcher*, 32(5), 19–25.

Gutiérrez, K., Rymes, B., & Larson, J. (1995). Script, counterscript, and underlife in the classroom: James Brown versus Brown v. Board of Education. *Harvard Educational Review*, 65(3), 445–471.

Hall, S. (2000). Encoding/decoding. In P. Marris & S. Thornham (Eds.), *Media studies: A reader* (2nd ed., pp. 51–61). New York, NY: NYU Press.

Harding, V. (1981). *There is a river: The Black struggle for freedom in America*. New York, NY: Houghton Mifflin Harcourt.

Jenkins, H. (2008). *Convergence culture: Where old and new media collide*. New York, NY: New York University Press.

Johnson, P. (2017). *B(l)ack like it never left: Race, resonance, and television* (Unpublished doctoral dissertation), University of California, Berkeley.

Karimi, R. (2006). How I found my inner DJ. In J. Chang (Ed.), *Total chaos: The art and aesthetics of Hip Hop* (pp. 219–232). New York, NY: Basic Books.

Ladson-Billings, G. (1995). Toward a theory of culturally relevant pedagogy. *American Educational Research Journal, 32*(3), 465–491.

Ladson-Billings, G. (2000). Racialized discourses and ethnic epistemologies. In N. Denzin & Y. Lincoln (Eds.), *Handbook of qualitative research* (2nd ed., pp. 257–277). Thousand Oaks, CA: Sage Publications.

Lave, J. (1996). Teaching, as learning, in practice. *Mind, Culture and Activity, 3,* 149–164.

Lee, C. D. (1995). A culturally based cognitive apprenticeship: Teaching African American high school students skills in literary interpretation. *Reading Research Quarterly, 30*(4), 608–630.

Morley, D. (2006). Unanswered questions in audience research. *The Communication Review, 9*(2), 101–121.

Paris, D. (2012). Culturally sustaining pedagogy: A needed change in stance, terminology, and practice. *Educational Researcher, 41*(3), 93–97.

Paris, D., & Alim, H. S. (2014). What are we seeking to sustain through culturally sustaining pedagogy? A loving critique forward. *Harvard Educational Review, 84*(1), 85–100.

Rogoff, B. (2003). *The cultural nature of human development.* New York, NY: Oxford University Press.

Rogoff, B., & Angelillo, C. (2002). Investigating the coordinated functioning of multifaceted cultural practices in human development. *Human Development, 45,* 211–225.

Schloss, J. G. (2004). *Making beats: The art of sample-based Hip Hop.* Middletown, CT: Wesleyan University Press.

Smith, L. T. (2012). *Decolonizing methodologies: Research and indigenous peoples.* London, UK: Zed Books.

Street, B. (2004). Futures of the ethnography of literacy? *Language and Education, 18*(4), 326–330.

Tejeda, C., Espinoza, M., & Gutiérrez, K. (2003). Toward a decolonizing pedagogy: Social justice reconsidered. In P. Trifonas (Ed.), *Pedagogy of difference: Rethinking education for social change* (pp. 10–40). New York, NY: Routledge.

Zuberi, T., & Bonilla-Silva, E. (Eds.). (2008). *White logic, white methods: Racism and methodology.* Lanham, MD: Rowman & Littlefield.

CHAPTER 15

An Ecological Framework for Enacting Culturally Sustaining Pedagogy

Carol D. Lee
Northwestern University

Culturally sustaining pedagogy is a powerful next-generation articulation of the construct of culturally relevant pedagogy conceptualized by Gloria Ladson-Billings (1994, 1995, 2001) over a decade ago. The original construct was warranted in response to the persistent educational "achievement gap" in the United States associated with race/ethnicity and class. Ladson-Billings (2006) appropriately reconceptualized the gap as the "education debt," documenting both the historical legacy of underresourcing schools for Black and Brown youth and youth living in poverty, and the economic and political debt that the country has accrued as a consequence of its policies. The argument was that teachers needed to design instruction in such a way as to build upon prior knowledge and experiences of youth and to emphasize building nurturing relationships with youth and their families. Paris (2012) and Alim (Alim & Paris, 2015; Paris & Alim, 2014) have expanded this warranting to argue that diverse funds of knowledge and culturally inherited ways of navigating the world need to be sustained as goods unto themselves. They further complicate our understandings of community cultural practices to include not only those historically connected to particular communities, but, equally important, contemporary youth culture, which typically spans across groups associated with race and ethnicity.

I enter this conversation to introduce additional warrants to support the argument about the centrality of culture in learning and instruction, and to hopefully expand the domains of development that are entailed in enacting and socializing cultural practices. I situate this argument from two theoretical orientations. The first is an ecological framework that views development of children and adults as situated within and across the demands of participation in the multiple routine sites of activity in which people are engaged (Bronfenbrenner & Morris, 1998). In some respects, the historical

views of culturally relevant pedagogy and the more recent views of culturally sustaining pedagogy are rooted in an ecological frame, in the sense that
these constructs are asking teachers to take into account aspects of youths'
lives outside the classroom not only as resources, but as targets of learning
to be sustained. In my thinking about ecological framing, we need to take
into consideration both teachers' and children's lives outside of school (Bernstein, 2014), as well as thinking of how classroom life is intersected with
school and district organizational practices as well as broader policy implications that include multiple actors. This ecological framing views these
intersecting levels as dynamically interacting. More specifically, the Bronfenbrenner ecological framework considers the routine sites in which the
child participates; continuities and discontinuities across such sites; what
adults and other caregivers take from their routine sites of participation that
they then bring into the socialization of the child; then the broader institutional configurations and ideologies that shape structures and policies in the
broader society; and, finally, the broader historical context.

The other framing I bring to bear is situated in the fields of human development and cognition. I raise these framings because I think they open up
opportunities to view attention to culture in instruction and learning as fundamental to human growth and development (Lee, 2010), and not simply
as politically correct moves we want educators to make on behalf of Black
and Brown youth and youth living in poverty, suggesting that those who
are White and middle- or upper-class are just human, and that hegemonic
practices in schooling aimed at these youth are just normal, and that these
privileged groups are somehow both homogenous and not subject to vulnerabilities. Indeed, as Margaret Beale Spencer (2006) asserts, to be human is
to be at risk. But at the same time, the nature of the vulnerabilities that human individuals and human communities face are clearly differentiated by
an array of societal positionings, particularly with regard to race, ethnicity,
class, gender, sexual orientation, and constructions of ability.

Charles Mills (1997) articulates what he calls *the racial contract*. Mills
draws on social contract theory—the idea that individuals give up individual rights to enter into implicit social contracts to be governed in a collective
to achieve goods and protections that would be difficult to achieve simply
as individuals—but argues that Western world hegemony is built on a racial
contract (Kendi, 2016). The terms of this racial contract confer personhood
on those designated as White and non-personhood on Black and Brown
people; in other words, this is an ideology of White supremacy. In the United States and other former colonial nations in Europe, the terms of this
racial contract were explicit—witness the enslavement of Africans in North,
Central, and South America and the Caribbean and the genocide against
the Indigenous populations of these regions. However, today—for example,
in the United States post–*Brown v. Board of Education* and the passage of
civil rights legislation—the articulation of subpersonhood is not explicit,

but implicitly engrained in a myriad of societal practices, including the ways in which inferior educational opportunities continue to be structured for schools serving majority Black and Brown populations and youth living in poverty. I raise this historic and ongoing ire of the ideology of White supremacy because I think it frames a web of normalized assumptions to which we are continuously having to argue against: to prove that Black and Brown communities have meaningful cultural practices; to prove that Black and Brown youth can learn; to prove that Black and Brown families are not characterized by deficit parenting practices, and so on. In many ways the normalizing assumptions today are not explicitly articulated in terms of race and ethnicity, but more so in terms of poverty. We see arguments about the culture of poverty (Jensen, 2009), how poverty affects the brain (Farah et al., 2006), how poor children come to school with insufficient language skills (Hart & Risley, 1995), how poor children lack executive functioning and executive control (Heckman, 2012), and how poor children need special development of what are now being called noncognitive skills (Heckman & Rubinstein, 2001). From my perspective, these are all code for Black and Brown inferiority, articulating an unexamined set of assumptions about what it means to be middle-class, and inferring homogeneity to both the privileged and the disenfranchised.

I want to push against these implicit deficit codes by articulating an argument rooted in contemporary understandings of cognition, human development and the neurosciences, perhaps an ironic twist to the ways that pseudoscience was invoked to justify African enslavement (Gould, 1981). I hope this reimagining of the warrants to support arguments about the centrality of culture in human learning and development also open up new areas that I think a culturally sustaining pedagogy needs to address, as well as cautions to consider around how we conceptualize culture.

From a human development perspective, we know that identity is multi-faceted (Gutierrez & Rogoff, 2003). There are issues of individual personal differences, of allegiances that emerge from participation in historically inherited practices associated with larger social configurations (e.g. ethnicity, nationality, religion), from patterned practices within families and family networks, from participating and viewing oneself as a member of particular groupings (e.g., a student, a lover of science, a gamer, a basketball player). Then there are aspects of identity that are influenced by how others see you, especially as these perceptions of others help to shape your opportunities to participate in particular practices and settings (Steele, Spencer, & Aronson, 2002). These issues of how others perceive you become complicated in interesting ways for people whose patterns of practices are hybrid, crossing politically and socially salient communities (e.g., people who are biracial, more recent immigrants, transgender persons), and for persons whose public statuses are the subject of discriminatory belief systems (e.g., constructions of race, particular immigrant groups, those with physical disabilities, the poor; Lee, 2009). Any of these dimensions of identity can be more or less salient in different contexts, and must be understood from a developmental perspective (e.g., how identity contingencies shift with across the life span; Spencer & Markstrom-Adams, 1990).

Building and sustaining a personal conception of positive identity is connected to how settings—including school—support positive physiological and psychological needs for safety, efficacy, relevance, and feeling connected through positive relationships (Maslow, 1943). And how such identity development unfolds over time is an outgrowth of the nature of sources of vulnerability that you face and the relationship between the kinds of supports that are available to you in response to the nature of the threats or sources of vulnerability. Spencer's (Spencer, 2006; Spencer et al., 2006) PVEST framework (Phenomenological Variant of Ecological Systems Theory) articulates these relationships, identifying how supports in relation to risks help to shape coping responses that become socialized over time in terms of more stable identities.

It is also important to recognize that how we perceive and experience the affordances and constraints in our environments influences and is influenced by physiological responses. For example, Adam (Adam et al., 2015) has documented how persistent experiences of discrimination can have negative health consequences (e.g., heart disease, diabetes, etc.), especially as these are experienced during adolescence. And it is equally important to recognize that our perceptions and responses to experience are embodied, are not merely psychological, but physiological as well. This also means that there can and are often features of contexts, of neighborhoods, for example, that can heighten negative physiological responses (e.g., food deserts, lack of green space, patterns of neighborhood violence that include both violence committed by members of a community against members of that community as well as violence perpetrated against members of communities by structures of the state) to sources of vulnerability. It is equally important, following the PVEST framework, to recognize (a) that objective conditions of challenge do not in themselves dictate how we experience these conditions and (b) that knowledge, beliefs, and relationships can buffer debilitating response to vulnerabilities (e.g., we see this in the resilience of generations of people of African descent to the horrors of enslavement).

From a cognitive perspective (Bransford, Brown, & Cocking, 1999), informed by an accumulation of evidence from the various fields of the neurosciences (cognitive, cultural, social) (Cacioppo, Visser, & Pickett, 2005; Neville & Bavelier, 2000; Organisation for Economic Co-operation and Development, 2007; Tomasello, 1999; Whitehead, 2010), we recognize that thinking, perceiving, and feeling are all intertwined; that regions of the brains do not operate in isolation; that the brain is fundamentally plastic over the life course (although some experiences heighten that plasticity); and that the working and development of physiological systems, including brain activity, are intimately intertwined with people's participation in cultural activities. We also know that human evolution has positioned the human species to survive by virtue of having multiple pathways through which to accomplish the fundamental tasks of navigating an ever-changing world—physically and psychologically (Lee, 2010; Quartz & Sejnowski, 2002). All humans face the same challenges of establishing and sustaining relationships; of meeting ego-related needs for safety, efficacy, and relevance; of maintaining physical health; and of learning to adapt to change. However, the goals toward which we work to achieve these ends and the kinds of supports that are useful for accomplishing these aims differ substantively across cultural and historical communities. Thus, diversity is not just an ideological good, it is a necessity for survival—both at the level of individuals as well as groups.

So what are the implications for how we think about the demands and goals of culturally sustaining pedagogy? Further, how do we think about the knowledge demands and organizational demands of designing instruction that encompasses these multiple goals?

CORE CONSTRUCTS REVISITED (RACE, ETHNICITY, CULTURE)

The design of culturally sustaining pedagogical practices requires a critical examination of the constructs of culture, race, and ethnicity. These constructs must be critically examined because their normative and historical conceptions have been either informed by or responsive to what Mills (1997) calls the racial contract (Lee, 2009). This contract demarcates human family groups on the basis of physiognomy associated under this ideology with the construct of race. However, more recent research in the biological sciences documents that there are no significant genetic differences across the so-called races (Long & Kittles, 2009). And using skin color as a marker of race runs into conundrums (e.g., peoples of dark skin complexion in Africa, India, and Malaysia; of medium-brown or tan skin complexion from Spain and Italy; of light skin color from Europe as well as, for example the San people, the indigenous population of South Africa, or the Tuareg of Mali). Ultimately, race is a social and political construct and must be attended to as such. This is different from understanding race as a window into cultural communities. Ethnicity, on the other hand, refers to shared cultural practices that span across generations and are associated with both shared and distributed geographical space (Helms & Talleyrand, 1997). I indicate distributed geographical space because national boundaries change, and ethnic populations immigrate across national boundaries and carry with them cultural practices that often become hybridized as they adapt to the new nations. I will illustrate this idea in the case of people of African descent across the African diaspora (e.g. North, Central, and South America and the Caribbean).

The enslavement of Africans, or what many call the African Holocaust, forcibly stole peoples from West Africa to be dispersed as enslaved persons in North, Central, and South America and the Caribbean. Practices associated with their ethnic communities of origin—which would largely at that time have been constituted as nation-states (e.g. the Akan, Yoruba)—were forbidden under enslavement. However, in acts of historic and cultural resilience, African-descent communities in the West crafted ways to sustain practices and belief systems that were part of what Boykin (Boykin, Jagers, Ellison, & Albury, 1997) calls deep culture structures pervasive across West Africa. In some areas—particularly Brazil and Cuba—Yoruba practices were sustained in easily identifiable ways (Murphy, 1993). These West African cultural practices and belief systems that have sustained peoples of African descent as ethnic communities include commitments to extended family networks; particular structural and rhetorical features of language; a belief in relations between ancestors and the living; particular religious practices; and the salience of rhythm and the importance of the drum, among others. A number of anthropological, linguistic, psychological, and sociological studies have documented these ethnic practices (King, 1976; Nobles, 1974; Smitherman, 1977; Thompson, 1983; L. Turner, 1949; P. Turner, 1993; Vass, 1979; Wahlman, 2001; Williams, 1990). A focus on race does not include any attention to these ethnic practices and their historical evolution, nor the function these practices have and continue to play as sources of resilience in African descent ethnic communities (Hilliard, 1995).

Another complication to the construct of race emerges from how to categorize children born from parents of different "races." This conundrum raises the historic dilemmas in the United States around blood quantum, particularly in reference to people of African descent and Indigenous populations in the Americas. In South and Central America these dilemmas become particularly complex because of the longstanding intermixing of African, Indigenous, and European peoples in these regions (Wade, 2001).

I raise the issue of ethnic communities as a repository of historically intergenerational cultural practices for several reasons. First, I think this idea of intergenerational cultural practices offers an important warrant for the idea of culturally sustaining practices; that is, are there practices that communities have sustained over time (albeit in hybrid forms and transformations) that have sustained communities to be resilient in the face of challenge? For example, if particular cultural practices and belief systems allowed people of African descent in the United States and the diaspora to survive and thrive through enslavement and Jim Crow—America's two centuries of legal apartheid—then it seems reasonable that sustaining these practices and strategic transformations in response to changing conditions is a worthwhile goal. If belief systems and practices around relationships with the natural world among Indigenous populations in the Americas have allowed for ecological resilience (see the Menominee Nation in Wisconsin), then it seems reasonable that such practices should be sustained

(Bang, Medin, & Altran, 2007; Lomawaima & McCarty, 2006; McCarty & Lee, 2014).

In these instances, membership in cultural communities, in this case defined by ethnicity, is defined by participation in practices, and not by race or skin color. Under this framing, people can self-identify as members of such communities, but there is also the question of being accepted by others in the community, by actually being able to participate in settings where the practices are central. For example, there are Yoruba priests and priestesses of European descent. This ultimately means that any cultural self-identification can be contested. And socializing students to understand such contestations as well as the affordances of sustaining particular practices, I think, should be a goal of culturally sustaining pedagogy.

A second important tenet regarding cultural membership is that people always belong to multiple cultural communities. Communities defined by ethnicity are just one source of community identification (Gutierrez & Rogoff, 2003). Others include metalevel communities associated with gender, sexual orientation, religion, age cohort, and profession, as well as special interest groups (e.g., video gamers, Hip Hop). Depending on the context, one or more of these identity markers may be more salient or not. As a consequence, any theorizing around culturally sustaining pedagogy needs to conceptualize the multiple cultural communities with which students may identify, and figuring out which of these community identifications and their attendant resources may be most useful for particular targets of development that the pedagogy hopes to foster. Expanding our understandings of cultural repertoires has been an explicit focus of the conceptualization of CSP by Paris and Alim.

Paris and Alim (2014) offer exemplars of instantiations of Hip Hop culture as windows into the ways that the current youth generation, in particular, constructs hybrid practices that draw from across traditional ethnic communities (Alim, Ibrahim, & Pennycook, 2008). They argue that these hybrid practices represent emerging demographic changes in the United States and, as a consequence, embody the breadth of resources on which a culturally sustaining pedagogy can draw. They also argue, consistent with traditional conceptualizations of culturally responsive instruction, that our goals should move beyond simply helping Black and Brown students and students in poverty access what can be called Dominant Academic American English and Eurocentric assimilationist goals. While I fundamentally agree with both of these propositions, I want to offer a related set of considerations.

As I indicated earlier, this tradition of scholarship must wrestle with the constraints of responding to the deficit tenets of the racial contract. The interdependence across communities and constructions of hybrid practices simply is what human communities do. The idea that there is a homogenous White, middle-class culture is a myth, a myth that has been idealized in an array of norms by which schools and children are evaluated. The idea that there is a homogenous standard of what it means to be an American is a myth. The idea that there is a singular dominant academic English is also a myth. Languages evolve. "American English" continues to be fundamentally shaped by multiple linguistic traditions: new words and syntactic forms, new genres. American popular culture—music, dance, media—has always evolved from diverse cultural traditions. As literacy scholars, we know that, for example, American literature is inherently diverse and hybrid. For example, the genre of magical realism includes Toni Morrison and William Faulkner, Amos Tutuola and Gabriel García Márquez, who said he didn't realize he could write down the kinds of stories his African-descent grandmother told until he read the German Jewish writer Franz Kafka. There is no academic domain that we teach in schools that is not influenced by contributions and practices from across historical and diverse cultural ethnic communities. And the new knowledge that evolves is hybrid. Understanding the hybridity of the undergirdings of disciplinary knowledge, understanding such knowledge as social constructions whose explanatory power evolves with time, should be a goal of CSP for all students. This is a revolutionary set of assumptions, but ones that are in some instances embraced and in other instances ignored or contested in the academy. For example, linguists certainly understand the hybrid influences on the development of American Englishes (we do speak different regional dialects of American English), but K–12 education does not. Literary critics in the academy (albeit distributed quite unequally across English departments in the academy) recognize the interconnections among Morrison, Faulkner, Márquez, and Kafka, but literature instruction in K–12 education clearly does not.

While not explicitly addressed, another conundrum that scholars of CSP must wrestle with is the dilemma of the traditional and modernity (Zakaria, 2008). This is a question for communities and for scholars. In some respects, W. E. B. Du Bois (1903, 1973) raised this dilemma when he described what he called double-consciousness among African Americans (wrestling with being Black and being American), and later the challenge that advances in integration should not mean that African Americans need to give up on their Blackness. This is a dilemma across the globe. There is no simple resolution to this question. However, raising and wrestling with it is a necessary first step. As we think about what should be sustained and why, we must realize that there are always competing demands around what is historically transmitted as tradition, and new practices and allegiances that are often hybrid and emergent. And this dilemma is certainly one about which scholars and practitioners of CSP must think. In some ways, Paris and Alim's (2014) caution about the need to interrogate some of the homophobic, racist, and misogynistic practices in current Hip Hop artifacts and practices is another lens on the kinds of dilemmas that this problem space invites and the critical engagement that it requires.

So, from my perspective, these foundational propositions require attention to the following questions:

- How and why do we seek to understand the multiple cultural communities with which students identify?
- In particular, for students who are members of communities that are politically marginalized, what functions can attention to historically intergenerational cultural practices (often associated with ethnicity) serve in terms of supporting positive identities, resilience, and critical analyses of institutional policies and practices that serve as sources of disenfranchisement?
- Toward what goals should culturally sustaining pedagogy strive?
- For all students, how does attention to examining how historic and contemporary institutional structures and policies function to maintain stereotypes serve the broader public good in a democracy? Attention to the broader public good in a democracy may provide leverage, for those whose positionings are sustained through hegemonic ideologies may be able to see how such ideologies actually work against the public good and constrain their own development.
- For all students, how can examinations of the hybrid and diverse underpinnings of traditional academic domains help to shape how students understand knowledge production?

PEDAGOGICAL IMPLICATIONS

I want to build on the goals for CSP as articulated by Paris and Alim by revisiting my earlier discussion of the multidimensional nature of human learning. No matter the goals for instruction, there are fundamental supports that need to be available. Instruction needs to support students in feeling efficacious, in seeing the relevance of targets of learning and of developing relationships that build a sense of belonging, and in socializing beliefs in the power of effort. It is possible that supports from outside of school, for example, from parents, can help students buffer the challenges that can arise when classroom instruction does not build these competencies. When the challenges that you are navigating are in tension with the expectations of schooling, managing these discontinuities is all the more difficult. A goal in CSP is to minimize these discontinuities in the contexts of schooling. And from both the CRP and CSP traditions, the goal is to minimize these discontinuities and to not view them as based on presumed deficits in communities and family life. My point here is that robust learning environments must address goals beyond cognitive skills alone (e.g., learning content that is presumed to be culturally relevant for some set of goals). The issue of supporting students in feeling efficacious and seeing the relevance of learning targets needs to draw from extant research on how people learn: the importance of drawing on relevant prior knowledge, of making problem solving public and explicit; the need to address generative concepts and to socialize epistemologies, to facilitate dialogue and metacognition; and opportunities to interrogate multiple points of view and misconceptions. The idea of generativity pushes against simplistic and restrictive content and requires that we teach knowledge, skills, epistemologies, and dispositions that can serve as problem-solving resources for a wide array of problems within domains as well as across domains and tasks. These domains and tasks—both within and across domains—can include not only what we think of as academic skills (which, as you will recall, I do not hand over solely to Eurocentric origins), but equally the problems of sustaining a democracy, resisting stereotypes, engaging in activism for that which is just, and learning to be resilient in the face of changing and evolving sources of threat.

Indeed, these are herculean tasks of teaching (whether as parents, as teachers, as mentors, or as coaches) and require ongoing lifelong commitment to learning and inquiry. This, among the challenges of instantiating CSP (and CRP), particularly in schools, requires significant infrastructure (e.g., what we do in teacher education, the requirements of licensing, supports for professional development within schools as learning organizations, curriculum, assessments, a diverse array of supports within schools and communities). It means, then, that those of us who are committed to these kinds of asset-based pedagogies must form alliances, must ourselves be producers, must put ourselves on the line in terms of participating in practice on the ground.

REFERENCES

Adam, E. K., Heissel, J. A., Zeiders, K. H., Richeson, J. A., Ross, E. C., Ehrlich, K. B., . . . Malanchuk, O. (2015). Developmental histories of perceived racial discrimination and diurnal cortisol profiles in adulthood: A 20-year prospective study. *Psychoneuroendocrinology, 62,* 279–291.

Alim, H. S., Ibrahim, A., & Pennycook, A. (2008). *Global linguistic flows: Hip Hop cultures, youth identities, and the politics of language.* New York, NY: Routledge.

Alim, H. S., & Paris, D. (2015). Whose language gap? Critical and culturally sustaining pedagogies as necessary challenges to racializing hegemony. *Journal of Linguistic Anthropology, 25*(1) [Invited forum, "Bridging 'the Language Gap'"], 66–86.

Bang, M., Medin, D. L., & Altran, S. (2007). Cultural mosaics and mental models of nature. *Proceedings of the National Academy of Sciences* (104), 13868–13874.

Bernstein, M. (2014). Three planes of practice: Examining intersections of reading identity and pedagogy. *English Teaching: Practice and Critique, 13*(3), 110–129.

Boykin, A. W., Jagers, R. J., Ellison, C. M., & Albury, A. (1997). Communalism: Conceptualization and measurement of an afrocultural social orientation. *Journal of Black Studies, 27*(3), 409–418.

Bransford, J., Brown, A., & Cocking, R. (1999). *How people learn: Brain, mind, experience and school.* Washington, DC: National Academy Press.

Bronfenbrenner, U., & Morris, P. A. (1998). The ecology of developmental processes. In W. Damon & R. M. Lerner (Eds.), *Handbook of child psychology: Theoretical models of human development, 5th Edition* (Vol. 1, pp. 993–1028). New York, NY: Wiley & Sons.

Cacioppo, J. T., Visser, P. S., & Pickett, C. L. (Eds.). (2005). *Social neuroscience: People thinking about thinking people.* Cambridge, MA: MIT Press.

Du Bois, W. E. B. (1903). *The souls of black folk.* New York, NY: Oxford University Press.

Du Bois, W. E. B. (1973). *The education of black people: Ten critiques 1906–1960.* New York, NY: Monthly Review Press.

Farah, M., Shera, D., Savage, J., Betancourt, L., Giannetta, J., Brodsky, N., . . . Hurt, H. (2006). Childhood poverty: Specific associations with neurocognitive development. *Brain Research, 1110*(1), 166–174.

Gould, S. J. (1981). *The mismeasure of man.* New York, NY: W.W. Norton.

Gutierrez, K., & Rogoff, B. (2003). Cultural ways of learning: Individual traits or repertoires of practice. *Educational Researcher, 32*(5), 19–25.

Hart, B., & Risley, T. R. (1995). *Meaningful differences in the everyday experience of young American children.* Baltimore, MD: Paul H. Brookes.

Heckman, J. J. (2012, September/October). An effective strategy for promoting social mobility. *Boston Review,* 10155–10162.

Heckman, J. J., & Rubinstein, Y. (2001). The importance of noncognitive skills: Lessons from the GED testing program. *American Economic Review, 91*(2), 145–149.

Helms, J. E., & Talleyrand, R. (1997). Race is not ethnicity. *American Psychologist, 52,* 1246–1247.

Hilliard, A. G. (1995). *The maroon within us: Selected essays on African American community socialization.* Baltimore, MD: Black Classic Press.

Jensen, E. (2009). *Teaching with poverty in mind: What being poor does to kids' brains and what schools can do about it.* Alexandria, VA: Association for Supervision and Curriculum Development

Kendi, I. (2016). *Stamped from the beginning: The definitive history of racist ideas in America.* New York, NY: Nation Books.

King, J. R. (1976). African survivals in the black community: Key factors in stability. *Journal of Afro-American Issues, 4*(2), 153–167.

Ladson-Billings, G. (1994). *The dreamkeepers.* San Francisco, CA: Jossey-Bass.

Ladson-Billings, G. (1995). Toward a theory of culturally relevant pedagogy. *American Educational Research Journal, 32*(3), 465–491.

Ladson-Billings, G. (2001). *Crossing over to Canaan: The journey of new teachers in diverse classrooms.* San Francisco, CA: Jossey-Bass.

Ladson-Billings, G. (2006). From the achievement gap to the education debt: Understanding achievement in U.S. schools. *Educational Researcher, 35*(7), 3–12.

Lee, C. D. (2009). Historical evolution of risk and equity: Interdisciplinary issues and critiques. *Review of Research in Education, 33,* 63–100.

Lee, C. D. (2010). Soaring above the clouds, delving the ocean's depths: Understanding the ecologies of human learning and the challenge for education science. *Educational Researcher, 39*(9), 643–655.

Lomawaima, K. T., & McCarty, T. L. (2006). *"To remain an Indian": Lessons in democracy from a century of Native American education.* New York, NY: Teachers College Press.

Long, J. C., & Kittles, R. (2009). Human genetic diversity and the non-existence of biological races. *Human Biology, 74*(4), 449–471.

Maslow, A. H. (1943). A theory of human motivation. *Psychological Review, 50*(4), 370.

McCarty, T., & Lee, T. (2014). Critical culturally sustaining/revitalizing pedagogy and indigenous education sovereignty. *Harvard Educational Review, 84*(1), 101–124.

Mills, C. W. (1997). *The racial contract.* Ithaca, NY: Cornell University Press.

Murphy, J. (1993). *Santeria: African spirits in America.* New York, NY: Beacon Press.

Neville, H. J., & Bavelier, D. (2000). Specificity and plasticity in neurocognitive development in humans. In M. S. Gazzaniga (Ed.), *The new cognitive neurosciences* (pp. 83–99). Cambridge, MA: The MIT Press.

Nobles, W. (1974). African roots and American fruit: The black family. *Journal of Social and Behavioral Sciences, 20*(2), 52–64.

Organisation for Economic Co-operation and Development. (2007). *Understanding the brain: The birth of a new learning science.* OECD/CERI International Conference. Paris, France.

Paris, D. (2012). Culturally sustaining pedagogy: A needed change in stance, terminology, and practice. *Educational Researcher, 41*(3), 93–97

Paris, D., & Alim, H. S. (2014). What are we seeking to sustain through culturally sustaining pedagogy? A loving critique forward. *Harvard Educational Review, 84*(1), 85–100.

Quartz, S. R., & Sejnowski, T. J. (2002). *Liars, lovers, and heroes: What the new brain science reveals about how we become who we are.* New York, NY: Morrow.

Smitherman, G. (1977). *Talkin and testifyin: The language of Black America.* Boston, MA: Houghton Mifflin.

Spencer, M. B. (2006). Phenomenology and ecological systems theory: Development of diverse groups. In W. Damon & R. M. Lerner (Eds.), *Handbook of child psychology* (6th ed., Vol. 1, pp. 829–893). New York, NY: Wiley.

Spencer, M. B., Harpalani, V., Cassidy, E., Jacobs, C., Donde, S., & Goss, T. N. (2006). Understanding vulnerability and resilience from a normative development perspective: Implications for racially and ethnically diverse youth. In D. Chicchetti & E. Cohen (Eds.), *Handbook of developmental psychopathology* (Vol. 1, pp. 627–672). Hoboken, NJ: Wiley.

Spencer, M. B., & Markstrom-Adams, C. (1990). Identity processes among racial and ethnic minority children in America. *Child Development, 61,* 290–310.

Steele, C. M., Spencer, S. J., & Aronson, J. (2002). Contending with group image: The psychology of stereotype and social identity threat. *Advances in Experimental Social Psychology, 34*, 379–440.

Thompson, R. F. (1983). *Flash of the spirit: African and Afro-American art and philosophy.* New York, NY: Random House.

Tomasello, M. (1999). *The cultural origins of human cognition.* Cambridge, MA: Harvard University Press.

Turner, L. (1949). *Africanisms in the Gullah dialect.* Chicago: University of Chicago Press.

Turner, P. (1993). *Heard it through the grapevine: Rumor in African American culture.* Berkeley, CA: University of California Press.

Vass, W. (1979). *The Bantu speaking heritage of the United States.* Los Angeles, CA: Center for Afro-american Studies, University of California, Los Angeles.

Wade, P. (2001). Racial identity and nationalism: A theoretical view from Latin America. *Ethnic and Racial Studies, 24*(5), 845–865.

Wahlman, M. S. (2001). *Signs and symbols: African images in African American quilts.* Atlanta, GA: Tinwood Books.

Whitehead, C. (2010). The culture ready brain. *Social Cognitive and Affective Neuroscience, 5*, 168–179.

Williams, S. (1990). The African character of African American language: Insights from the Creole connection. In J. E. Holloway (Ed.), *Africanisms in American culture* (pp. 397–425). Bloomington, IN: University of Indiana Press.

Zakaria, F. (2008). *The post-American world.* New York, NY: W. W. Norton.

Index

Note: Page numbers followed by "n" indicate material in numbered endnotes.